BATMAN
LEGENDS OF THE DARK KNIGHT™

VOLUME 1

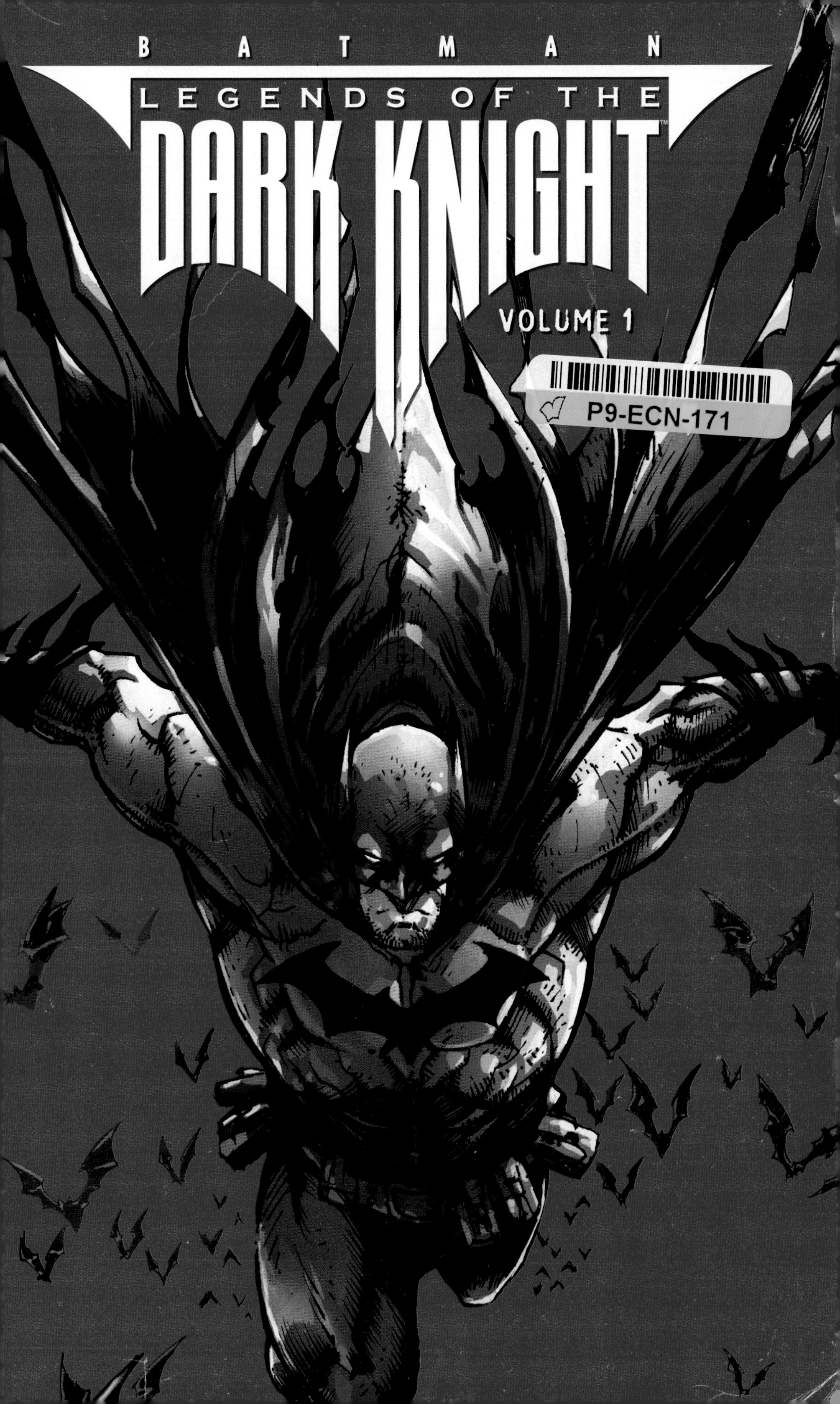

BATMAN

LEGENDS OF THE

DARK KNIGHT

VOLUME 1

Damon LINDELOF · Jonathan LARSEN · Tom TAYLOR · B. Clay MOORE
Steve NILES · T.J. FIXMAN · Andrew DABB · Joshua Hale FIALKOV
WRITERS

Jeff LEMIRE · J.G. JONES · Nicola SCOTT · Wayne FAUCHER
Ben TEMPLESMITH · Trevor HAIRSINE · Christopher MITTEN
Giorgio PONTRELLI · Tan Eng HUAT · Phil HESTER · Eric GAPSTUR
ARTISTS

Jose VILLARRUBIA · Paul MOUNTS · Ben TEMPLESMITH
Allen PASSALAQUA · Antonio FABELA · David LOPEZ &
SANTI CASAS of Ikari STUDIO · Jim CHARALAMPIDIS
COLORISTS

Saida TEMOFONTE
LETTERER

Ethan VAN SCIVER with Brian MILLER of HI-FI
COLLECTION COVER ARTISTS

BATMAN created by BOB KANE

HANK KANALZ BEN ABERNATHY EDITORS–ORIGINAL SERIES
KRISTY QUINN ASSOCIATE EDITOR–ORIGINAL SERIES
RACHEL PINNELAS EDITOR
ROBBIN BROSTERMAN DESIGN DIRECTOR–BOOKS
DAMIAN RYLAND PUBLICATION DESIGN

HANK KANALZ SENIOR VP – VERTIGO & INTEGRATED PUBLISHING

DIANE NELSON PRESIDENT
DAN DIDIO and JIM LEE CO-PUBLISHERS
GEOFF JOHNS CHIEF CREATIVE OFFICER
JOHN ROOD EXECUTIVE VP–SALES, MARKETING AND BUSINESS DEVELOPMENT
AMY GENKINS SENIOR VP–BUSINESS AND LEGAL AFFAIRS
NAIRI GARDINER SENIOR VP–FINANCE
JEFF BOISON VP – PUBLISHING PLANNING
JOHN CUNNINGHAM VP–MARKETING
TERRI CUNNINGHAM VP – EDITORIAL ADMINISTRATION
AMIT DESAI SENIOR VP – FRANCHISE MANAGEMENT
BOB HARRAS SENIOR VP – EDITOR-IN-CHIEF, DC COMICS
JASON JAMES VP – INTERACTIVE MARKETING
ALISON GILL SENIOR VP–MANUFACTURING AND OPERATIONS
JAY KOGAN VP–BUSINESS AND LEGAL AFFAIRS, PUBLISHING
JACK MAHAN VP–BUSINESS AFFAIRS, TALENT
NICK NAPOLITANO VP–MANUFACTURING ADMINISTRATION
RICH PALERMO VP – BUSINESS AFFAIRS, MEDIA
COURTNEY SIMMONS SENIOR VP–PUBLICITY
BOB WAYNE SENIOR VP–SALES

BATMAN: LEGENDS OF THE DARK KNIGHT VOLUME 1

DC COMICS, 1700 BROADWAY, NEW YORK, NY 10019
A WARNER BROS. ENTERTAINMENT COMPANY.
PRINTED BY RR DONNELLEY, SALEM, VA, USA. 8/2/13.
ISBN: 978-1-4012-4239-8. FIRST PRINTING.

LIBRARY OF CONGRESS CATALOGING-IN-PUBLICATION DATA

BATMAN : LEGENDS OF THE DARK KNIGHT, VOLUME 1.
PAGES CM
"ORIGINALLY PUBLISHED IN SINGLE MAGAZINE FORM IN LEGENDS OF THE DARK KNIGHT 1-5."
ISBN 978-1-4012-4239-8
1. GRAPHIC NOVELS. I. TITLE: LEGENDS OF THE DARK KNIGHT, VOLUME 1.
PN6728.B36B4245 2013
741.5'973—DC23
2013018257

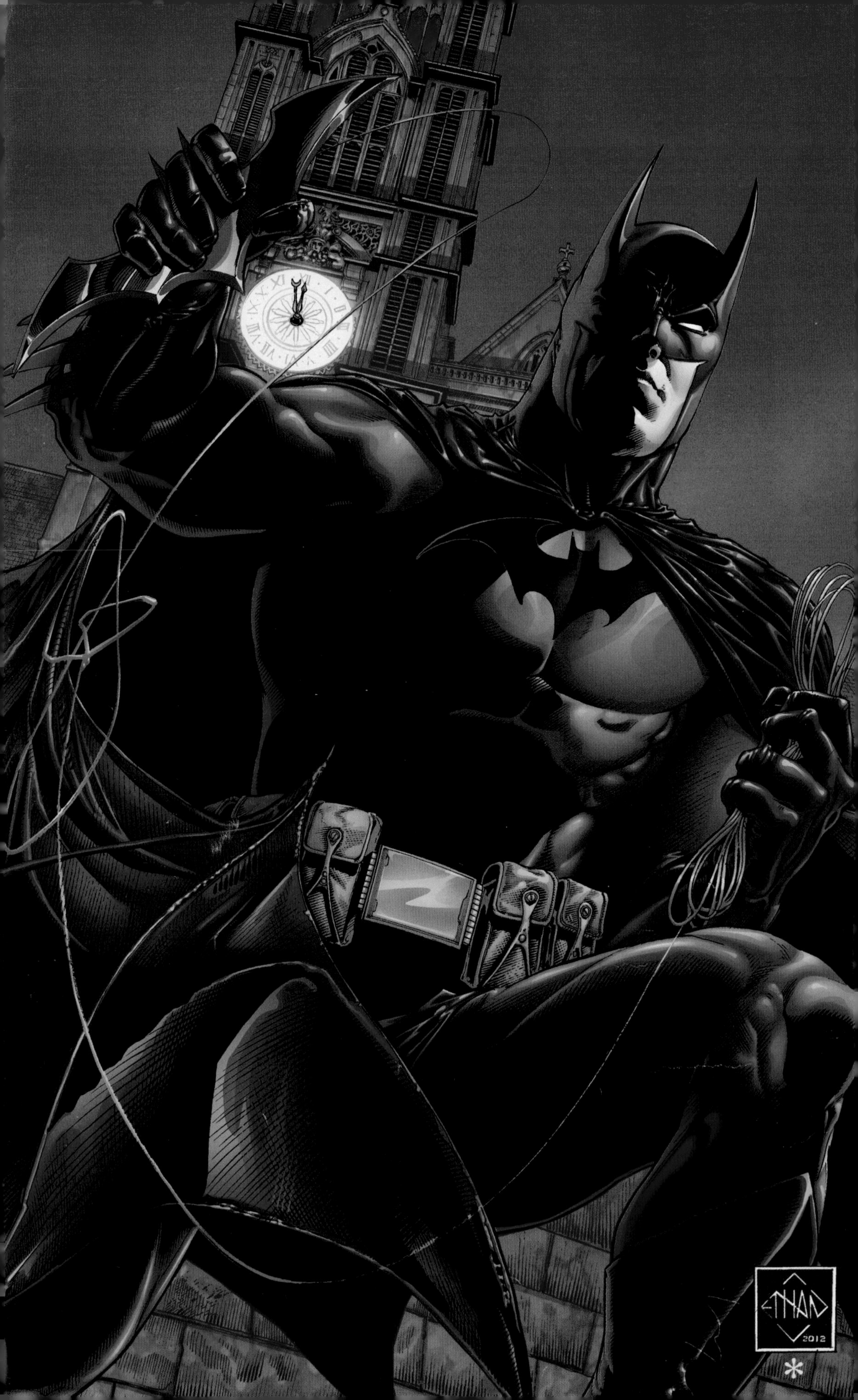
2012

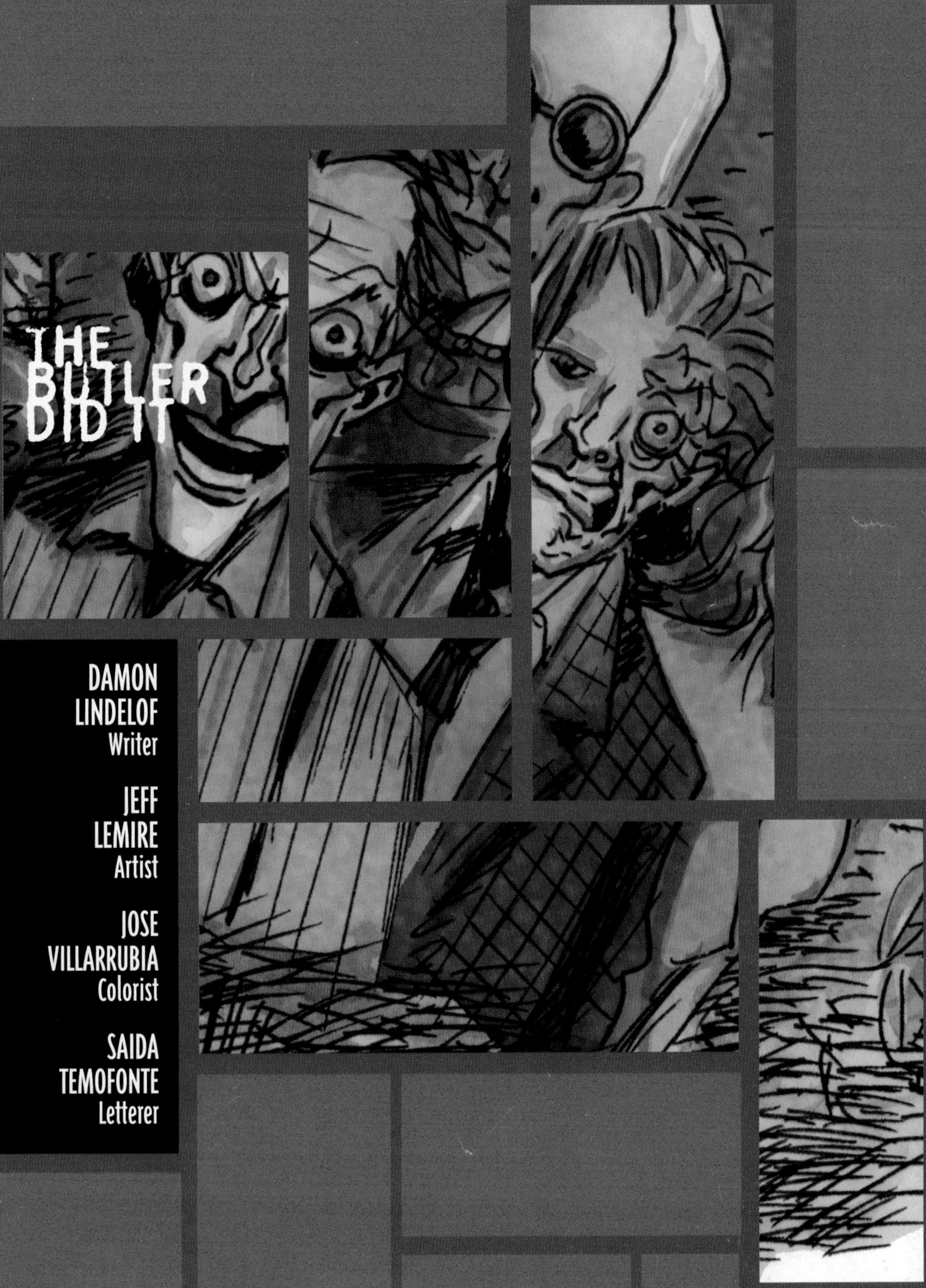
THE BUTLER DID IT

DAMON LINDELOF
Writer

JEFF LEMIRE
Artist

JOSE VILLARRUBIA
Colorist

SAIDA TEMOFONTE
Letterer

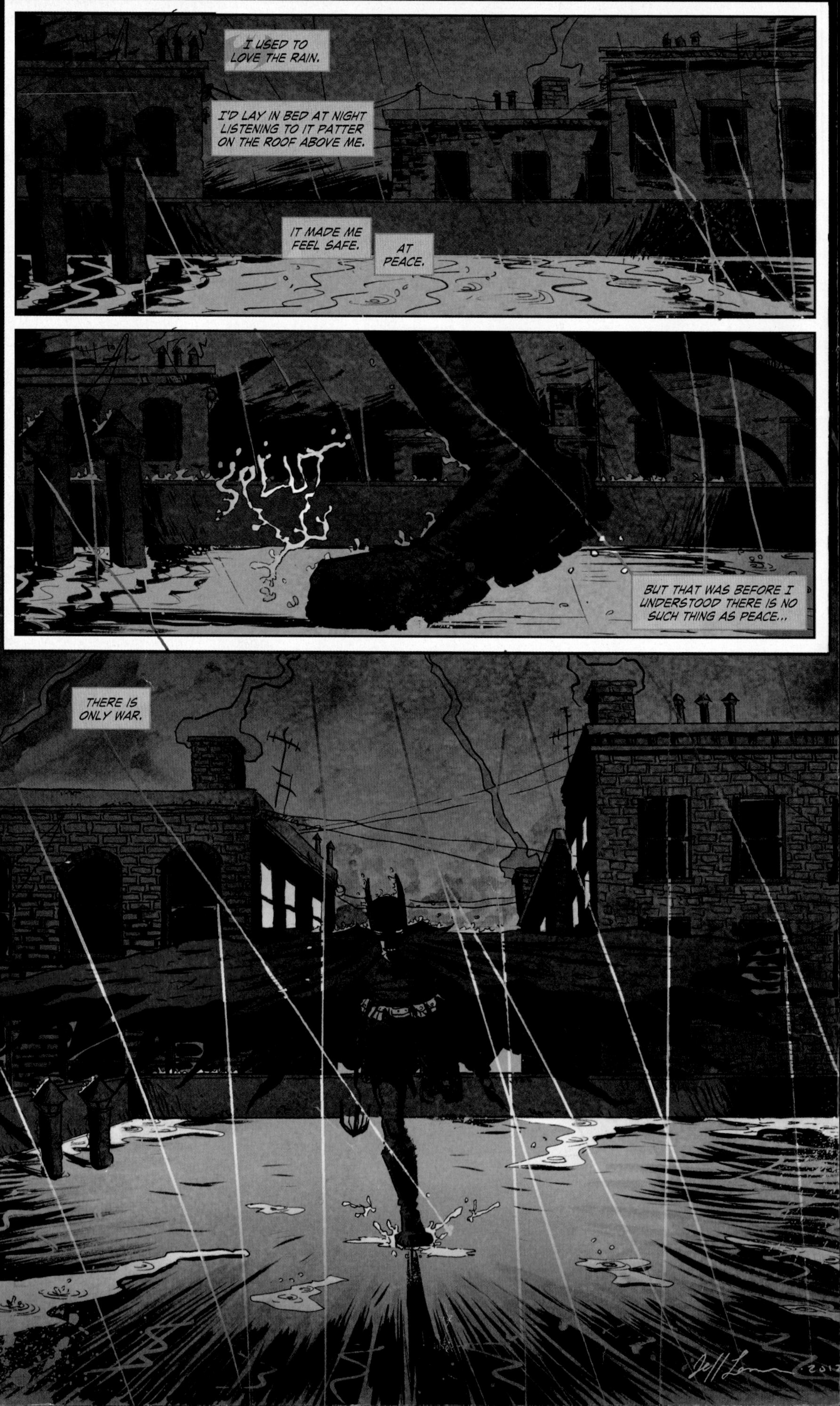
I USED TO LOVE THE RAIN.
I'D LAY IN BED AT NIGHT LISTENING TO IT PATTER ON THE ROOF ABOVE ME.
IT MADE ME FEEL SAFE.
AT PEACE.
BUT THAT WAS BEFORE I UNDERSTOOD THERE IS NO SUCH THING AS PEACE...
THERE IS ONLY WAR.

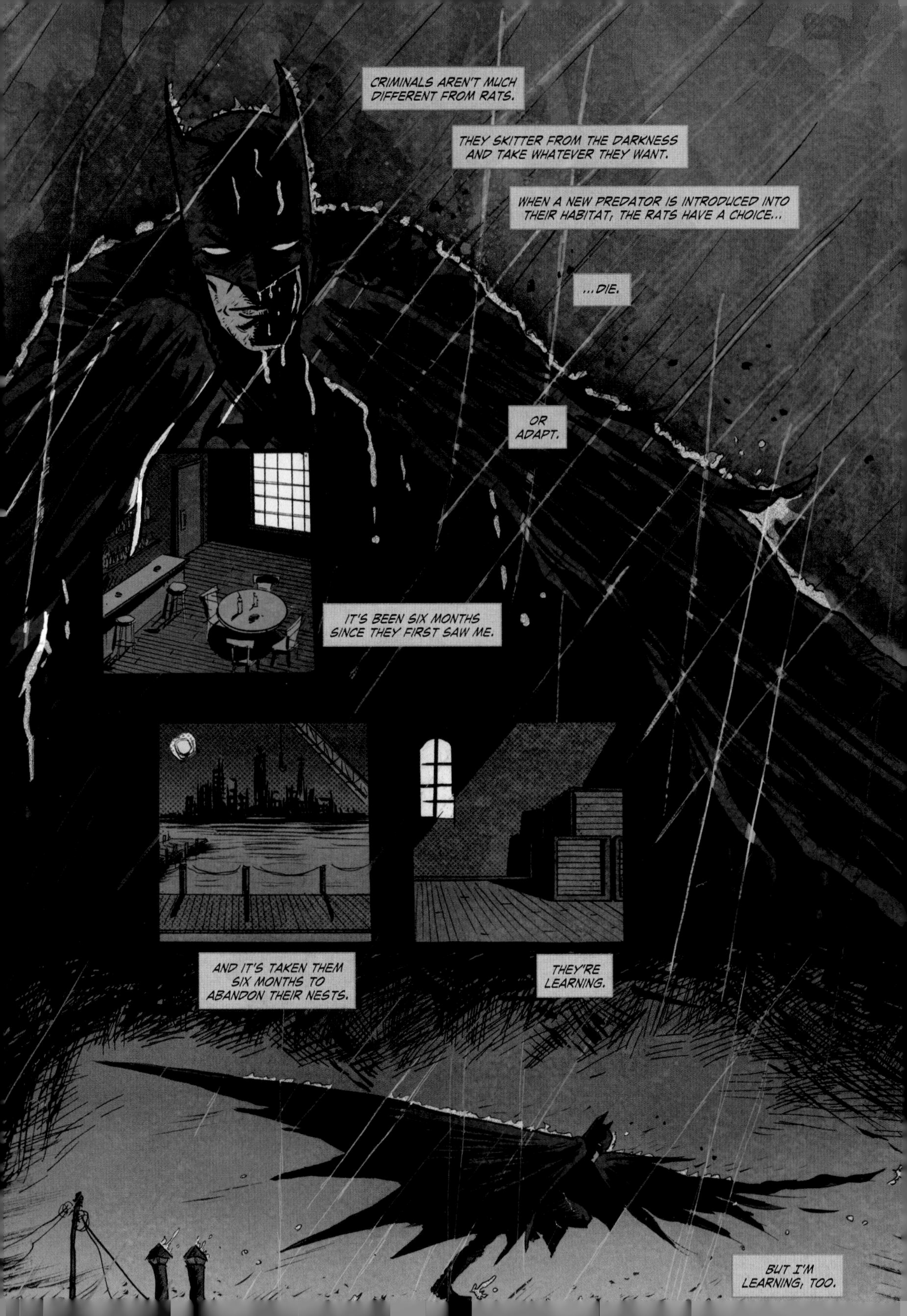
CRIMINALS AREN'T MUCH DIFFERENT FROM RATS.
THEY SKITTER FROM THE DARKNESS AND TAKE WHATEVER THEY WANT.
WHEN A NEW PREDATOR IS INTRODUCED INTO THEIR HABITAT, THE RATS HAVE A CHOICE...
...DIE.
OR ADAPT.
IT'S BEEN SIX MONTHS SINCE THEY FIRST SAW ME.
AND IT'S TAKEN THEM SIX MONTHS TO ABANDON THEIR NESTS.
THEY'RE LEARNING.
BUT I'M LEARNING, TOO.

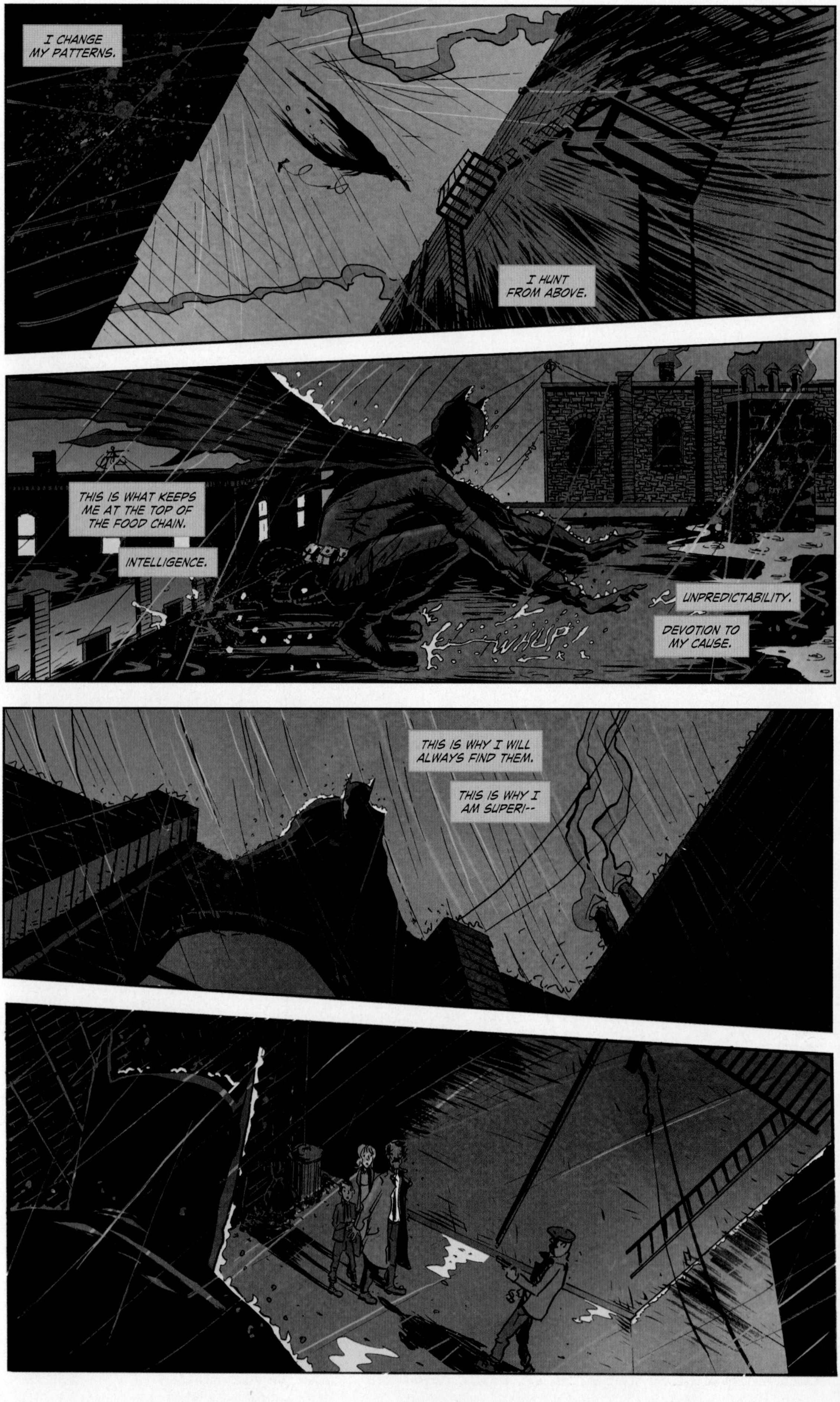
I CHANGE MY PATTERNS.
I HUNT FROM ABOVE.
THIS IS WHAT KEEPS ME AT THE TOP OF THE FOOD CHAIN.
INTELLIGENCE.
UNPREDICTABILITY.
DEVOTION TO MY CAUSE.
WHUP!
THIS IS WHY I WILL ALWAYS FIND THEM.
THIS IS WHY I AM SUPERI--

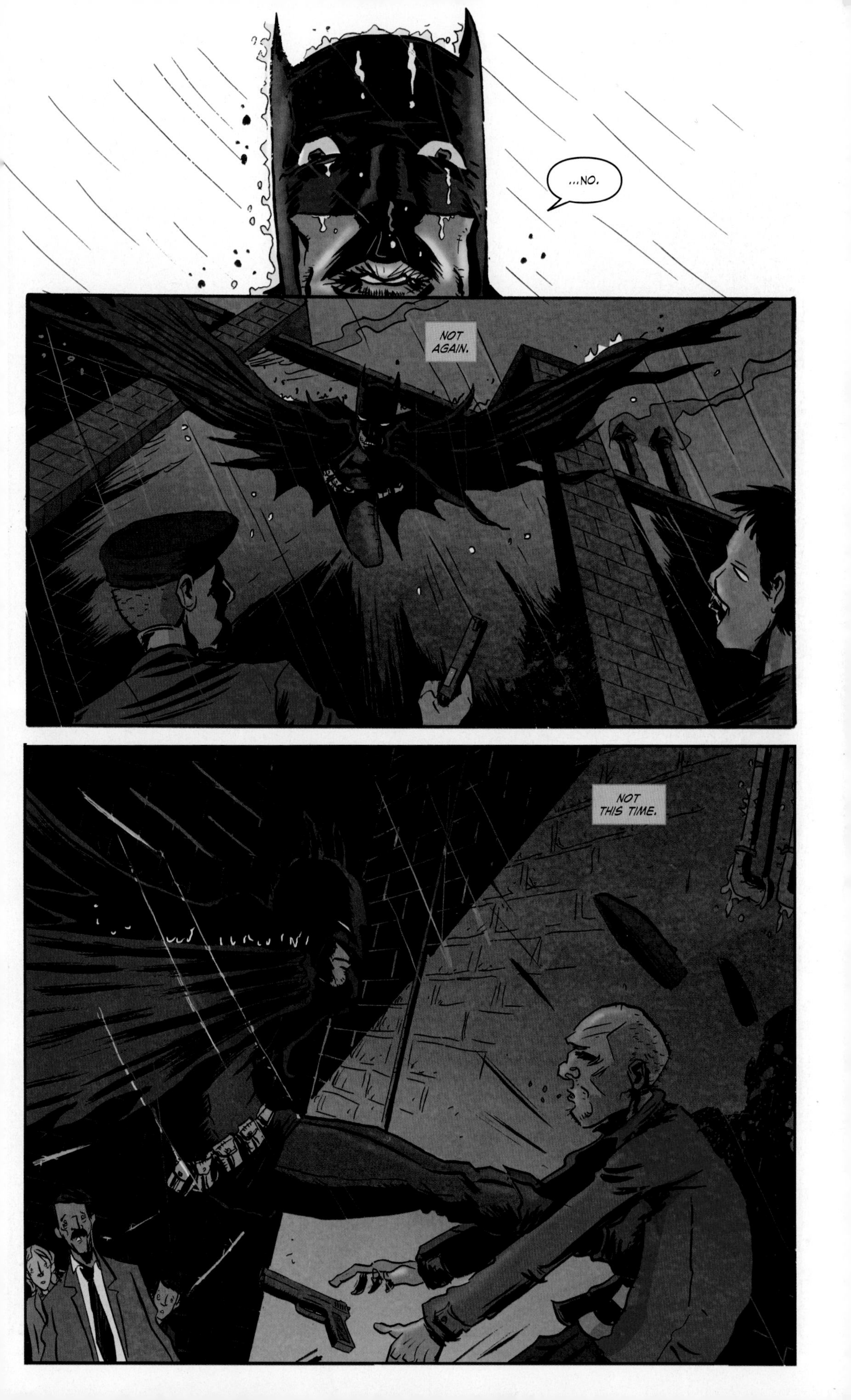
...NO.
NOT AGAIN.
NOT THIS TIME.

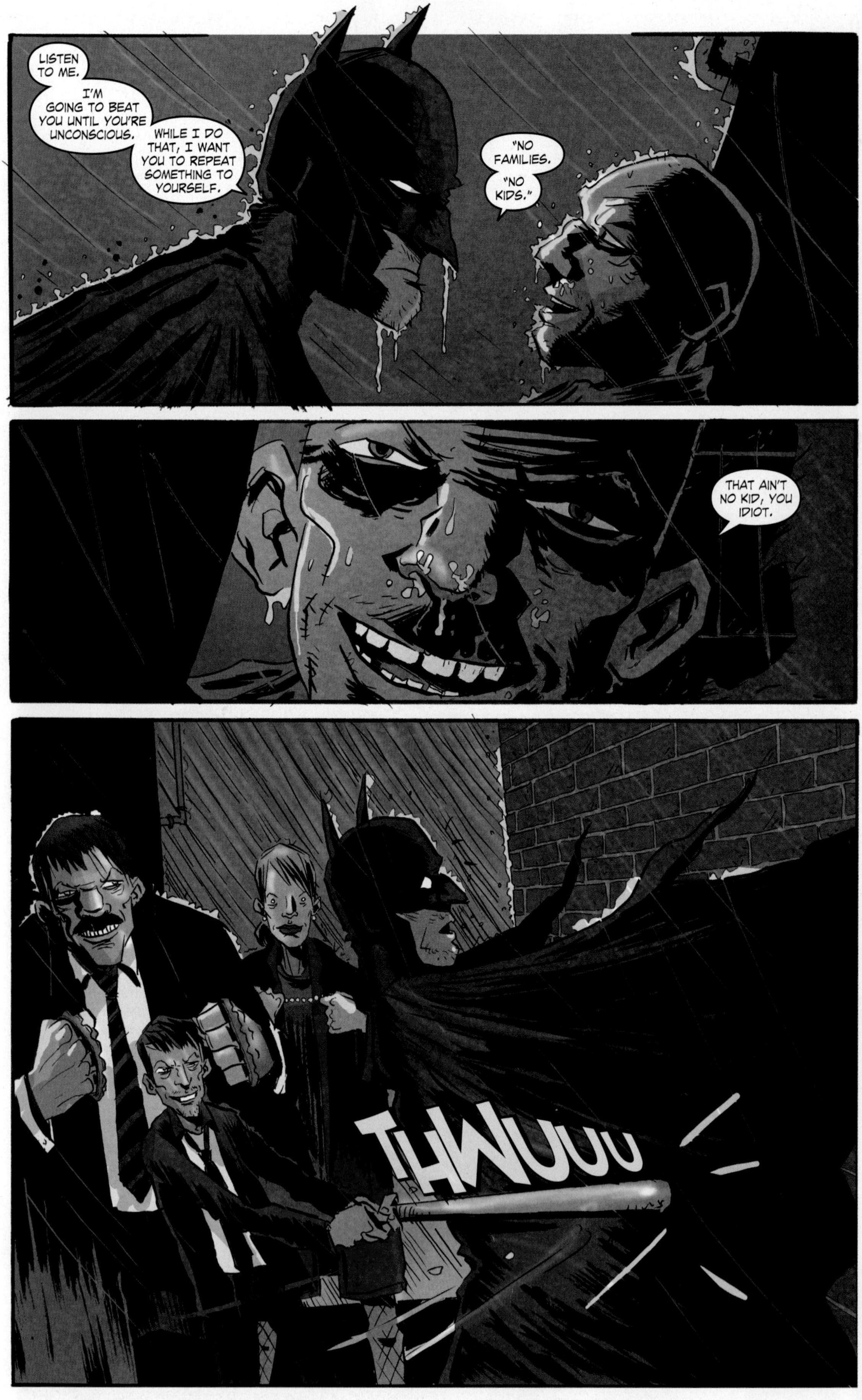
LISTEN TO ME.
I'M GOING TO BEAT YOU UNTIL YOU'RE UNCONSCIOUS.
WHILE I DO THAT, I WANT YOU TO REPEAT SOMETHING TO YOURSELF.
"NO FAMILIES.
"NO KIDS."
THAT AIN'T NO KID, YOU IDIOT.
THWUUU

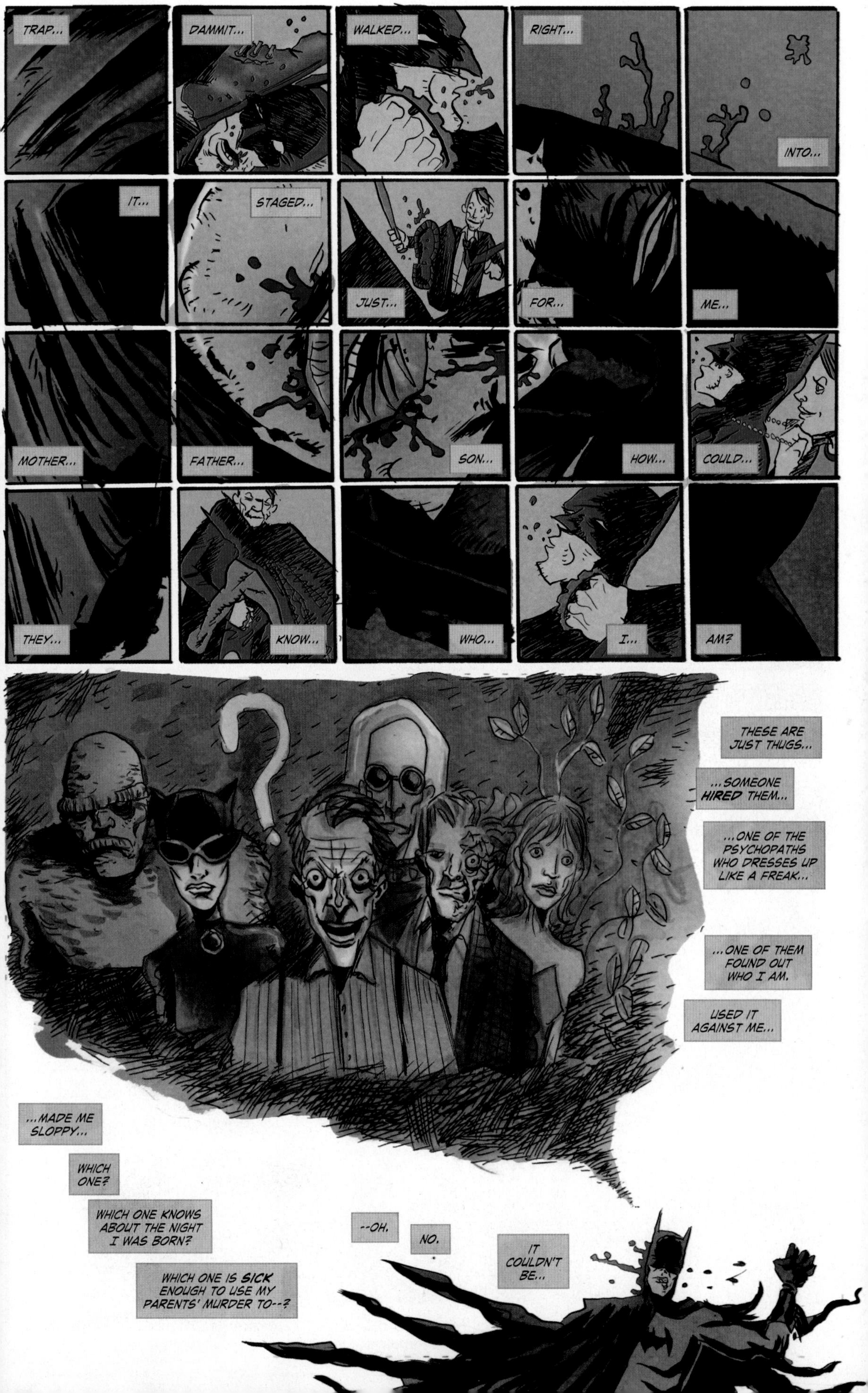
TRAP...
DAMMIT...
WALKED...
RIGHT...
INTO...
IT...
STAGED...
JUST...
FOR...
ME...
MOTHER...
FATHER...
SON...
HOW...
COULD...
THEY...
KNOW...
WHO...
I...
AM?
THESE ARE JUST THUGS...
...SOMEONE HIRED THEM...
...ONE OF THE PSYCHOPATHS WHO DRESSES UP LIKE A FREAK...
...ONE OF THEM FOUND OUT WHO I AM.
USED IT AGAINST ME...
...MADE ME SLOPPY...
WHICH ONE?
WHICH ONE KNOWS ABOUT THE NIGHT I WAS BORN?
WHICH ONE IS SICK ENOUGH TO USE MY PARENTS' MURDER TO--?
--OH.
NO.
IT COULDN'T BE...

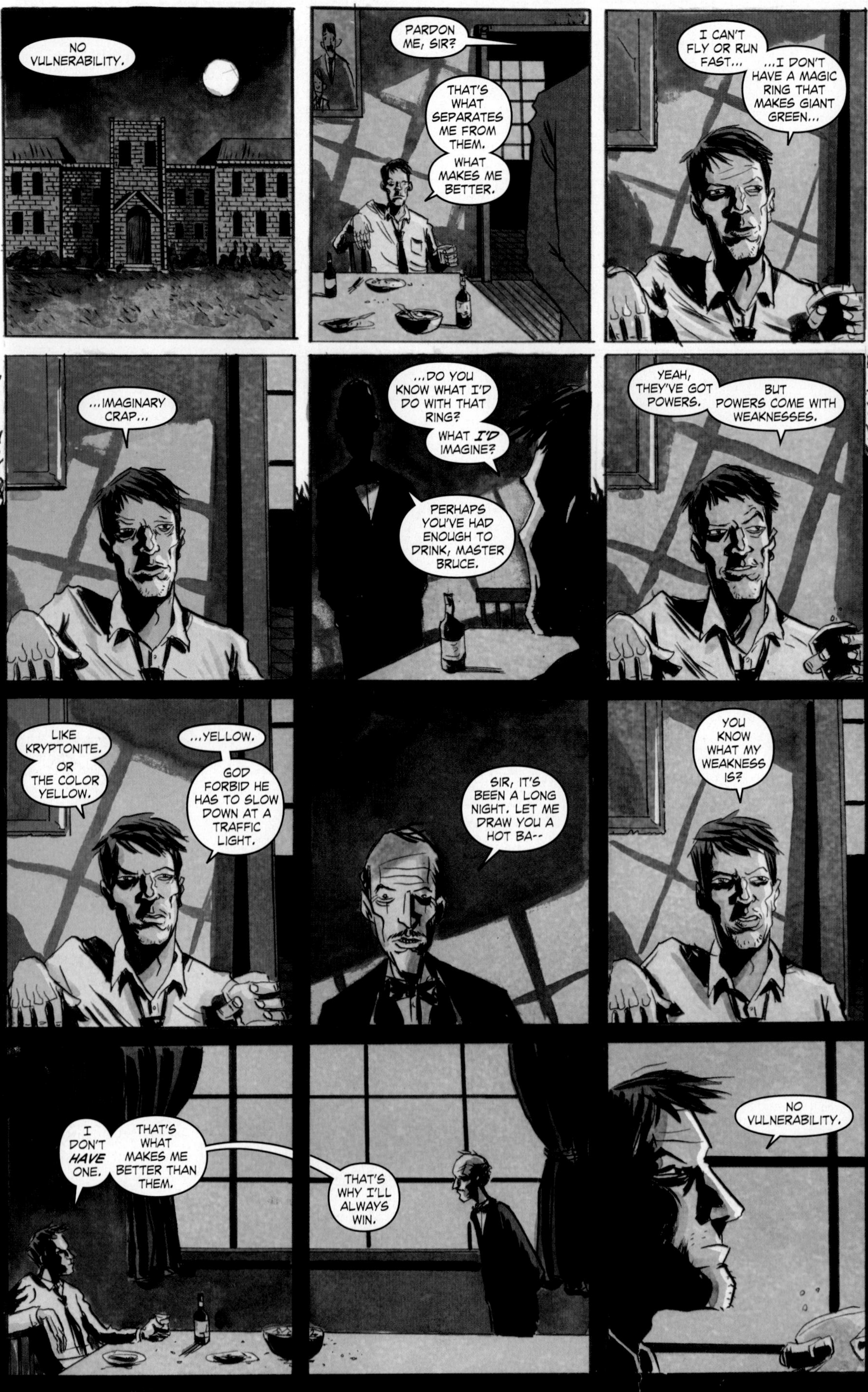
NO VULNERABILITY.
PARDON ME, SIR?
THAT'S WHAT SEPARATES ME FROM THEM.
WHAT MAKES ME BETTER.
I CAN'T FLY OR RUN FAST...
...I DON'T HAVE A MAGIC RING THAT MAKES GIANT GREEN...
...IMAGINARY CRAP...
...DO YOU KNOW WHAT I'D DO WITH THAT RING?
WHAT *I'D* IMAGINE?
PERHAPS YOU'VE HAD ENOUGH TO DRINK, MASTER BRUCE.
YEAH, THEY'VE GOT POWERS.
BUT POWERS COME WITH WEAKNESSES.
LIKE KRYPTONITE. OR THE COLOR YELLOW.
...YELLOW.
GOD FORBID HE HAS TO SLOW DOWN AT A TRAFFIC LIGHT.
SIR, IT'S BEEN A LONG NIGHT. LET ME DRAW YOU A HOT BA--
YOU KNOW WHAT MY WEAKNESS IS?
I DON'T *HAVE* ONE.
THAT'S WHAT MAKES ME BETTER THAN THEM.
THAT'S WHY I'LL ALWAYS WIN.
NO VULNERABILITY.

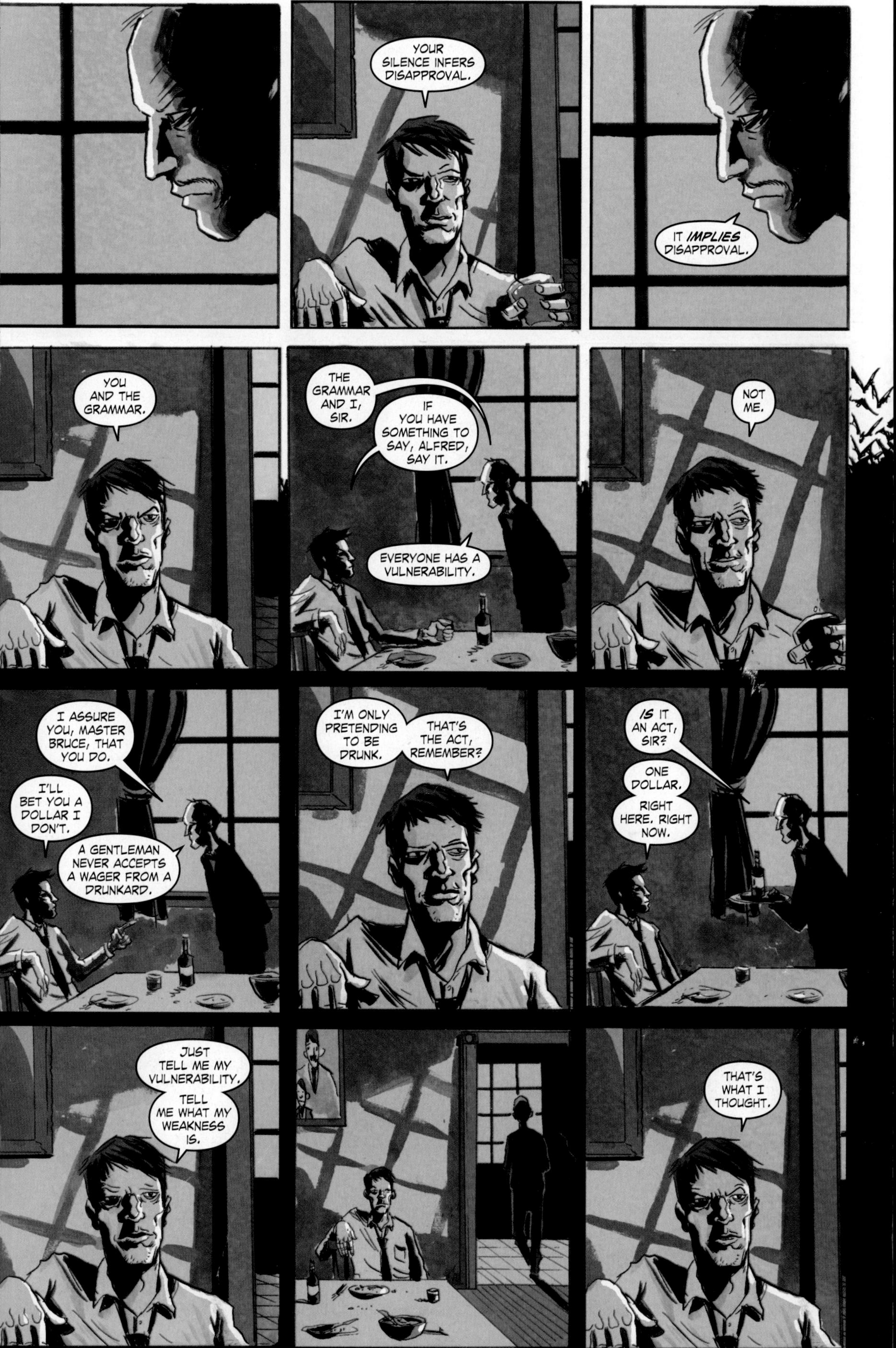
YOUR SILENCE INFERS DISAPPROVAL.
IT *IMPLIES* DISAPPROVAL.
YOU AND THE GRAMMAR.
THE GRAMMAR AND I, SIR.
IF YOU HAVE SOMETHING TO SAY, ALFRED, SAY IT.
EVERYONE HAS A VULNERABILITY.
NOT ME.
I ASSURE YOU, MASTER BRUCE, THAT YOU DO.
I'LL BET YOU A DOLLAR I DON'T.
A GENTLEMAN NEVER ACCEPTS A WAGER FROM A DRUNKARD.
I'M ONLY PRETENDING TO BE DRUNK.
THAT'S THE ACT, REMEMBER?
IS IT AN ACT, SIR?
ONE DOLLAR.
RIGHT HERE. RIGHT NOW.
JUST TELL ME MY VULNERABILITY.
TELL ME WHAT MY WEAKNESS IS.
THAT'S WHAT I THOUGHT.

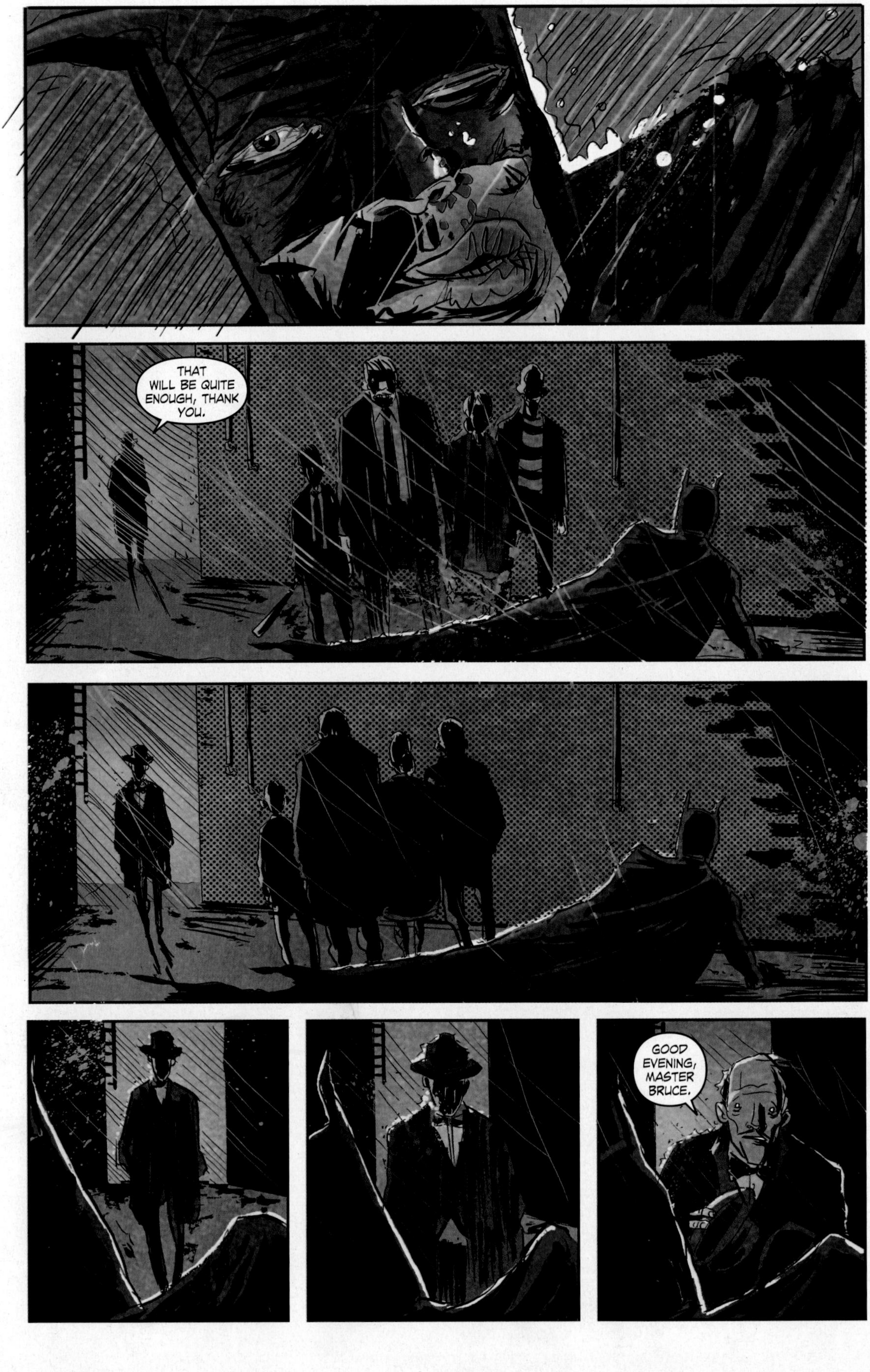
THAT WILL BE QUITE ENOUGH, THANK YOU.
GOOD EVENING, MASTER BRUCE.

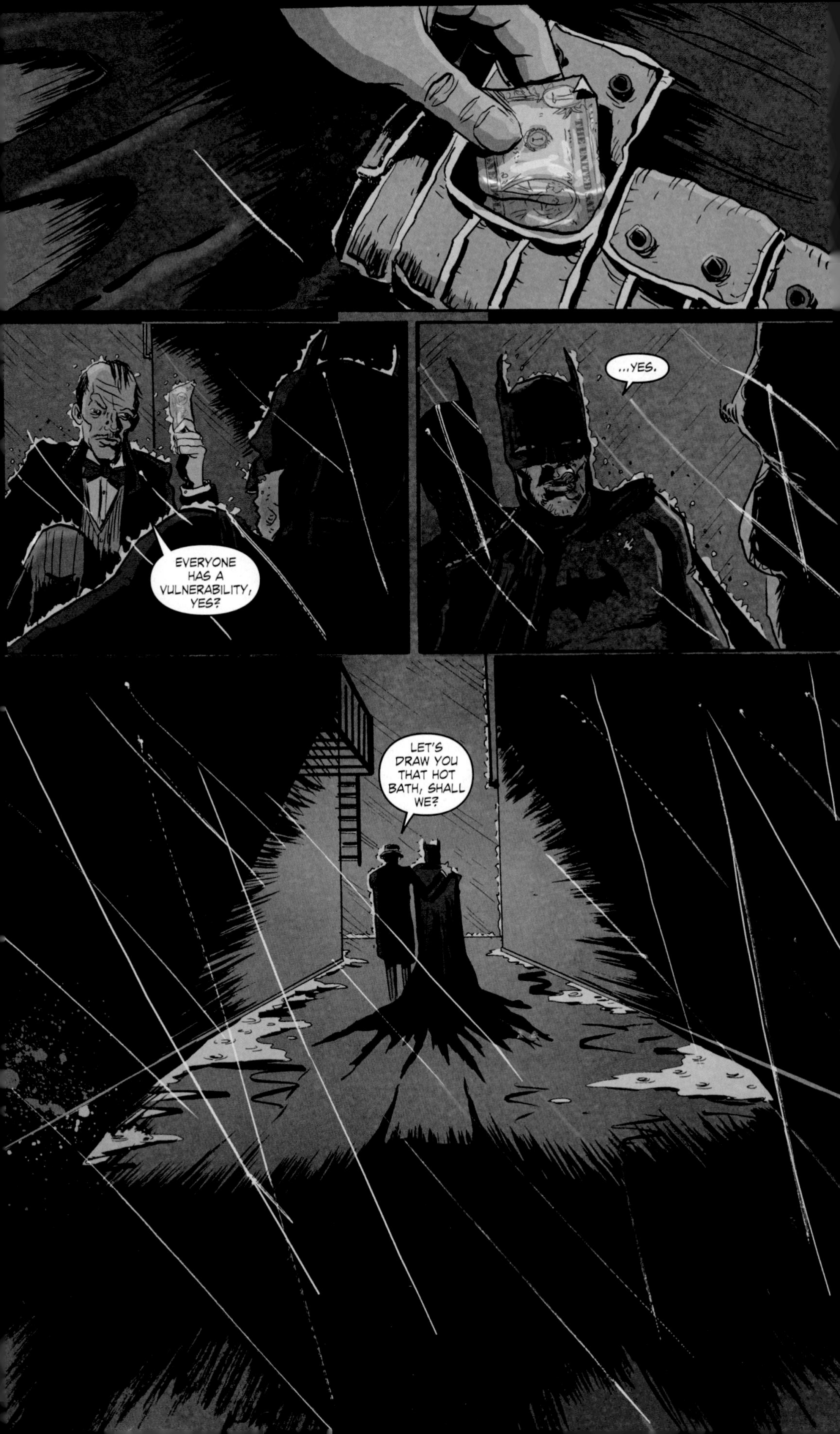
EVERYONE HAS A VULNERABILITY, YES?
...YES.
LET'S DRAW YOU THAT HOT BATH, SHALL WE?

ALL OF THE ABOVE

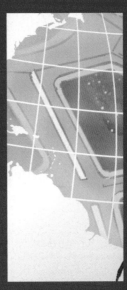

JONATHAN LARSEN
Writer

J.G. JONES
Artist

PAUL MOUNTS
Colorist

SAIDA TEMOFONTE
Letterer

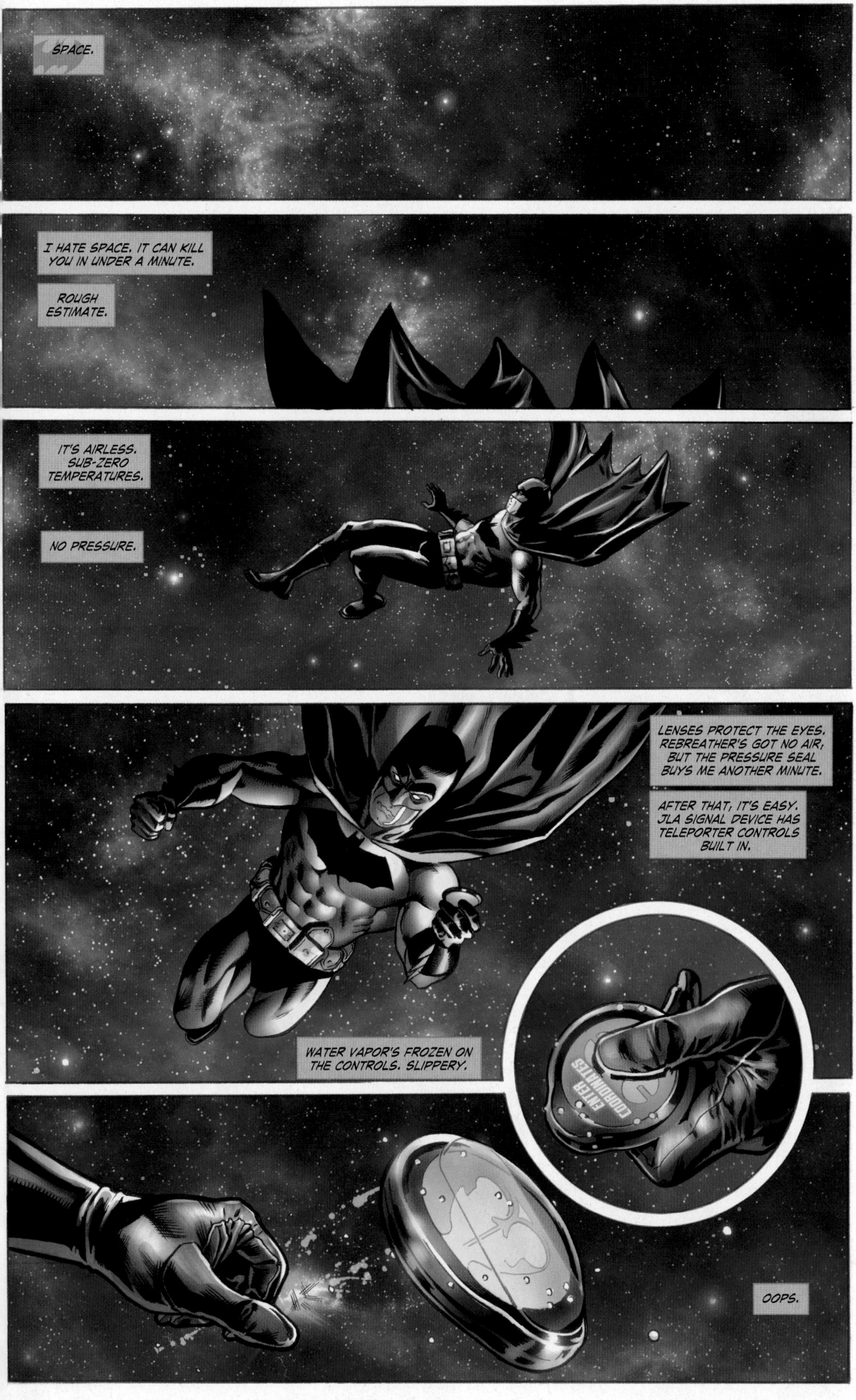
SPACE.
I HATE SPACE. IT CAN KILL YOU IN UNDER A MINUTE.
ROUGH ESTIMATE.
IT'S AIRLESS. SUB-ZERO TEMPERATURES.
NO PRESSURE.
LENSES PROTECT THE EYES. REBREATHER'S GOT NO AIR, BUT THE PRESSURE SEAL BUYS ME ANOTHER MINUTE.
AFTER THAT, IT'S EASY. JLA SIGNAL DEVICE HAS TELEPORTER CONTROLS BUILT IN.
WATER VAPOR'S FROZEN ON THE CONTROLS. SLIPPERY.
ENTER COORDINATES
OOPS.

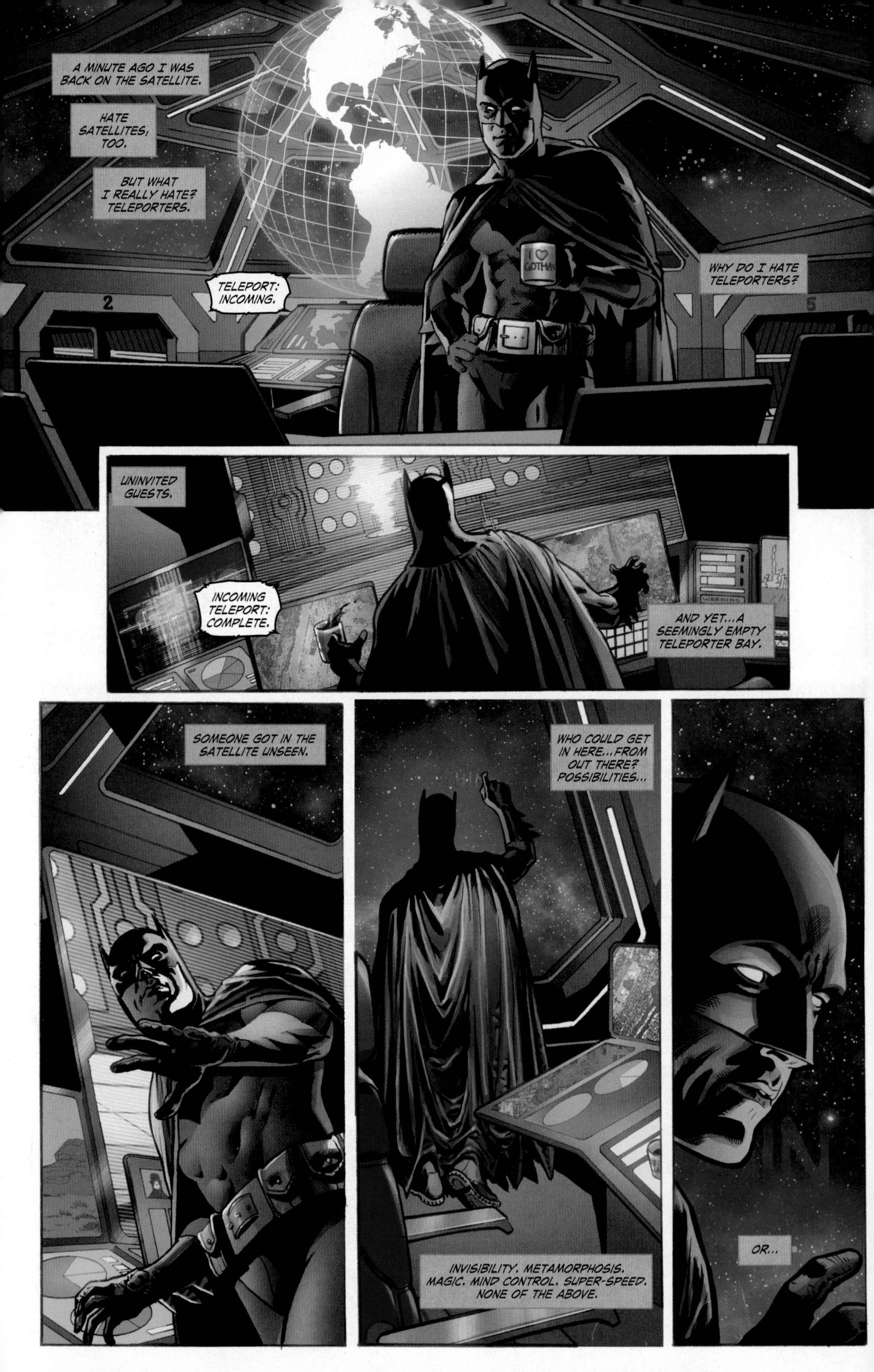

A MINUTE AGO I WAS BACK ON THE SATELLITE.
HATE SATELLITES, TOO.
BUT WHAT I REALLY HATE? TELEPORTERS.
TELEPORT: INCOMING.
WHY DO I HATE TELEPORTERS?
I ♥ GOTHAM
UNINVITED GUESTS.
INCOMING TELEPORT: COMPLETE.
AND YET...A SEEMINGLY EMPTY TELEPORTER BAY.
WARNING
SOMEONE GOT IN THE SATELLITE UNSEEN.
WHO COULD GET IN HERE...FROM OUT THERE? POSSIBILITIES...
INVISIBILITY. METAMORPHOSIS. MAGIC. MIND CONTROL. SUPER-SPEED. NONE OF THE ABOVE.
OR...

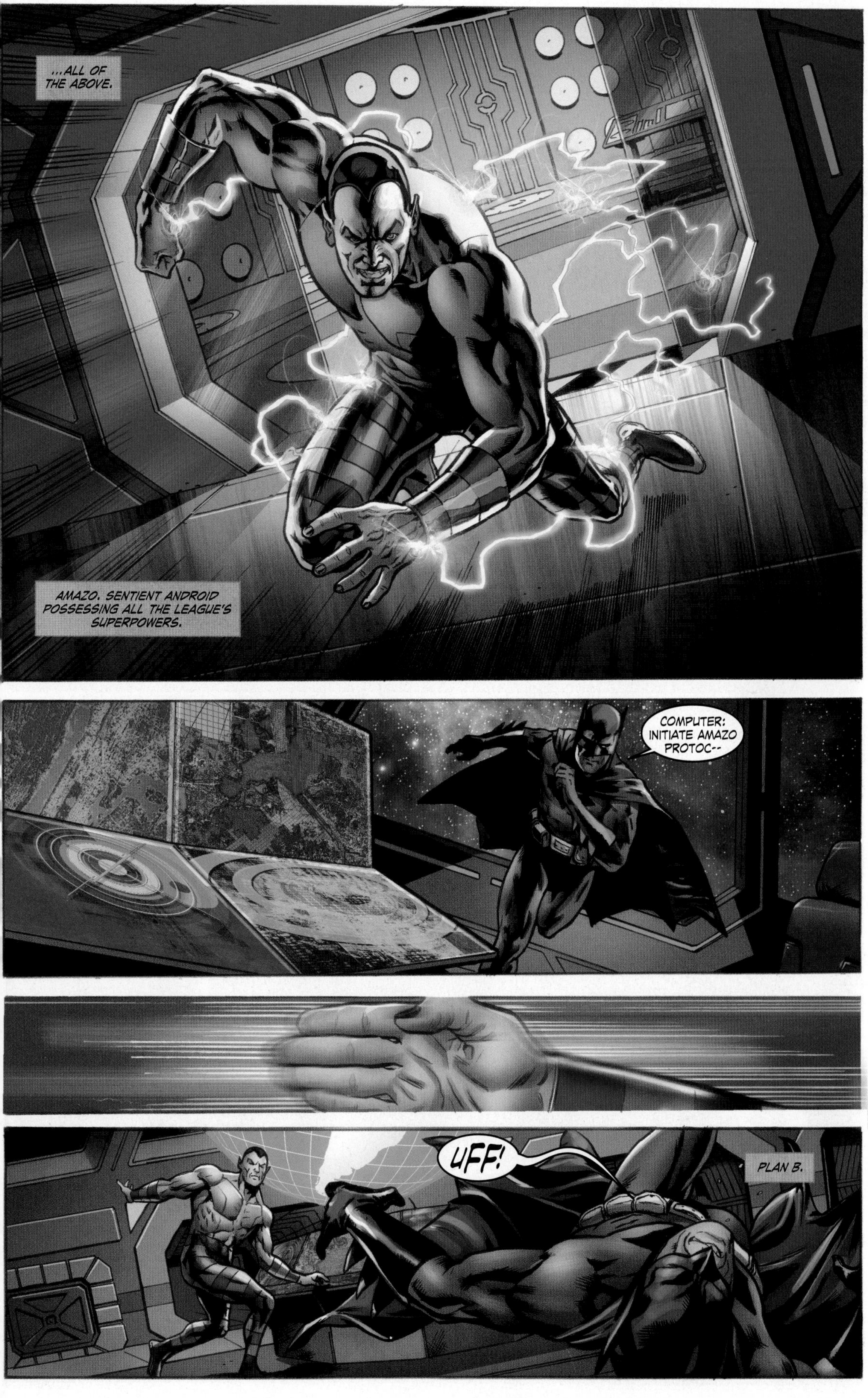
...ALL OF THE ABOVE.
AMAZO. SENTIENT ANDROID POSSESSING ALL THE LEAGUE'S SUPERPOWERS.
COMPUTER: INITIATE AMAZO PROTOC--
UFF!
PLAN B.

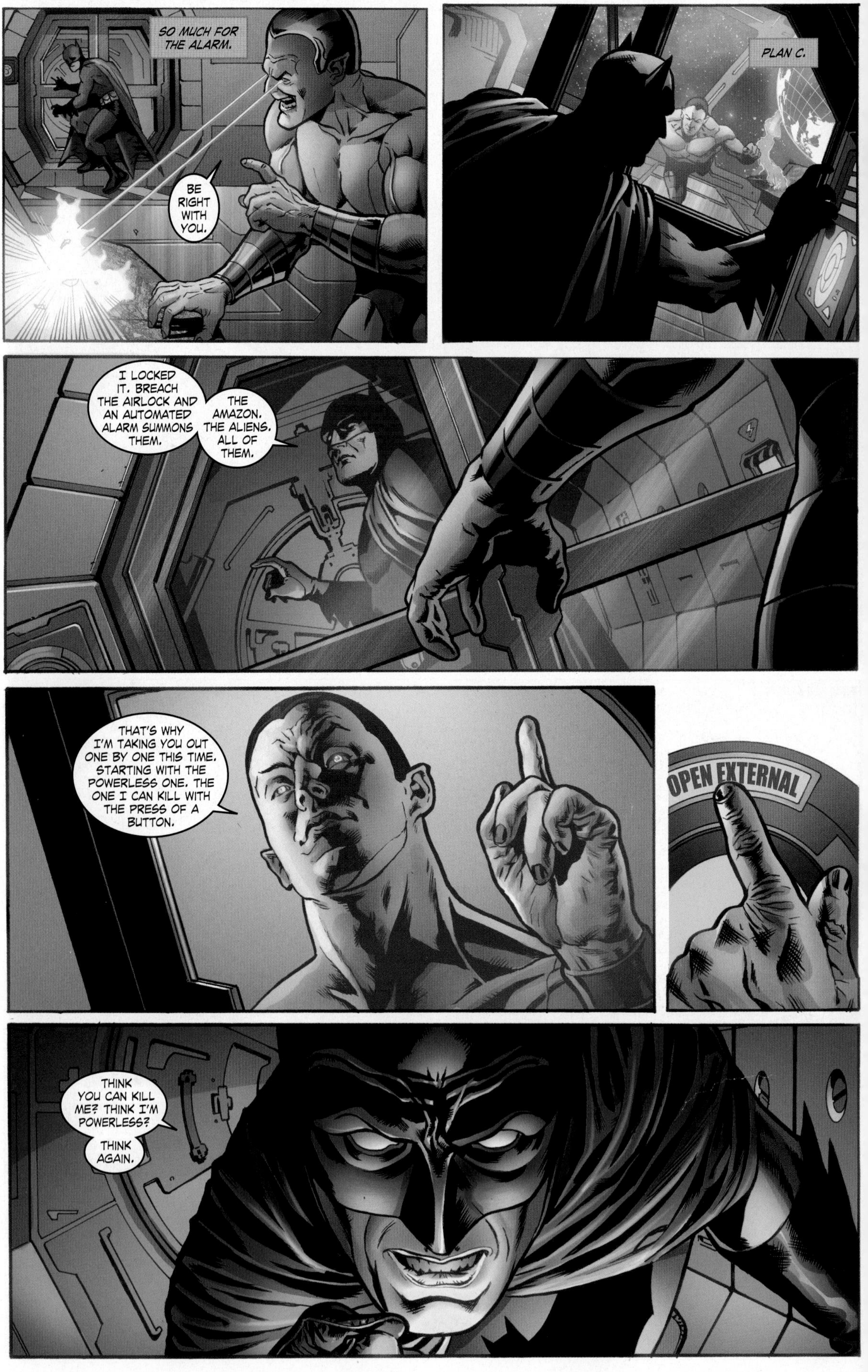
SO MUCH FOR THE ALARM.
BE RIGHT WITH YOU.
PLAN C.
I LOCKED IT. BREACH THE AIRLOCK AND AN AUTOMATED ALARM SUMMONS THEM.
THE AMAZON. THE ALIENS. ALL OF THEM.
THAT'S WHY I'M TAKING YOU OUT ONE BY ONE THIS TIME. STARTING WITH THE POWERLESS ONE. THE ONE I CAN KILL WITH THE PRESS OF A BUTTON.
OPEN EXTERNAL
THINK YOU CAN KILL ME? THINK I'M POWERLESS?
THINK AGAIN.

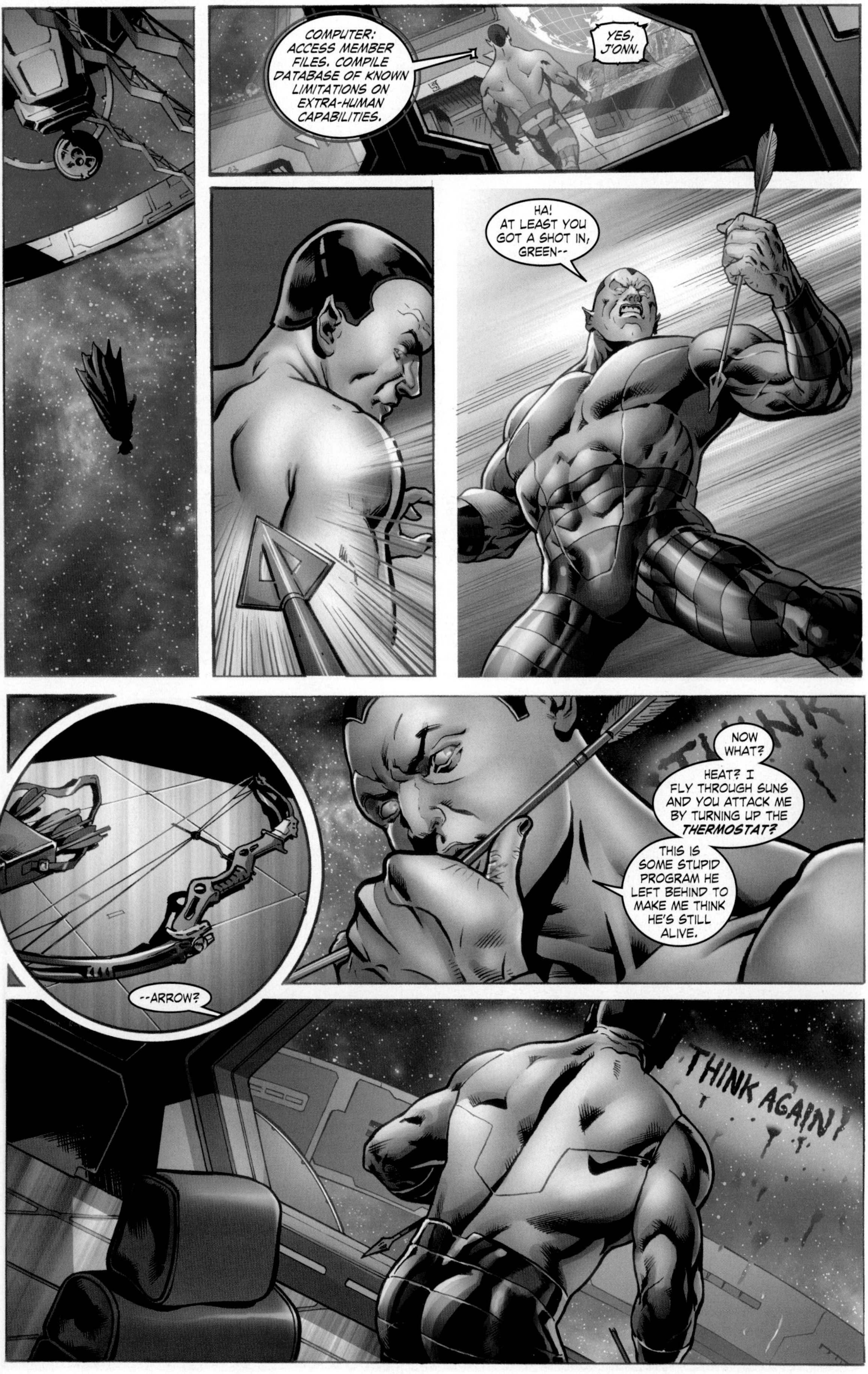
COMPUTER: ACCESS MEMBER FILES. COMPILE DATABASE OF KNOWN LIMITATIONS ON EXTRA-HUMAN CAPABILITIES.
YES, J'ONN.
HA! AT LEAST YOU GOT A SHOT IN, GREEN--
--ARROW?
NOW WHAT?
HEAT? I FLY THROUGH SUNS AND YOU ATTACK ME BY TURNING UP THE *THERMOSTAT?*
THIS IS SOME STUPID PROGRAM HE LEFT BEHIND TO MAKE ME THINK HE'S STILL ALIVE.
THINK AGAIN

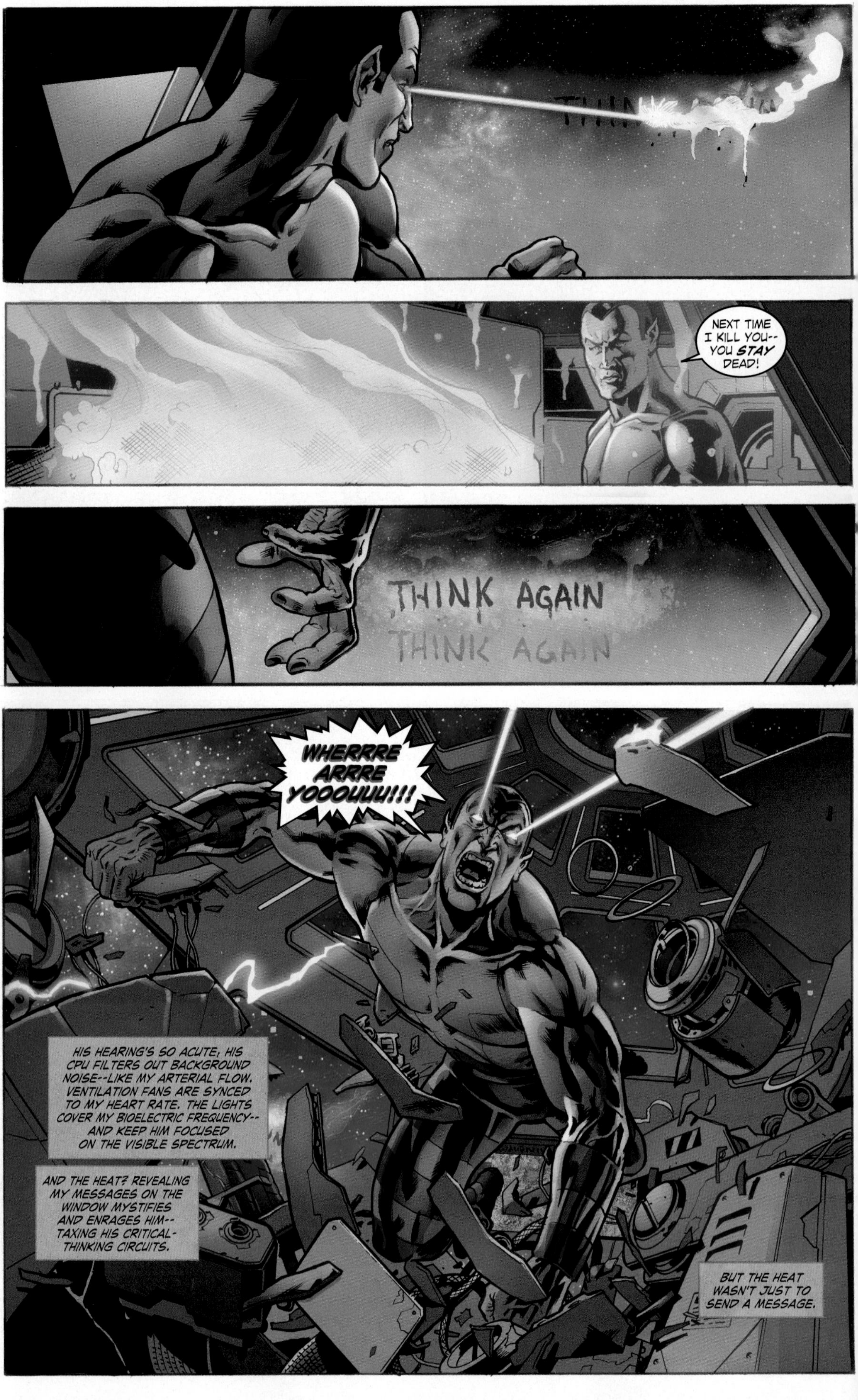
NEXT TIME I KILL YOU-- YOU STAY DEAD!
THINK AGAIN
THINK AGAIN
WHERRRE ARRRE YOOOUUU!!!
HIS HEARING'S SO ACUTE; HIS CPU FILTERS OUT BACKGROUND NOISE--LIKE MY ARTERIAL FLOW. VENTILATION FANS ARE SYNCED TO MY HEART RATE. THE LIGHTS COVER MY BIOELECTRIC FREQUENCY-- AND KEEP HIM FOCUSED ON THE VISIBLE SPECTRUM.
AND THE HEAT? REVEALING MY MESSAGES ON THE WINDOW MYSTIFIES AND ENRAGES HIM-- TAXING HIS CRITICAL-THINKING CIRCUITS.
BUT THE HEAT WASN'T JUST TO SEND A MESSAGE.

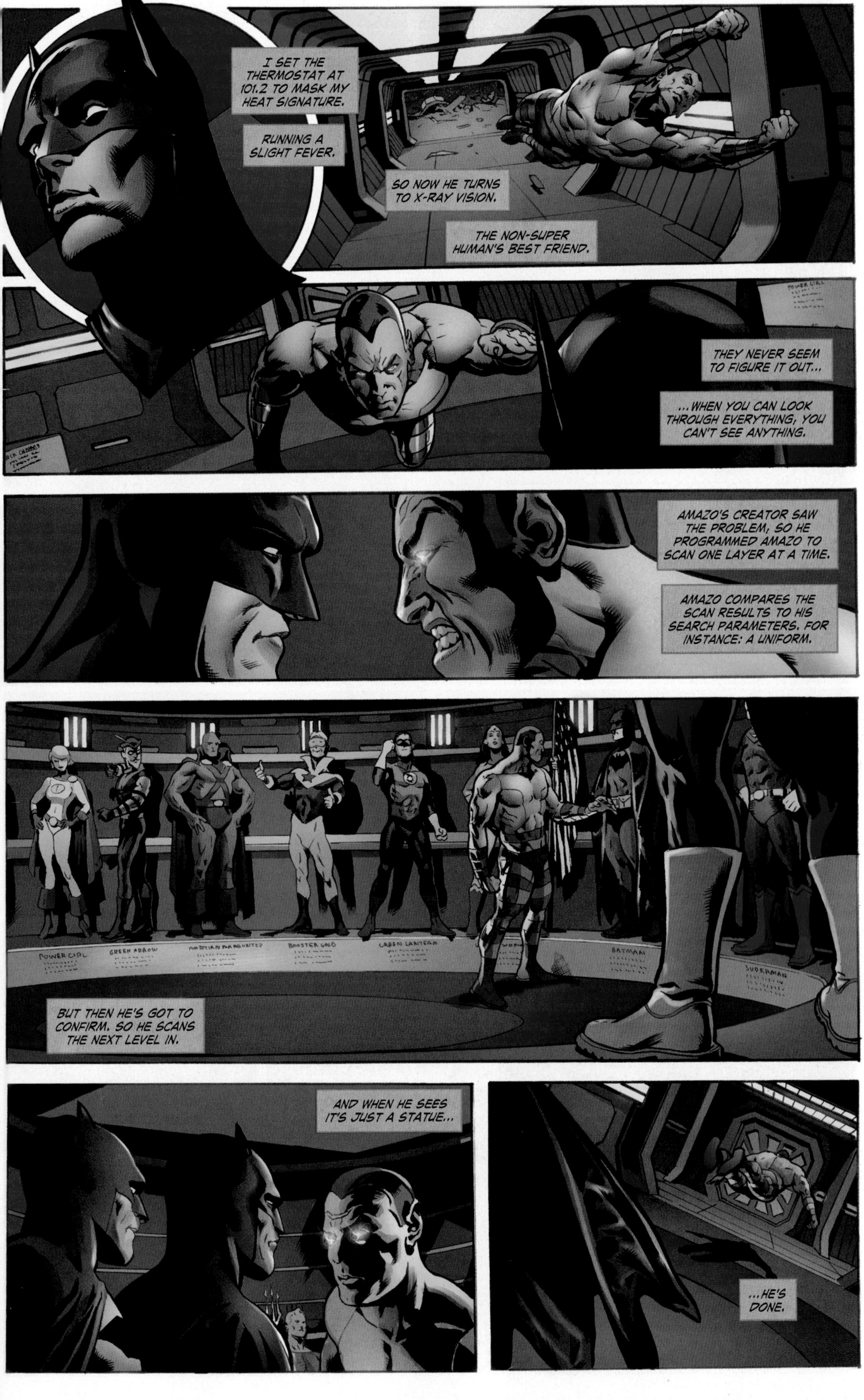
I SET THE THERMOSTAT AT 101.2 TO MASK MY HEAT SIGNATURE.
RUNNING A SLIGHT FEVER.
SO NOW HE TURNS TO X-RAY VISION.
THE NON-SUPER HUMAN'S BEST FRIEND.
THEY NEVER SEEM TO FIGURE IT OUT...
...WHEN YOU CAN LOOK THROUGH EVERYTHING, YOU CAN'T SEE ANYTHING.
AMAZO'S CREATOR SAW THE PROBLEM, SO HE PROGRAMMED AMAZO TO SCAN ONE LAYER AT A TIME.
AMAZO COMPARES THE SCAN RESULTS TO HIS SEARCH PARAMETERS. FOR INSTANCE: A UNIFORM.
POWER GIRL
GREEN ARROW
BOOSTER GOLD
GREEN LANTERN
BATMAN
SUPERMAN
BUT THEN HE'S GOT TO CONFIRM. SO HE SCANS THE NEXT LEVEL IN.
AND WHEN HE SEES IT'S JUST A STATUE...
...HE'S DONE.

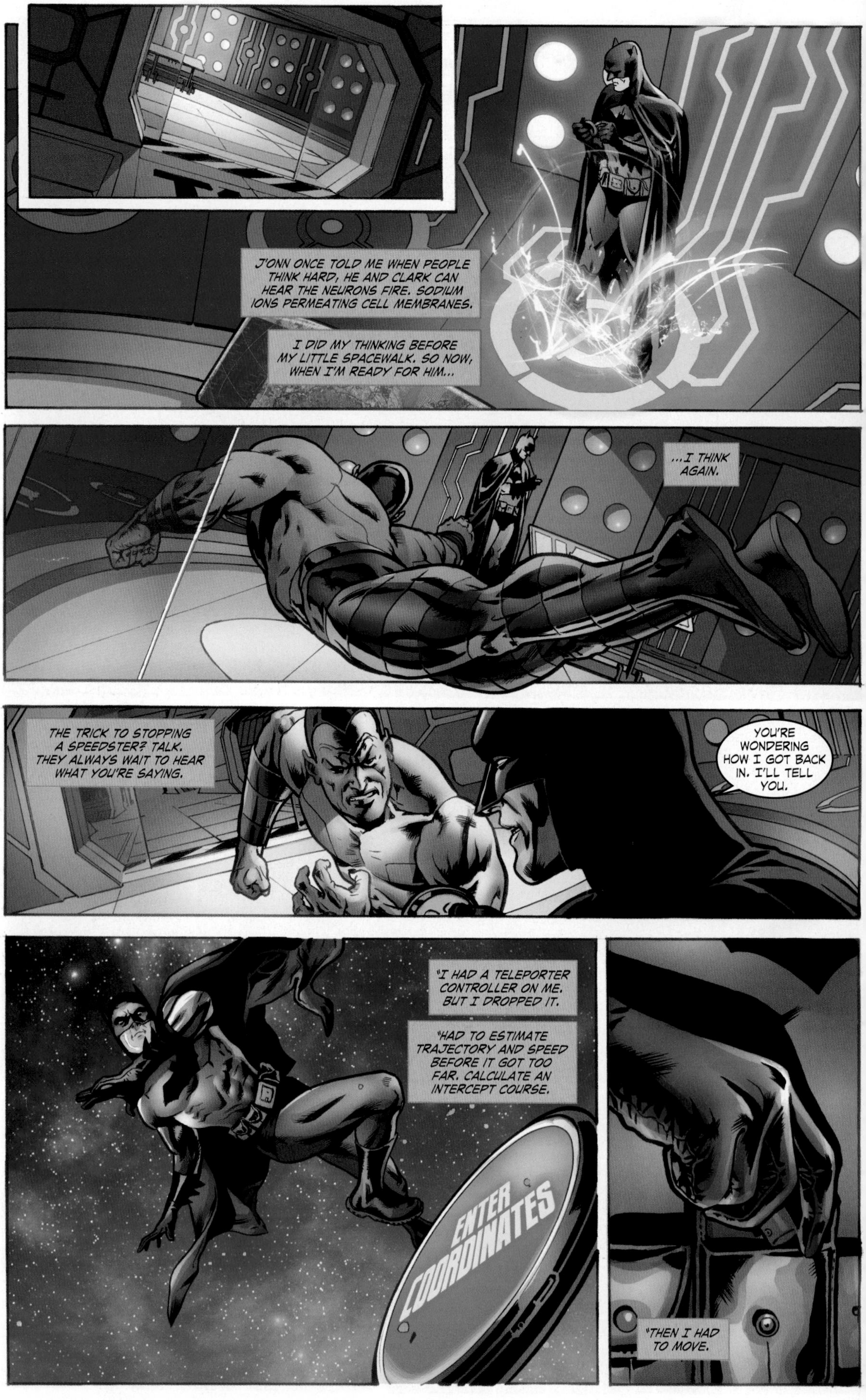
J'ONN ONCE TOLD ME WHEN PEOPLE THINK HARD, HE AND CLARK CAN HEAR THE NEURONS FIRE. SODIUM IONS PERMEATING CELL MEMBRANES.
I DID MY THINKING BEFORE MY LITTLE SPACEWALK. SO NOW, WHEN I'M READY FOR HIM...
...I THINK AGAIN.
THE TRICK TO STOPPING A SPEEDSTER? TALK. THEY ALWAYS WAIT TO HEAR WHAT YOU'RE SAYING.
YOU'RE WONDERING HOW I GOT BACK IN. I'LL TELL YOU.
"I HAD A TELEPORTER CONTROLLER ON ME. BUT I DROPPED IT.
"HAD TO ESTIMATE TRAJECTORY AND SPEED BEFORE IT GOT TOO FAR. CALCULATE AN INTERCEPT COURSE.
ENTER COORDINATES
"THEN I HAD TO MOVE.

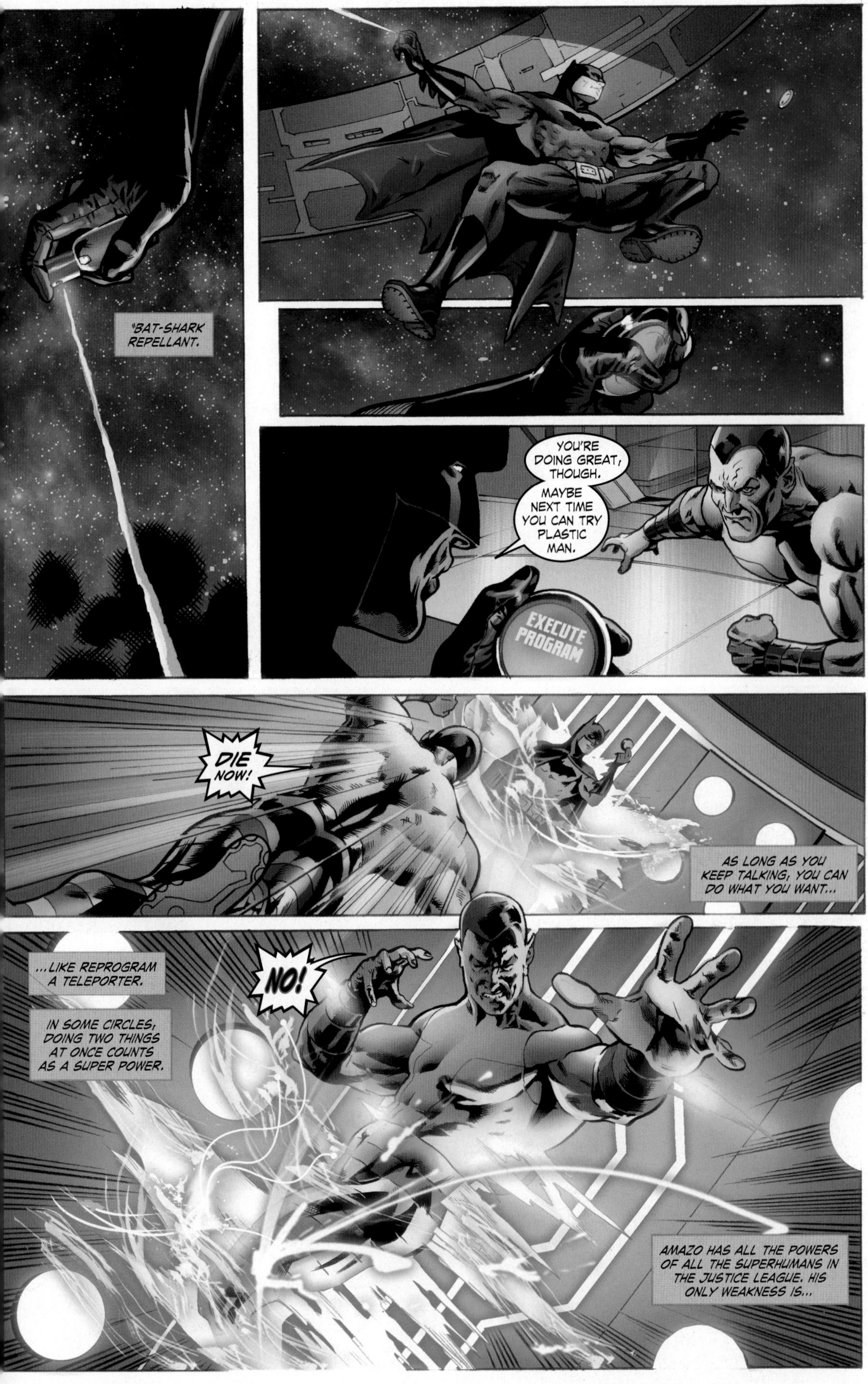
"BAT-SHARK REPELLANT.
YOU'RE DOING GREAT, THOUGH.
MAYBE NEXT TIME YOU CAN TRY PLASTIC MAN.
EXECUTE PROGRAM
DIE NOW!
AS LONG AS YOU KEEP TALKING, YOU CAN DO WHAT YOU WANT...
...LIKE REPROGRAM A TELEPORTER.
IN SOME CIRCLES, DOING TWO THINGS AT ONCE COUNTS AS A SUPER POWER.
NO!
AMAZO HAS ALL THE POWERS OF ALL THE SUPERHUMANS IN THE JUSTICE LEAGUE. HIS ONLY WEAKNESS IS...

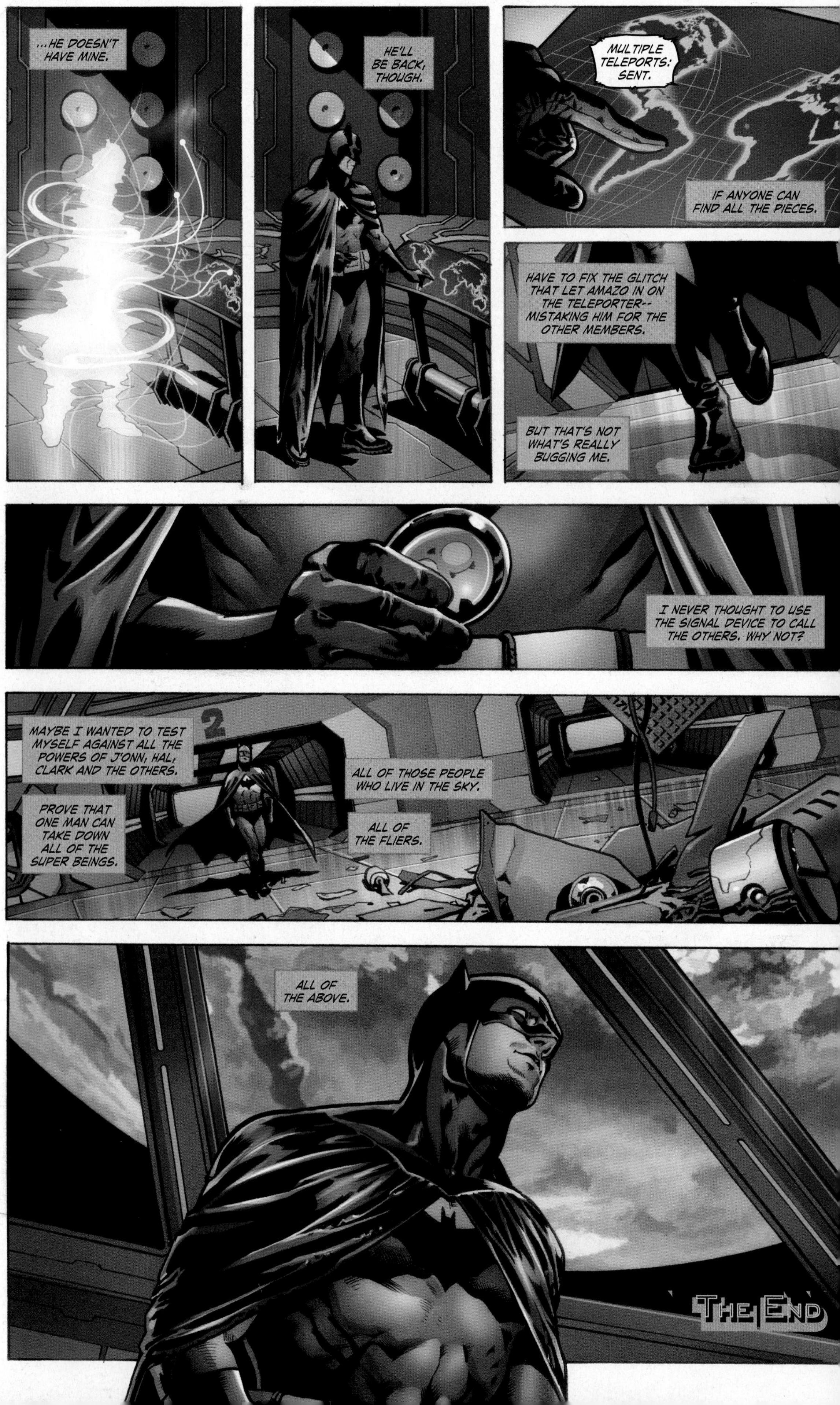
...HE DOESN'T HAVE MINE.
HE'LL BE BACK, THOUGH.
MULTIPLE TELEPORTS: SENT.
IF ANYONE CAN FIND ALL THE PIECES.
HAVE TO FIX THE GLITCH THAT LET AMAZO IN ON THE TELEPORTER-- MISTAKING HIM FOR THE OTHER MEMBERS.
BUT THAT'S NOT WHAT'S REALLY BUGGING ME.
I NEVER THOUGHT TO USE THE SIGNAL DEVICE TO CALL THE OTHERS. WHY NOT?
MAYBE I WANTED TO TEST MYSELF AGAINST ALL THE POWERS OF J'ONN, HAL, CLARK AND THE OTHERS.
PROVE THAT ONE MAN CAN TAKE DOWN ALL OF THE SUPER BEINGS.
ALL OF THOSE PEOPLE WHO LIVE IN THE SKY.
ALL OF THE FLIERS.
ALL OF THE ABOVE.
THE END

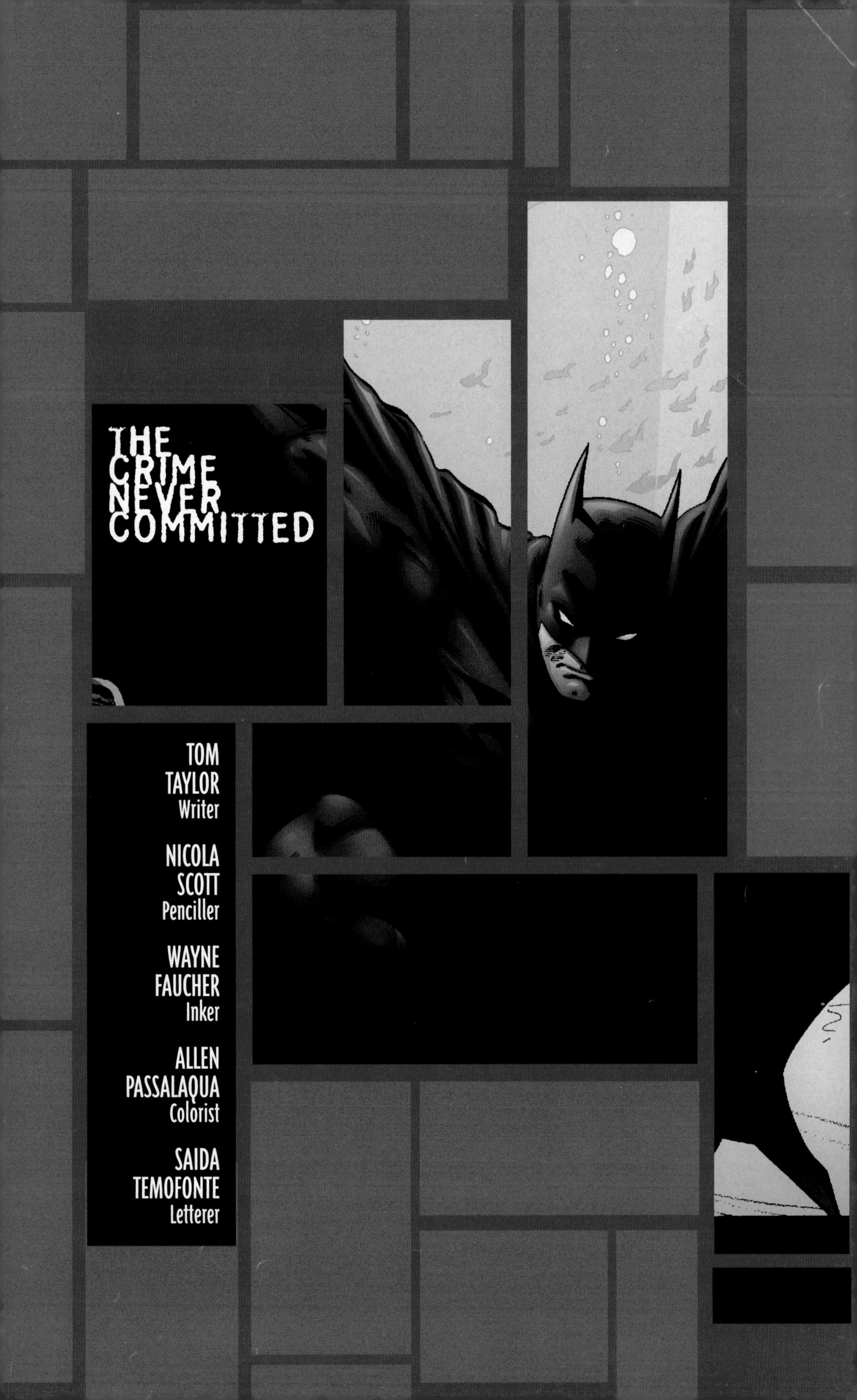

THE CRIME NEVER COMMITTED
TOM TAYLOR Writer
NICOLA SCOTT Penciller
WAYNE FAUCHER Inker
ALLEN PASSALAQUA Colorist
SAIDA TEMOFONTE Letterer

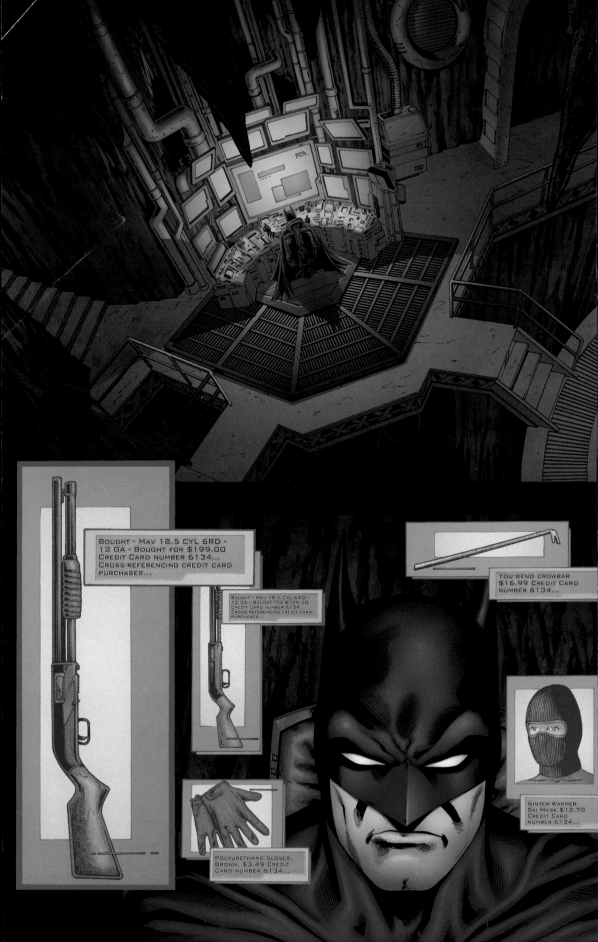

BOUGHT - MAV 18.5 CYL 6RD - 12 GA - BOUGHT FOR $199.00 CREDIT CARD NUMBER 6134... CROSS-REFERENCING CREDIT CARD PURCHASES...

BOUGHT - MAV 18.5 CYL 6RD - 12 GA - BOUGHT FOR $199.00 CREDIT CARD NUMBER 6134... CROSS-REFERENCING CREDIT CARD PURCHASES...

YOU-BEND CROWBAR $16.99 CREDIT CARD NUMBER 6134...

POLYURETHANE GLOVES, BROWN, $3.49 CREDIT CARD NUMBER 6134...

WINTER WARMER SKI MASK $12.70 CREDIT CARD NUMBER 6134...

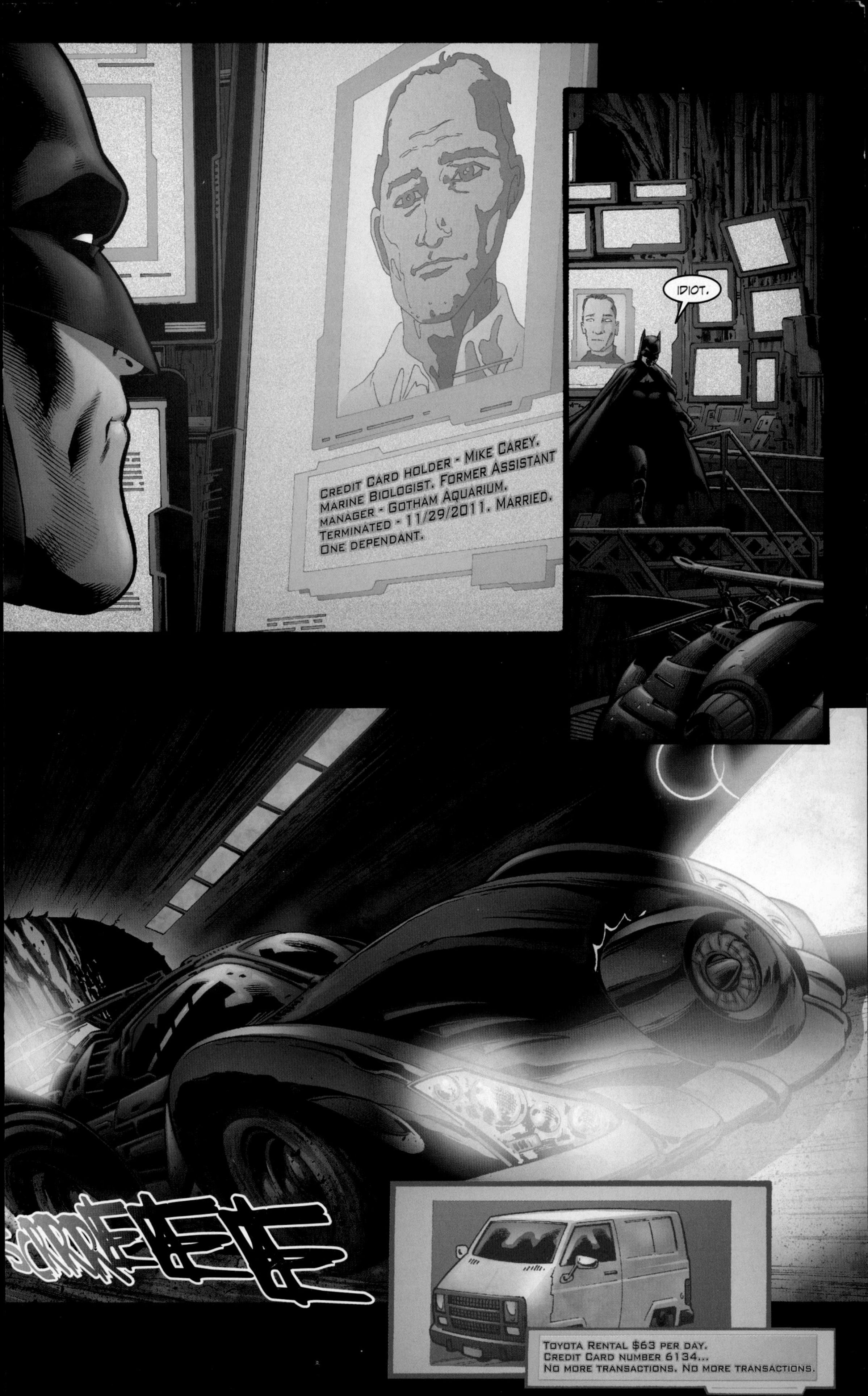
CREDIT CARD HOLDER - MIKE CAREY. MARINE BIOLOGIST. FORMER ASSISTANT MANAGER - GOTHAM AQUARIUM. TERMINATED - 11/29/2011. MARRIED. ONE DEPENDANT.
IDIOT.
TOYOTA RENTAL $63 PER DAY. CREDIT CARD NUMBER 6134... NO MORE TRANSACTIONS. NO MORE TRANSACTIONS.

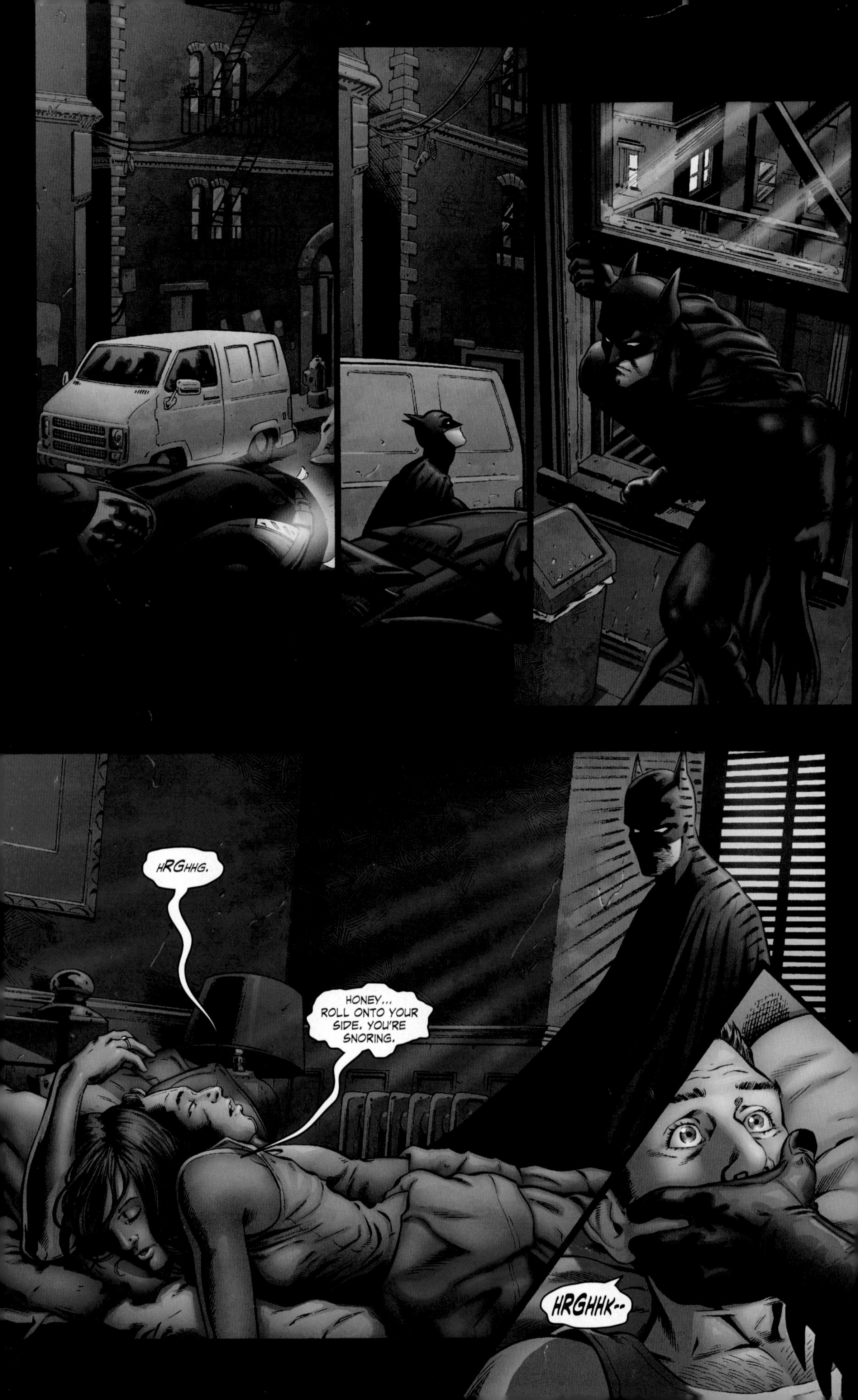
HRGHHG.
HONEY... ROLL ONTO YOUR SIDE. YOU'RE SNORING.
HRGHHK--

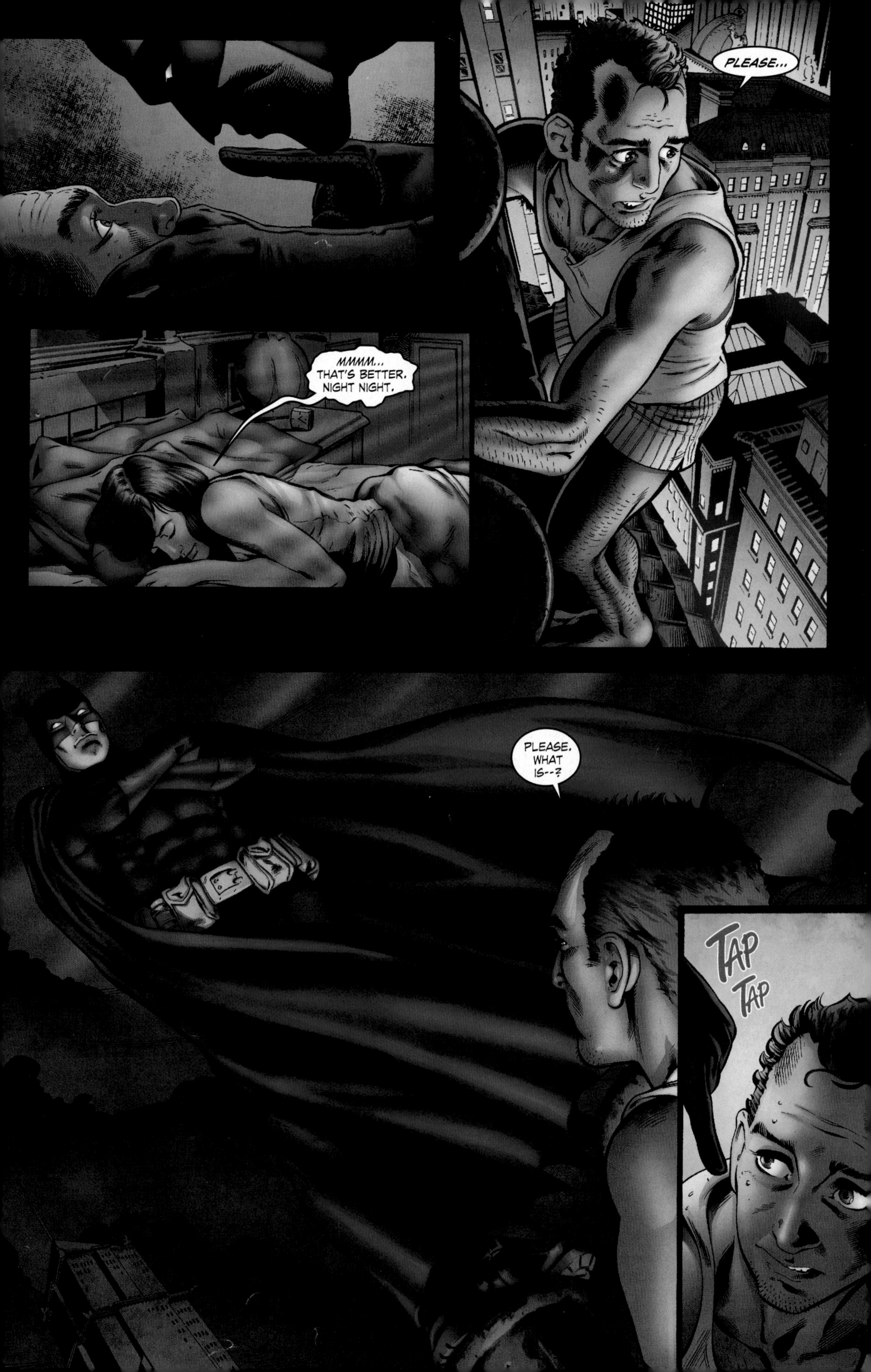
PLEASE...
MMMM... THAT'S BETTER. NIGHT NIGHT.
PLEASE. WHAT IS--?
TAP TAP

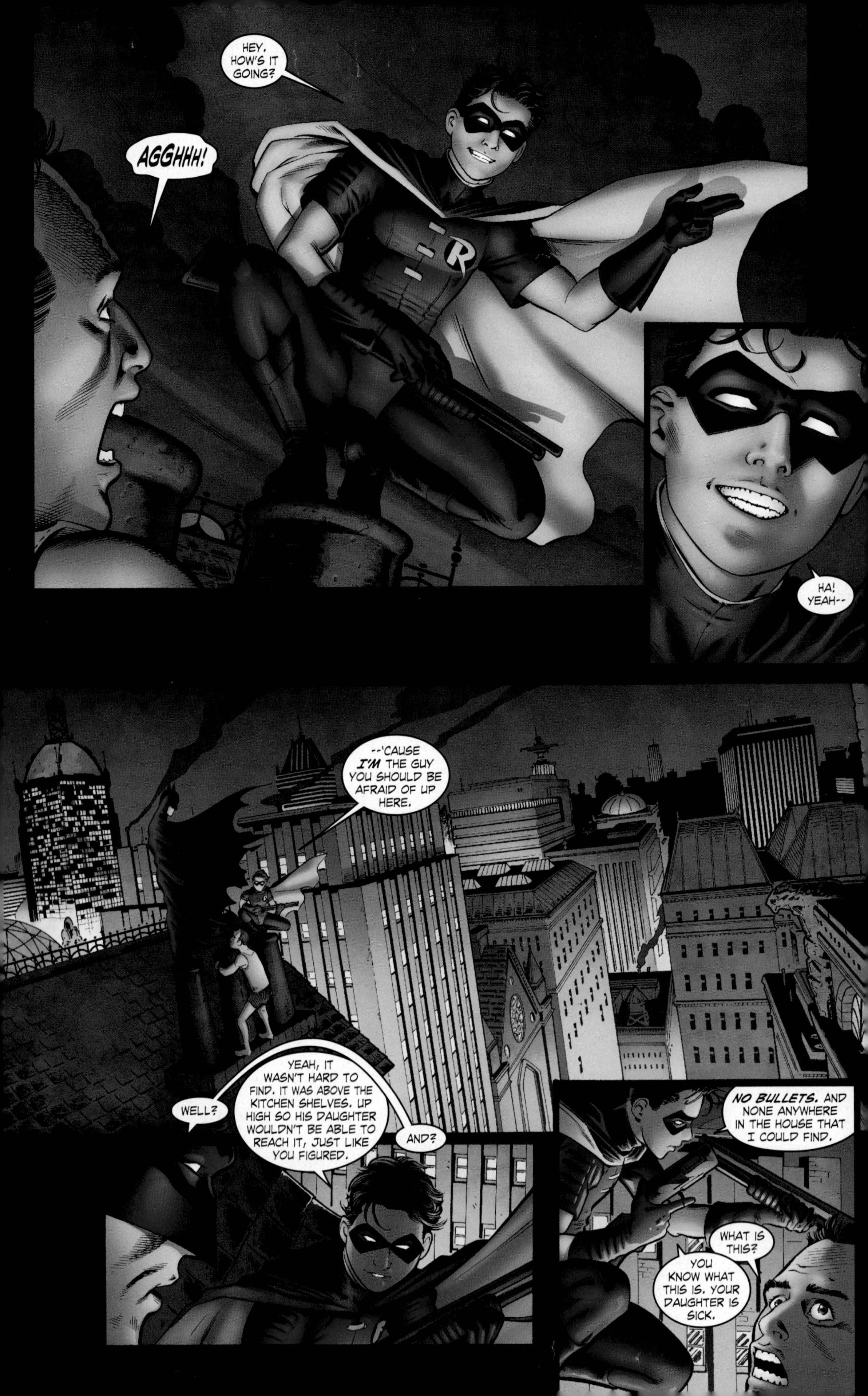
HEY. HOW'S IT GOING?
AGGHHH!
HA! YEAH--
--'CAUSE I'M THE GUY YOU SHOULD BE AFRAID OF UP HERE.
WELL?
YEAH, IT WASN'T HARD TO FIND. IT WAS ABOVE THE KITCHEN SHELVES. UP HIGH SO HIS DAUGHTER WOULDN'T BE ABLE TO REACH IT, JUST LIKE YOU FIGURED.
AND?
NO BULLETS. AND NONE ANYWHERE IN THE HOUSE THAT I COULD FIND.
WHAT IS THIS?
YOU KNOW WHAT THIS IS. YOUR DAUGHTER IS SICK.

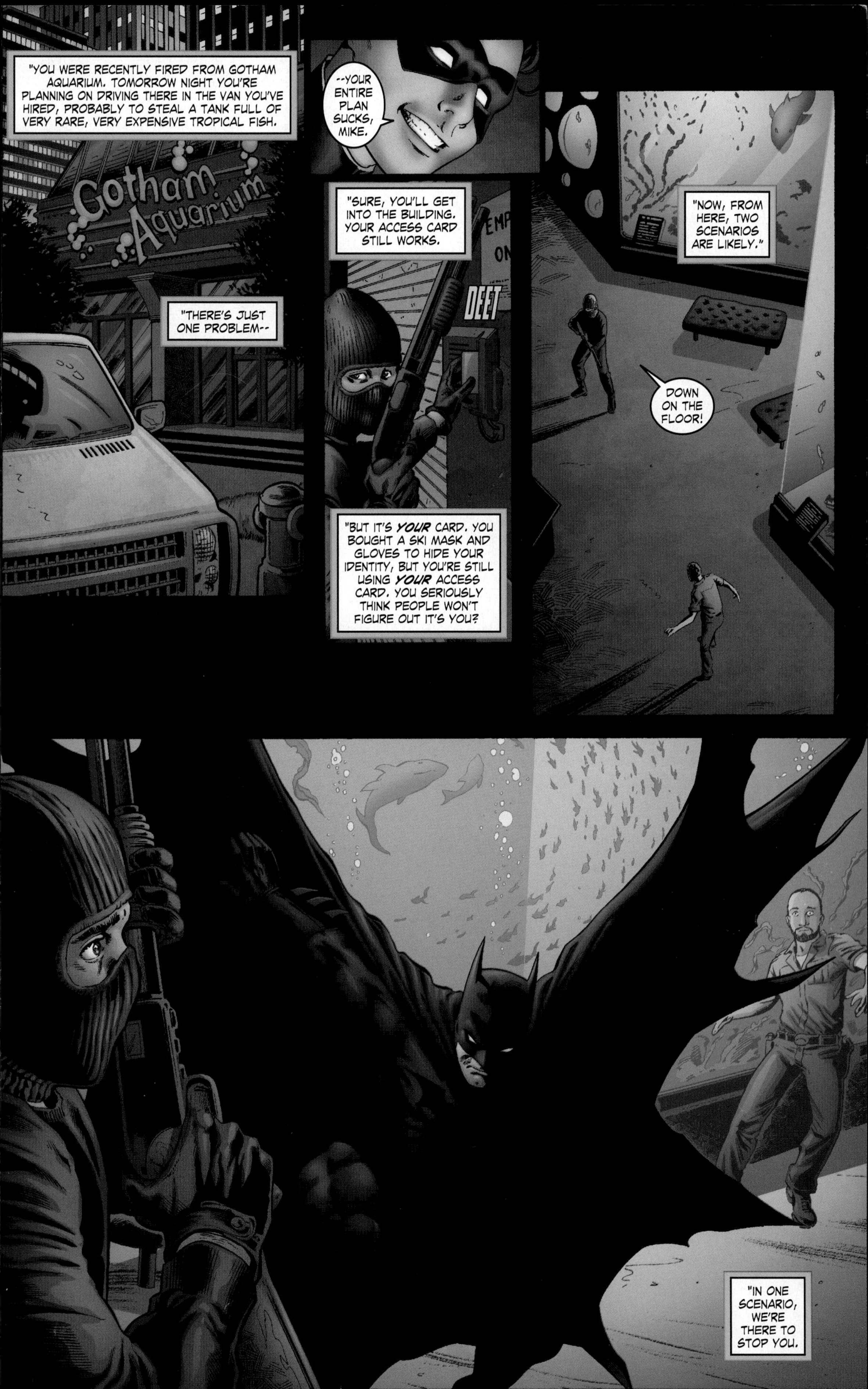
"YOU WERE RECENTLY FIRED FROM GOTHAM AQUARIUM. TOMORROW NIGHT YOU'RE PLANNING ON DRIVING THERE IN THE VAN YOU'VE HIRED, PROBABLY TO STEAL A TANK FULL OF VERY RARE, VERY EXPENSIVE TROPICAL FISH.
Gotham Aquarium
"THERE'S JUST ONE PROBLEM--
--YOUR ENTIRE PLAN SUCKS, MIKE.
"SURE, YOU'LL GET INTO THE BUILDING. YOUR ACCESS CARD STILL WORKS.
DEET
"BUT IT'S YOUR CARD. YOU BOUGHT A SKI MASK AND GLOVES TO HIDE YOUR IDENTITY, BUT YOU'RE STILL USING YOUR ACCESS CARD. YOU SERIOUSLY THINK PEOPLE WON'T FIGURE OUT IT'S YOU?
"NOW, FROM HERE, TWO SCENARIOS ARE LIKELY."
DOWN ON THE FLOOR!
"IN ONE SCENARIO, WE'RE THERE TO STOP YOU.

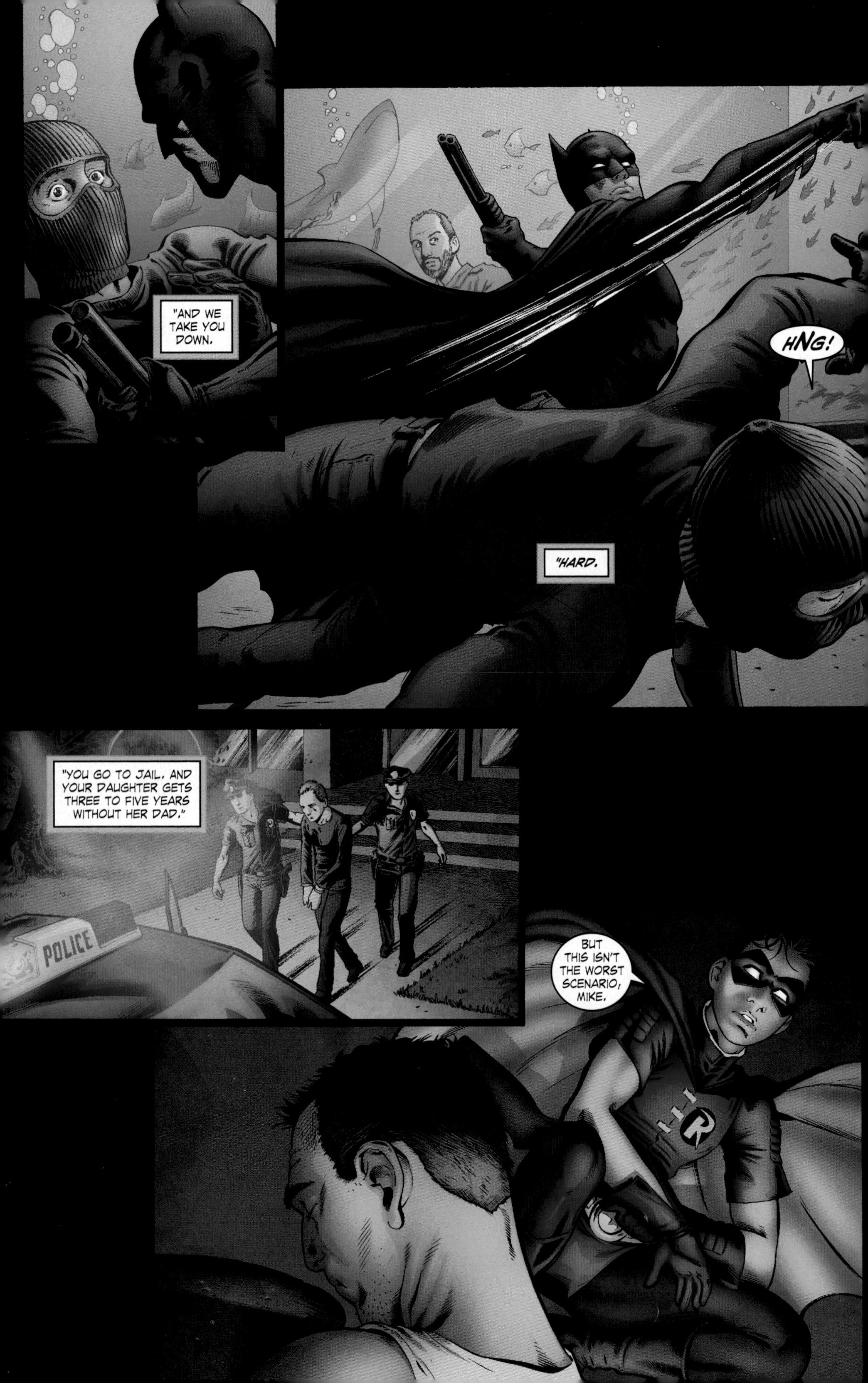
"AND WE TAKE YOU DOWN.
HNG!
"HARD.
"YOU GO TO JAIL. AND YOUR DAUGHTER GETS THREE TO FIVE YEARS WITHOUT HER DAD."
POLICE
BUT THIS ISN'T THE WORST SCENARIO, MIKE.

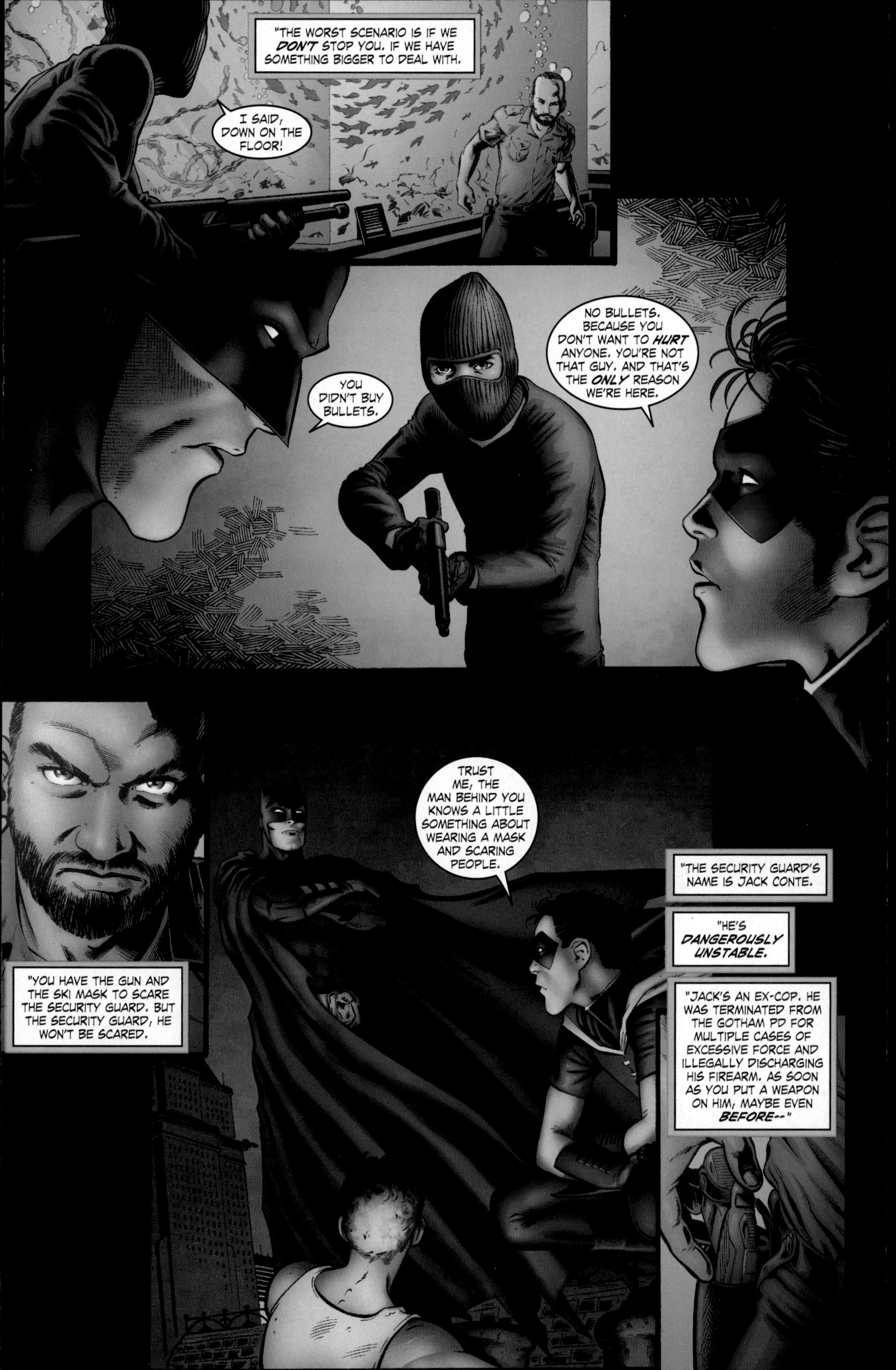
"THE WORST SCENARIO IS IF WE DON'T STOP YOU. IF WE HAVE SOMETHING BIGGER TO DEAL WITH.
I SAID, DOWN ON THE FLOOR!
YOU DIDN'T BUY BULLETS.
NO BULLETS. BECAUSE YOU DON'T WANT TO HURT ANYONE. YOU'RE NOT THAT GUY. AND THAT'S THE ONLY REASON WE'RE HERE.
"YOU HAVE THE GUN AND THE SKI MASK TO SCARE THE SECURITY GUARD. BUT THE SECURITY GUARD, HE WON'T BE SCARED.
TRUST ME, THE MAN BEHIND YOU KNOWS A LITTLE SOMETHING ABOUT WEARING A MASK AND SCARING PEOPLE.
"THE SECURITY GUARD'S NAME IS JACK CONTE.
"HE'S DANGEROUSLY UNSTABLE.
"JACK'S AN EX-COP. HE WAS TERMINATED FROM THE GOTHAM PD FOR MULTIPLE CASES OF EXCESSIVE FORCE AND ILLEGALLY DISCHARGING HIS FIREARM. AS SOON AS YOU PUT A WEAPON ON HIM, MAYBE EVEN BEFORE--"

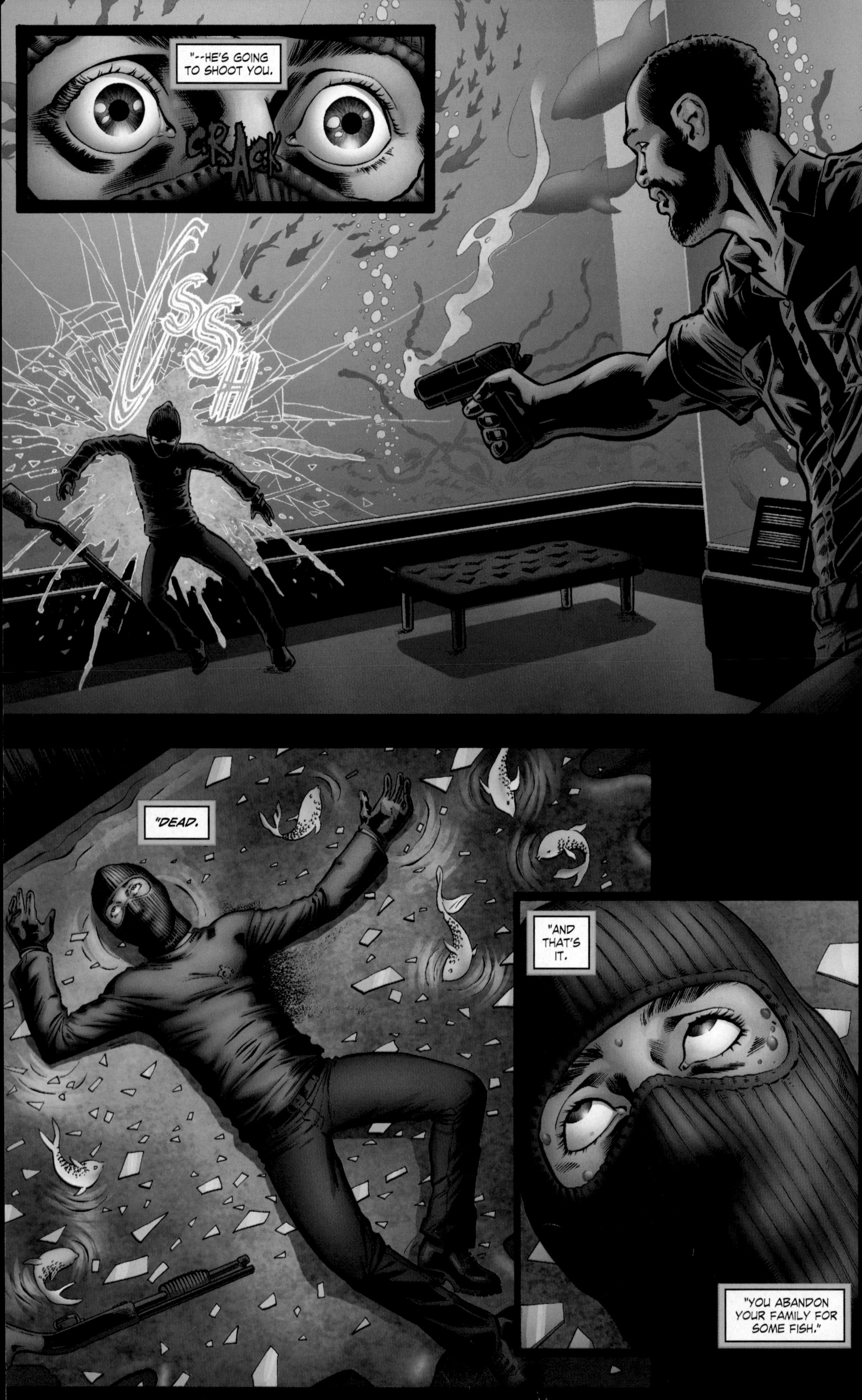
"--HE'S GOING TO SHOOT YOU.
CRACK
SSSH
"DEAD.
"AND THAT'S IT.
"YOU ABANDON YOUR FAMILY FOR SOME FISH."

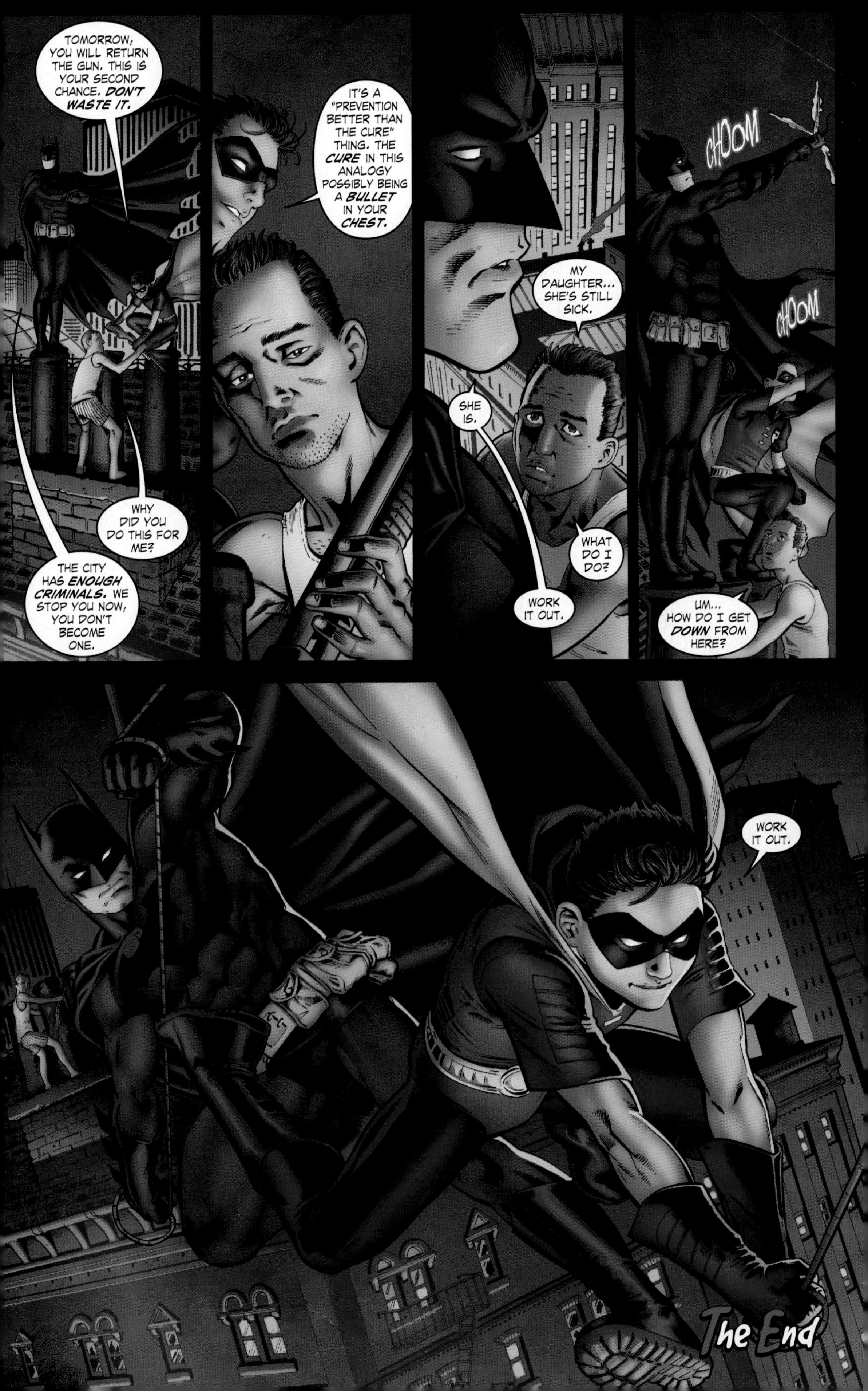
TOMORROW, YOU WILL RETURN THE GUN. THIS IS YOUR SECOND CHANCE. DON'T WASTE IT.
WHY DID YOU DO THIS FOR ME?
THE CITY HAS ENOUGH CRIMINALS. WE STOP YOU NOW, YOU DON'T BECOME ONE.
IT'S A "PREVENTION BETTER THAN THE CURE" THING. THE CURE IN THIS ANALOGY POSSIBLY BEING A BULLET IN YOUR CHEST.
MY DAUGHTER... SHE'S STILL SICK.
SHE IS.
WHAT DO I DO?
WORK IT OUT.
CHOOM
CHOOM
UM... HOW DO I GET DOWN FROM HERE?
WORK IT OUT.
The End

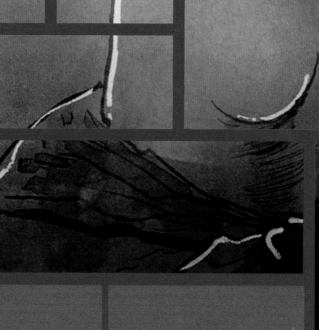

CRISIS IN IDENTITY

B. CLAY MOORE
Writer

BEN TEMPLESMITH
Artist & Colorist

SAIDA TEMOFONTE
Letterer

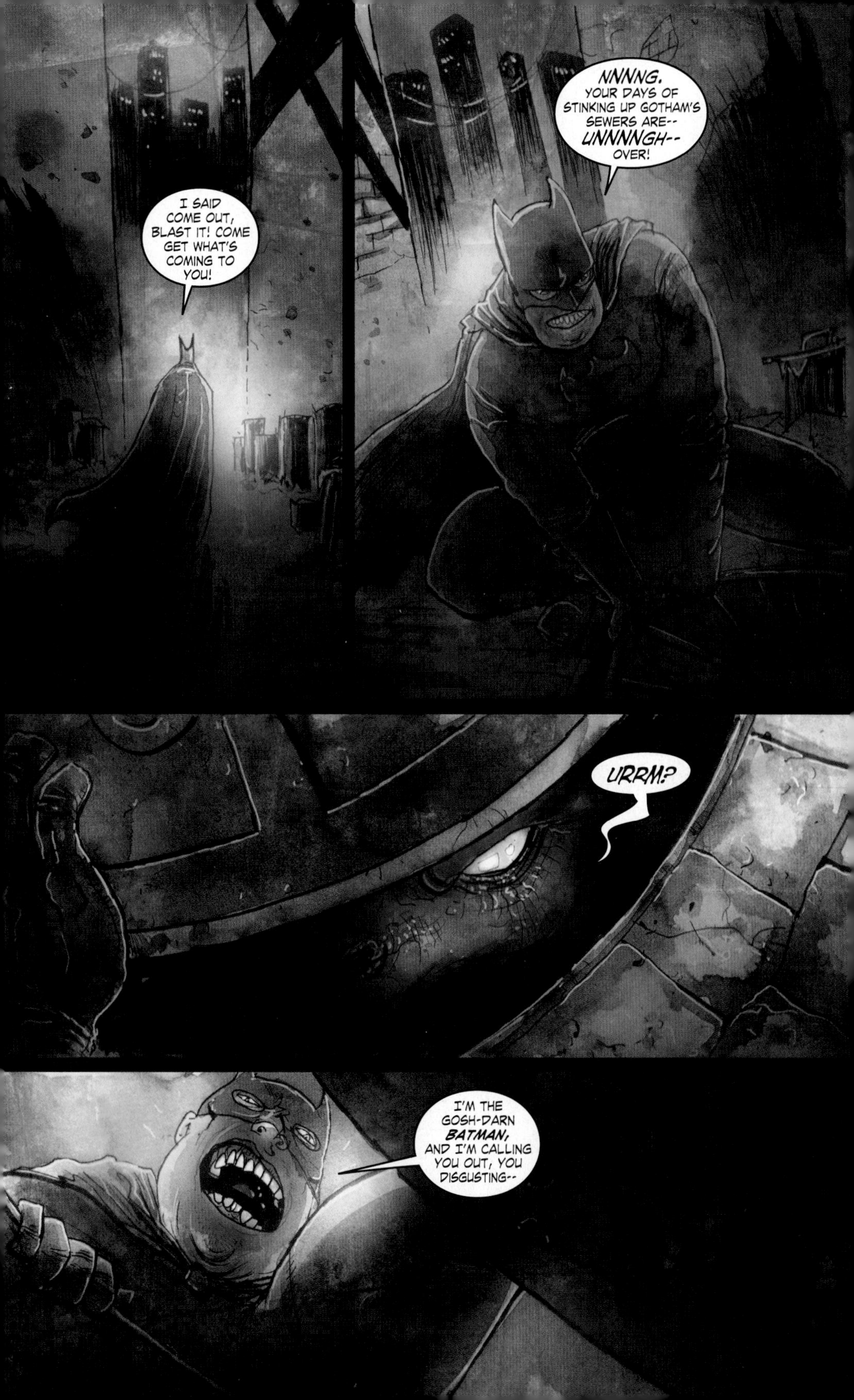
I SAID COME OUT, BLAST IT! COME GET WHAT'S COMING TO YOU!
NNNNG. YOUR DAYS OF STINKING UP GOTHAM'S SEWERS ARE-- UNNNNGH-- OVER!
URRM?
I'M THE GOSH-DARN BATMAN, AND I'M CALLING YOU OUT, YOU DISGUSTING--

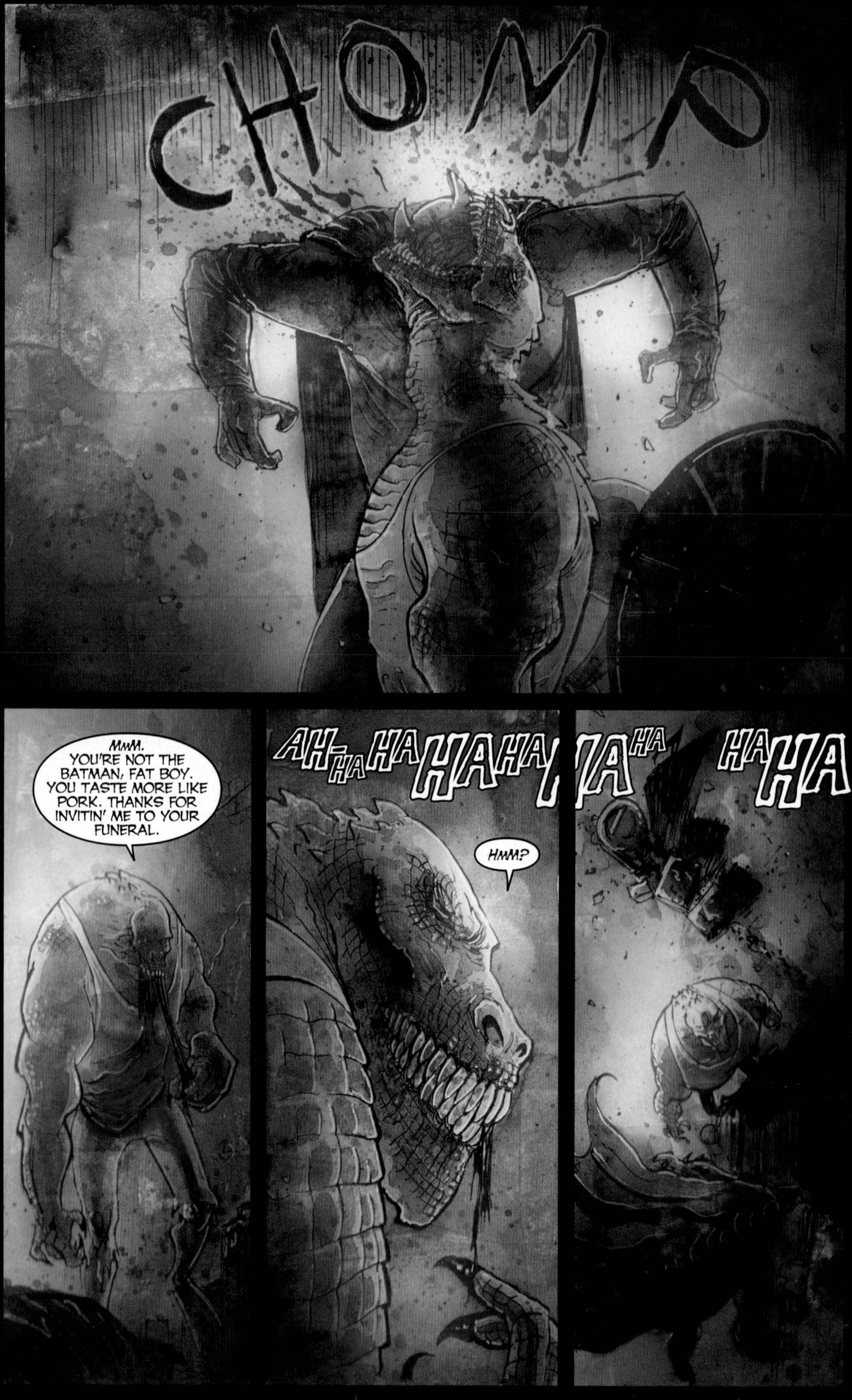
CHOMP
MMM. YOU'RE NOT THE BATMAN, FAT BOY. YOU TASTE MORE LIKE PORK. THANKS FOR INVITIN' ME TO YOUR FUNERAL.
AH-HA HA HAHAHA HA HA HA HA HA
HMM?

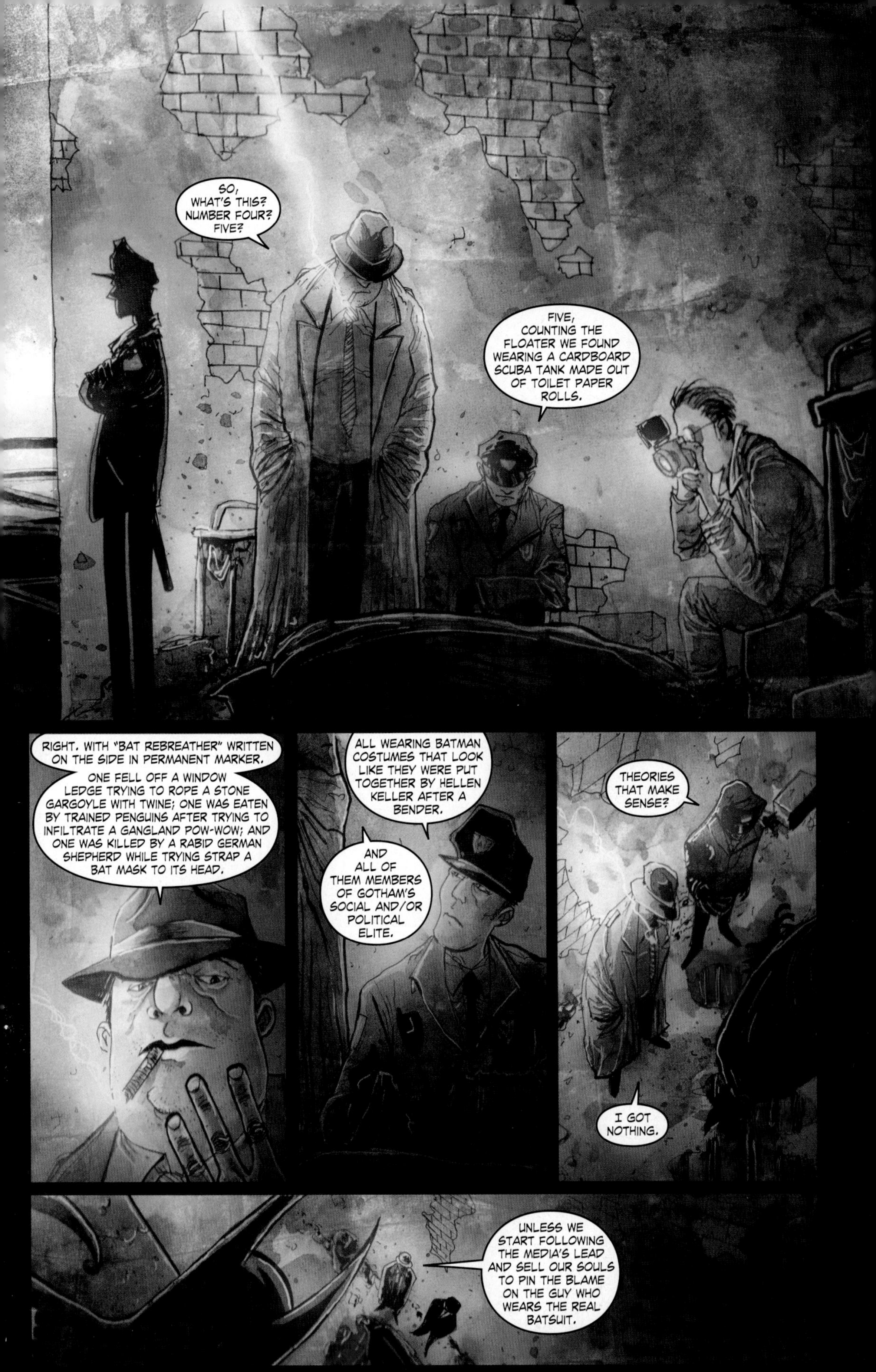
SO, WHAT'S THIS? NUMBER FOUR? FIVE?
FIVE, COUNTING THE FLOATER WE FOUND WEARING A CARDBOARD SCUBA TANK MADE OUT OF TOILET PAPER ROLLS.
RIGHT. WITH "BAT REBREATHER" WRITTEN ON THE SIDE IN PERMANENT MARKER.
ONE FELL OFF A WINDOW LEDGE TRYING TO ROPE A STONE GARGOYLE WITH TWINE; ONE WAS EATEN BY TRAINED PENGUINS AFTER TRYING TO INFILTRATE A GANGLAND POW-WOW; AND ONE WAS KILLED BY A RABID GERMAN SHEPHERD WHILE TRYING STRAP A BAT MASK TO ITS HEAD.
ALL WEARING BATMAN COSTUMES THAT LOOK LIKE THEY WERE PUT TOGETHER BY HELLEN KELLER AFTER A BENDER.
AND ALL OF THEM MEMBERS OF GOTHAM'S SOCIAL AND/OR POLITICAL ELITE.
THEORIES THAT MAKE SENSE?
I GOT NOTHING.
UNLESS WE START FOLLOWING THE MEDIA'S LEAD AND SELL OUR SOULS TO PIN THE BLAME ON THE GUY WHO WEARS THE REAL BATSUIT.

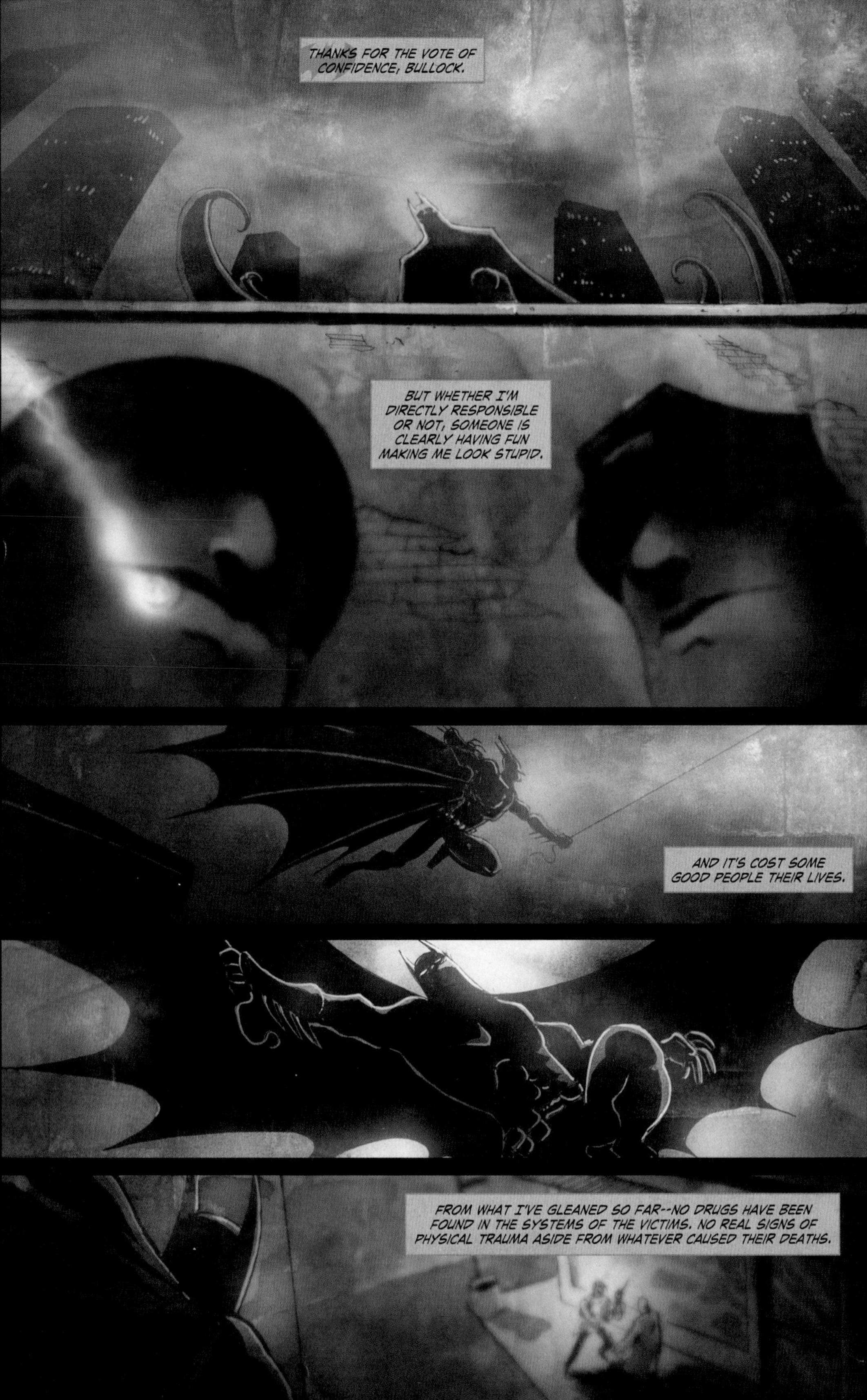
THANKS FOR THE VOTE OF CONFIDENCE, BULLOCK.
BUT WHETHER I'M DIRECTLY RESPONSIBLE OR NOT, SOMEONE IS CLEARLY HAVING FUN MAKING ME LOOK STUPID.
AND IT'S COST SOME GOOD PEOPLE THEIR LIVES.
FROM WHAT I'VE GLEANED SO FAR--NO DRUGS HAVE BEEN FOUND IN THE SYSTEMS OF THE VICTIMS. NO REAL SIGNS OF PHYSICAL TRAUMA ASIDE FROM WHATEVER CAUSED THEIR DEATHS.

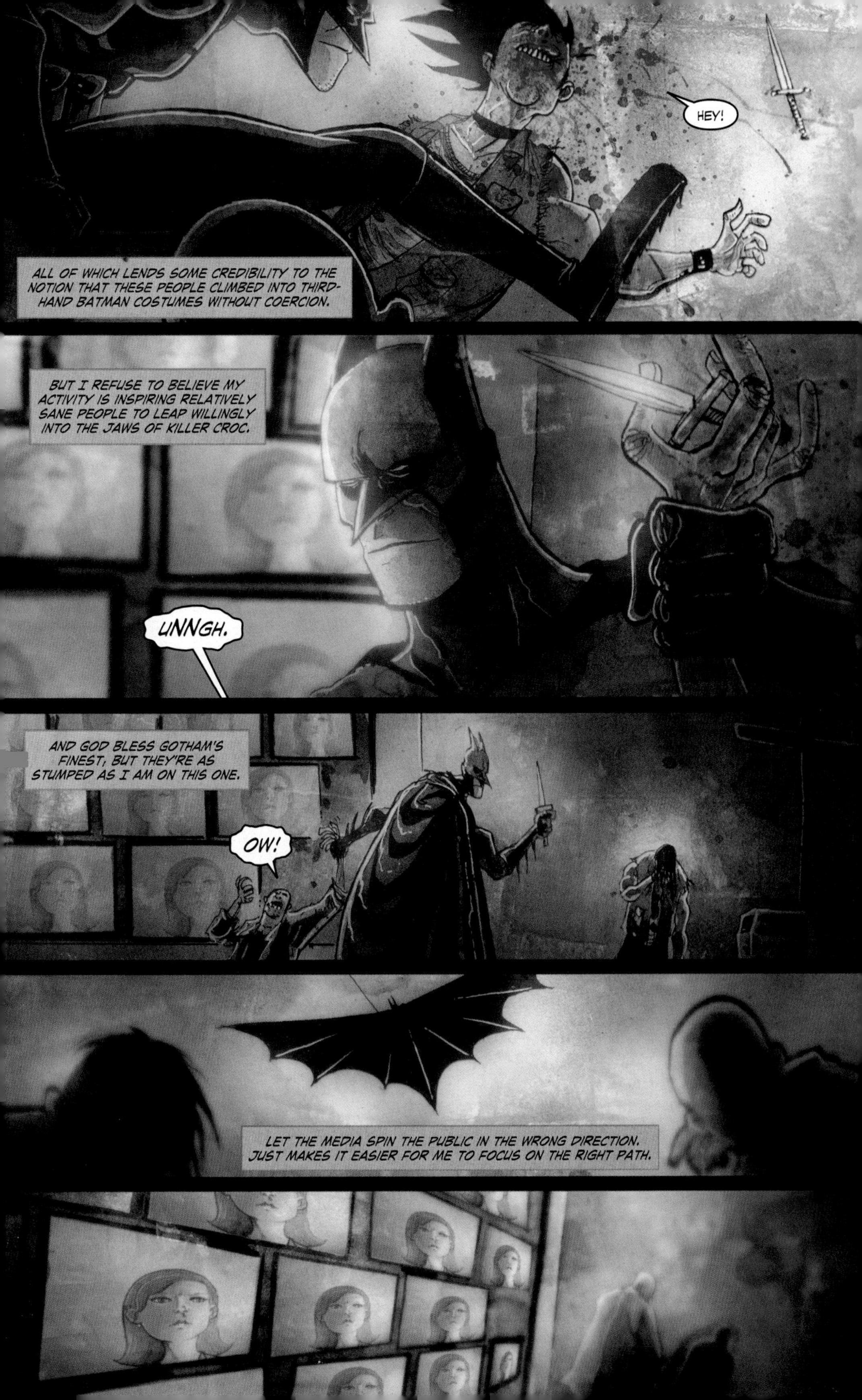

HEY!
ALL OF WHICH LENDS SOME CREDIBILITY TO THE NOTION THAT THESE PEOPLE CLIMBED INTO THIRD-HAND BATMAN COSTUMES WITHOUT COERCION.
BUT I REFUSE TO BELIEVE MY ACTIVITY IS INSPIRING RELATIVELY SANE PEOPLE TO LEAP WILLINGLY INTO THE JAWS OF KILLER CROC.
UNNGH.
AND GOD BLESS GOTHAM'S FINEST, BUT THEY'RE AS STUMPED AS I AM ON THIS ONE.
OW!
LET THE MEDIA SPIN THE PUBLIC IN THE WRONG DIRECTION. JUST MAKES IT EASIER FOR ME TO FOCUS ON THE RIGHT PATH.

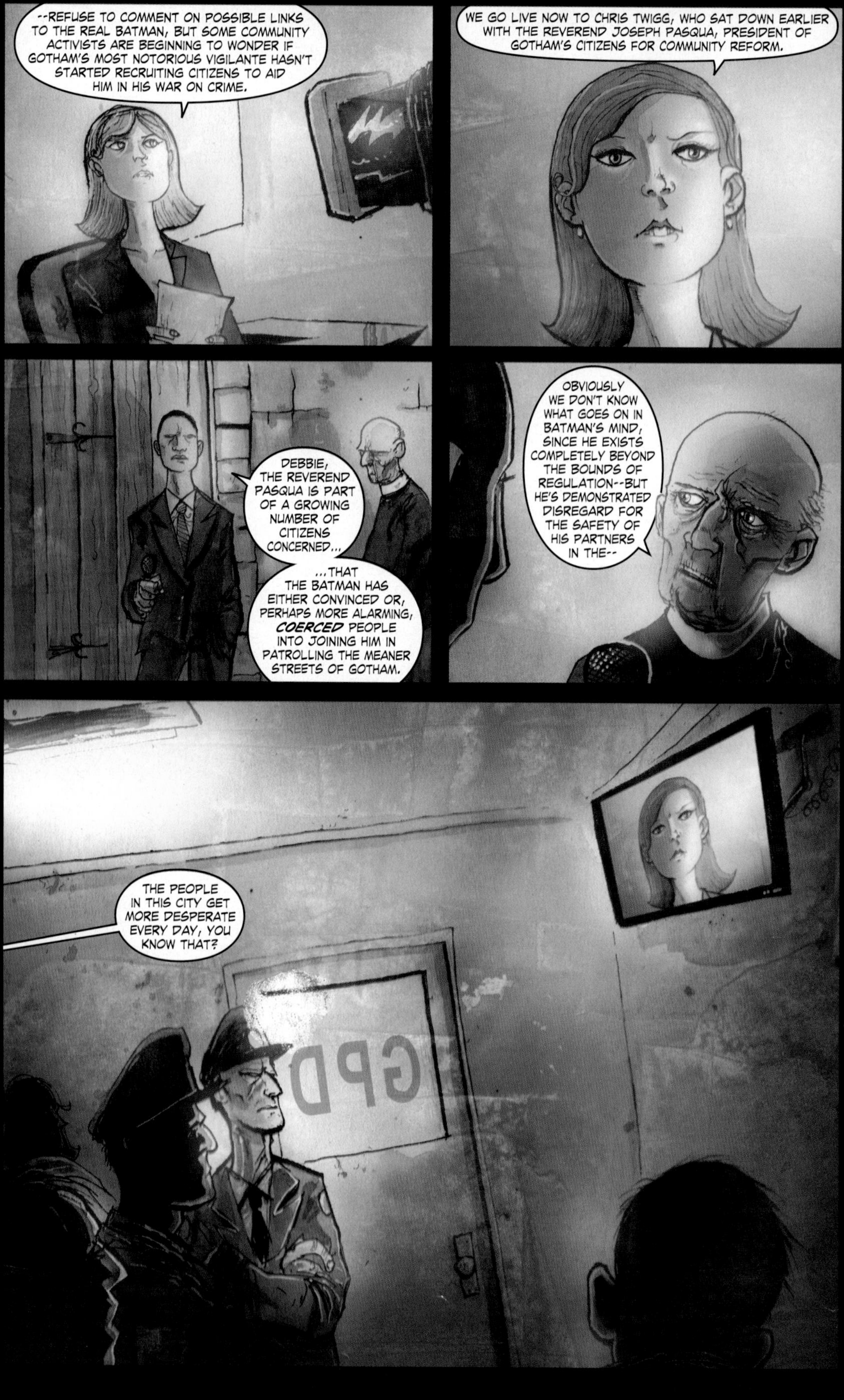
--REFUSE TO COMMENT ON POSSIBLE LINKS TO THE REAL BATMAN, BUT SOME COMMUNITY ACTIVISTS ARE BEGINNING TO WONDER IF GOTHAM'S MOST NOTORIOUS VIGILANTE HASN'T STARTED RECRUITING CITIZENS TO AID HIM IN HIS WAR ON CRIME.
WE GO LIVE NOW TO CHRIS TWIGG, WHO SAT DOWN EARLIER WITH THE REVEREND JOSEPH PASQUA, PRESIDENT OF GOTHAM'S CITIZENS FOR COMMUNITY REFORM.
DEBBIE, THE REVEREND PASQUA IS PART OF A GROWING NUMBER OF CITIZENS CONCERNED...
...THAT THE BATMAN HAS EITHER CONVINCED OR, PERHAPS MORE ALARMING, COERCED PEOPLE INTO JOINING HIM IN PATROLLING THE MEANER STREETS OF GOTHAM.
OBVIOUSLY WE DON'T KNOW WHAT GOES ON IN BATMAN'S MIND, SINCE HE EXISTS COMPLETELY BEYOND THE BOUNDS OF REGULATION--BUT HE'S DEMONSTRATED DISREGARD FOR THE SAFETY OF HIS PARTNERS IN THE--
THE PEOPLE IN THIS CITY GET MORE DESPERATE EVERY DAY, YOU KNOW THAT?
GPD

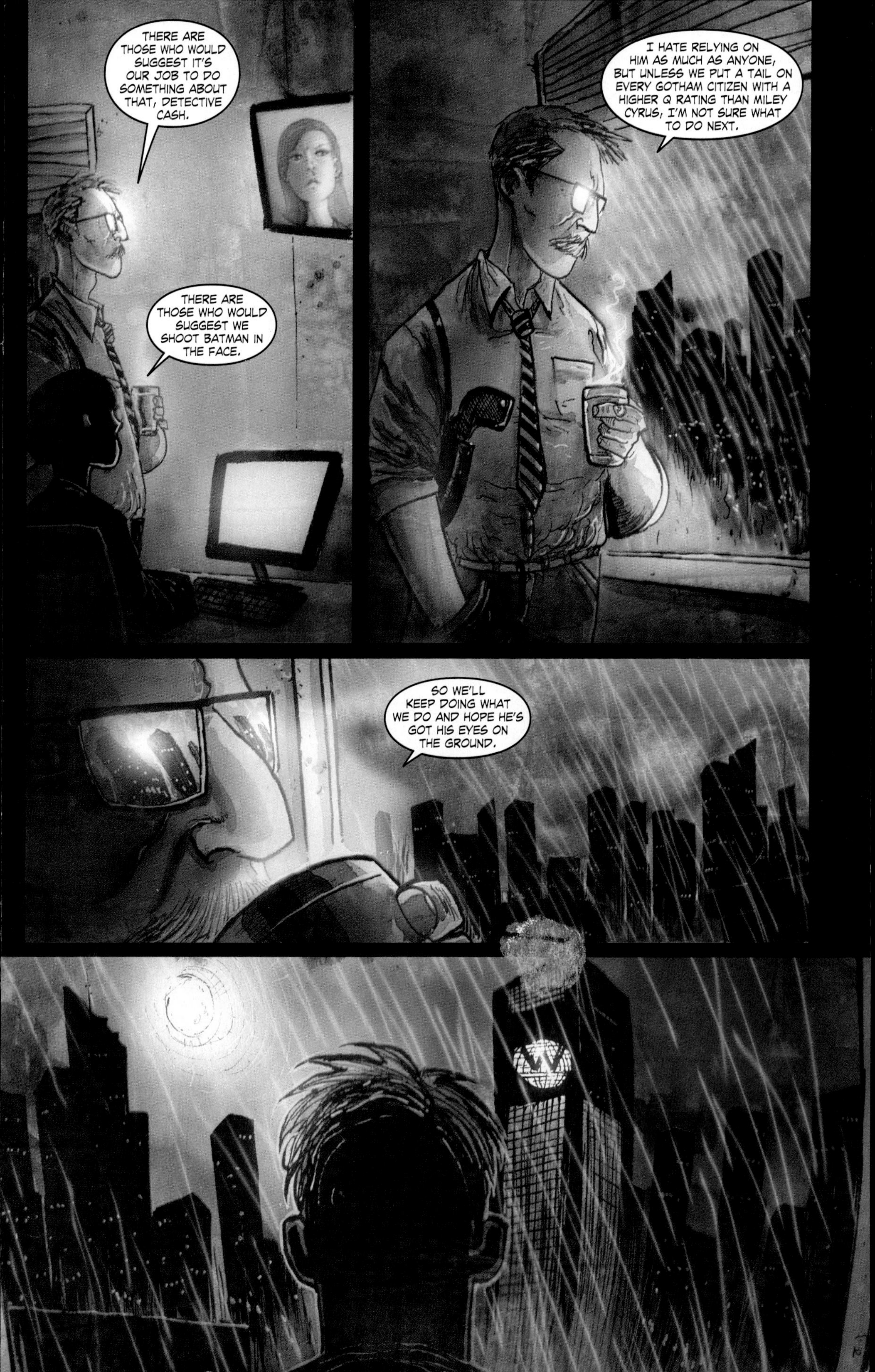
THERE ARE THOSE WHO WOULD SUGGEST IT'S OUR JOB TO DO SOMETHING ABOUT THAT, DETECTIVE CASH.
THERE ARE THOSE WHO WOULD SUGGEST WE SHOOT BATMAN IN THE FACE.
I HATE RELYING ON HIM AS MUCH AS ANYONE, BUT UNLESS WE PUT A TAIL ON EVERY GOTHAM CITIZEN WITH A HIGHER Q RATING THAN MILEY CYRUS, I'M NOT SURE WHAT TO DO NEXT.
SO WE'LL KEEP DOING WHAT WE DO AND HOPE HE'S GOT HIS EYES ON THE GROUND.

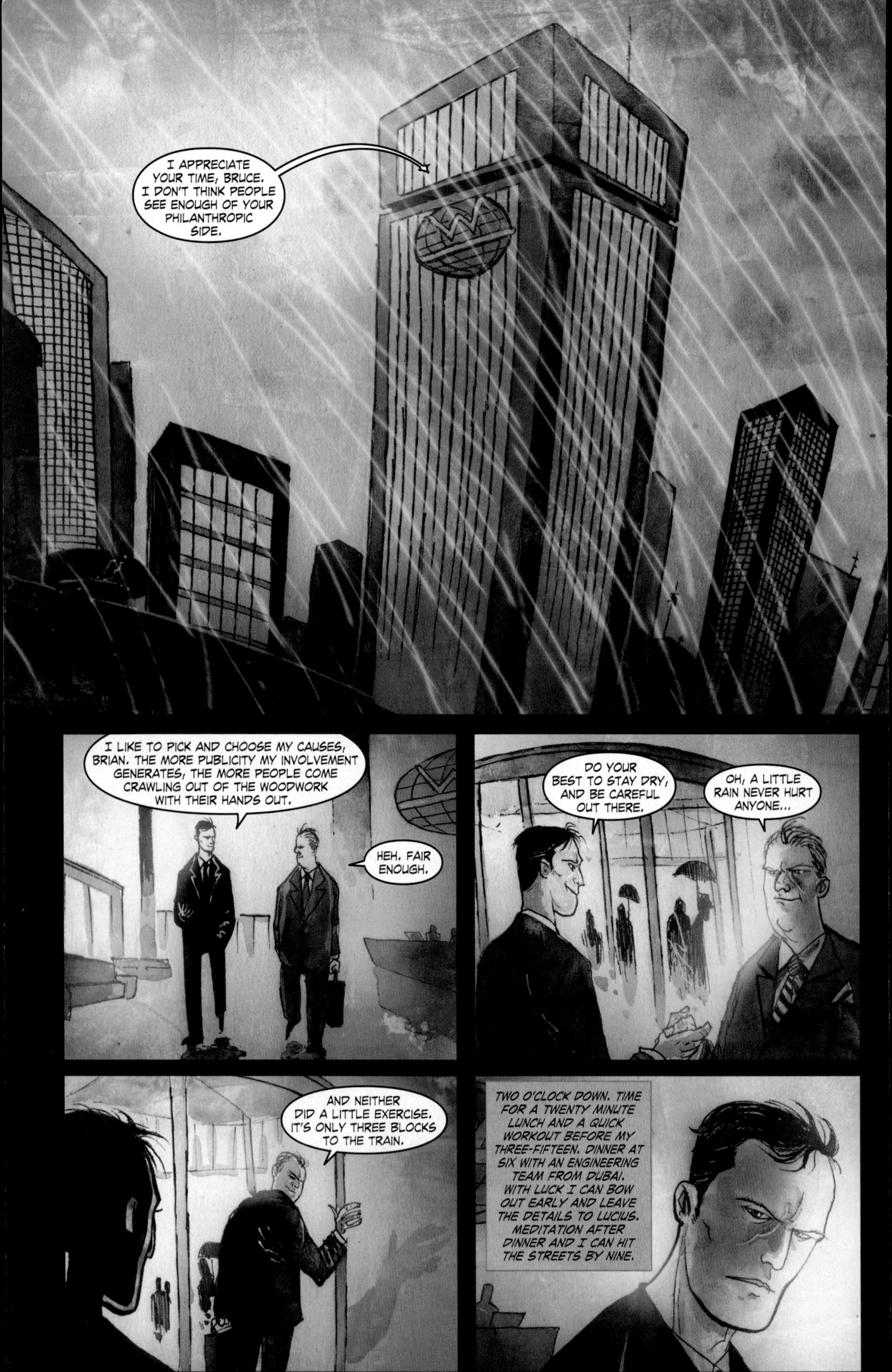
I APPRECIATE YOUR TIME, BRUCE. I DON'T THINK PEOPLE SEE ENOUGH OF YOUR PHILANTHROPIC SIDE.
I LIKE TO PICK AND CHOOSE MY CAUSES, BRIAN. THE MORE PUBLICITY MY INVOLVEMENT GENERATES, THE MORE PEOPLE COME CRAWLING OUT OF THE WOODWORK WITH THEIR HANDS OUT.
HEH. FAIR ENOUGH.
DO YOUR BEST TO STAY DRY, AND BE CAREFUL OUT THERE.
OH, A LITTLE RAIN NEVER HURT ANYONE...
AND NEITHER DID A LITTLE EXERCISE. IT'S ONLY THREE BLOCKS TO THE TRAIN.
TWO O'CLOCK DOWN. TIME FOR A TWENTY MINUTE LUNCH AND A QUICK WORKOUT BEFORE MY THREE-FIFTEEN. DINNER AT SIX WITH AN ENGINEERING TEAM FROM DUBAI. WITH LUCK I CAN BOW OUT EARLY AND LEAVE THE DETAILS TO LUCIUS. MEDITATION AFTER DINNER AND I CAN HIT THE STREETS BY NINE.

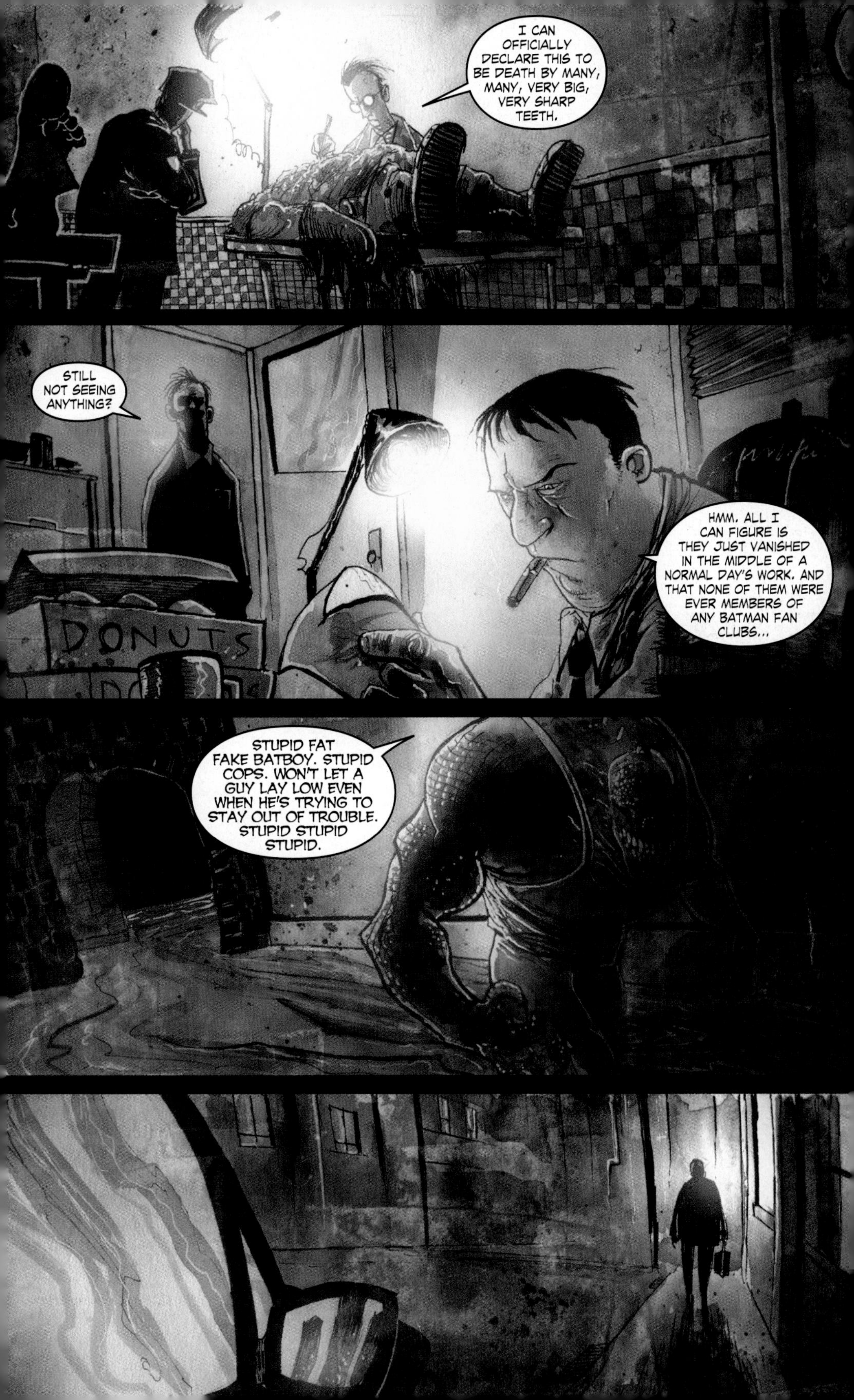
I CAN OFFICIALLY DECLARE THIS TO BE DEATH BY MANY, MANY, VERY BIG, VERY SHARP TEETH.
STILL NOT SEEING ANYTHING?
HMM. ALL I CAN FIGURE IS THEY JUST VANISHED IN THE MIDDLE OF A NORMAL DAY'S WORK. AND THAT NONE OF THEM WERE EVER MEMBERS OF ANY BATMAN FAN CLUBS...
DONUTS
STUPID FAT FAKE BATBOY. STUPID COPS. WON'T LET A GUY LAY LOW EVEN WHEN HE'S TRYING TO STAY OUT OF TROUBLE. STUPID STUPID STUPID.

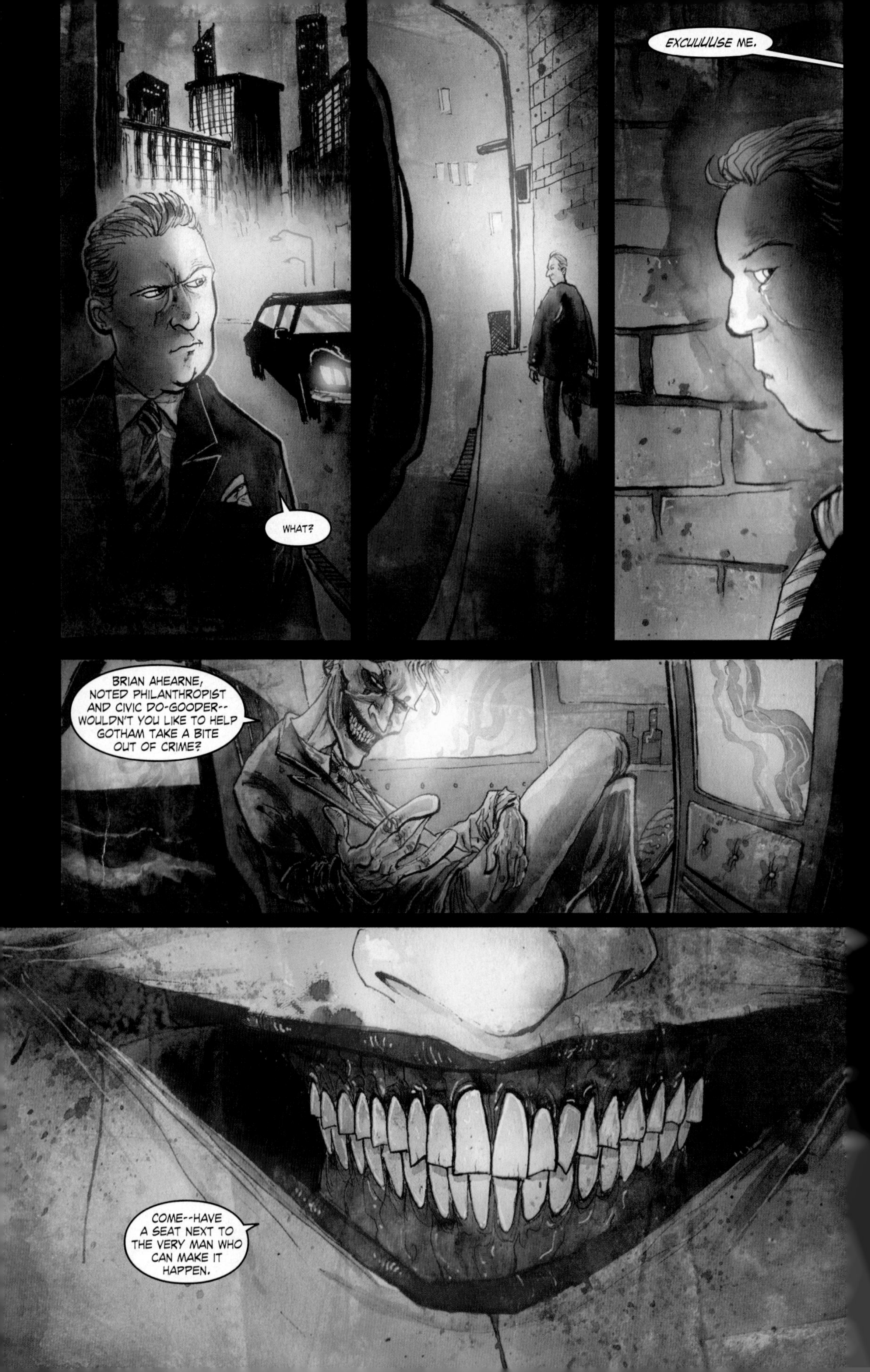
WHAT?
EXCUUUUSE ME.
BRIAN AHEARNE, NOTED PHILANTHROPIST AND CIVIC DO-GOODER--WOULDN'T YOU LIKE TO HELP GOTHAM TAKE A BITE OUT OF CRIME?
COME--HAVE A SEAT NEXT TO THE VERY MAN WHO CAN MAKE IT HAPPEN.

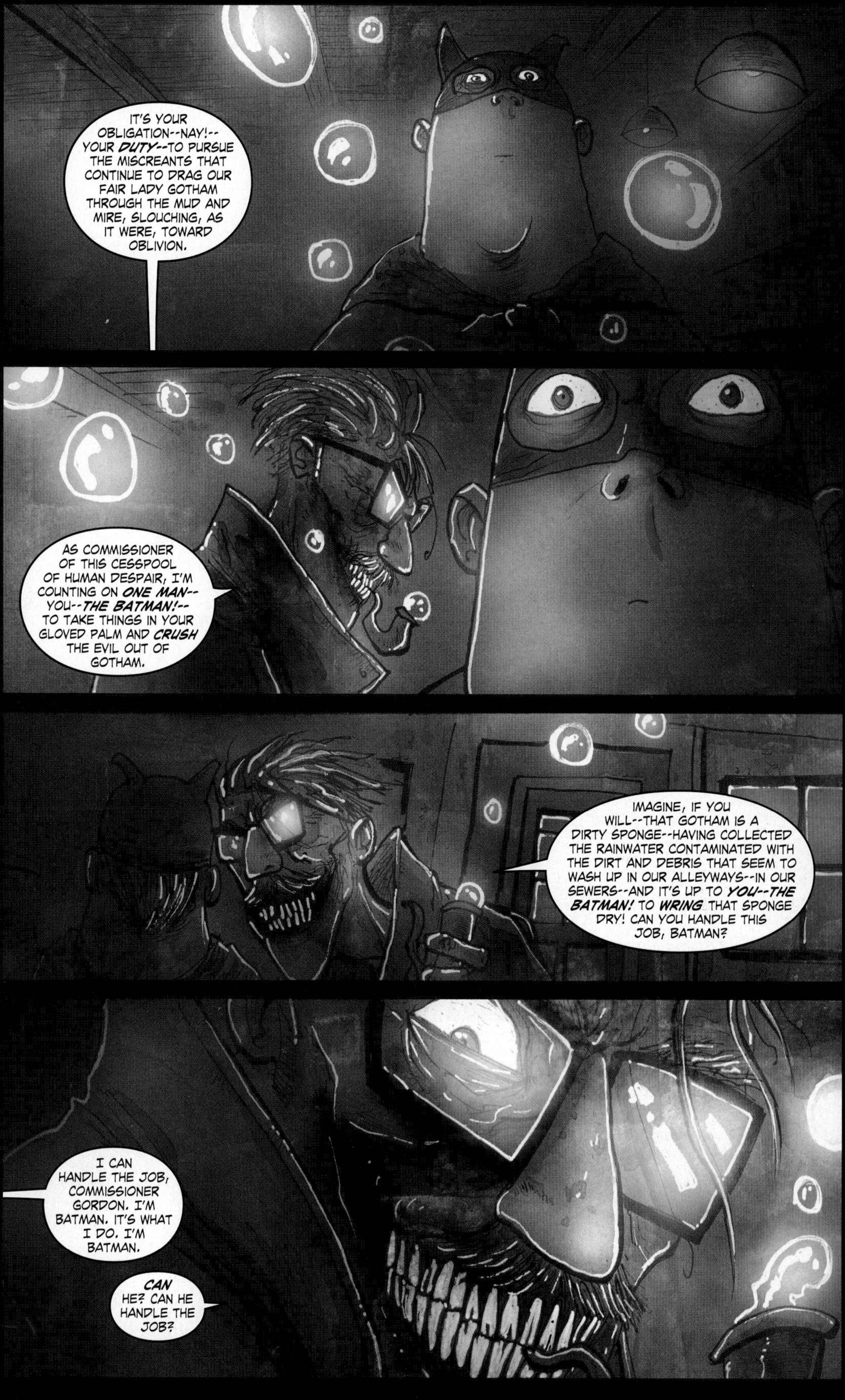
IT'S YOUR OBLIGATION--NAY!--YOUR DUTY--TO PURSUE THE MISCREANTS THAT CONTINUE TO DRAG OUR FAIR LADY GOTHAM THROUGH THE MUD AND MIRE, SLOUCHING, AS IT WERE, TOWARD OBLIVION.
AS COMMISSIONER OF THIS CESSPOOL OF HUMAN DESPAIR, I'M COUNTING ON ONE MAN--YOU--THE BATMAN!--TO TAKE THINGS IN YOUR GLOVED PALM AND CRUSH THE EVIL OUT OF GOTHAM.
IMAGINE, IF YOU WILL--THAT GOTHAM IS A DIRTY SPONGE--HAVING COLLECTED THE RAINWATER CONTAMINATED WITH THE DIRT AND DEBRIS THAT SEEM TO WASH UP IN OUR ALLEYWAYS--IN OUR SEWERS--AND IT'S UP TO YOU--THE BATMAN! TO WRING THAT SPONGE DRY! CAN YOU HANDLE THIS JOB, BATMAN?
I CAN HANDLE THE JOB, COMMISSIONER GORDON. I'M BATMAN. IT'S WHAT I DO. I'M BATMAN.
CAN HE? CAN HE HANDLE THE JOB?

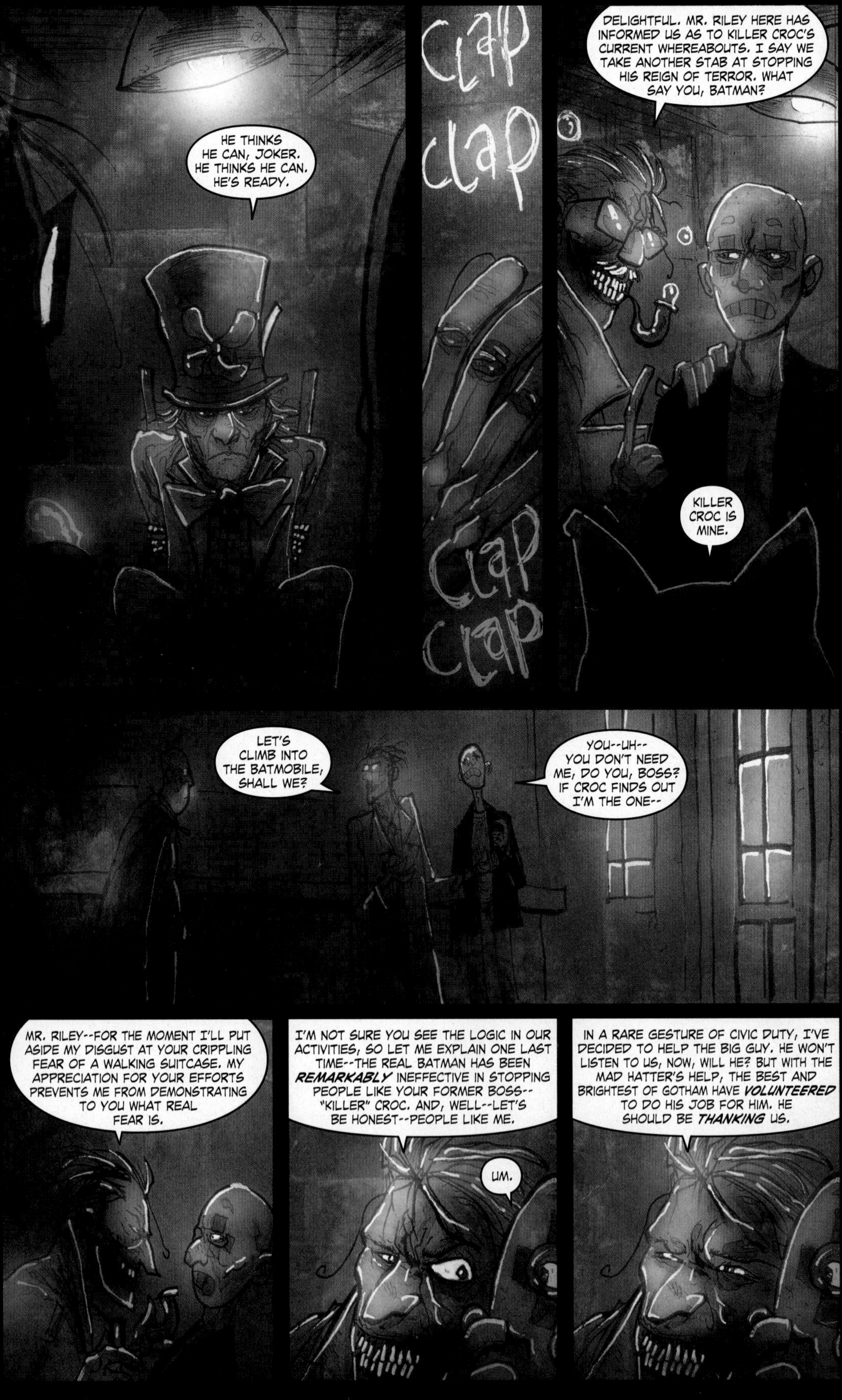
HE THINKS HE CAN, JOKER. HE THINKS HE CAN. HE'S READY.
CLAP CLAP
CLAP CLAP
DELIGHTFUL. MR. RILEY HERE HAS INFORMED US AS TO KILLER CROC'S CURRENT WHEREABOUTS. I SAY WE TAKE ANOTHER STAB AT STOPPING HIS REIGN OF TERROR. WHAT SAY YOU, BATMAN?
KILLER CROC IS MINE.
LET'S CLIMB INTO THE BATMOBILE, SHALL WE?
YOU--UH-- YOU DON'T NEED ME, DO YOU, BOSS? IF CROC FINDS OUT I'M THE ONE--
MR. RILEY--FOR THE MOMENT I'LL PUT ASIDE MY DISGUST AT YOUR CRIPPLING FEAR OF A WALKING SUITCASE. MY APPRECIATION FOR YOUR EFFORTS PREVENTS ME FROM DEMONSTRATING TO YOU WHAT REAL FEAR IS.
I'M NOT SURE YOU SEE THE LOGIC IN OUR ACTIVITIES, SO LET ME EXPLAIN ONE LAST TIME--THE REAL BATMAN HAS BEEN REMARKABLY INEFFECTIVE IN STOPPING PEOPLE LIKE YOUR FORMER BOSS-- "KILLER" CROC. AND, WELL--LET'S BE HONEST--PEOPLE LIKE ME.
UM.
IN A RARE GESTURE OF CIVIC DUTY, I'VE DECIDED TO HELP THE BIG GUY. HE WON'T LISTEN TO US, NOW, WILL HE? BUT WITH THE MAD HATTER'S HELP, THE BEST AND BRIGHTEST OF GOTHAM HAVE VOLUNTEERED TO DO HIS JOB FOR HIM. HE SHOULD BE THANKING US.

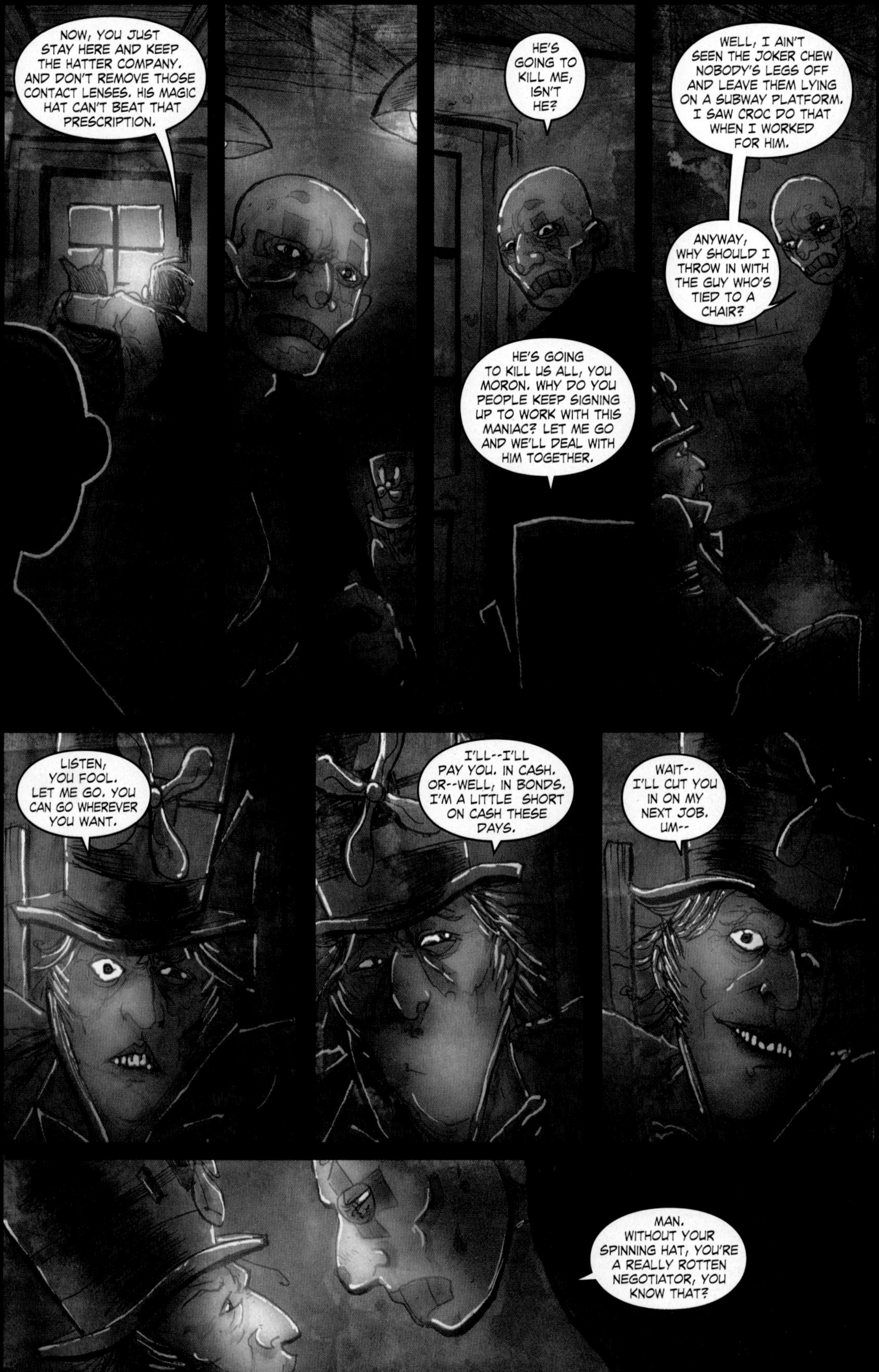
NOW, YOU JUST STAY HERE AND KEEP THE HATTER COMPANY. AND DON'T REMOVE THOSE CONTACT LENSES. HIS MAGIC HAT CAN'T BEAT THAT PRESCRIPTION.
HE'S GOING TO KILL ME, ISN'T HE?
WELL, I AIN'T SEEN THE JOKER CHEW NOBODY'S LEGS OFF AND LEAVE THEM LYING ON A SUBWAY PLATFORM. I SAW CROC DO THAT WHEN I WORKED FOR HIM.
ANYWAY, WHY SHOULD I THROW IN WITH THE GUY WHO'S TIED TO A CHAIR?
HE'S GOING TO KILL US ALL, YOU MORON. WHY DO YOU PEOPLE KEEP SIGNING UP TO WORK WITH THIS MANIAC? LET ME GO AND WE'LL DEAL WITH HIM TOGETHER.
LISTEN, YOU FOOL. LET ME GO. YOU CAN GO WHEREVER YOU WANT.
I'LL--I'LL PAY YOU. IN CASH. OR--WELL, IN BONDS. I'M A LITTLE SHORT ON CASH THESE DAYS.
WAIT-- I'LL CUT YOU IN ON MY NEXT JOB. UM--
MAN. WITHOUT YOUR SPINNING HAT, YOU'RE A REALLY ROTTEN NEGOTIATOR, YOU KNOW THAT?

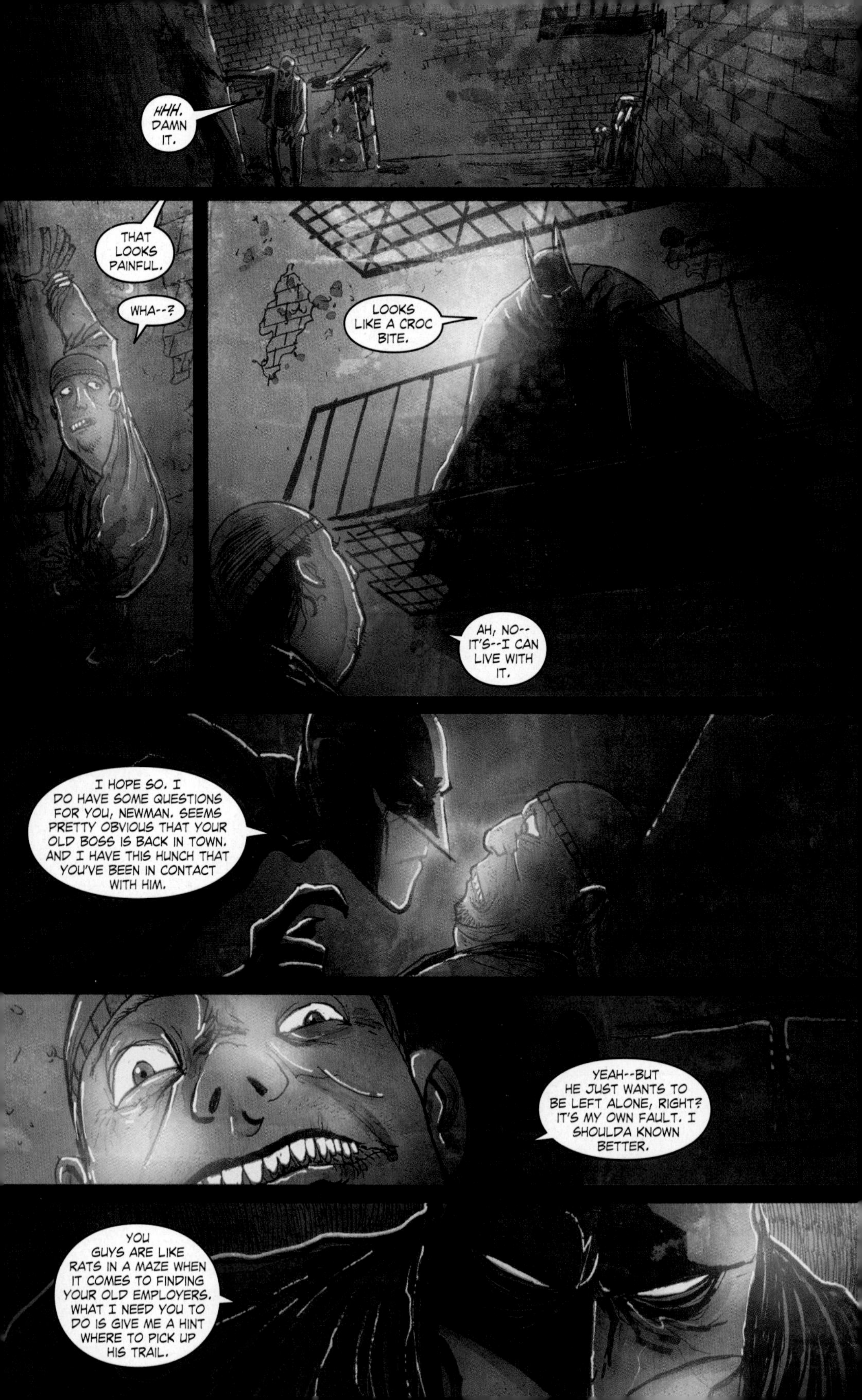
HHH. DAMN IT.
THAT LOOKS PAINFUL.
WHA--?
LOOKS LIKE A CROC BITE.
AH, NO-- IT'S--I CAN LIVE WITH IT.
I HOPE SO. I DO HAVE SOME QUESTIONS FOR YOU, NEWMAN. SEEMS PRETTY OBVIOUS THAT YOUR OLD BOSS IS BACK IN TOWN. AND I HAVE THIS HUNCH THAT YOU'VE BEEN IN CONTACT WITH HIM.
YEAH--BUT HE JUST WANTS TO BE LEFT ALONE, RIGHT? IT'S MY OWN FAULT. I SHOULDA KNOWN BETTER.
YOU GUYS ARE LIKE RATS IN A MAZE WHEN IT COMES TO FINDING YOUR OLD EMPLOYERS. WHAT I NEED YOU TO DO IS GIVE ME A HINT WHERE TO PICK UP HIS TRAIL.

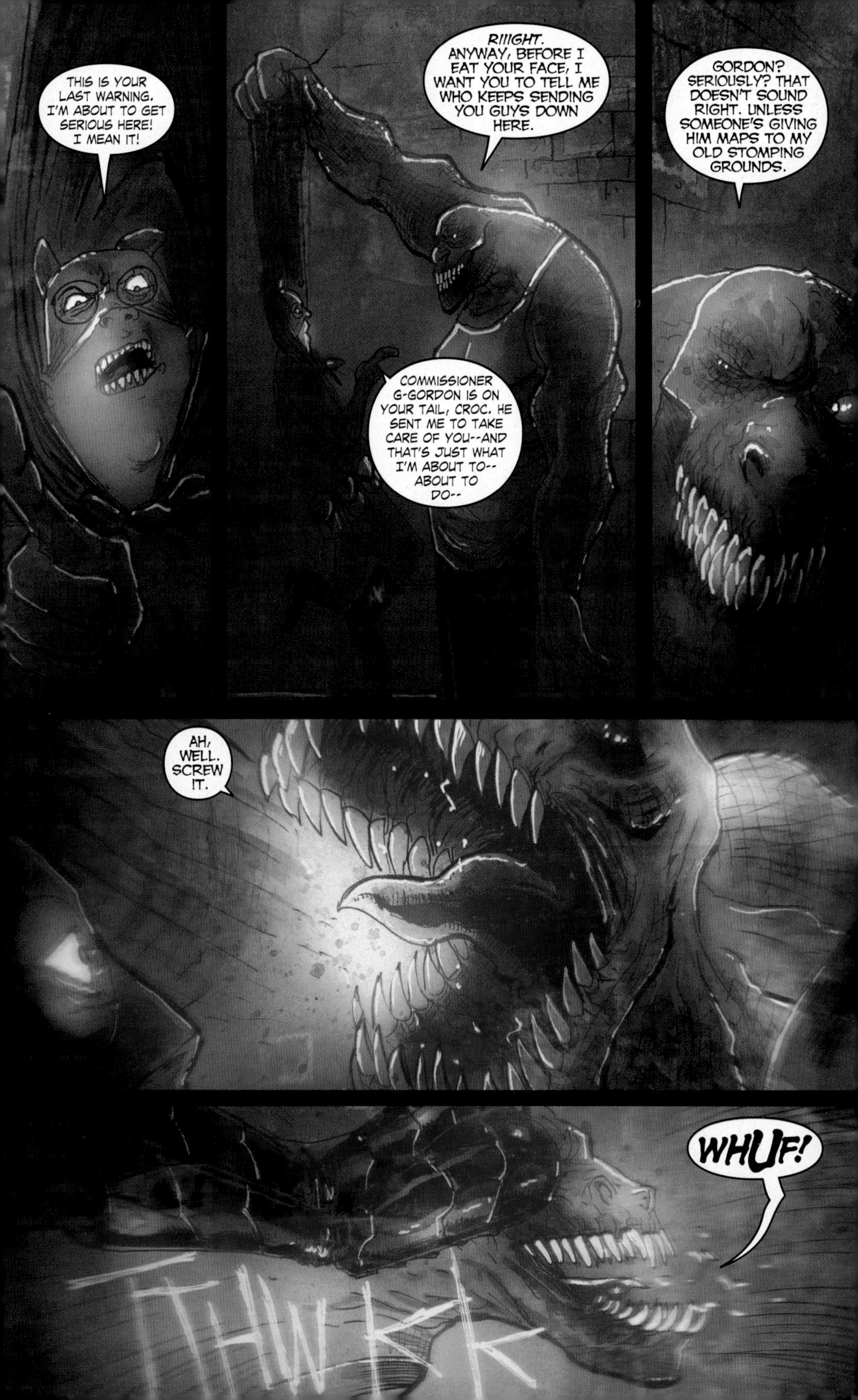
THIS IS YOUR LAST WARNING. I'M ABOUT TO GET SERIOUS HERE! I MEAN IT!
RIIIGHT. ANYWAY, BEFORE I EAT YOUR FACE, I WANT YOU TO TELL ME WHO KEEPS SENDING YOU GUYS DOWN HERE.
COMMISSIONER G-GORDON IS ON YOUR TAIL, CROC. HE SENT ME TO TAKE CARE OF YOU--AND THAT'S JUST WHAT I'M ABOUT TO--ABOUT TO DO--
GORDON? SERIOUSLY? THAT DOESN'T SOUND RIGHT. UNLESS SOMEONE'S GIVING HIM MAPS TO MY OLD STOMPING GROUNDS.
AH, WELL. SCREW IT.
WHUF!
THWKK

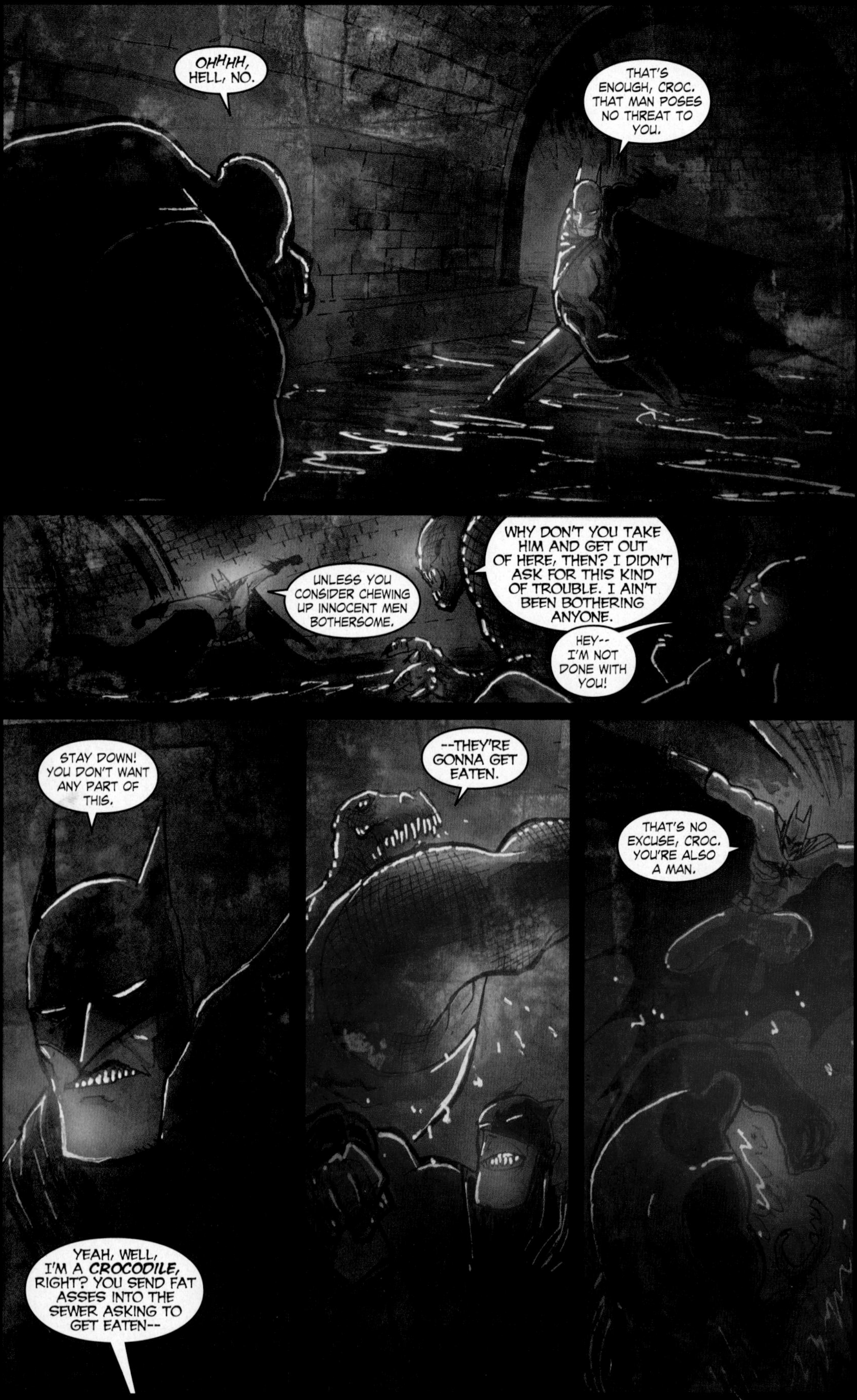
OHHHH, HELL, NO.
THAT'S ENOUGH, CROC. THAT MAN POSES NO THREAT TO YOU.
WHY DON'T YOU TAKE HIM AND GET OUT OF HERE, THEN? I DIDN'T ASK FOR THIS KIND OF TROUBLE. I AIN'T BEEN BOTHERING ANYONE.
UNLESS YOU CONSIDER CHEWING UP INNOCENT MEN BOTHERSOME.
HEY-- I'M NOT DONE WITH YOU!
STAY DOWN! YOU DON'T WANT ANY PART OF THIS.
YEAH, WELL, I'M A CROCODILE, RIGHT? YOU SEND FAT ASSES INTO THE SEWER ASKING TO GET EATEN--
--THEY'RE GONNA GET EATEN.
THAT'S NO EXCUSE, CROC. YOU'RE ALSO A MAN.

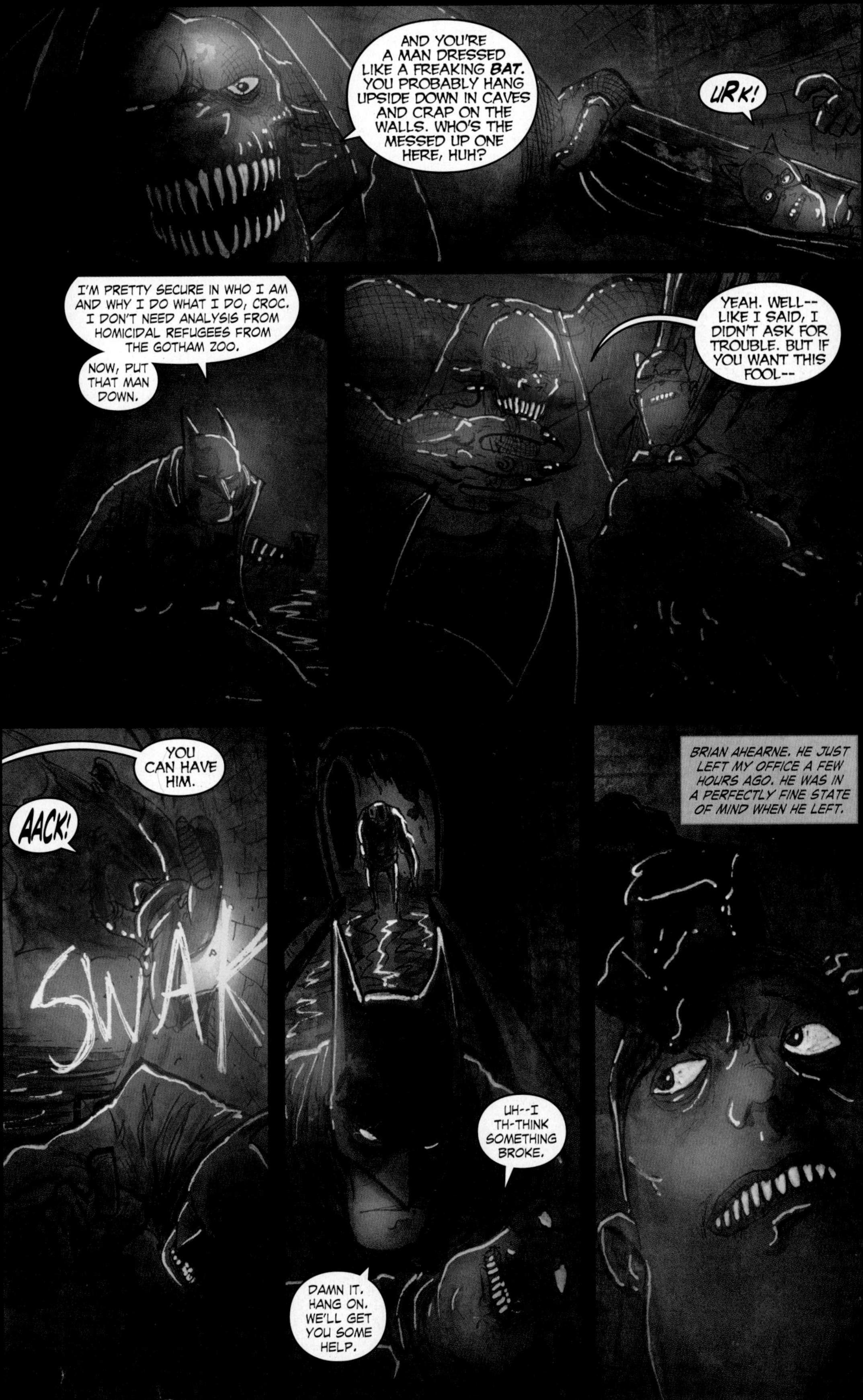
AND YOU'RE A MAN DRESSED LIKE A FREAKING BAT. YOU PROBABLY HANG UPSIDE DOWN IN CAVES AND CRAP ON THE WALLS. WHO'S THE MESSED UP ONE HERE, HUH?
URK!
I'M PRETTY SECURE IN WHO I AM AND WHY I DO WHAT I DO, CROC. I DON'T NEED ANALYSIS FROM HOMICIDAL REFUGEES FROM THE GOTHAM ZOO.
NOW, PUT THAT MAN DOWN.
YEAH. WELL-- LIKE I SAID, I DIDN'T ASK FOR TROUBLE. BUT IF YOU WANT THIS FOOL--
YOU CAN HAVE HIM.
AACK!
SWAK
UH--I TH-THINK SOMETHING BROKE.
DAMN IT. HANG ON. WE'LL GET YOU SOME HELP.
BRIAN AHEARNE. HE JUST LEFT MY OFFICE A FEW HOURS AGO. HE WAS IN A PERFECTLY FINE STATE OF MIND WHEN HE LEFT.

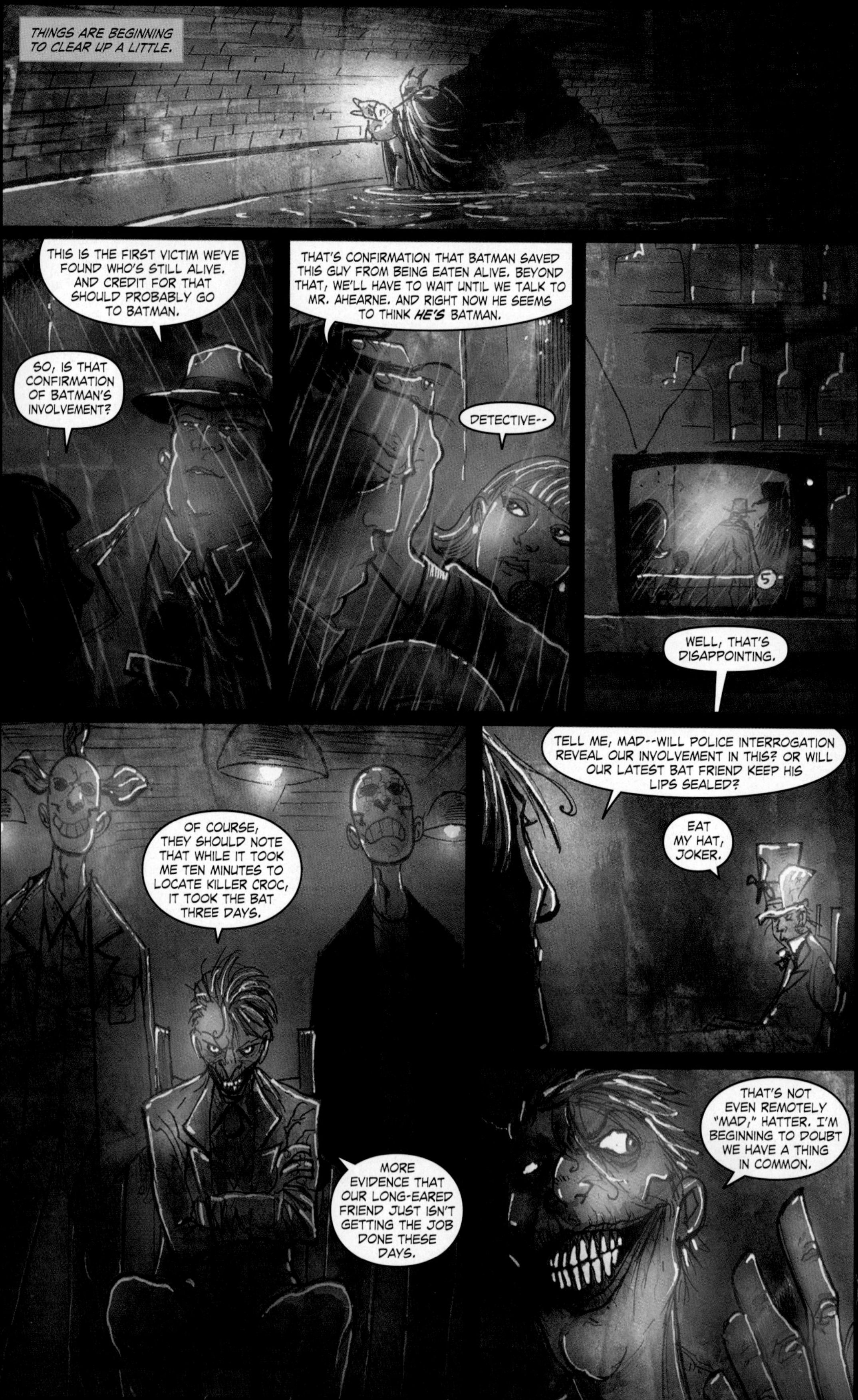
THINGS ARE BEGINNING TO CLEAR UP A LITTLE.
THIS IS THE FIRST VICTIM WE'VE FOUND WHO'S STILL ALIVE. AND CREDIT FOR THAT SHOULD PROBABLY GO TO BATMAN.
SO, IS THAT CONFIRMATION OF BATMAN'S INVOLVEMENT?
THAT'S CONFIRMATION THAT BATMAN SAVED THIS GUY FROM BEING EATEN ALIVE. BEYOND THAT, WE'LL HAVE TO WAIT UNTIL WE TALK TO MR. AHEARNE. AND RIGHT NOW HE SEEMS TO THINK *HE'S* BATMAN.
DETECTIVE--
5
WELL, THAT'S DISAPPOINTING.
OF COURSE, THEY SHOULD NOTE THAT WHILE IT TOOK ME TEN MINUTES TO LOCATE KILLER CROC, IT TOOK THE BAT THREE DAYS.
MORE EVIDENCE THAT OUR LONG-EARED FRIEND JUST ISN'T GETTING THE JOB DONE THESE DAYS.
TELL ME, MAD--WILL POLICE INTERROGATION REVEAL OUR INVOLVEMENT IN THIS? OR WILL OUR LATEST BAT FRIEND KEEP HIS LIPS SEALED?
EAT MY HAT, JOKER.
THAT'S NOT EVEN REMOTELY "MAD," HATTER. I'M BEGINNING TO DOUBT WE HAVE A THING IN COMMON.

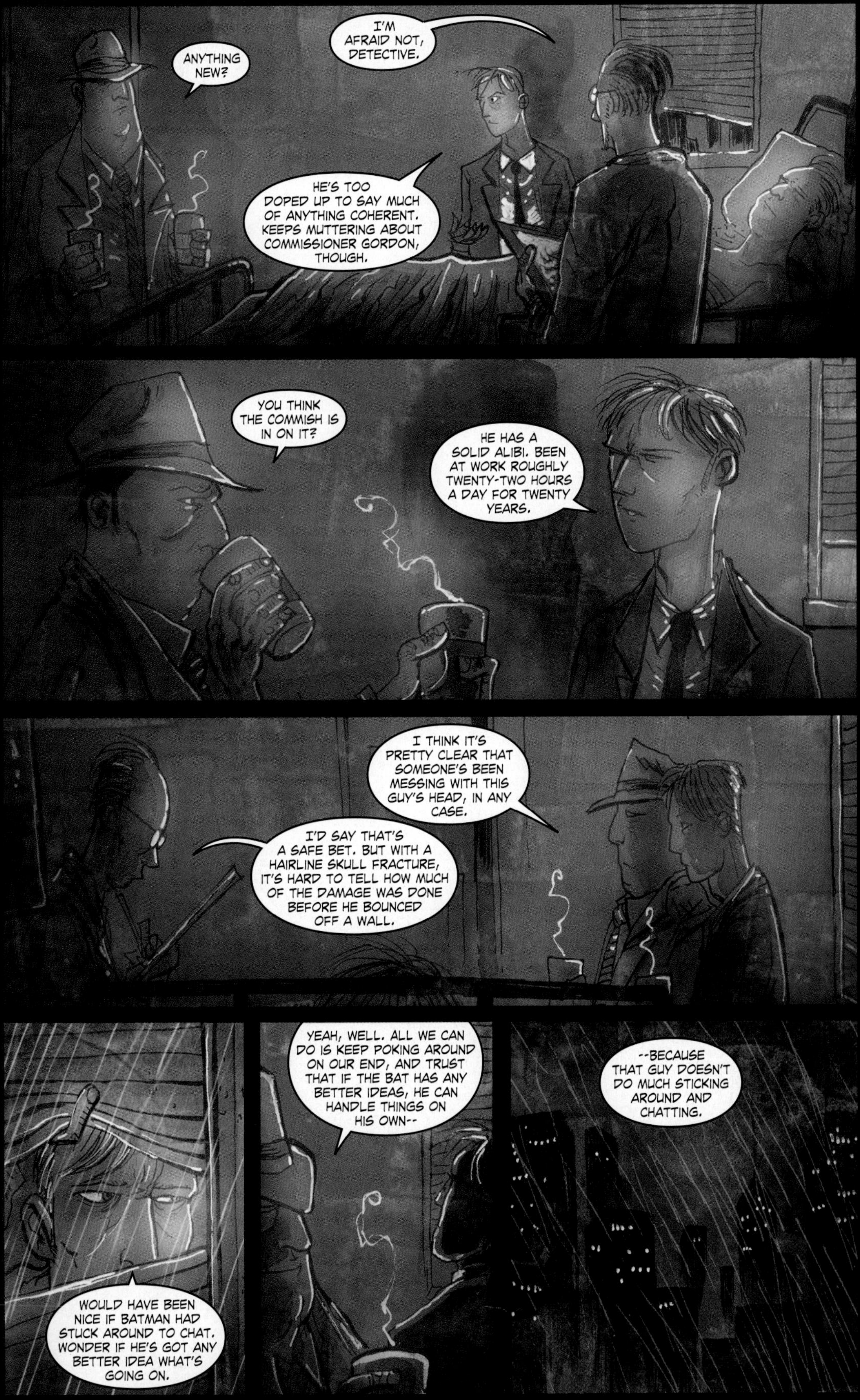

ANYTHING NEW?
I'M AFRAID NOT, DETECTIVE.
HE'S TOO DOPED UP TO SAY MUCH OF ANYTHING COHERENT. KEEPS MUTTERING ABOUT COMMISSIONER GORDON, THOUGH.
YOU THINK THE COMMISH IS IN ON IT?
HE HAS A SOLID ALIBI. BEEN AT WORK ROUGHLY TWENTY-TWO HOURS A DAY FOR TWENTY YEARS.
I THINK IT'S PRETTY CLEAR THAT SOMEONE'S BEEN MESSING WITH THIS GUY'S HEAD, IN ANY CASE.
I'D SAY THAT'S A SAFE BET. BUT WITH A HAIRLINE SKULL FRACTURE, IT'S HARD TO TELL HOW MUCH OF THE DAMAGE WAS DONE BEFORE HE BOUNCED OFF A WALL.
WOULD HAVE BEEN NICE IF BATMAN HAD STUCK AROUND TO CHAT. WONDER IF HE'S GOT ANY BETTER IDEA WHAT'S GOING ON.
YEAH, WELL. ALL WE CAN DO IS KEEP POKING AROUND ON OUR END, AND TRUST THAT IF THE BAT HAS ANY BETTER IDEAS, HE CAN HANDLE THINGS ON HIS OWN--
--BECAUSE THAT GUY DOESN'T DO MUCH STICKING AROUND AND CHATTING.

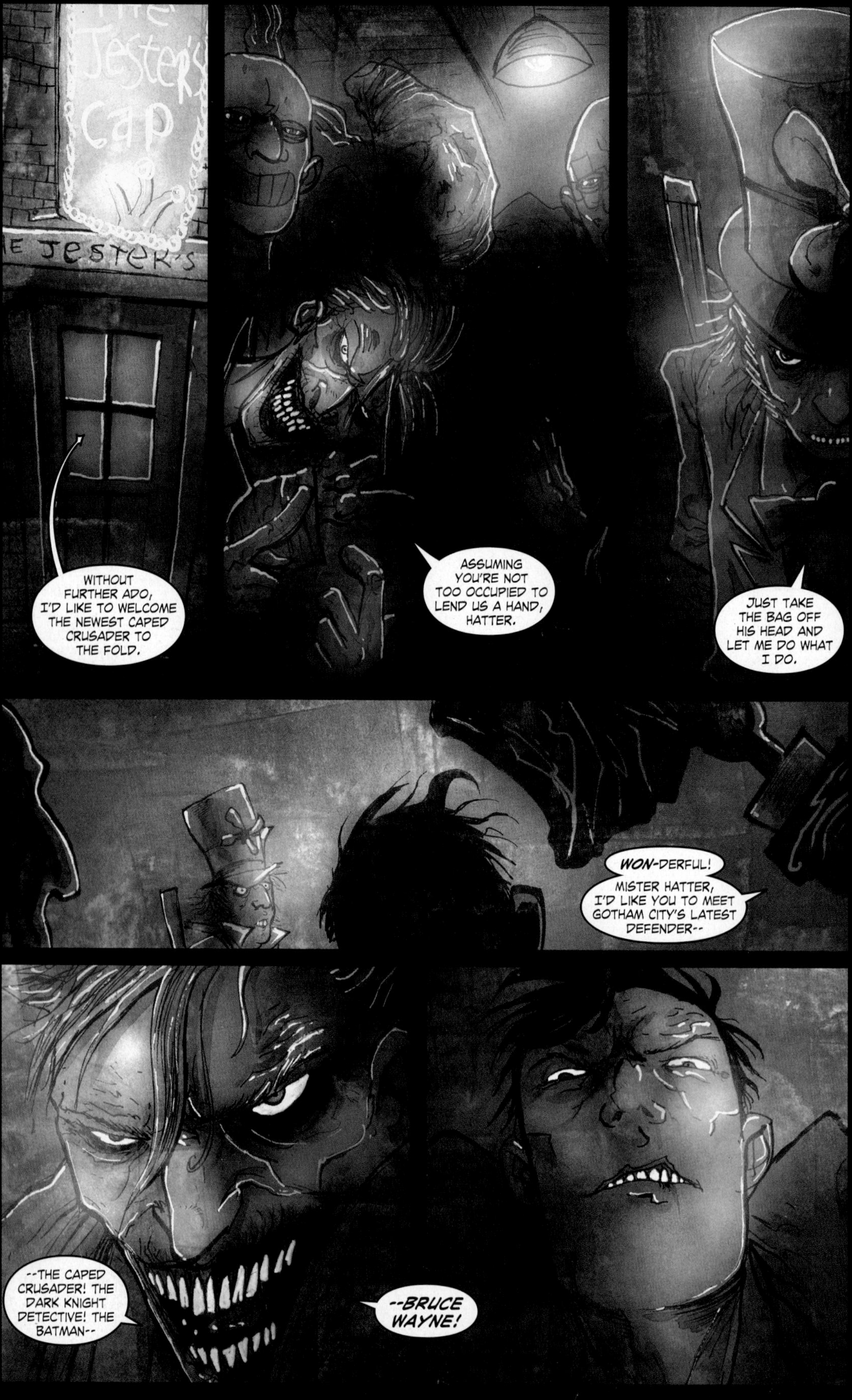
The Jester's Cap
E JESTER'S
WITHOUT FURTHER ADO, I'D LIKE TO WELCOME THE NEWEST CAPED CRUSADER TO THE FOLD.
ASSUMING YOU'RE NOT TOO OCCUPIED TO LEND US A HAND, HATTER.
JUST TAKE THE BAG OFF HIS HEAD AND LET ME DO WHAT I DO.
WON-DERFUL!
MISTER HATTER, I'D LIKE YOU TO MEET GOTHAM CITY'S LATEST DEFENDER--
--THE CAPED CRUSADER! THE DARK KNIGHT DETECTIVE! THE BATMAN--
--BRUCE WAYNE!

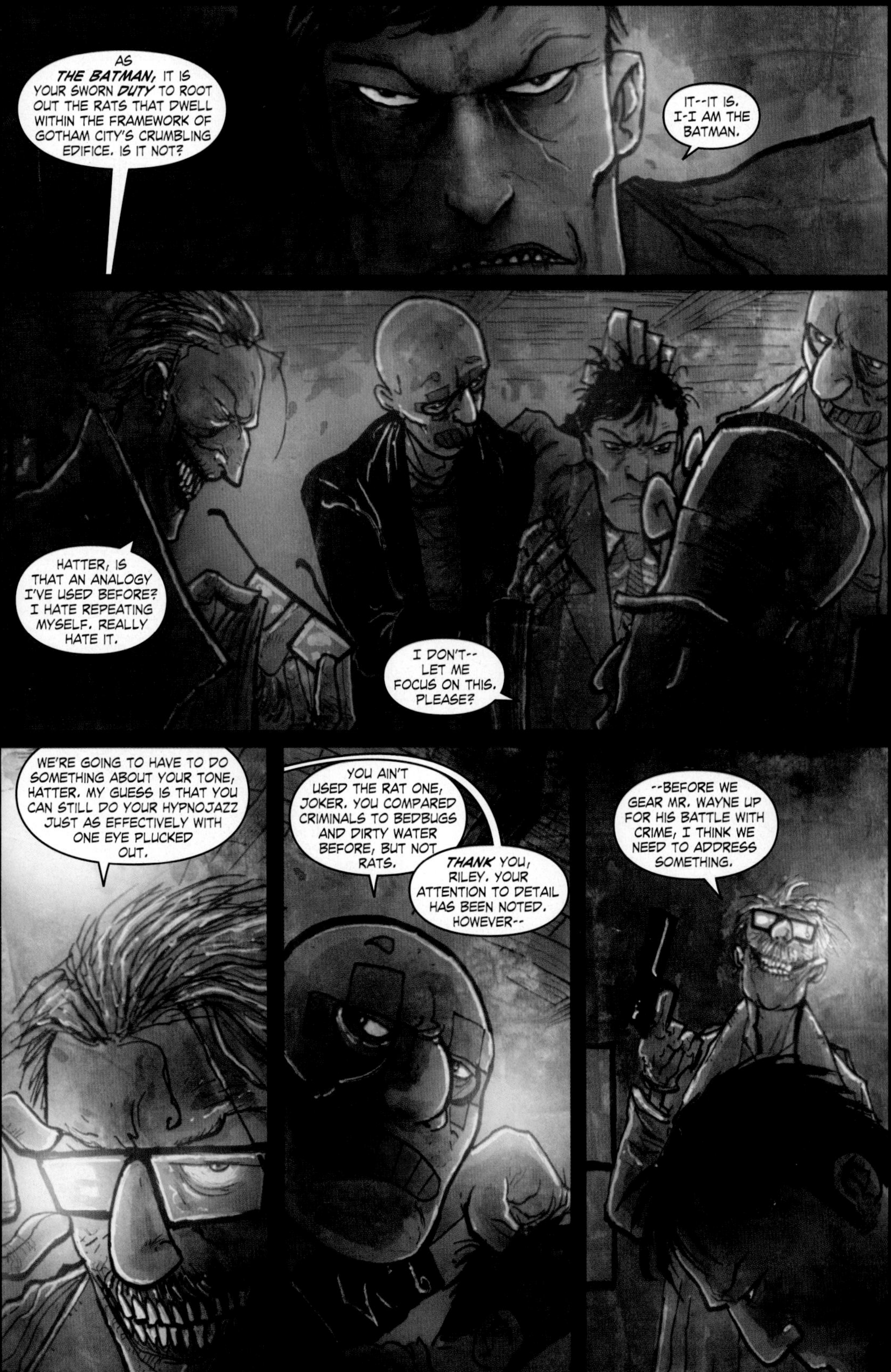
AS THE BATMAN, IT IS YOUR SWORN DUTY TO ROOT OUT THE RATS THAT DWELL WITHIN THE FRAMEWORK OF GOTHAM CITY'S CRUMBLING EDIFICE. IS IT NOT?
IT--IT IS. I-I AM THE BATMAN.
HATTER, IS THAT AN ANALOGY I'VE USED BEFORE? I HATE REPEATING MYSELF. REALLY HATE IT.
I DON'T-- LET ME FOCUS ON THIS. PLEASE?
WE'RE GOING TO HAVE TO DO SOMETHING ABOUT YOUR TONE, HATTER. MY GUESS IS THAT YOU CAN STILL DO YOUR HYPNOJAZZ JUST AS EFFECTIVELY WITH ONE EYE PLUCKED OUT.
YOU AIN'T USED THE RAT ONE, JOKER. YOU COMPARED CRIMINALS TO BEDBUGS AND DIRTY WATER BEFORE, BUT NOT RATS.
THANK YOU, RILEY. YOUR ATTENTION TO DETAIL HAS BEEN NOTED. HOWEVER--
--BEFORE WE GEAR MR. WAYNE UP FOR HIS BATTLE WITH CRIME, I THINK WE NEED TO ADDRESS SOMETHING.

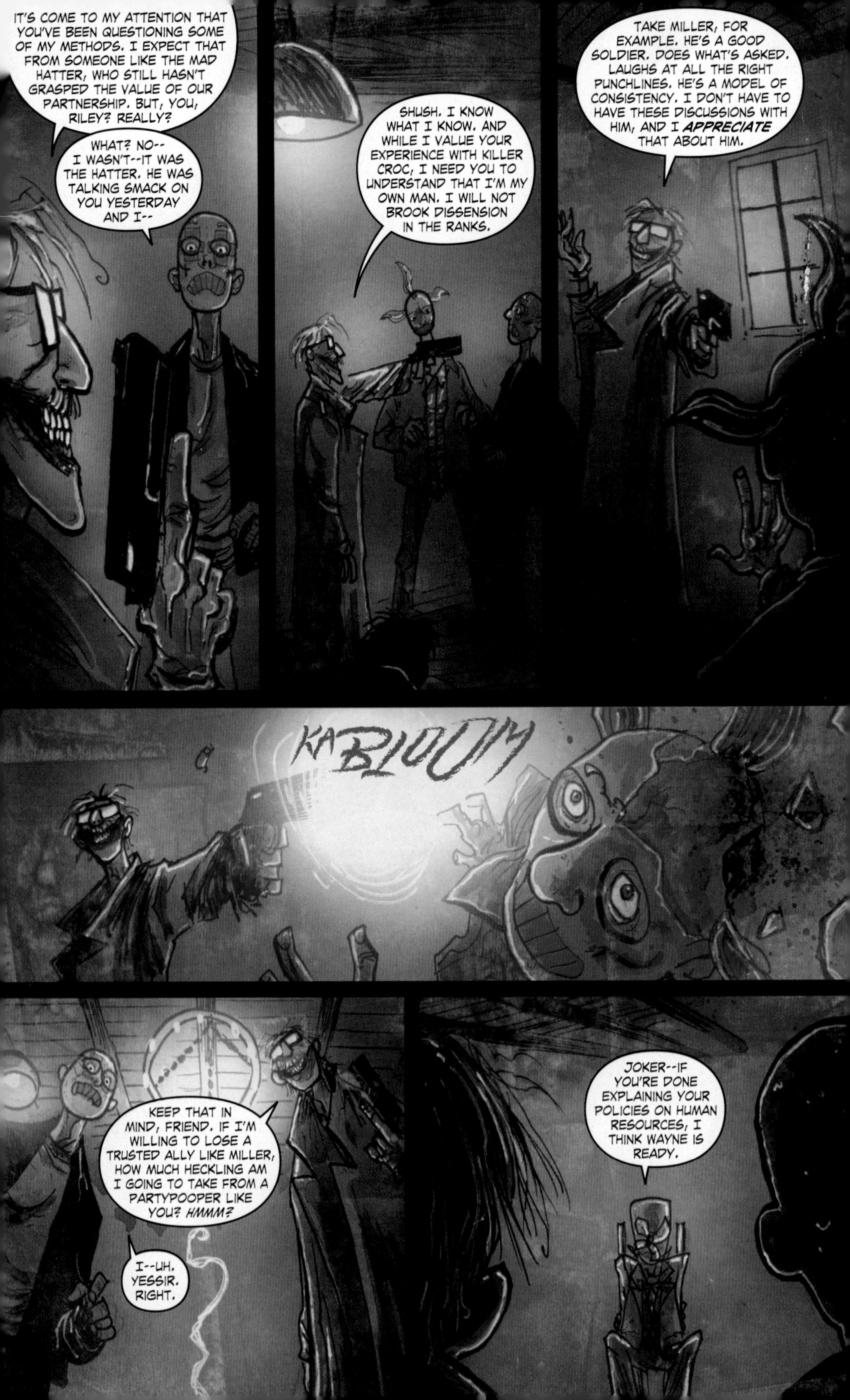
IT'S COME TO MY ATTENTION THAT YOU'VE BEEN QUESTIONING SOME OF MY METHODS. I EXPECT THAT FROM SOMEONE LIKE THE MAD HATTER, WHO STILL HASN'T GRASPED THE VALUE OF OUR PARTNERSHIP. BUT, YOU, RILEY? REALLY?
WHAT? NO-- I WASN'T--IT WAS THE HATTER. HE WAS TALKING SMACK ON YOU YESTERDAY AND I--
SHUSH. I KNOW WHAT I KNOW. AND WHILE I VALUE YOUR EXPERIENCE WITH KILLER CROC, I NEED YOU TO UNDERSTAND THAT I'M MY OWN MAN. I WILL NOT BROOK DISSENSION IN THE RANKS.
TAKE MILLER, FOR EXAMPLE. HE'S A GOOD SOLDIER. DOES WHAT'S ASKED. LAUGHS AT ALL THE RIGHT PUNCHLINES. HE'S A MODEL OF CONSISTENCY. I DON'T HAVE TO HAVE THESE DISCUSSIONS WITH HIM, AND I ***APPRECIATE*** THAT ABOUT HIM.
KABLOOM
KEEP THAT IN MIND, FRIEND. IF I'M WILLING TO LOSE A TRUSTED ALLY LIKE MILLER, HOW MUCH HECKLING AM I GOING TO TAKE FROM A PARTYPOOPER LIKE YOU? *HMMM?*
I--UH. YESSIR. RIGHT.
JOKER--IF YOU'RE DONE EXPLAINING YOUR POLICIES ON HUMAN RESOURCES, I THINK WAYNE IS READY.

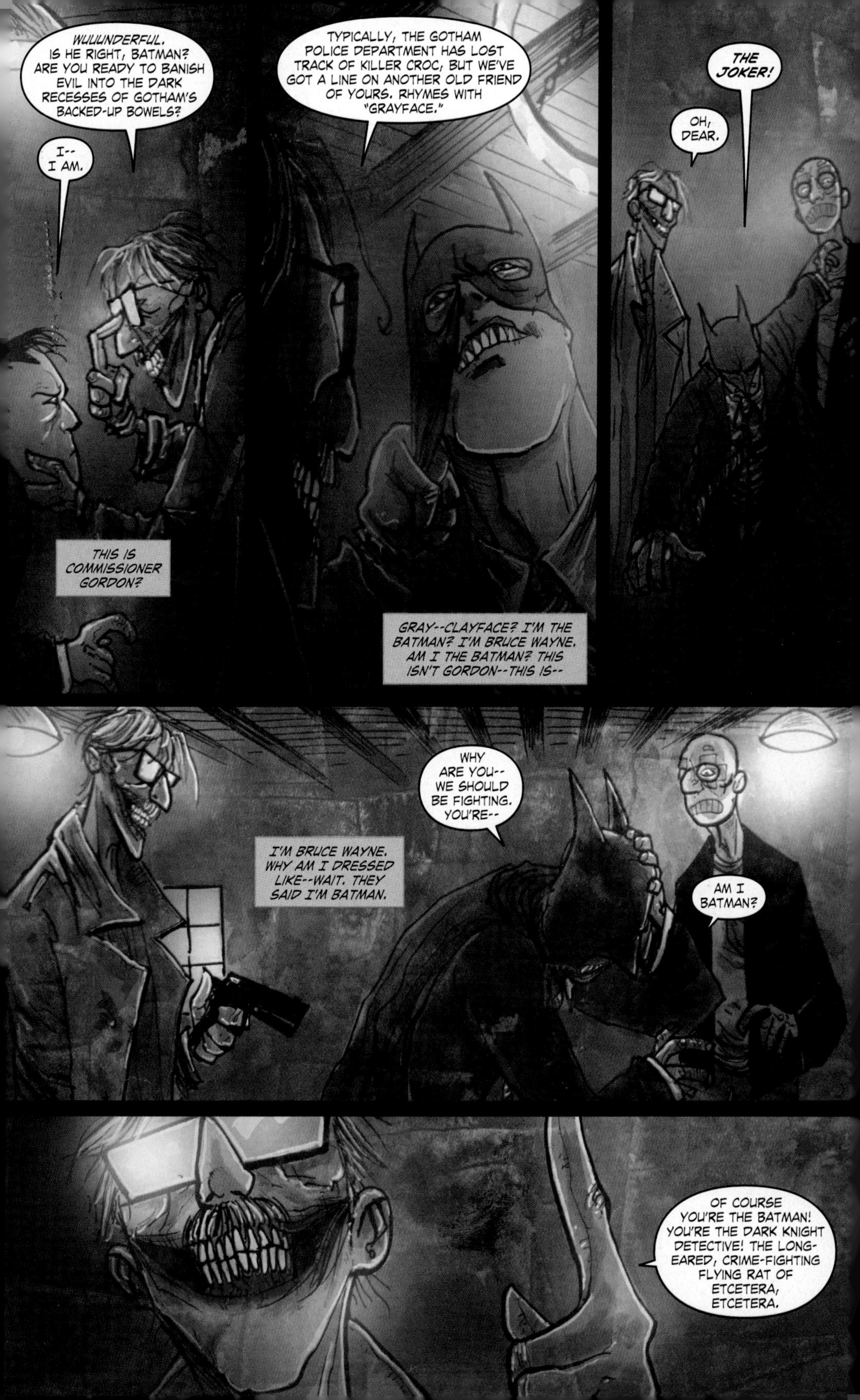
WUUUNDERFUL. IS HE RIGHT, BATMAN? ARE YOU READY TO BANISH EVIL INTO THE DARK RECESSES OF GOTHAM'S BACKED-UP BOWELS?
I-- I AM.
THIS IS COMMISSIONER GORDON?
TYPICALLY, THE GOTHAM POLICE DEPARTMENT HAS LOST TRACK OF KILLER CROC, BUT WE'VE GOT A LINE ON ANOTHER OLD FRIEND OF YOURS. RHYMES WITH "GRAYFACE."
GRAY--CLAYFACE? I'M THE BATMAN? I'M BRUCE WAYNE. AM I THE BATMAN? THIS ISN'T GORDON--THIS IS--
THE JOKER!
OH, DEAR.
I'M BRUCE WAYNE. WHY AM I DRESSED LIKE--WAIT. THEY SAID I'M BATMAN.
WHY ARE YOU-- WE SHOULD BE FIGHTING. YOU'RE--
AM I BATMAN?
OF COURSE YOU'RE THE BATMAN! YOU'RE THE DARK KNIGHT DETECTIVE! THE LONG-EARED, CRIME-FIGHTING FLYING RAT OF ETCETERA, ETCETERA.

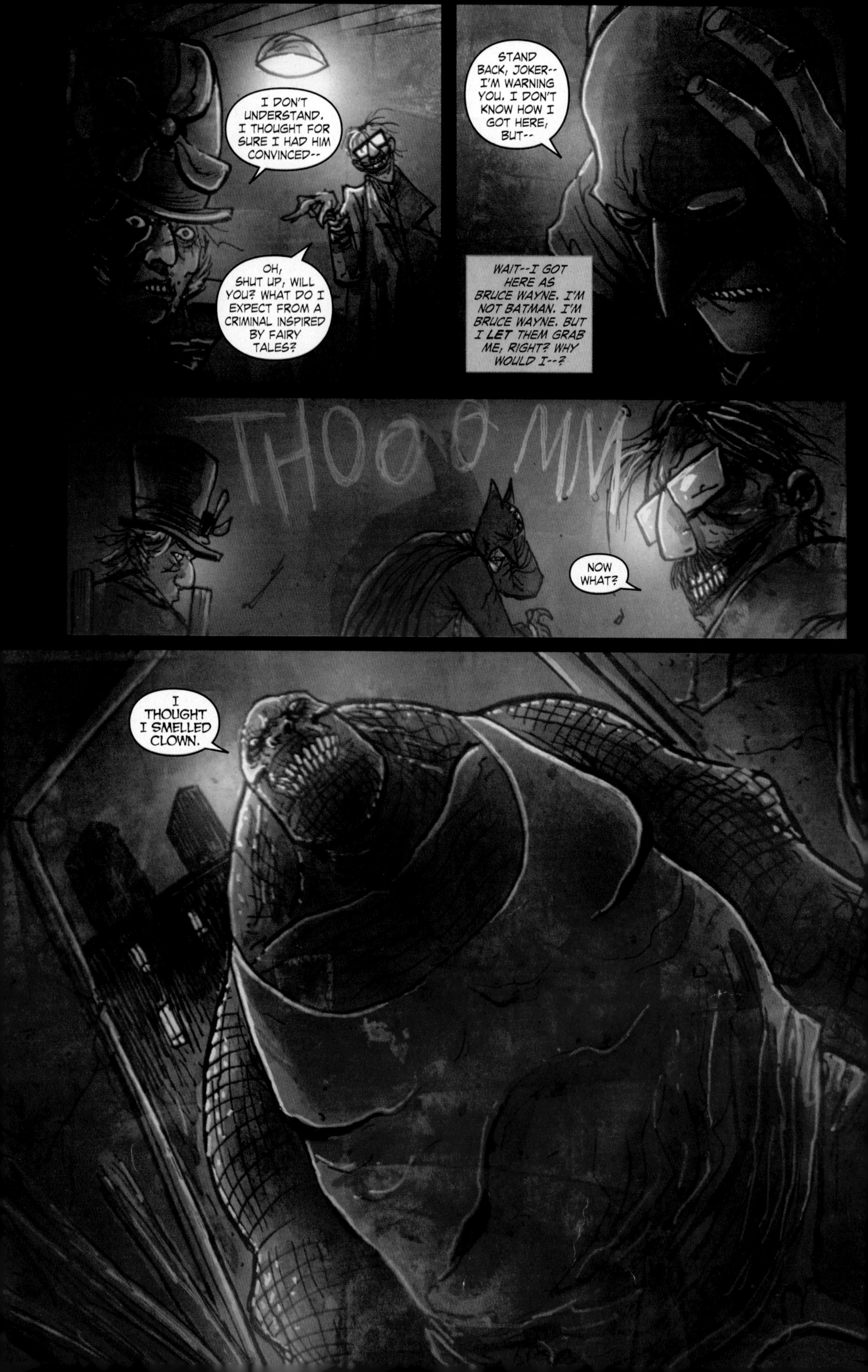
I DON'T UNDERSTAND. I THOUGHT FOR SURE I HAD HIM CONVINCED--
OH, SHUT UP, WILL YOU? WHAT DO I EXPECT FROM A CRIMINAL INSPIRED BY FAIRY TALES?
STAND BACK, JOKER-- I'M WARNING YOU. I DON'T KNOW HOW I GOT HERE, BUT--
WAIT--I GOT HERE AS BRUCE WAYNE. I'M NOT BATMAN. I'M BRUCE WAYNE. BUT I LET THEM GRAB ME, RIGHT? WHY WOULD I--?
THOOOOMM
NOW WHAT?
I THOUGHT I SMELLED CLOWN.

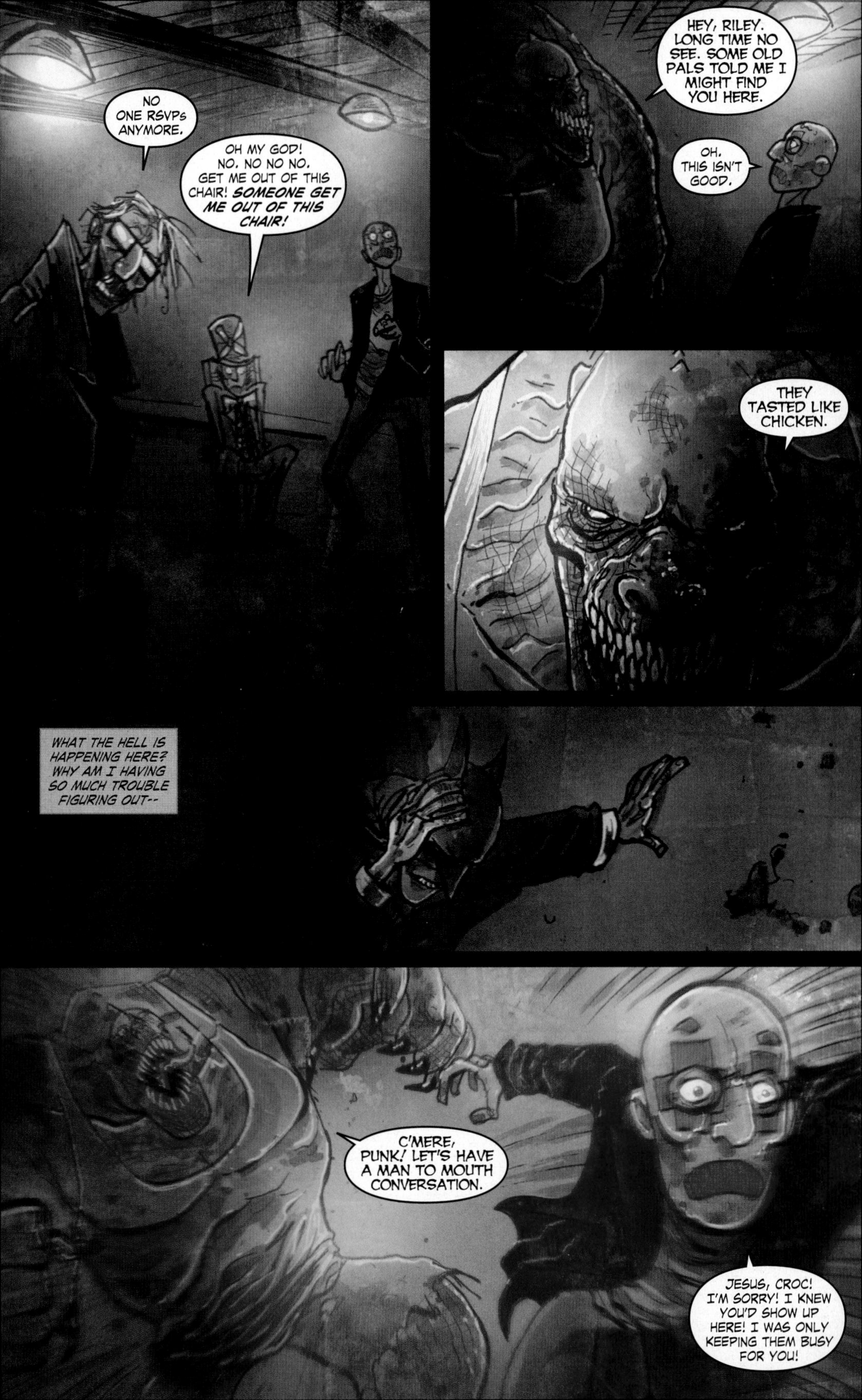
NO ONE RSVPs ANYMORE.
OH MY GOD! NO. NO NO NO. GET ME OUT OF THIS CHAIR! SOMEONE GET ME OUT OF THIS CHAIR!
HEY, RILEY. LONG TIME NO SEE. SOME OLD PALS TOLD ME I MIGHT FIND YOU HERE.
OH. THIS ISN'T GOOD.
THEY TASTED LIKE CHICKEN.
WHAT THE HELL IS HAPPENING HERE? WHY AM I HAVING SO MUCH TROUBLE FIGURING OUT--
C'MERE, PUNK! LET'S HAVE A MAN TO MOUTH CONVERSATION.
JESUS, CROC! I'M SORRY! I KNEW YOU'D SHOW UP HERE! I WAS ONLY KEEPING THEM BUSY FOR YOU!

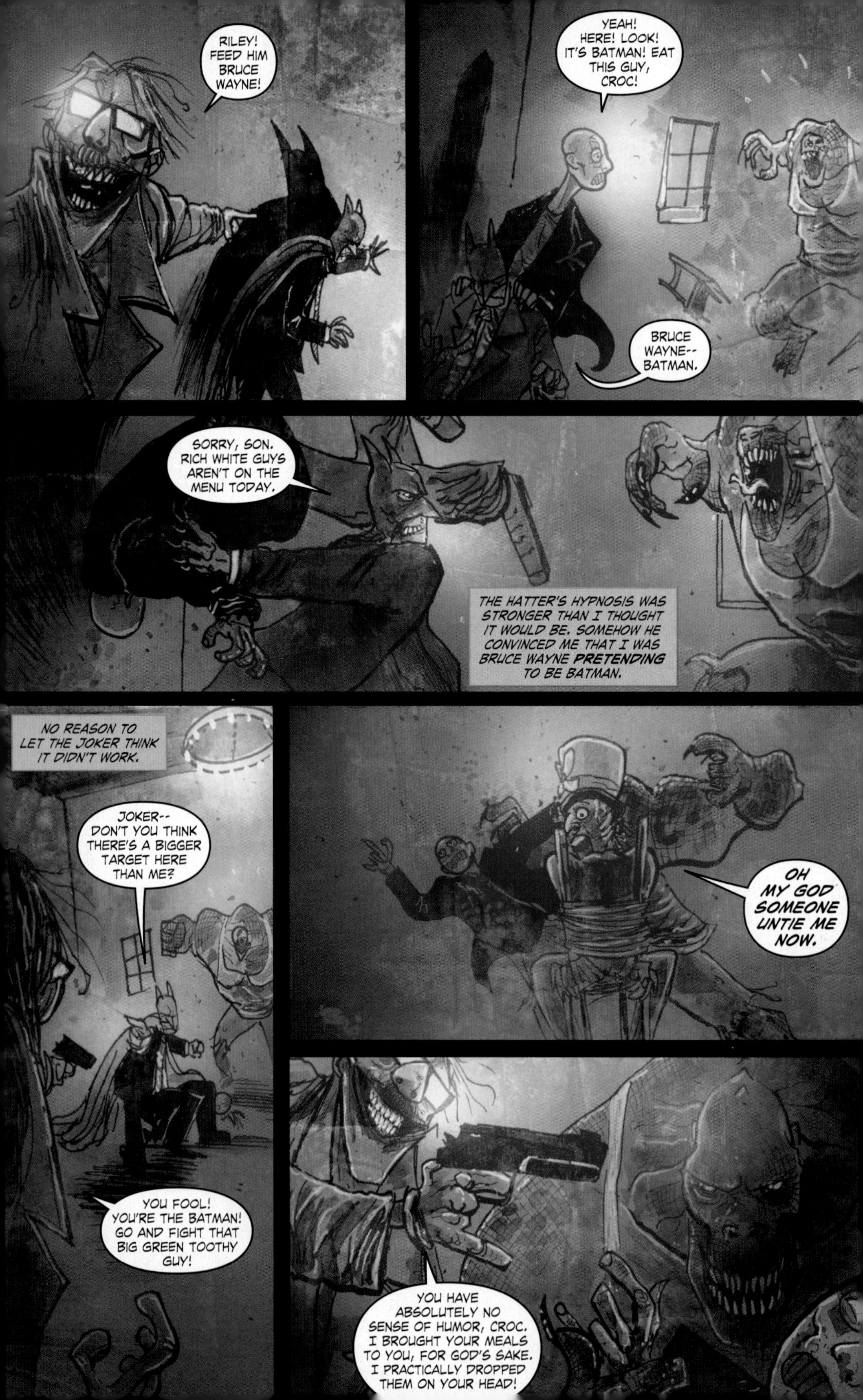
RILEY! FEED HIM BRUCE WAYNE!
YEAH! HERE! LOOK! IT'S BATMAN! EAT THIS GUY, CROC!
BRUCE WAYNE-- BATMAN.
SORRY, SON. RICH WHITE GUYS AREN'T ON THE MENU TODAY.
THE HATTER'S HYPNOSIS WAS STRONGER THAN I THOUGHT IT WOULD BE. SOMEHOW HE CONVINCED ME THAT I WAS BRUCE WAYNE PRETENDING TO BE BATMAN.
NO REASON TO LET THE JOKER THINK IT DIDN'T WORK.
JOKER-- DON'T YOU THINK THERE'S A BIGGER TARGET HERE THAN ME?
YOU FOOL! YOU'RE THE BATMAN! GO AND FIGHT THAT BIG GREEN TOOTHY GUY!
OH MY GOD SOMEONE UNTIE ME NOW.
YOU HAVE ABSOLUTELY NO SENSE OF HUMOR, CROC. I BROUGHT YOUR MEALS TO YOU, FOR GOD'S SAKE. I PRACTICALLY DROPPED THEM ON YOUR HEAD!

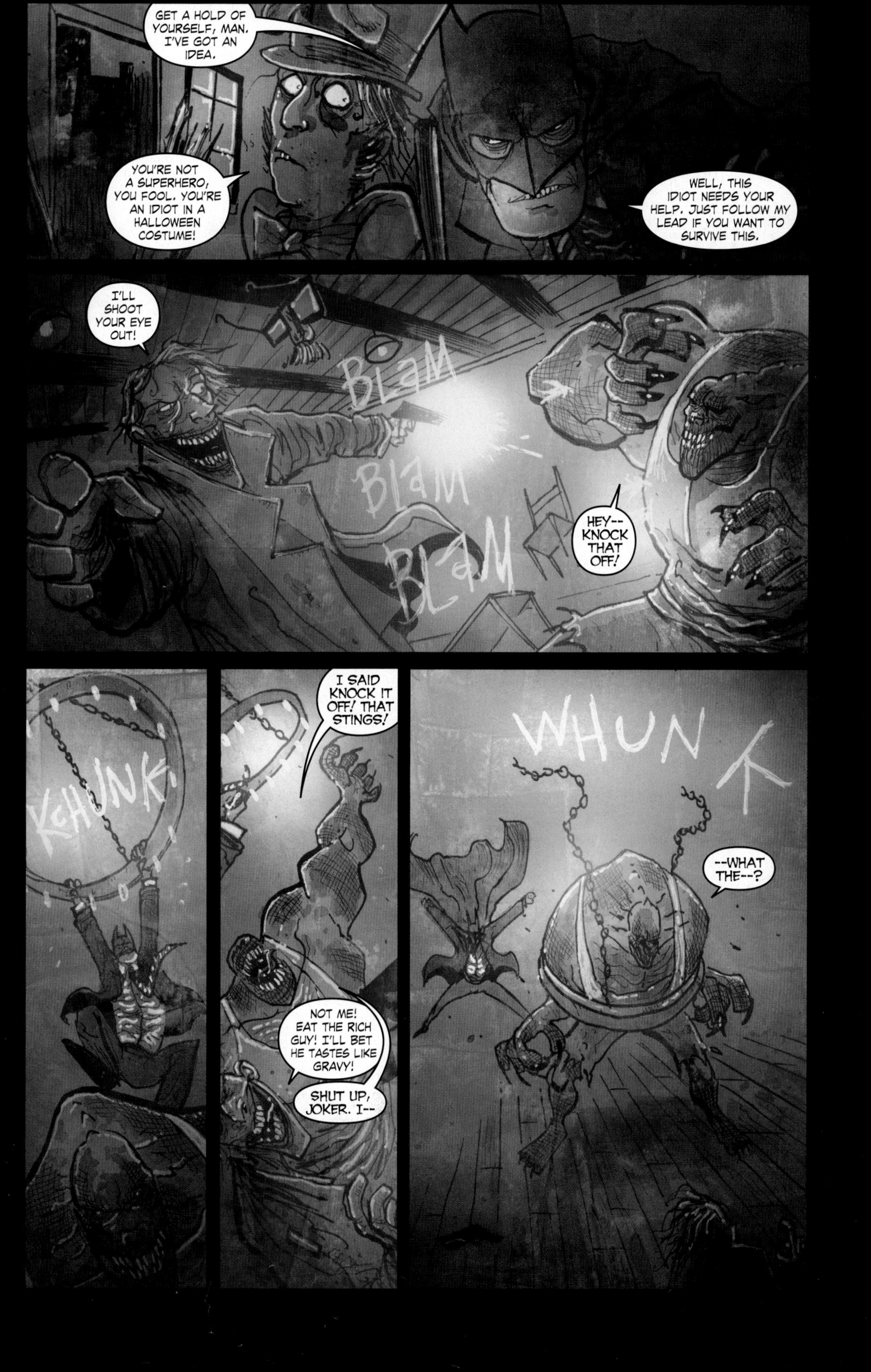
GET A HOLD OF YOURSELF, MAN. I'VE GOT AN IDEA.
YOU'RE NOT A SUPERHERO, YOU FOOL. YOU'RE AN IDIOT IN A HALLOWEEN COSTUME!
WELL, THIS IDIOT NEEDS YOUR HELP. JUST FOLLOW MY LEAD IF YOU WANT TO SURVIVE THIS.
I'LL SHOOT YOUR EYE OUT!
BLAM
BLAM
BLAM
HEY-- KNOCK THAT OFF!
KCHUNK
I SAID KNOCK IT OFF! THAT STINGS!
NOT ME! EAT THE RICH GUY! I'LL BET HE TASTES LIKE GRAVY!
SHUT UP, JOKER. I--
WHUNK
--WHAT THE--?

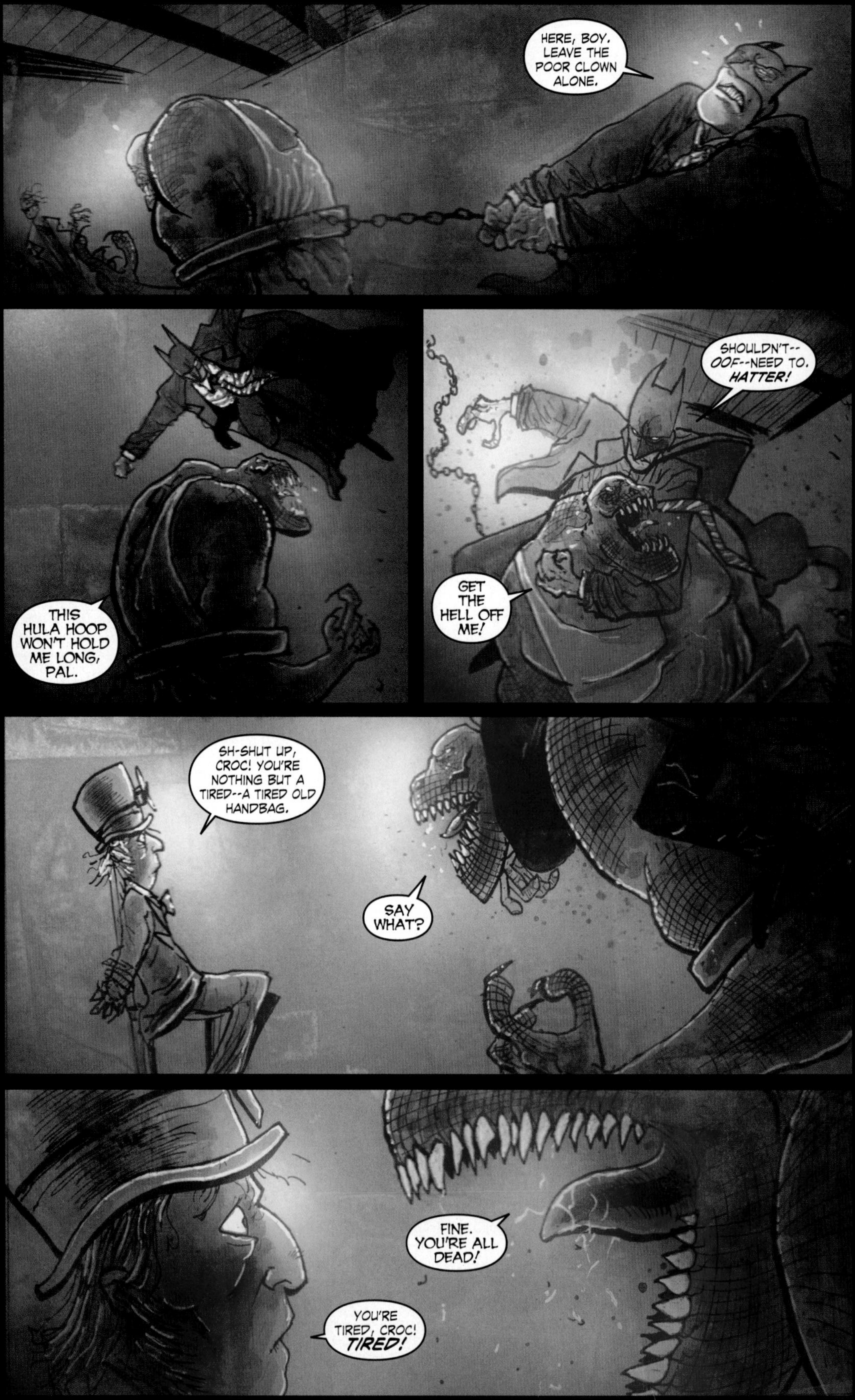
HERE, BOY. LEAVE THE POOR CLOWN ALONE.
THIS HULA HOOP WON'T HOLD ME LONG, PAL.
SHOULDN'T--OOF--NEED TO. HATTER!
GET THE HELL OFF ME!
SH-SHUT UP, CROC! YOU'RE NOTHING BUT A TIRED--A TIRED OLD HANDBAG.
SAY WHAT?
FINE. YOU'RE ALL DEAD!
YOU'RE TIRED, CROC! TIRED!

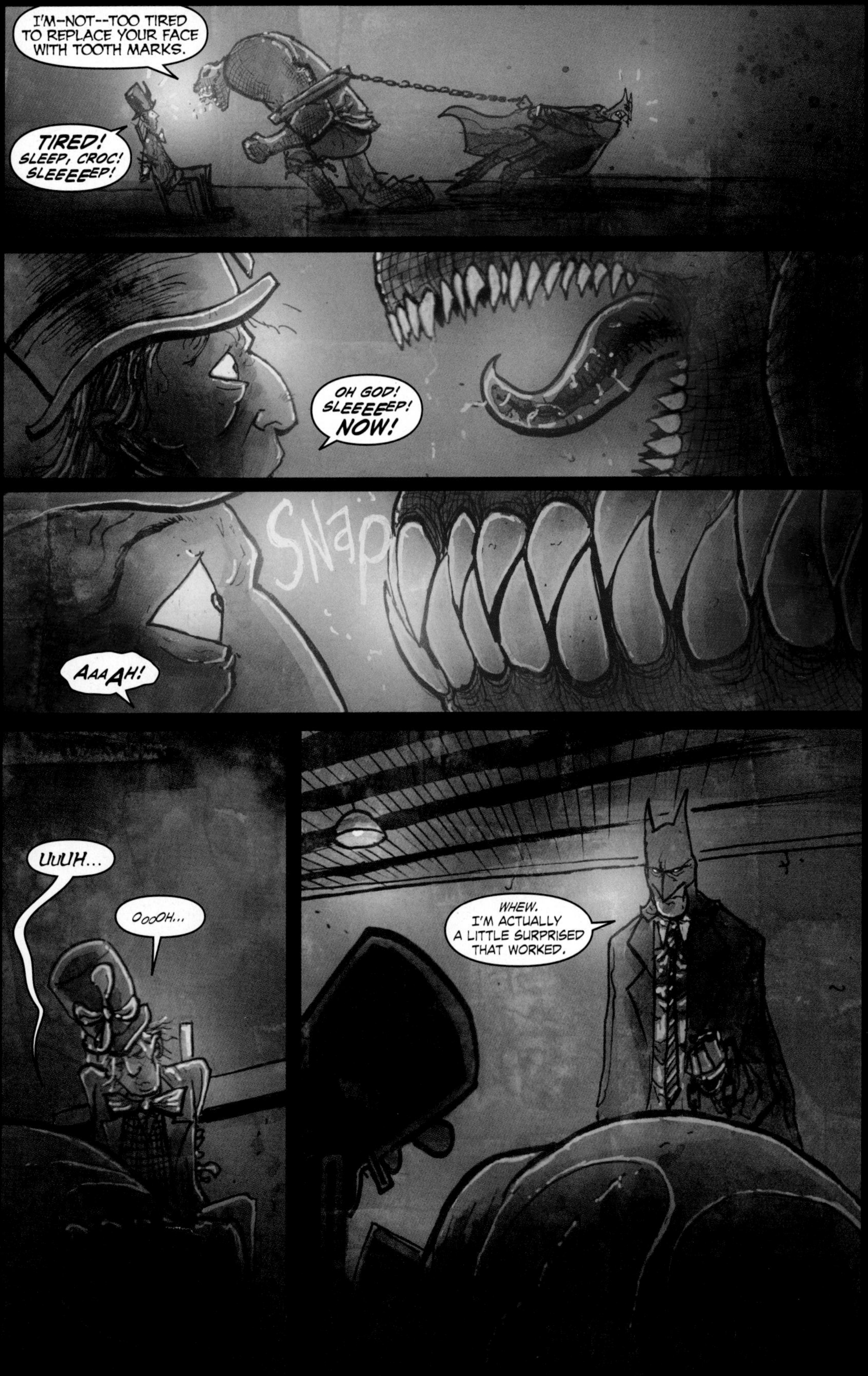
I'M--NOT--TOO TIRED TO REPLACE YOUR FACE WITH TOOTH MARKS.
TIRED! SLEEP, CROC! SLEEEEEEP!
OH GOD! SLEEEEEEP! NOW!
SNAP
AAAAH!
UUUH...
OOOOH...
WHEW. I'M ACTUALLY A LITTLE SURPRISED THAT WORKED.

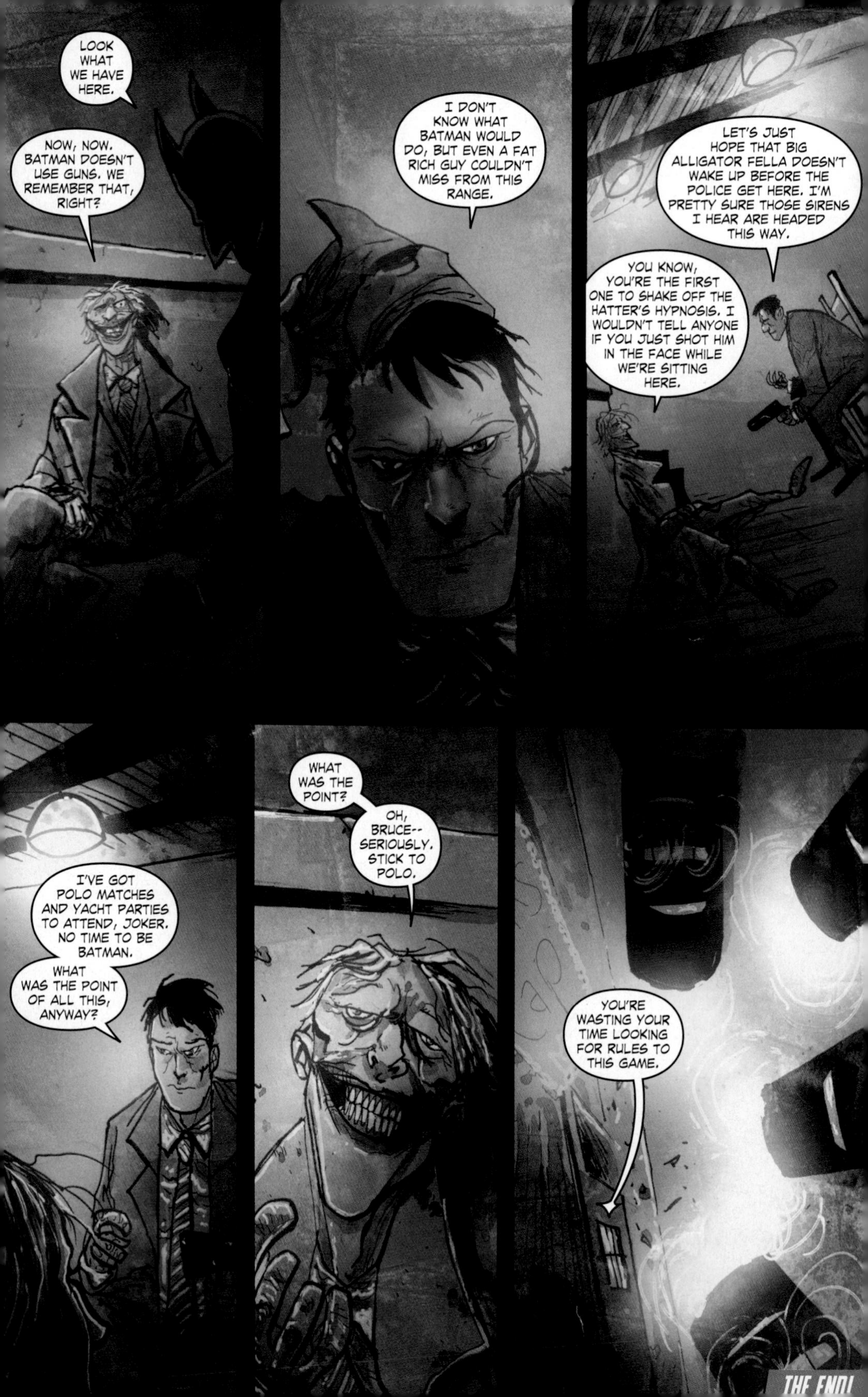
LOOK WHAT WE HAVE HERE.
NOW, NOW. BATMAN DOESN'T USE GUNS. WE REMEMBER THAT, RIGHT?
I DON'T KNOW WHAT BATMAN WOULD DO, BUT EVEN A FAT RICH GUY COULDN'T MISS FROM THIS RANGE.
LET'S JUST HOPE THAT BIG ALLIGATOR FELLA DOESN'T WAKE UP BEFORE THE POLICE GET HERE. I'M PRETTY SURE THOSE SIRENS I HEAR ARE HEADED THIS WAY.
YOU KNOW, YOU'RE THE FIRST ONE TO SHAKE OFF THE HATTER'S HYPNOSIS. I WOULDN'T TELL ANYONE IF YOU JUST SHOT HIM IN THE FACE WHILE WE'RE SITTING HERE.
I'VE GOT POLO MATCHES AND YACHT PARTIES TO ATTEND, JOKER. NO TIME TO BE BATMAN.
WHAT WAS THE POINT OF ALL THIS, ANYWAY?
WHAT WAS THE POINT?
OH, BRUCE-- SERIOUSLY. STICK TO POLO.
YOU'RE WASTING YOUR TIME LOOKING FOR RULES TO THIS GAME.
THE END!

LETTERS TO BATMAN

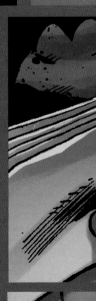

STEVE NILES
Writer

TREVOR HAIRSINE
Artist

ANTONIO FABELA
Colorist

SAIDA TEMOFONTE
Letterer

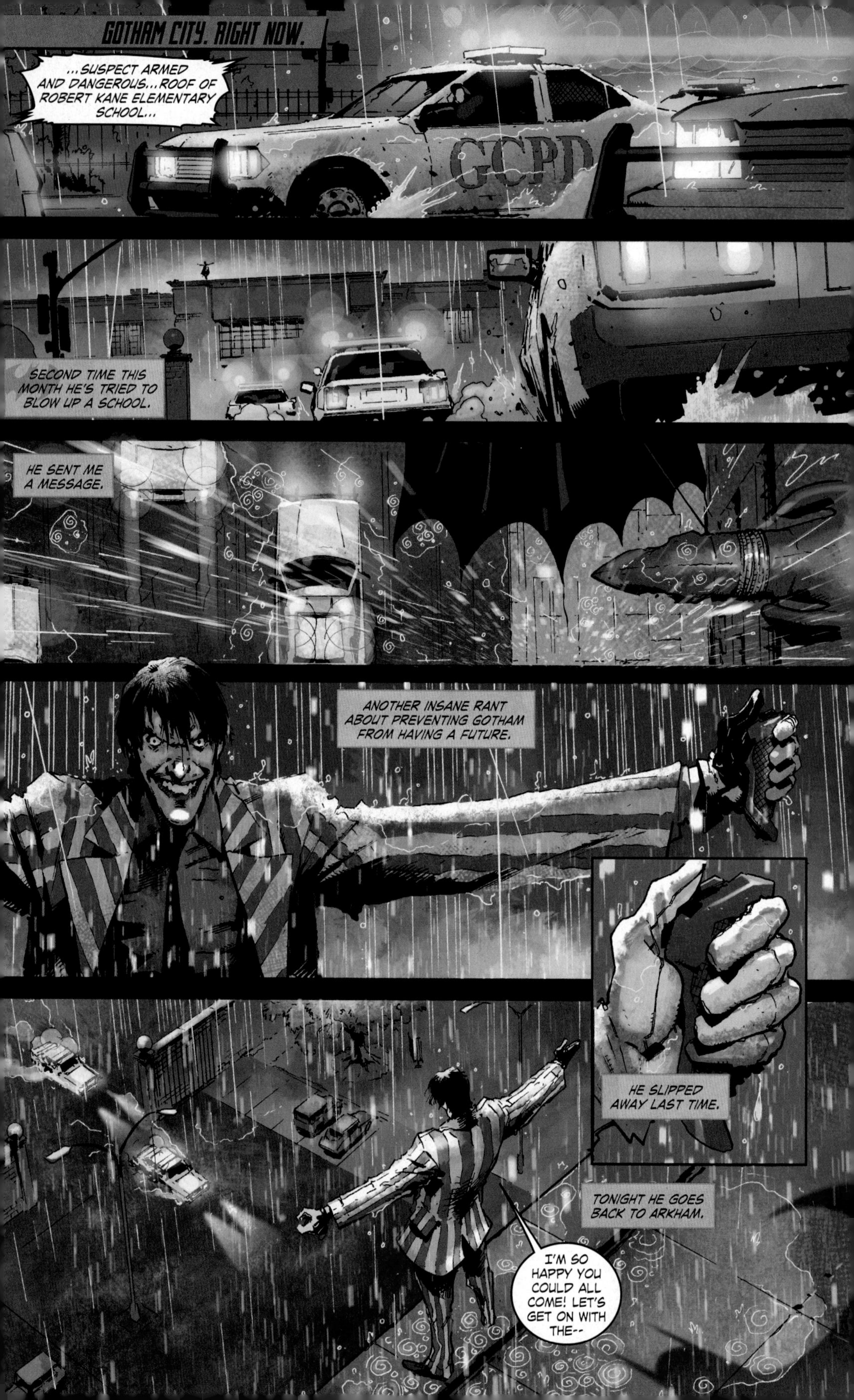
GOTHAM CITY. RIGHT NOW.
...SUSPECT ARMED AND DANGEROUS...ROOF OF ROBERT KANE ELEMENTARY SCHOOL...
GCPD
SECOND TIME THIS MONTH HE'S TRIED TO BLOW UP A SCHOOL.
HE SENT ME A MESSAGE.
ANOTHER INSANE RANT ABOUT PREVENTING GOTHAM FROM HAVING A FUTURE.
HE SLIPPED AWAY LAST TIME.
TONIGHT HE GOES BACK TO ARKHAM.
I'M SO HAPPY YOU COULD ALL COME! LET'S GET ON WITH THE--

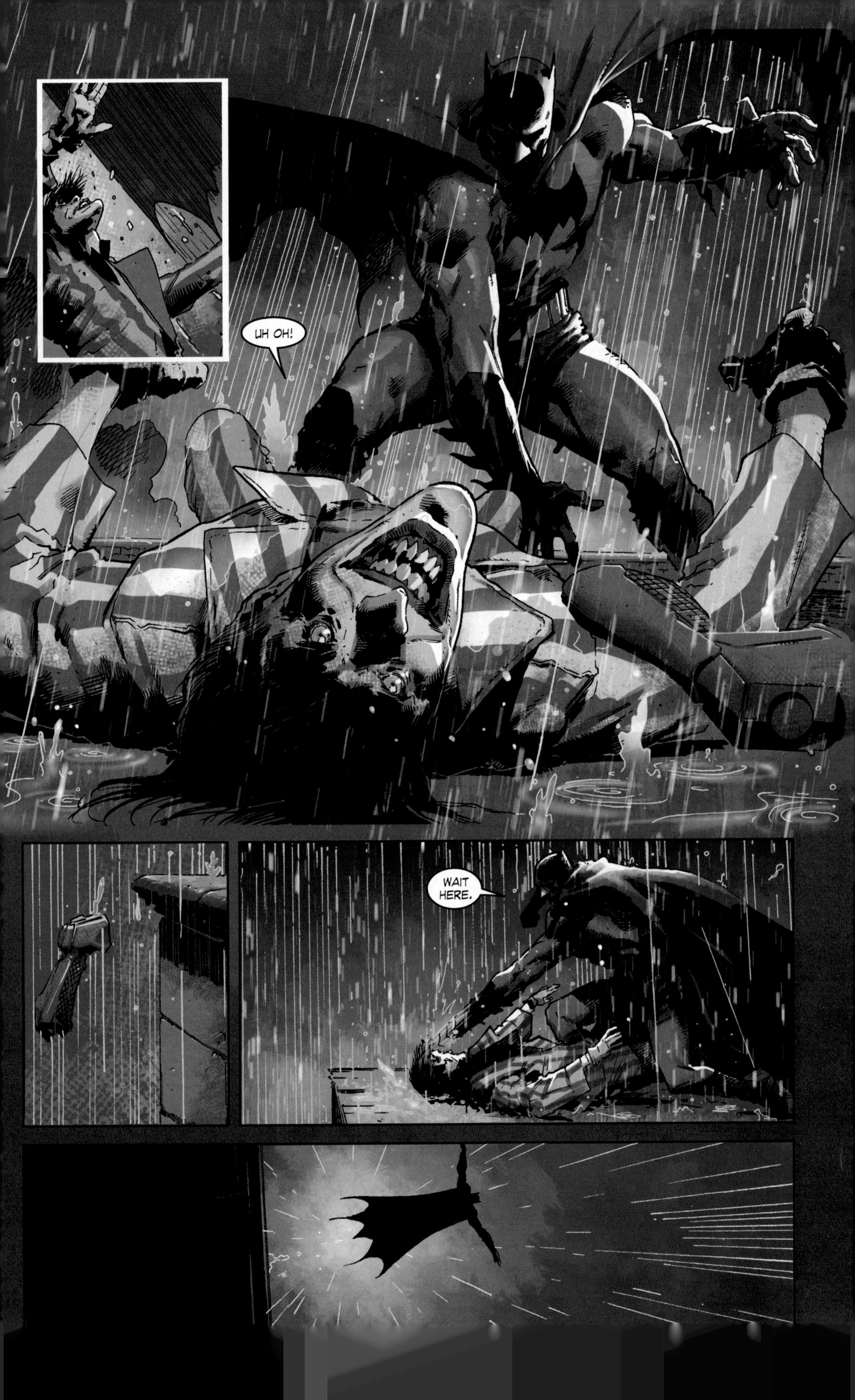
UH OH!
WAIT HERE.

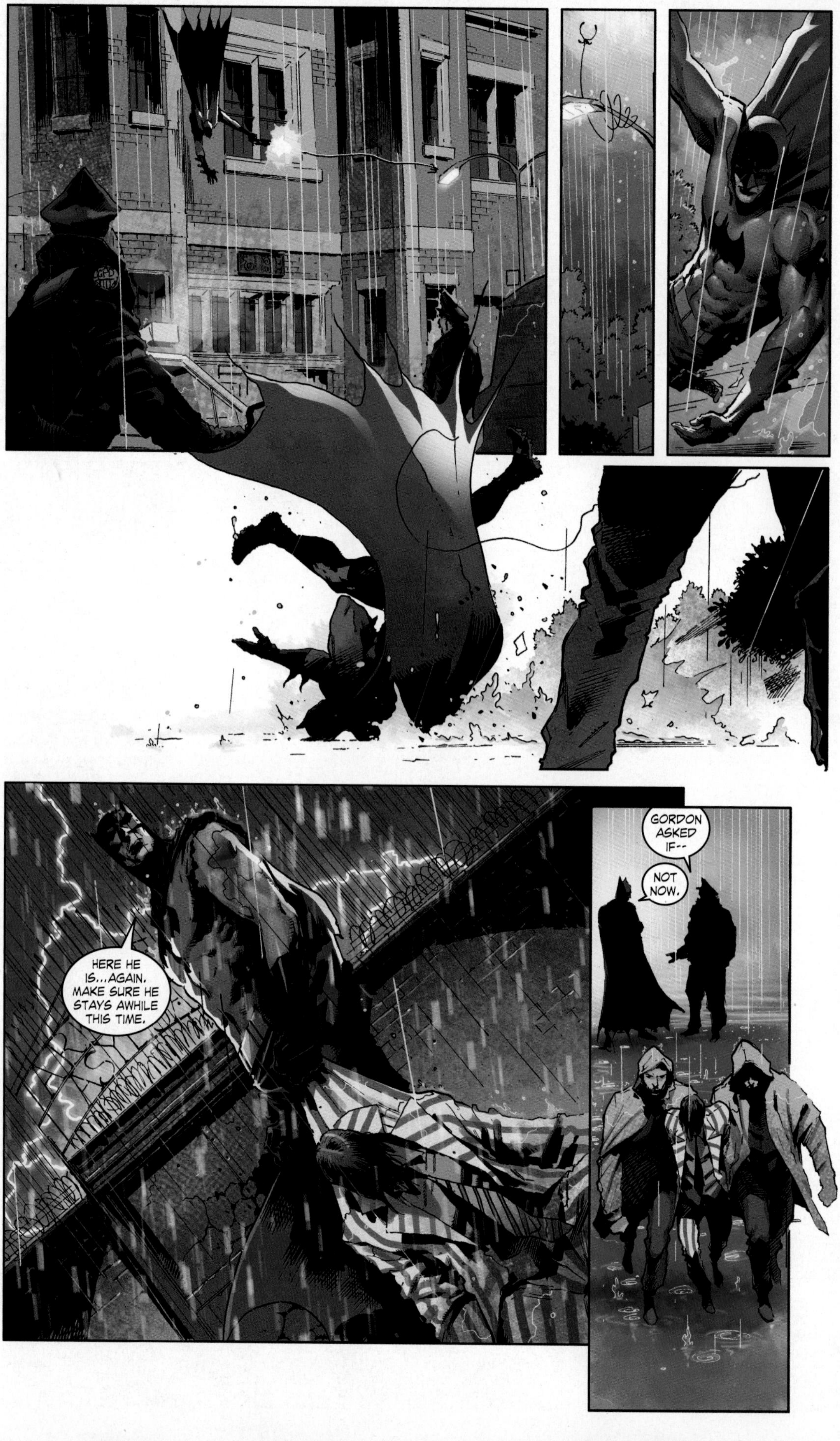
HERE HE IS...AGAIN. MAKE SURE HE STAYS AWHILE THIS TIME.
GORDON ASKED IF--
NOT NOW.

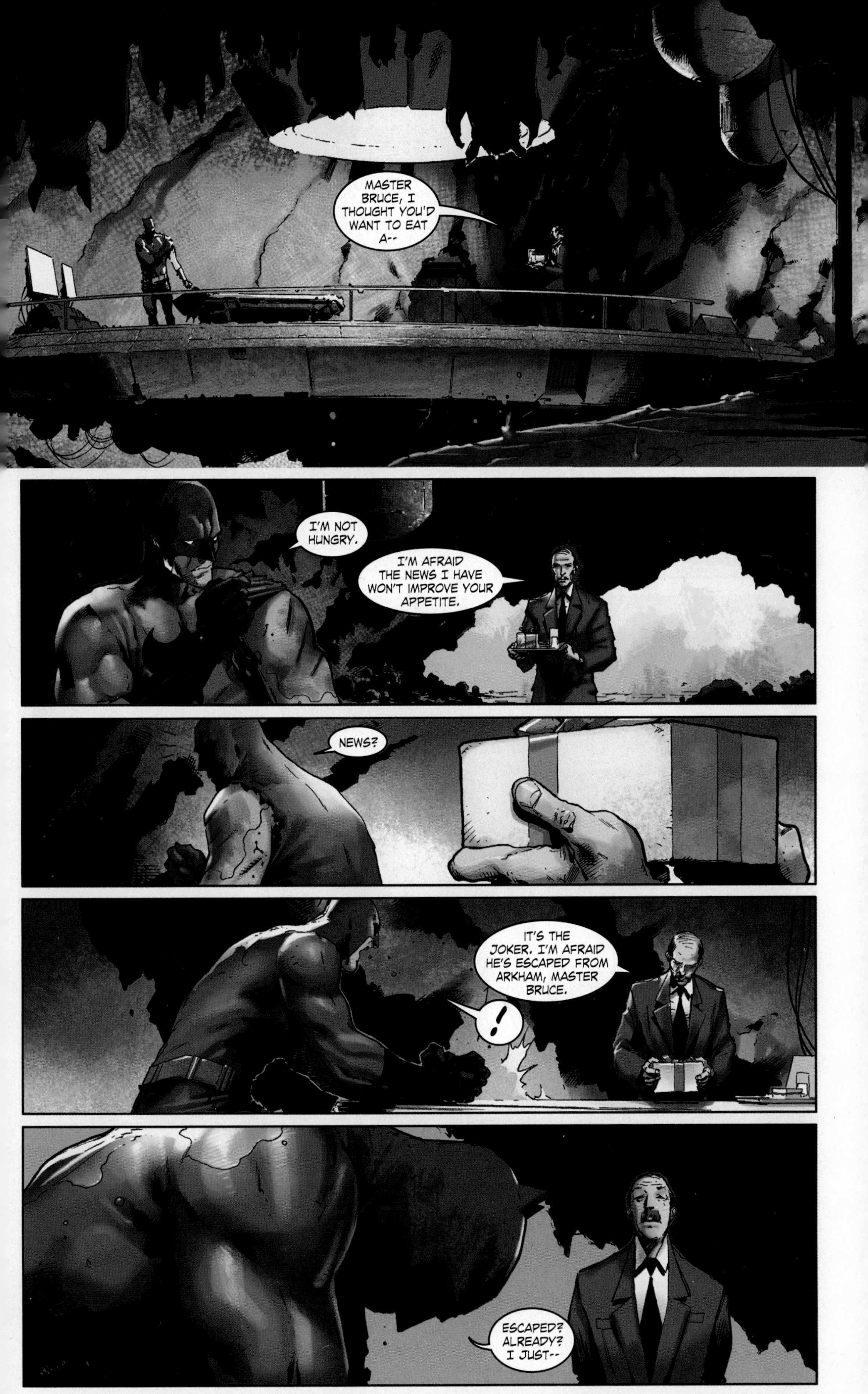
MASTER BRUCE, I THOUGHT YOU'D WANT TO EAT A--
I'M NOT HUNGRY.
I'M AFRAID THE NEWS I HAVE WON'T IMPROVE YOUR APPETITE.
NEWS?
IT'S THE JOKER. I'M AFRAID HE'S ESCAPED FROM ARKHAM, MASTER BRUCE.
!
ESCAPED? ALREADY? I JUST--

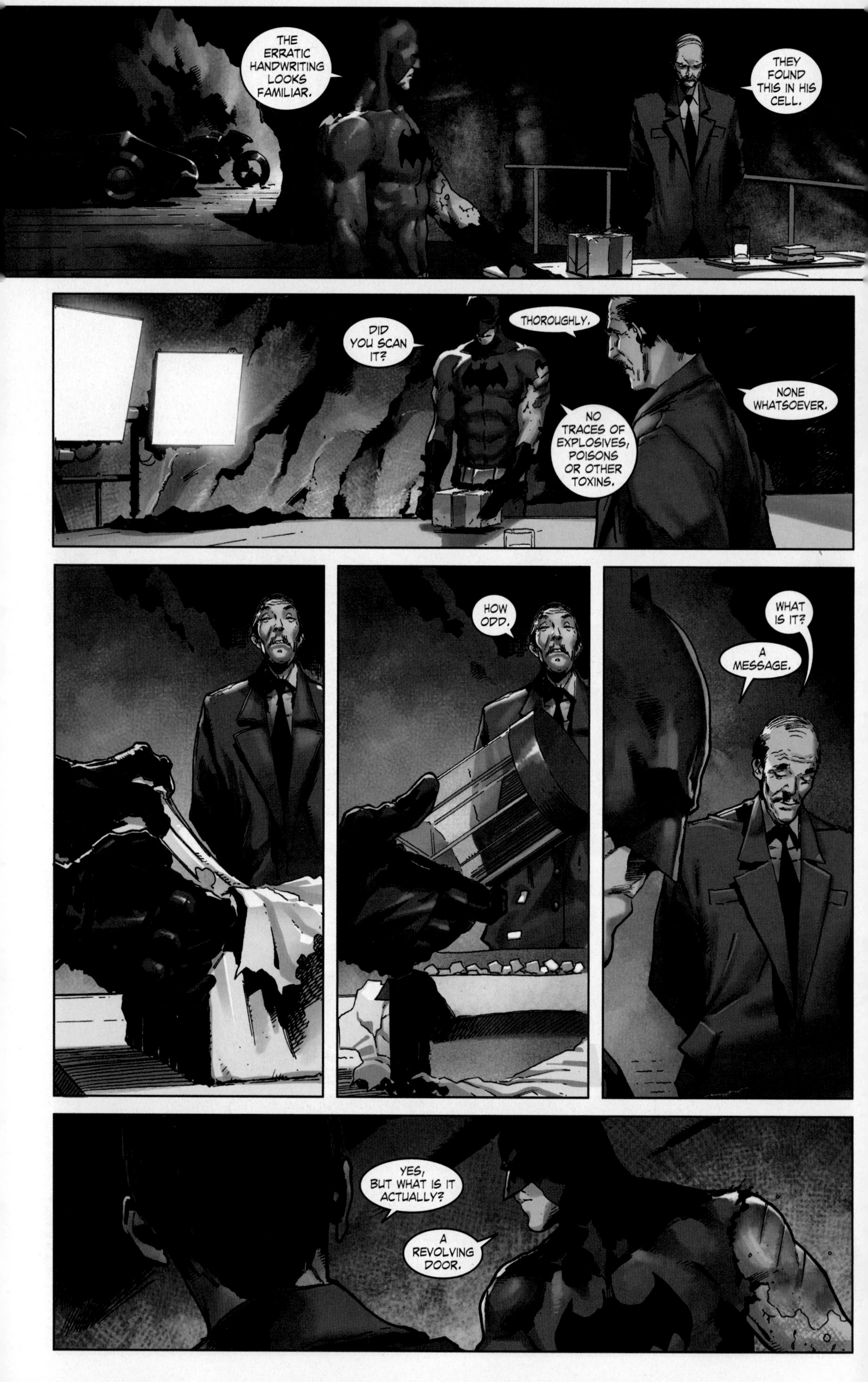
THE ERRATIC HANDWRITING LOOKS FAMILIAR.
THEY FOUND THIS IN HIS CELL.
DID YOU SCAN IT?
THOROUGHLY.
NO TRACES OF EXPLOSIVES, POISONS OR OTHER TOXINS.
NONE WHATSOEVER.
HOW ODD.
WHAT IS IT?
A MESSAGE.
YES, BUT WHAT IS IT ACTUALLY?
A REVOLVING DOOR.

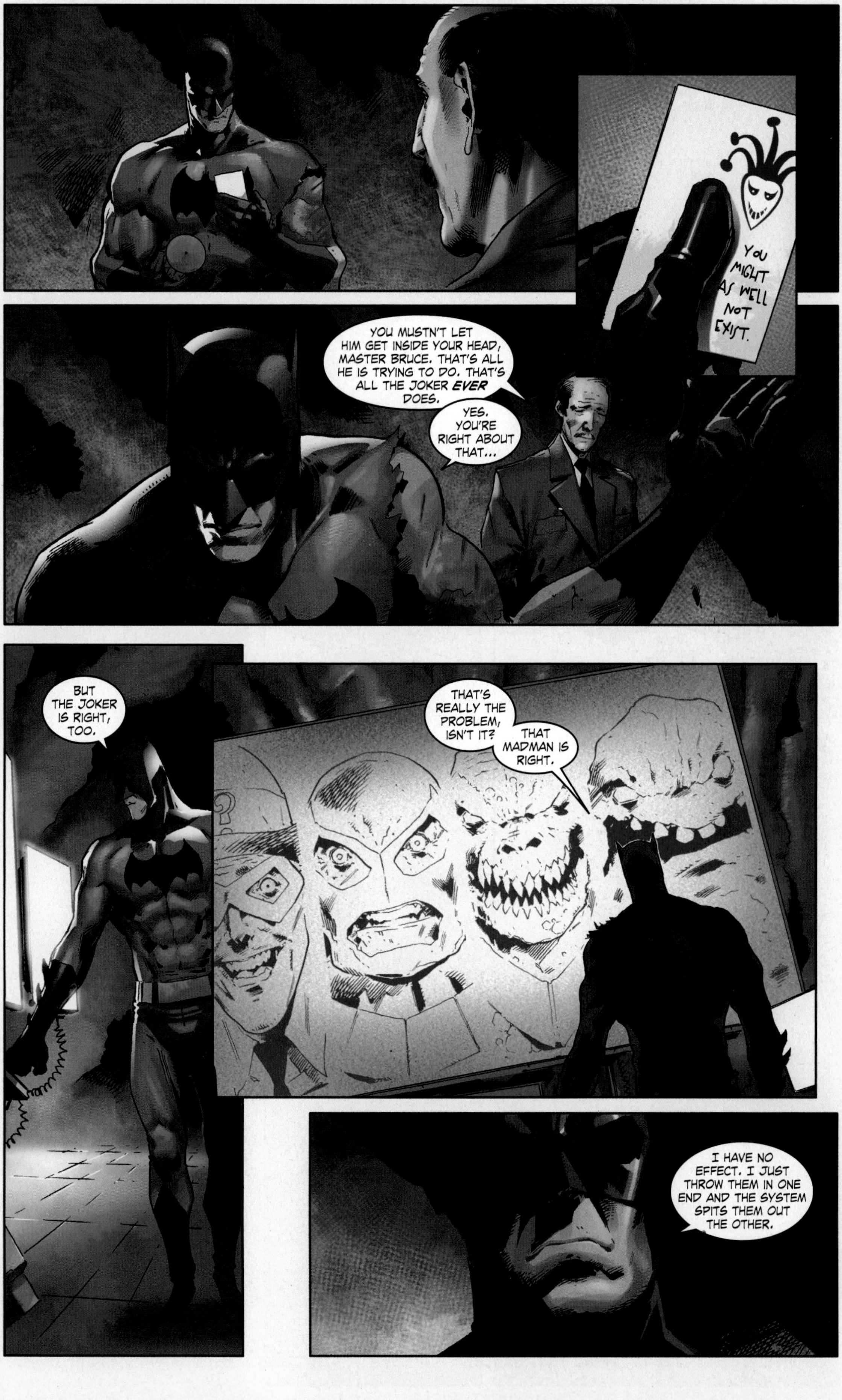
YOU MIGHT AS WELL NOT EXIST.
YOU MUSTN'T LET HIM GET INSIDE YOUR HEAD, MASTER BRUCE. THAT'S ALL HE IS TRYING TO DO. THAT'S ALL THE JOKER ***EVER*** DOES.
YES. YOU'RE RIGHT ABOUT THAT...
BUT THE JOKER IS RIGHT, TOO.
THAT'S REALLY THE PROBLEM, ISN'T IT?
THAT MADMAN IS RIGHT.
I HAVE NO EFFECT. I JUST THROW THEM IN ONE END AND THE SYSTEM SPITS THEM OUT THE OTHER.

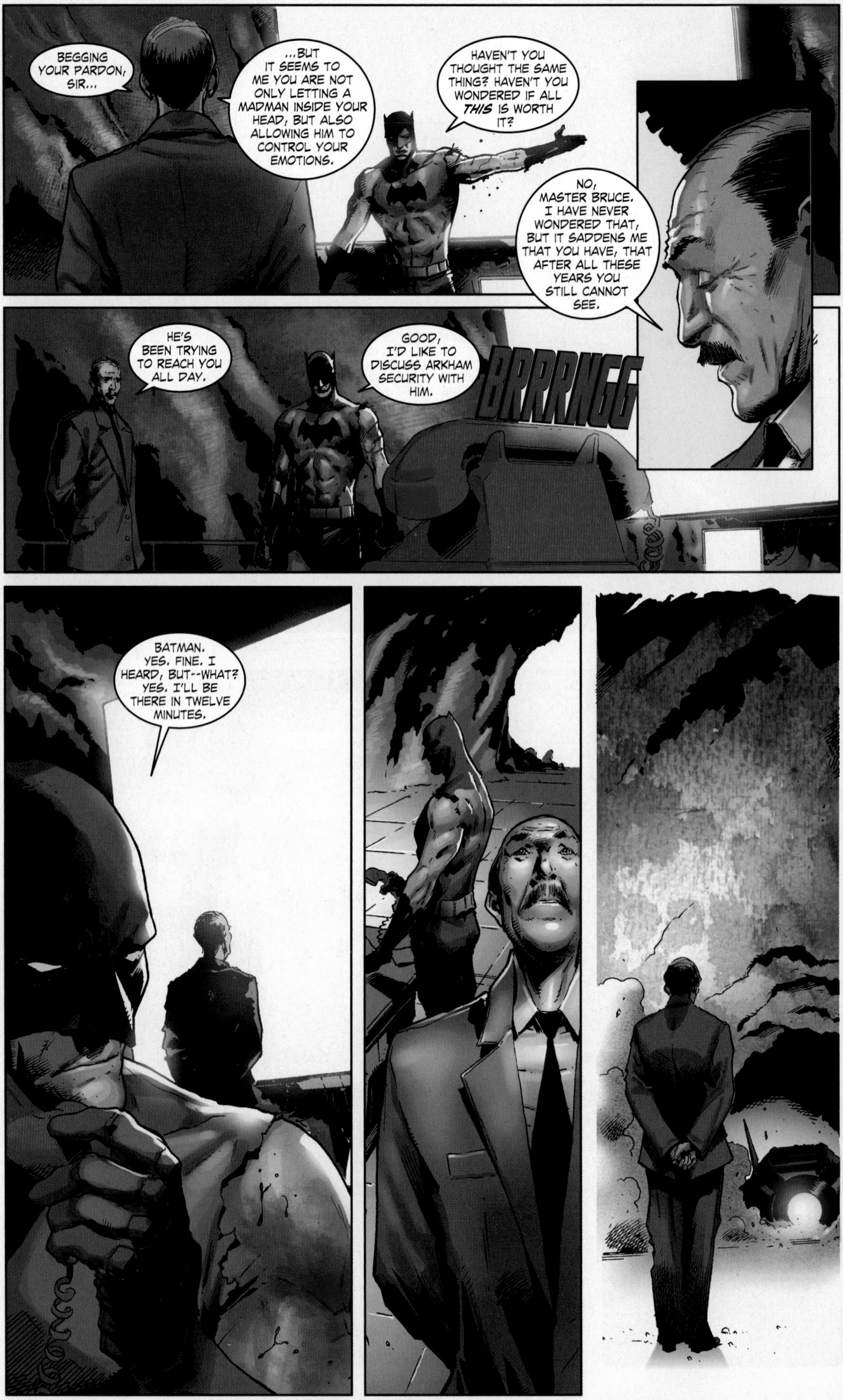
BEGGING YOUR PARDON, SIR...
...BUT IT SEEMS TO ME YOU ARE NOT ONLY LETTING A MADMAN INSIDE YOUR HEAD, BUT ALSO ALLOWING HIM TO CONTROL YOUR EMOTIONS.
HAVEN'T YOU THOUGHT THE SAME THING? HAVEN'T YOU WONDERED IF ALL *THIS* IS WORTH IT?
NO, MASTER BRUCE. I HAVE NEVER WONDERED THAT, BUT IT SADDENS ME THAT YOU HAVE, THAT AFTER ALL THESE YEARS YOU STILL CANNOT SEE.
BRRRNGG
HE'S BEEN TRYING TO REACH YOU ALL DAY.
GOOD, I'D LIKE TO DISCUSS ARKHAM SECURITY WITH HIM.
BATMAN. YES. FINE. I HEARD, BUT--WHAT? YES. I'LL BE THERE IN TWELVE MINUTES.

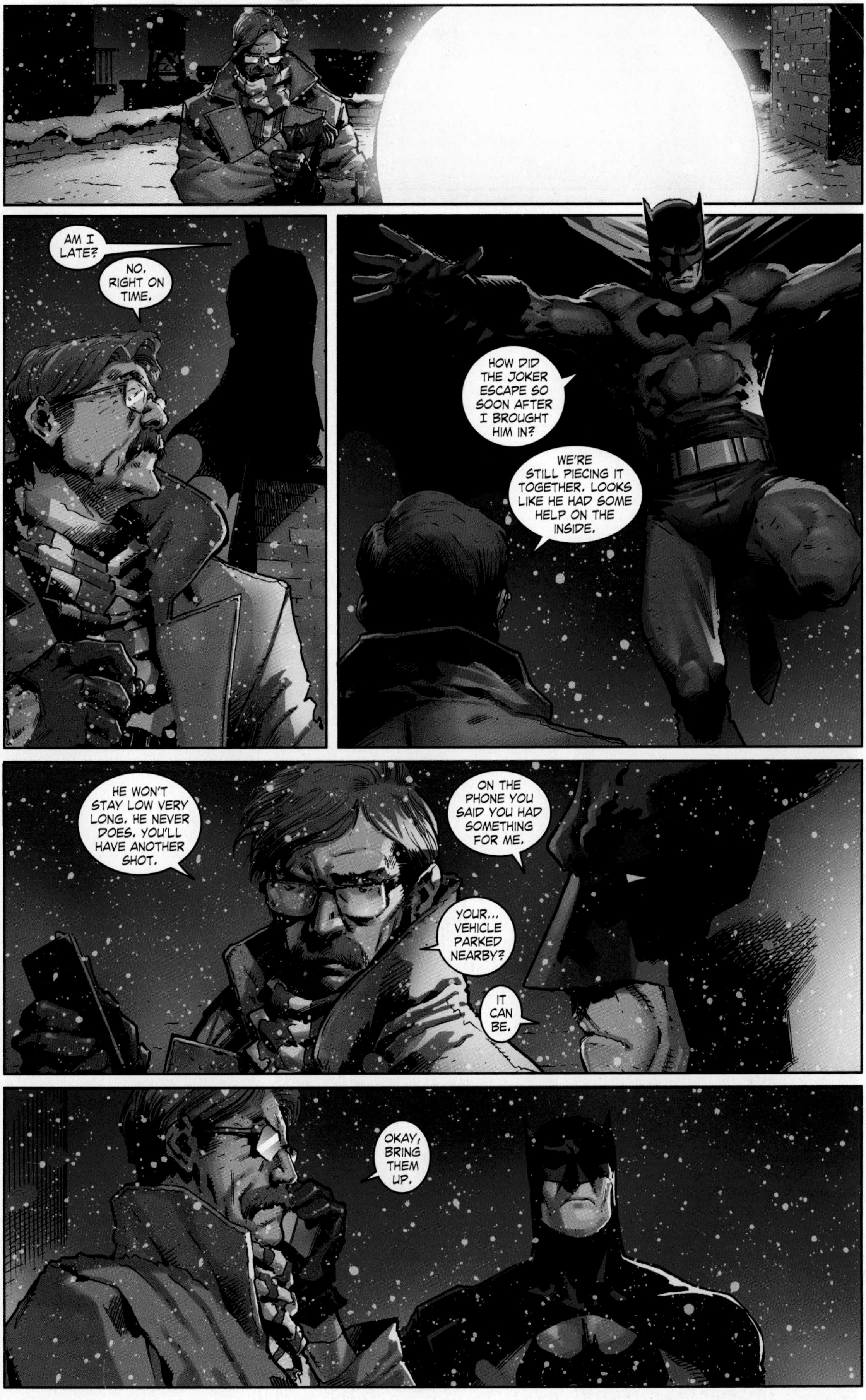

AM I LATE?
NO. RIGHT ON TIME.
HOW DID THE JOKER ESCAPE SO SOON AFTER I BROUGHT HIM IN?
WE'RE STILL PIECING IT TOGETHER. LOOKS LIKE HE HAD SOME HELP ON THE INSIDE.
HE WON'T STAY LOW VERY LONG. HE NEVER DOES. YOU'LL HAVE ANOTHER SHOT.
ON THE PHONE YOU SAID YOU HAD SOMETHING FOR ME.
YOUR... VEHICLE PARKED NEARBY?
IT CAN BE.
OKAY, BRING THEM UP.

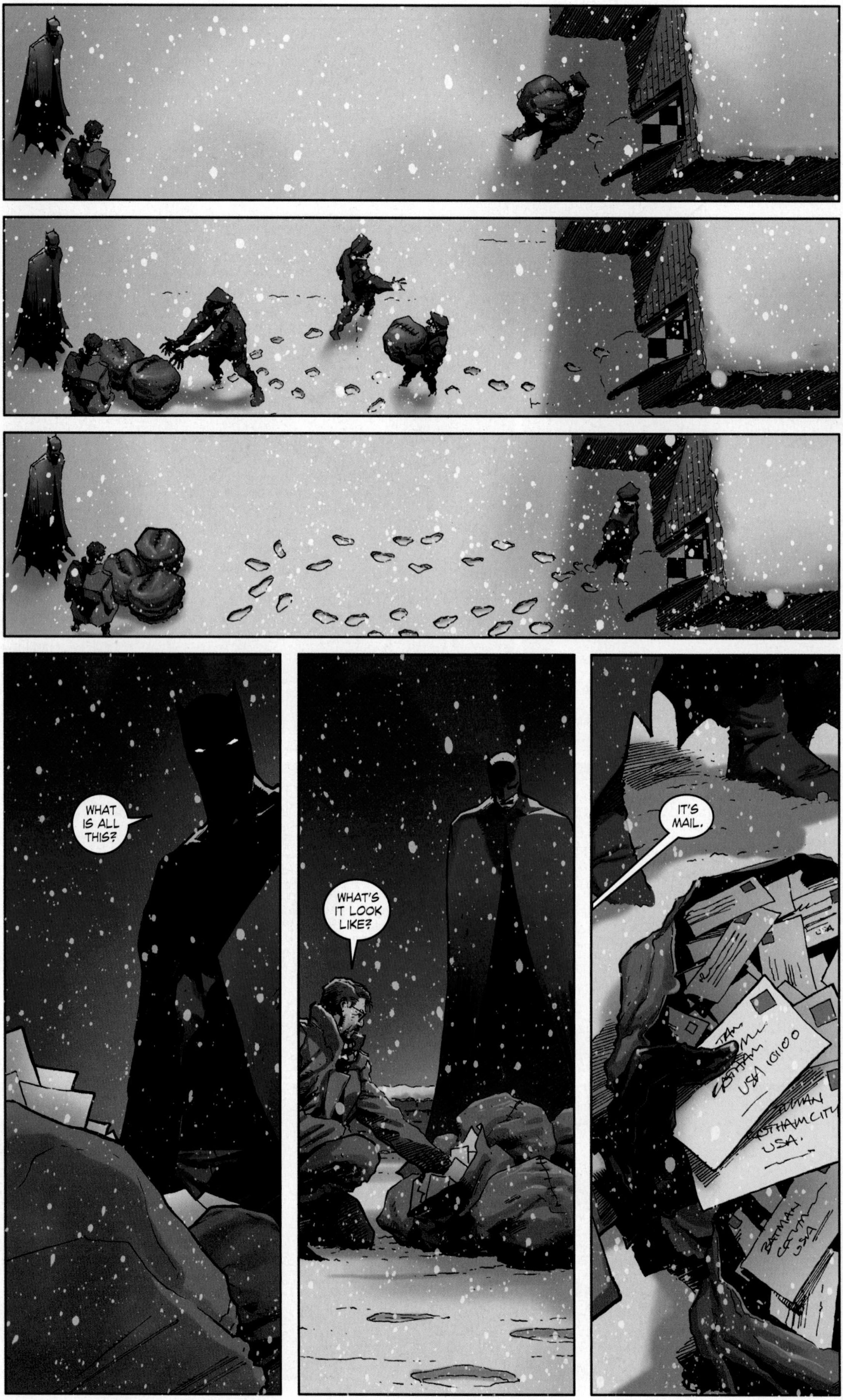
WHAT IS ALL THIS?
WHAT'S IT LOOK LIKE?
IT'S MAIL.

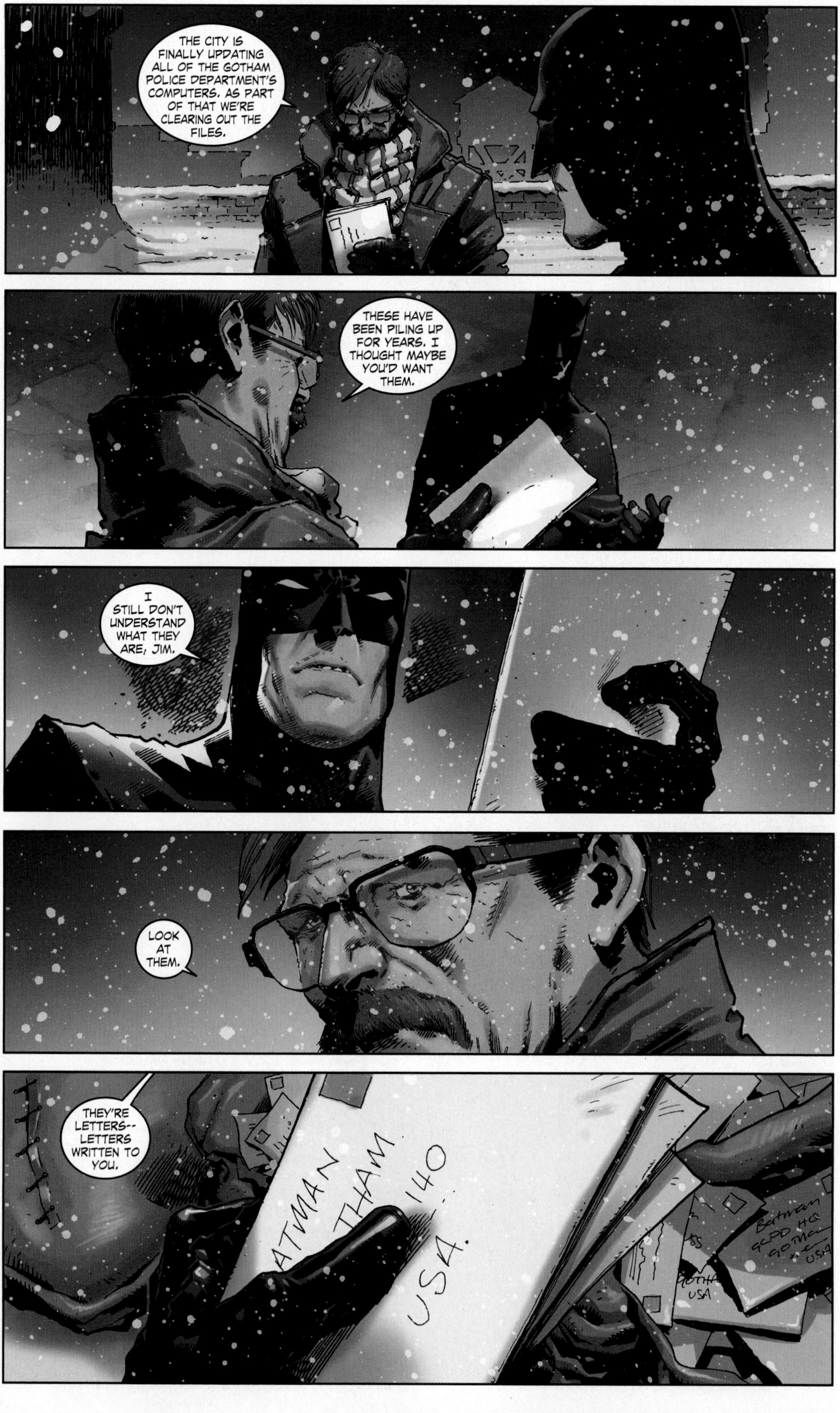
THE CITY IS FINALLY UPDATING ALL OF THE GOTHAM POLICE DEPARTMENT'S COMPUTERS. AS PART OF THAT WE'RE CLEARING OUT THE FILES.
THESE HAVE BEEN PILING UP FOR YEARS. I THOUGHT MAYBE YOU'D WANT THEM.
I STILL DON'T UNDERSTAND WHAT THEY ARE, JIM.
LOOK AT THEM.
THEY'RE LETTERS-- LETTERS WRITTEN TO YOU.
ATMAN
THAM
140
USA.

WHAT ARE THOSE?

LETTERS. GORDON HAS BEEN RECEIVING THEM FOR YEARS. HE ASKED ME TO TAKE THEM OFF HIS HANDS. WHAT'S THE STATUS OF JOKER'S ESCAPE?

THEY ARE ALL TO YOU? AREN'T YOU GOING TO READ THEM?

NO.

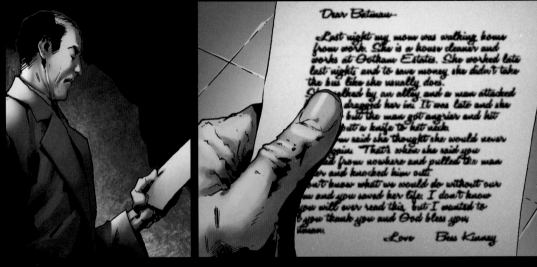

Dear Batman—

Last night my mom was walking home from work. She is a house cleaner and works at Gotham Estates. She worked late last nights and to save money she didn't take the bus like she usually does.

She walked by an alley, and a man attacked her and dragged her in. It was late and she ... but the man got angrier and hit ... put a knife to her neck ...

... she said she thought she would never ... again. That's where she said you ... ed from nowhere and pulled the man ... er and knocked him out ...

... don't know what we would do without our ... u and you saved her life. I don't know ... you will ever read this, but I wanted to ... t you thank you and God bless you.

Love Bess Kinney

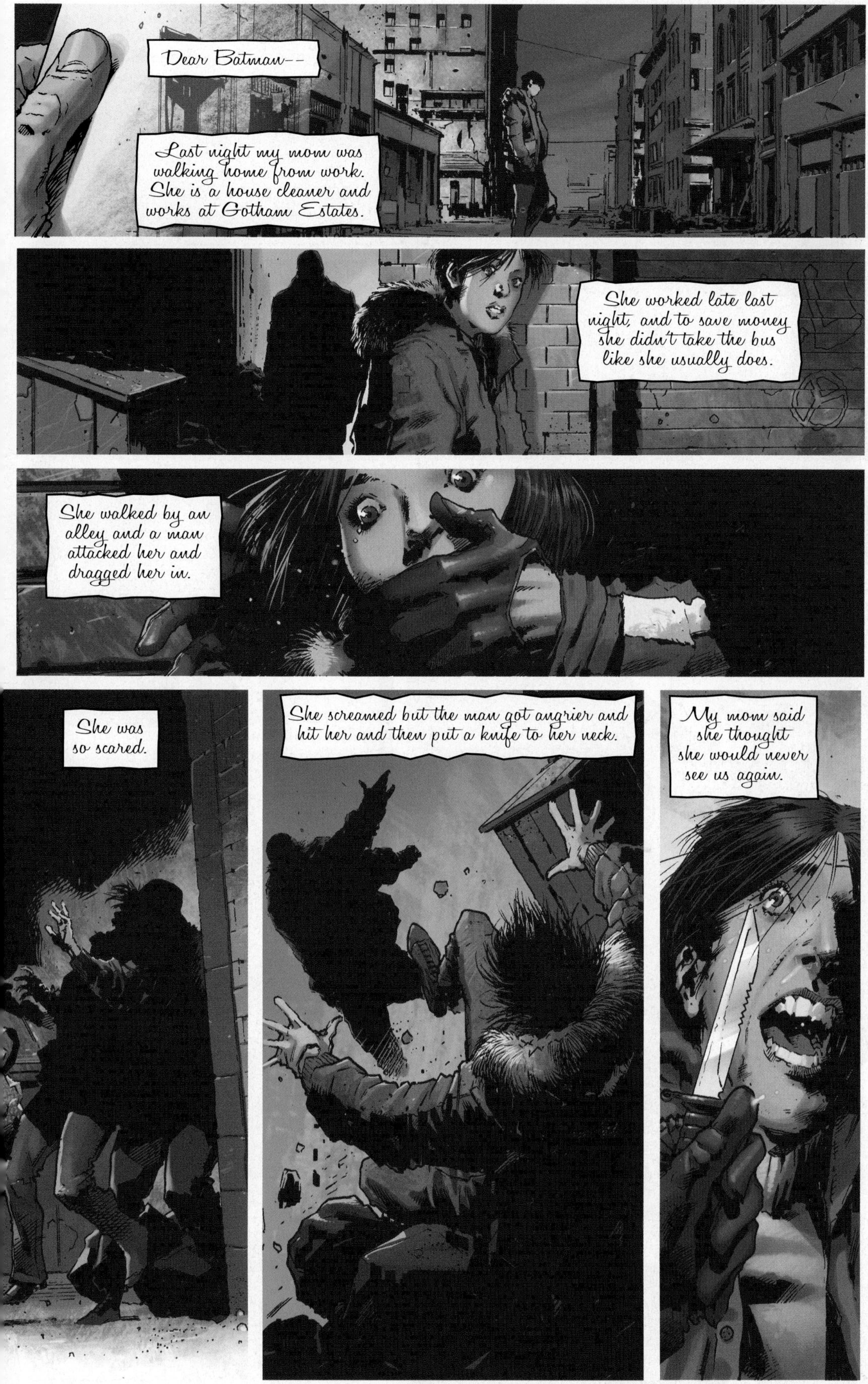
Dear Batman--
Last night my mom was walking home from work. She is a house cleaner and works at Gotham Estates.
She worked late last night, and to save money she didn't take the bus like she usually does.
She walked by an alley and a man attacked her and dragged her in.
She was so scared.
She screamed but the man got angrier and hit her and then put a knife to her neck.
My mom said she thought she would never see us again.

That's when she said you appeared from nowhere and pulled the man off her and knocked him out.

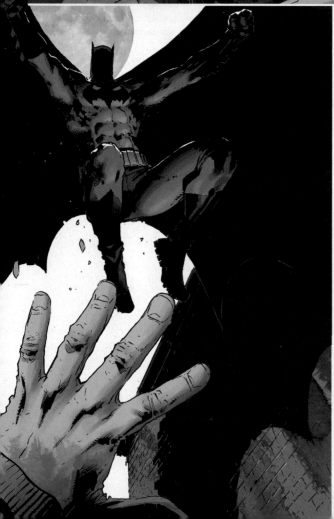

I don't know what we would do without our mom and you saved her life.

I don't know if you will ever read this, but I wanted to tell you thank you and God bless you, Batman.

Love,
Bess Kinney

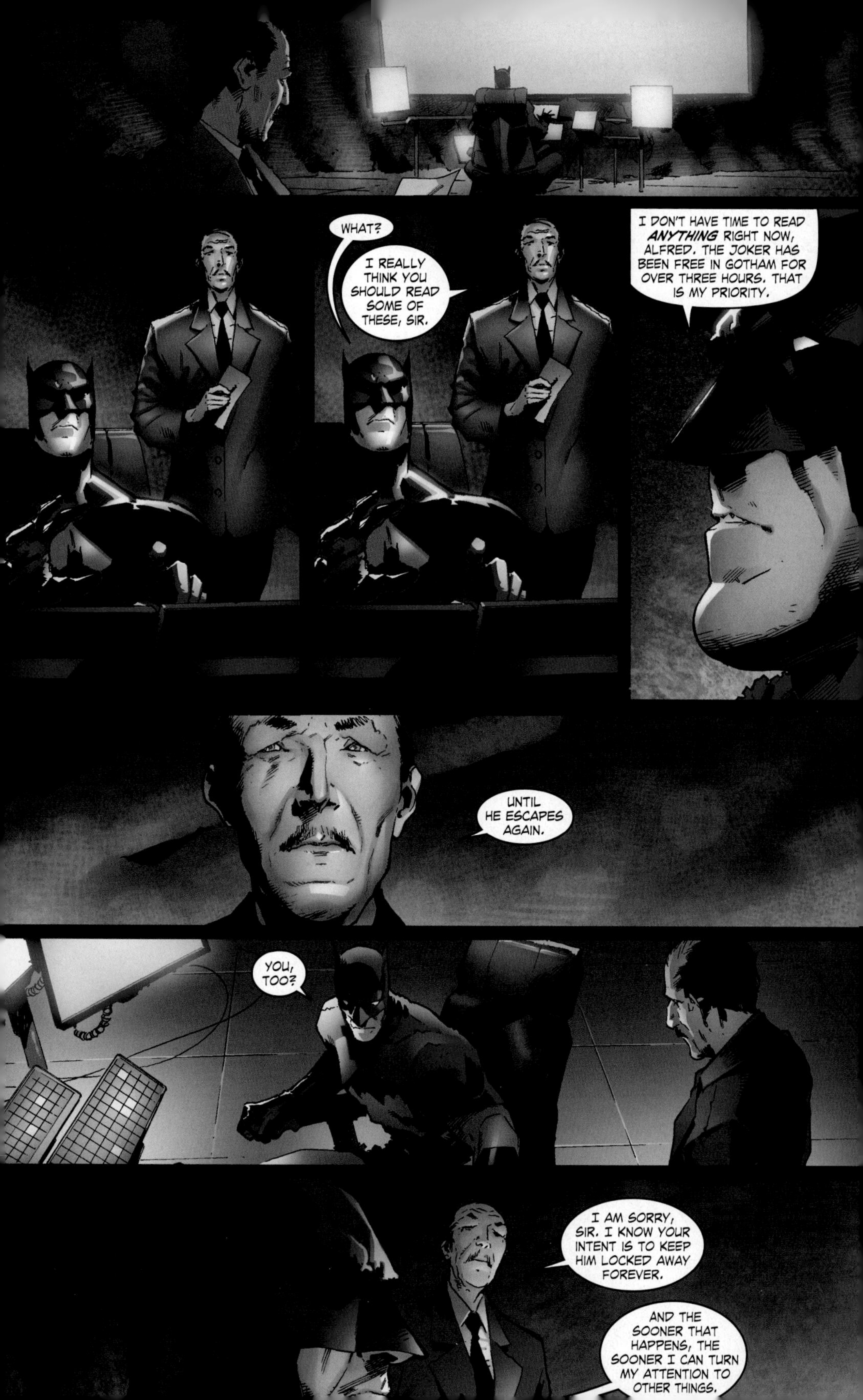
WHAT?
I REALLY THINK YOU SHOULD READ SOME OF THESE, SIR.
I DON'T HAVE TIME TO READ ANYTHING RIGHT NOW, ALFRED. THE JOKER HAS BEEN FREE IN GOTHAM FOR OVER THREE HOURS. THAT IS MY PRIORITY.
UNTIL HE ESCAPES AGAIN.
YOU, TOO?
I AM SORRY, SIR. I KNOW YOUR INTENT IS TO KEEP HIM LOCKED AWAY FOREVER.
AND THE SOONER THAT HAPPENS, THE SOONER I CAN TURN MY ATTENTION TO OTHER THINGS.

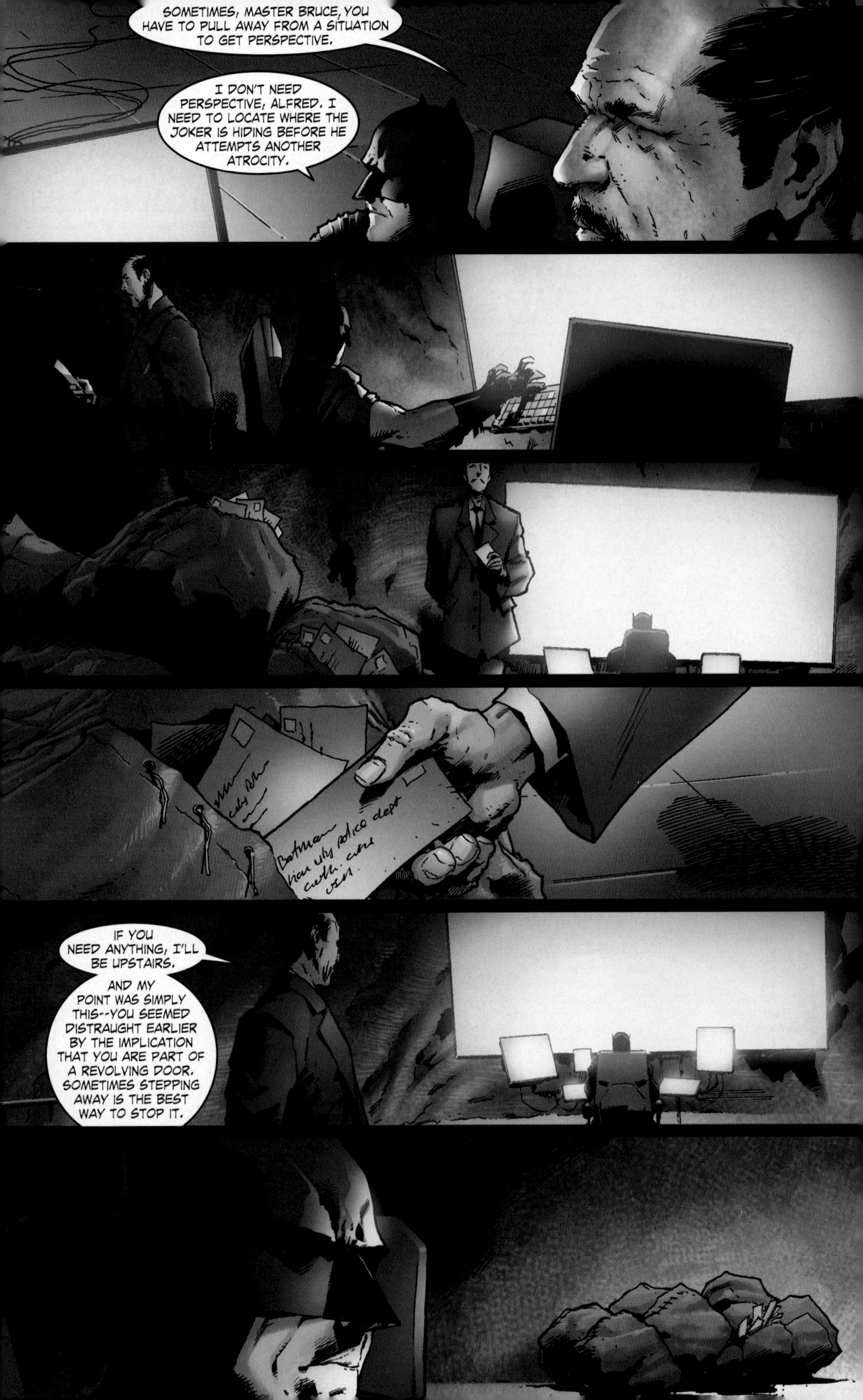
SOMETIMES, MASTER BRUCE, YOU HAVE TO PULL AWAY FROM A SITUATION TO GET PERSPECTIVE.
I DON'T NEED PERSPECTIVE, ALFRED. I NEED TO LOCATE WHERE THE JOKER IS HIDING BEFORE HE ATTEMPTS ANOTHER ATROCITY.
IF YOU NEED ANYTHING, I'LL BE UPSTAIRS.
AND MY POINT WAS SIMPLY THIS--YOU SEEMED DISTRAUGHT EARLIER BY THE IMPLICATION THAT YOU ARE PART OF A REVOLVING DOOR. SOMETIMES STEPPING AWAY IS THE BEST WAY TO STOP IT.

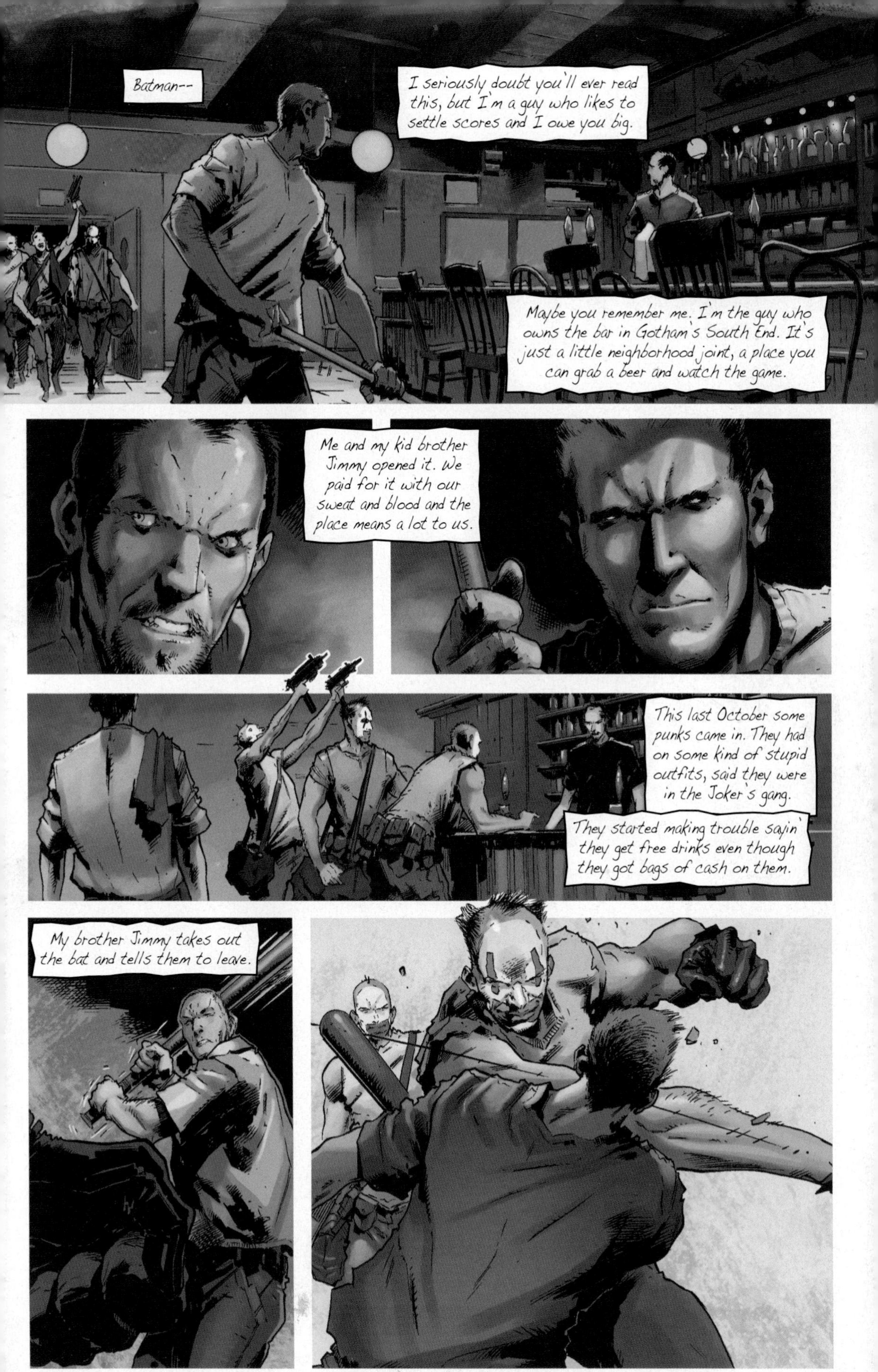
Batman--
I seriously doubt you'll ever read this, but I'm a guy who likes to settle scores and I owe you big.
Maybe you remember me. I'm the guy who owns the bar in Gotham's South End. It's just a little neighborhood joint, a place you can grab a beer and watch the game.
Me and my kid brother Jimmy opened it. We paid for it with our sweat and blood and the place means a lot to us.
This last October some punks came in. They had on some kind of stupid outfits, said they were in the Joker's gang.
They started making trouble sayin' they get free drinks even though they got bags of cash on them.
My brother Jimmy takes out the bat and tells them to leave.

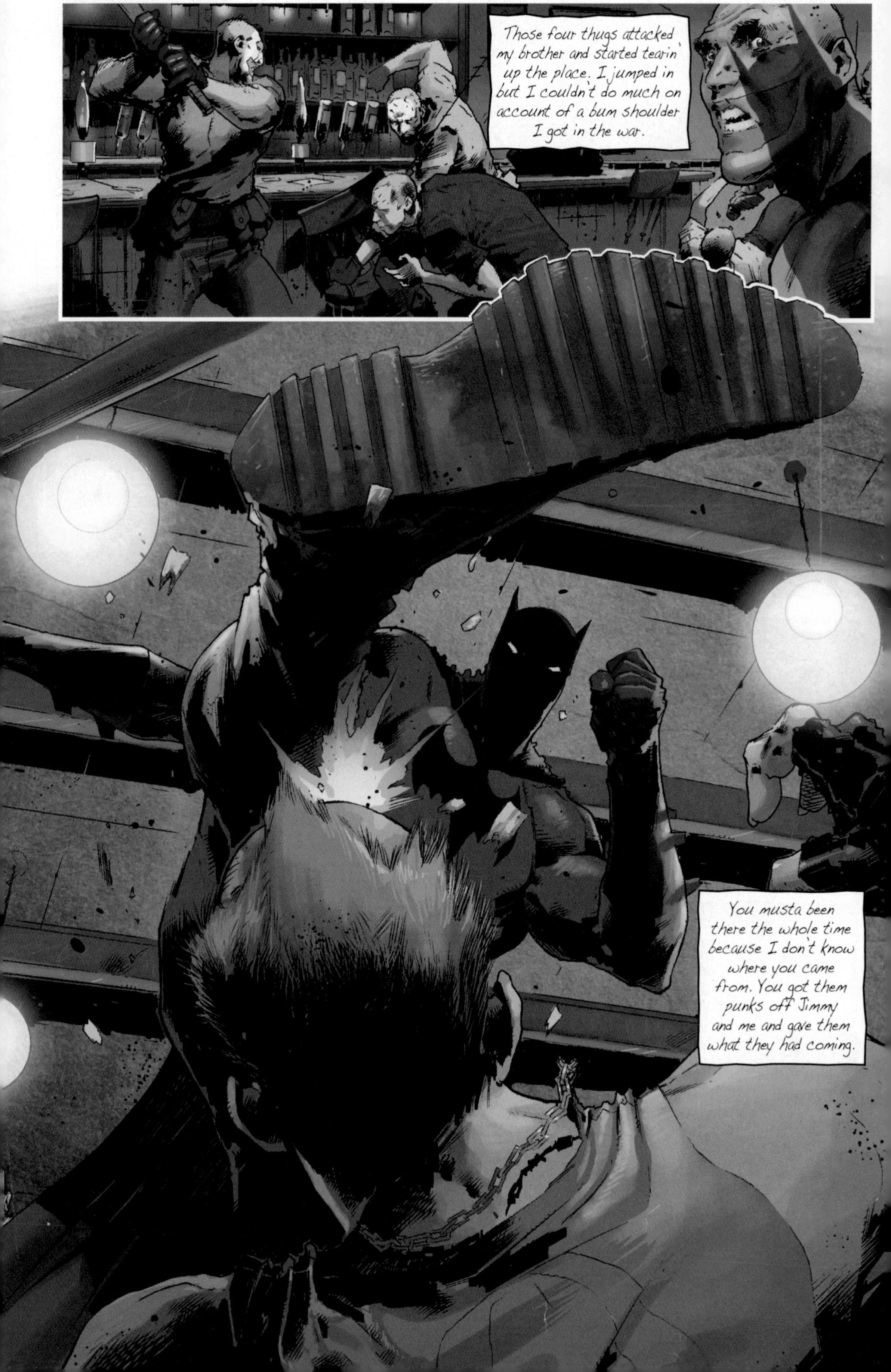
Those four thugs attacked my brother and started tearin' up the place. I jumped in but I couldn't do much on account of a bum shoulder I got in the war.
You musta been there the whole time because I don't know where you came from. You got them punks off Jimmy and me and gave them what they had coming.

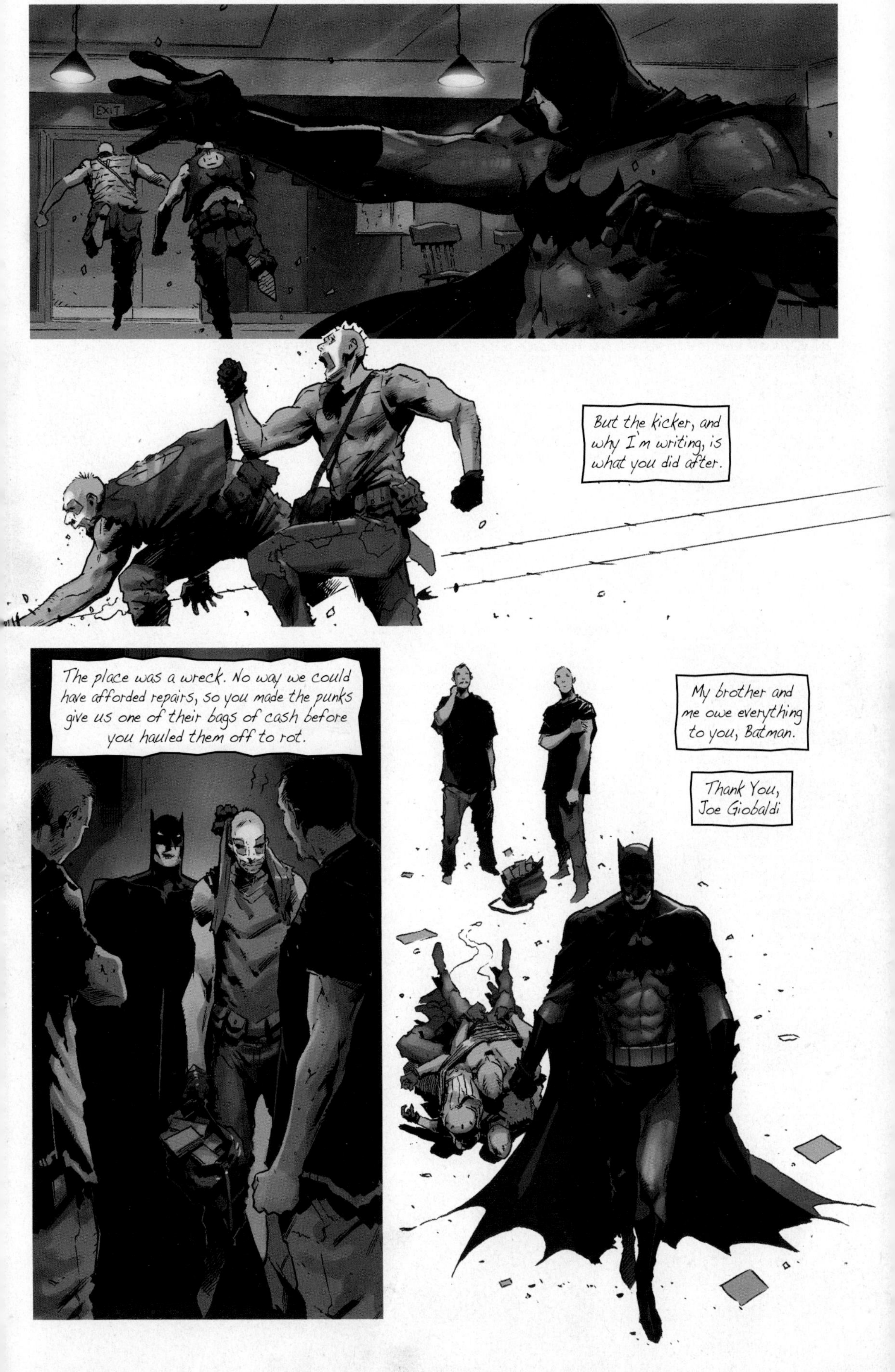
EXIT
But the kicker, and why I'm writing, is what you did after.
The place was a wreck. No way we could have afforded repairs, so you made the punks give us one of their bags of cash before you hauled them off to rot.
My brother and me owe everything to you, Batman.
Thank You, Joe Giobaldi

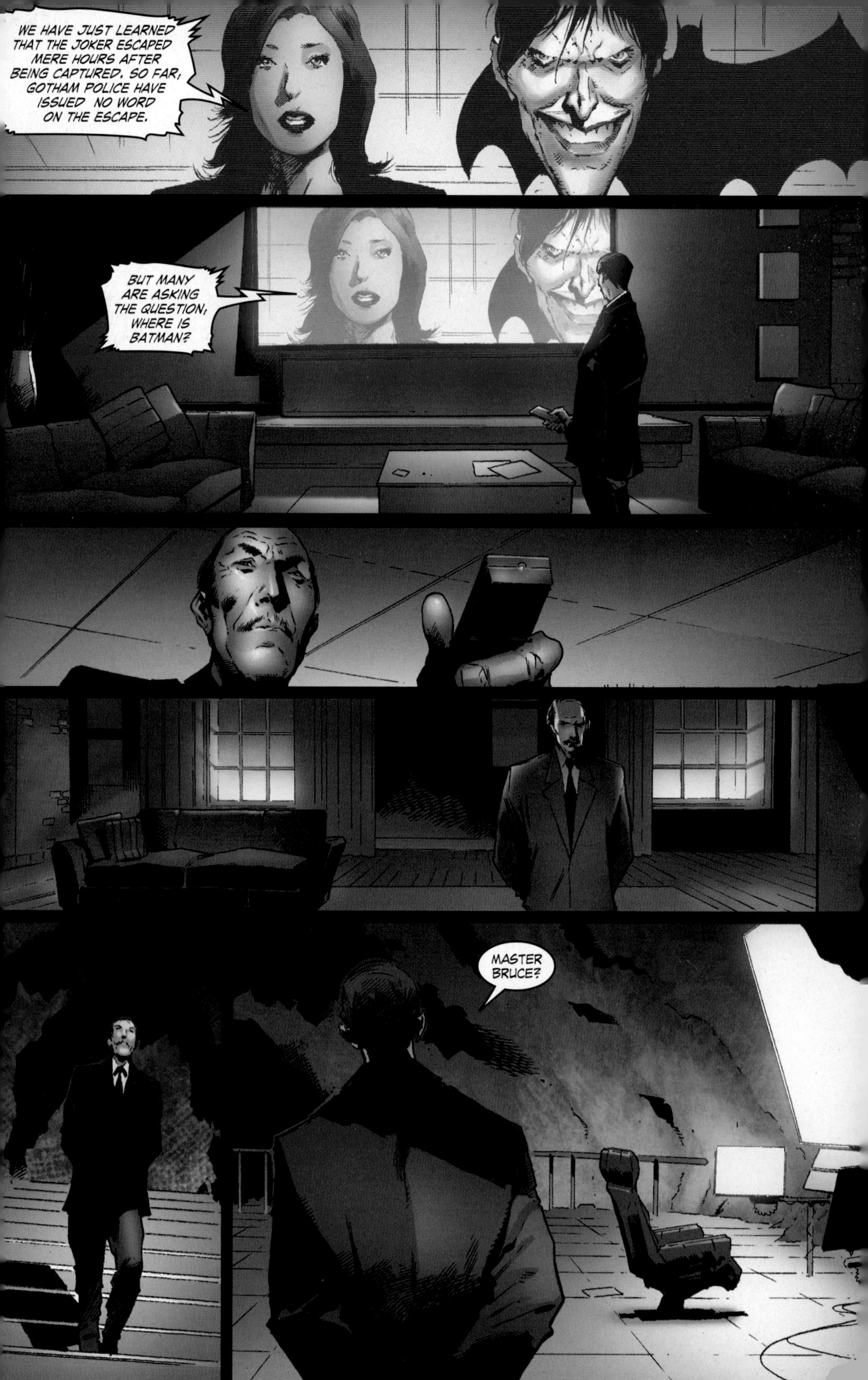
WE HAVE JUST LEARNED THAT THE JOKER ESCAPED MERE HOURS AFTER BEING CAPTURED. SO FAR, GOTHAM POLICE HAVE ISSUED NO WORD ON THE ESCAPE.
BUT MANY ARE ASKING THE QUESTION, WHERE IS BATMAN?
MASTER BRUCE?

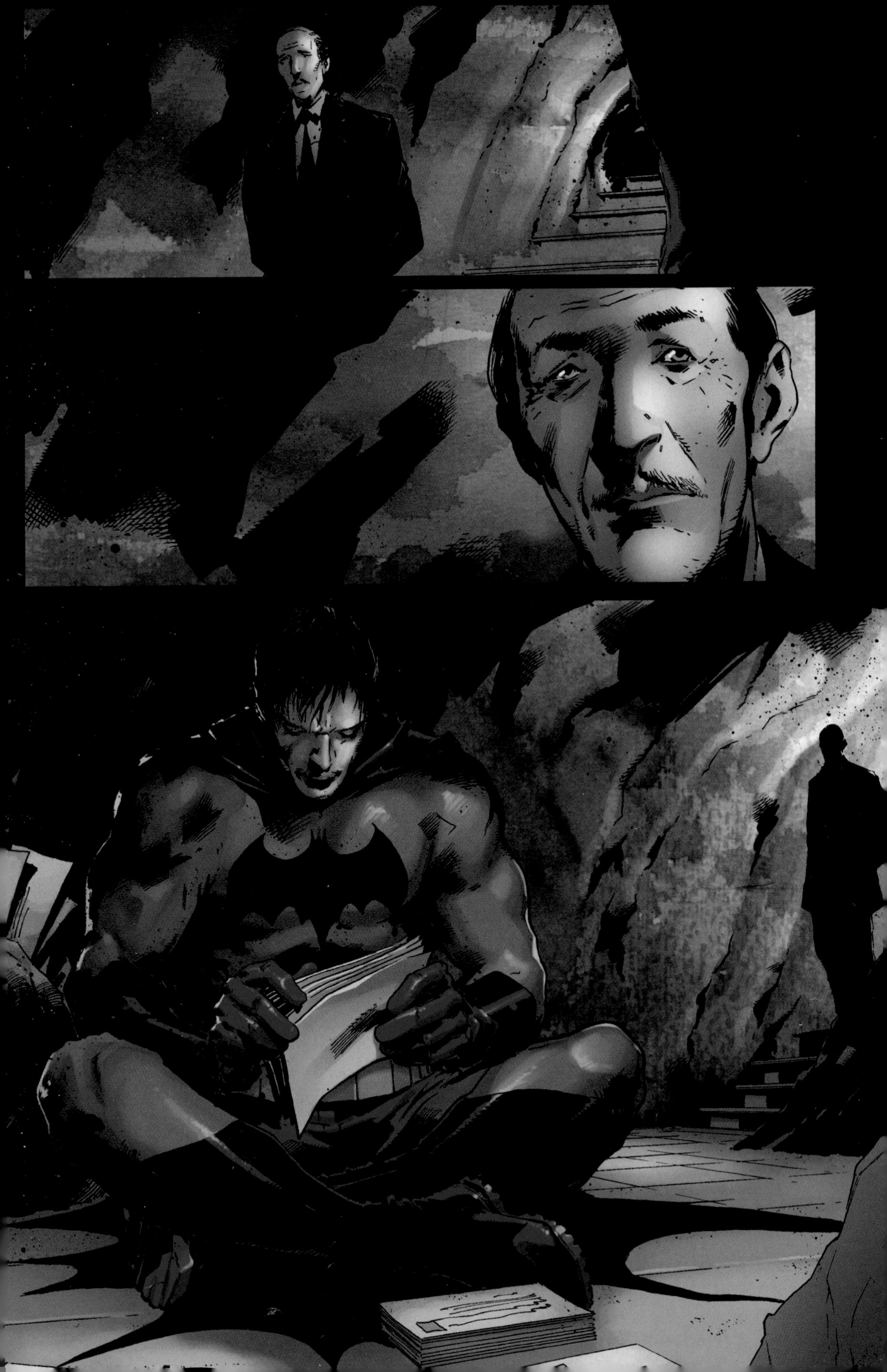

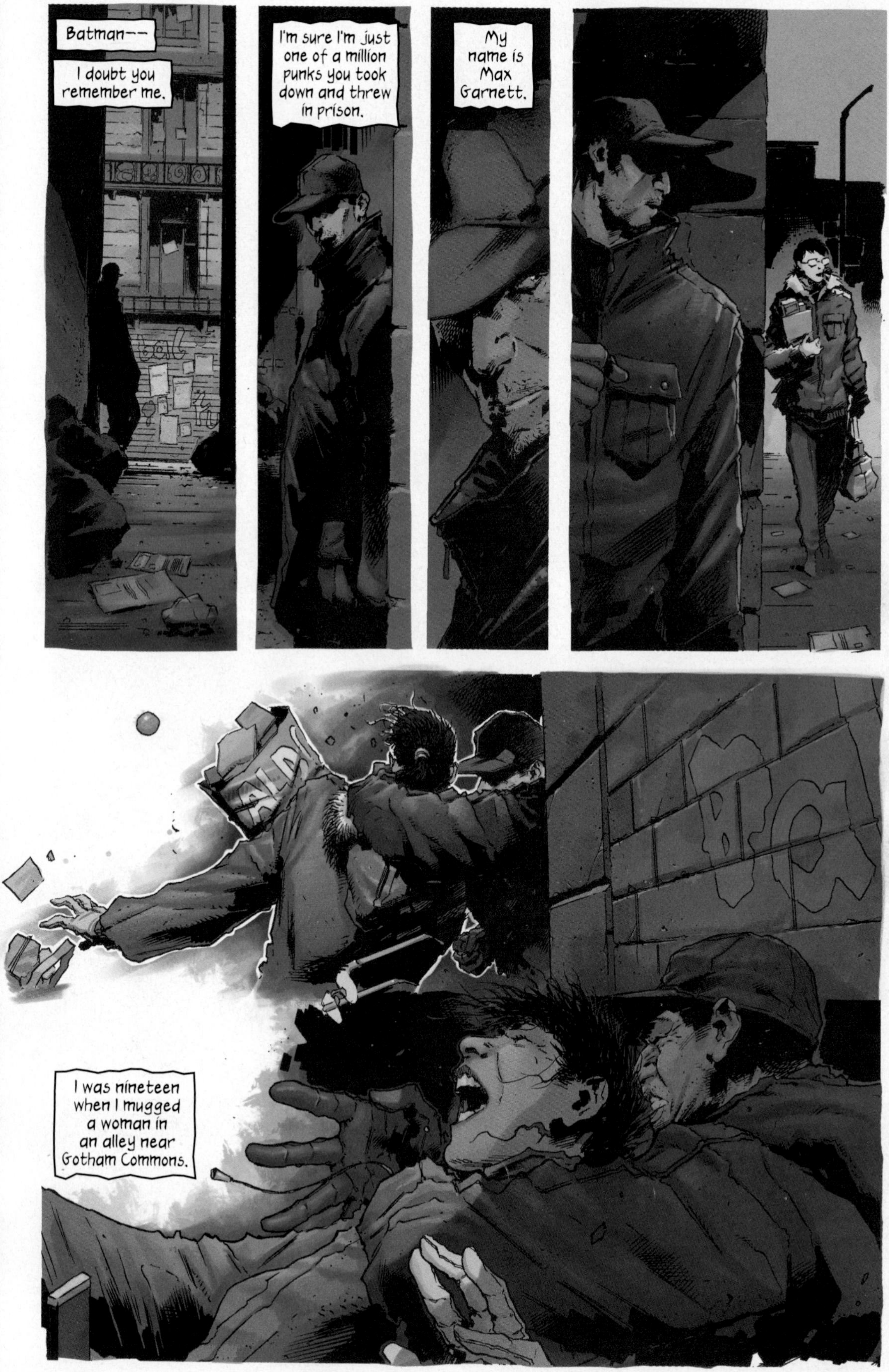
Batman--
I doubt you remember me.
I'm sure I'm just one of a million punks you took down and threw in prison.
My name is Max Garnett.
I was nineteen when I mugged a woman in an alley near Gotham Commons.

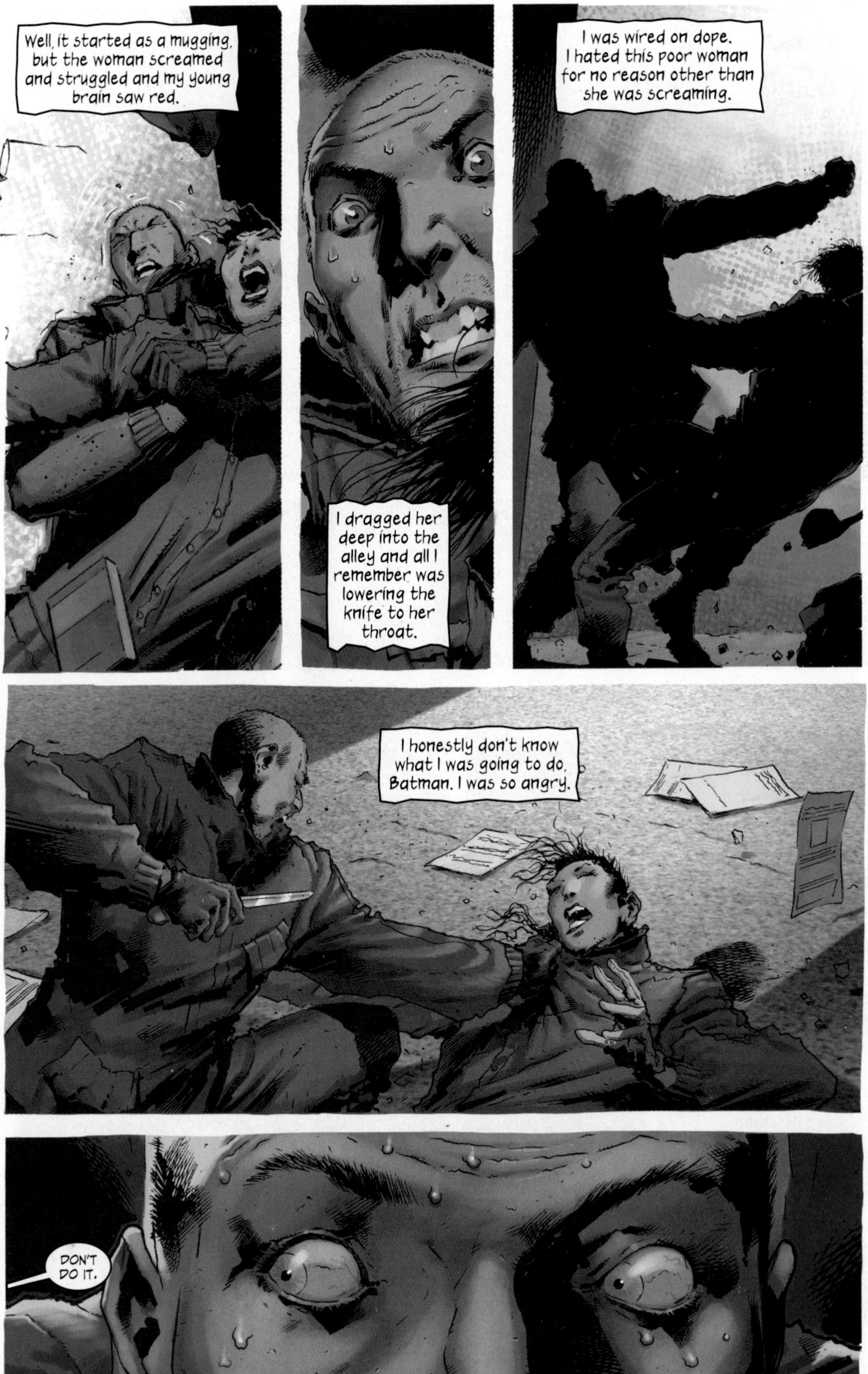
Well, it started as a mugging, but the woman screamed and struggled and my young brain saw red.
I dragged her deep into the alley and all I remember was lowering the knife to her throat.
I was wired on dope. I hated this poor woman for no reason other than she was screaming.
I honestly don't know what I was going to do, Batman. I was so angry.
DON'T DO IT.

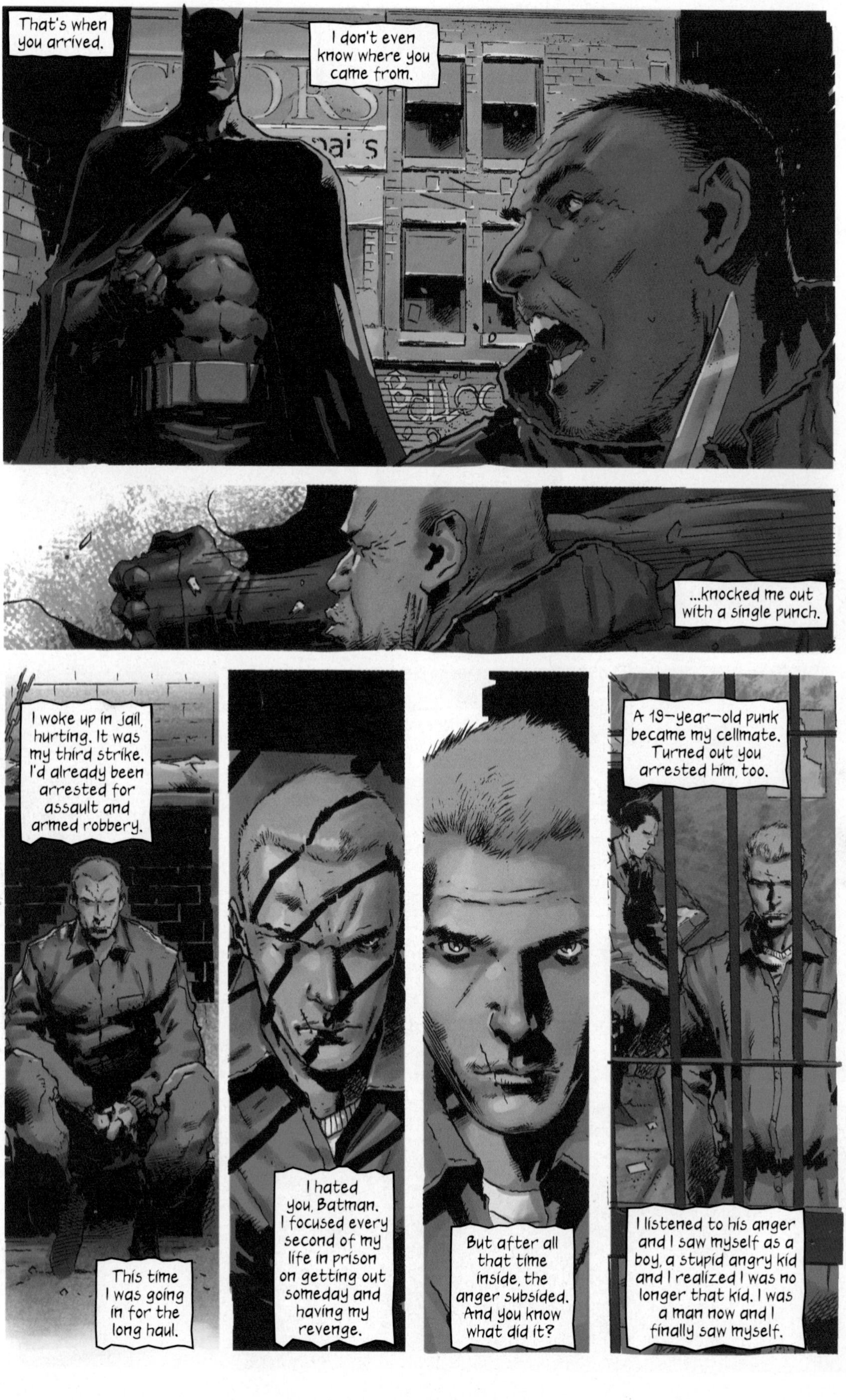
That's when you arrived.
I don't even know where you came from.
...knocked me out with a single punch.
I woke up in jail, hurting. It was my third strike. I'd already been arrested for assault and armed robbery.
This time I was going in for the long haul.
I hated you, Batman. I focused every second of my life in prison on getting out someday and having my revenge.
But after all that time inside, the anger subsided. And you know what did it?
A 19-year-old punk became my cellmate. Turned out you arrested him, too.
I listened to his anger and I saw myself as a boy, a stupid angry kid and I realized I was no longer that kid. I was a man now and I finally saw myself.

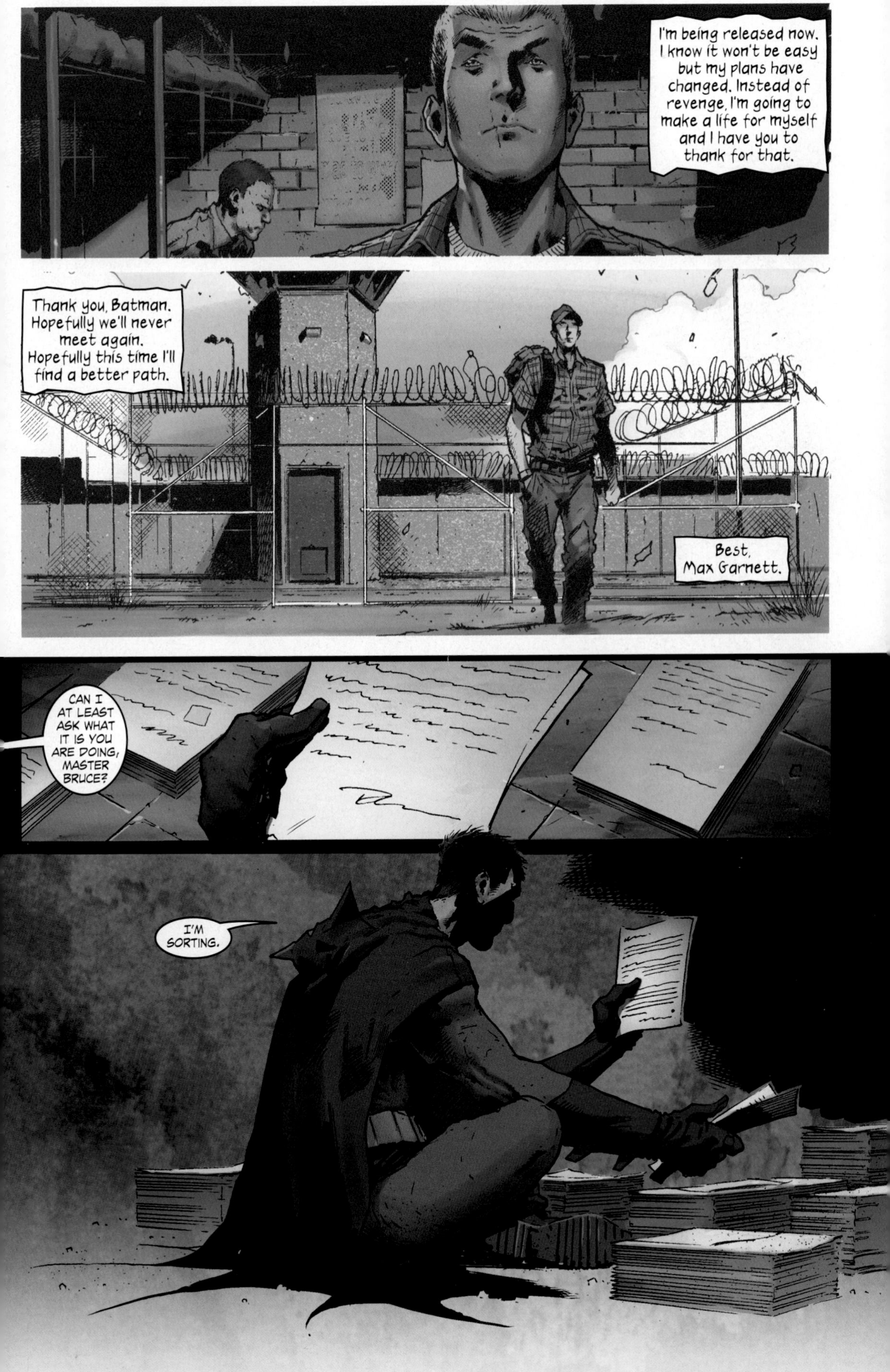
I'm being released now. I know it won't be easy but my plans have changed. Instead of revenge, I'm going to make a life for myself and I have you to thank for that.
Thank you, Batman. Hopefully we'll never meet again. Hopefully this time I'll find a better path.
Best, Max Garnett.
CAN I AT LEAST ASK WHAT IT IS YOU ARE DOING, MASTER BRUCE?
I'M SORTING.

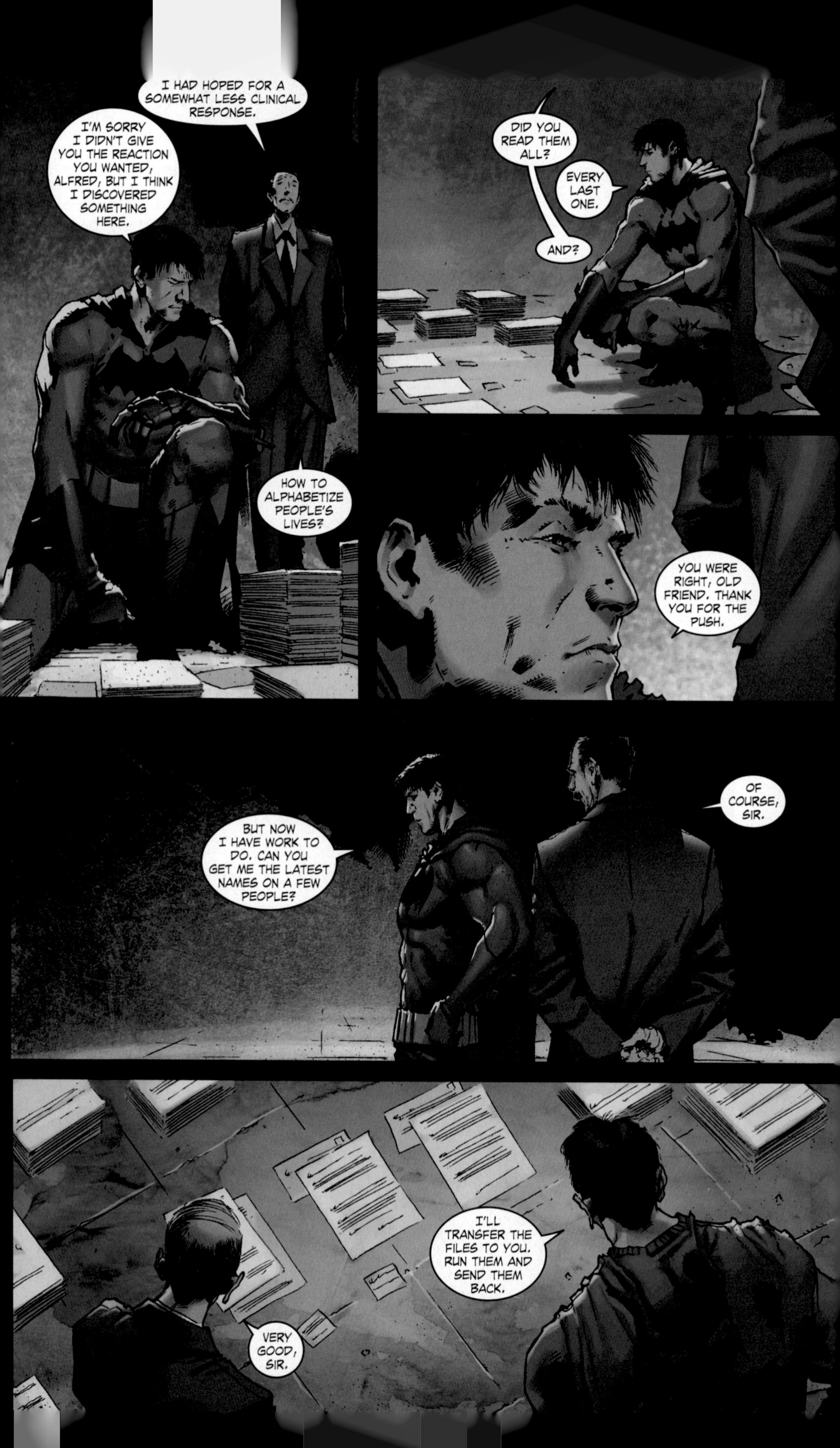
I'M SORRY I DIDN'T GIVE YOU THE REACTION YOU WANTED, ALFRED, BUT I THINK I DISCOVERED SOMETHING HERE.
I HAD HOPED FOR A SOMEWHAT LESS CLINICAL RESPONSE.
HOW TO ALPHABETIZE PEOPLE'S LIVES?
DID YOU READ THEM ALL?
EVERY LAST ONE.
AND?
YOU WERE RIGHT, OLD FRIEND. THANK YOU FOR THE PUSH.
BUT NOW I HAVE WORK TO DO. CAN YOU GET ME THE LATEST NAMES ON A FEW PEOPLE?
OF COURSE, SIR.
I'LL TRANSFER THE FILES TO YOU. RUN THEM AND SEND THEM BACK.
VERY GOOD, SIR.

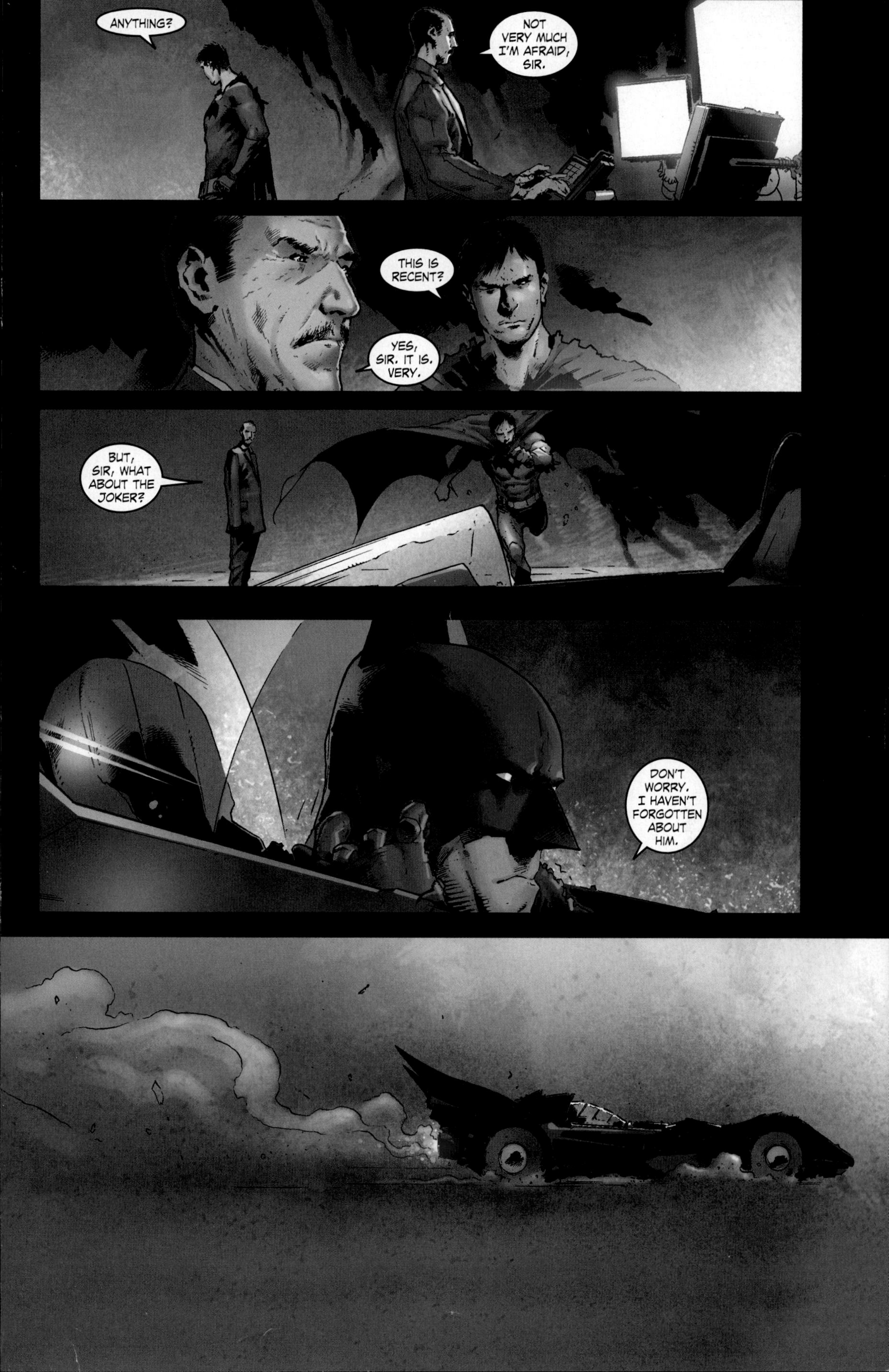
ANYTHING?
NOT VERY MUCH I'M AFRAID, SIR.
THIS IS RECENT?
YES, SIR. IT IS. VERY.
BUT, SIR, WHAT ABOUT THE JOKER?
DON'T WORRY. I HAVEN'T FORGOTTEN ABOUT HIM.

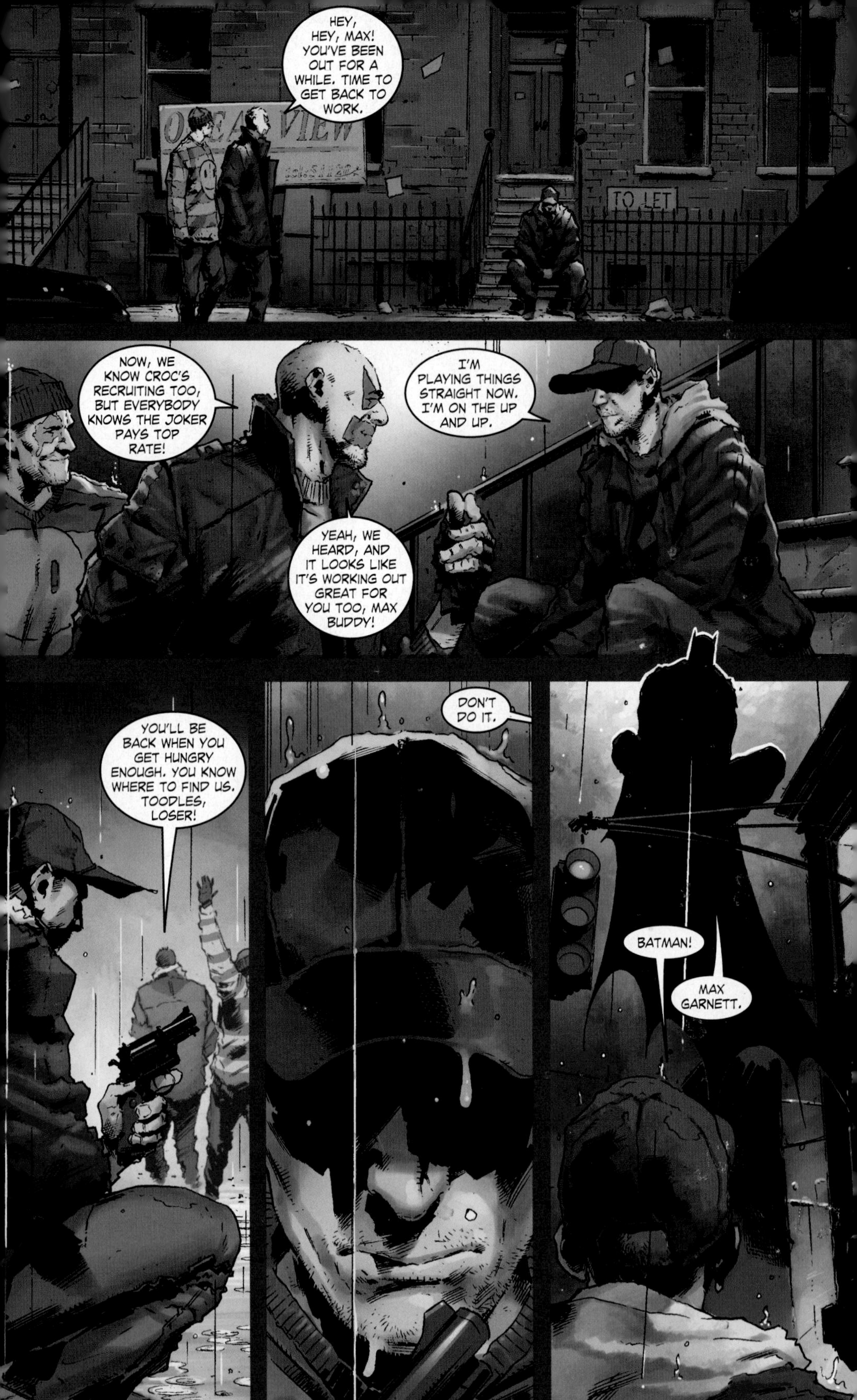
HEY, HEY, MAX! YOU'VE BEEN OUT FOR A WHILE. TIME TO GET BACK TO WORK.
TO LET
NOW, WE KNOW CROC'S RECRUITING TOO, BUT EVERYBODY KNOWS THE JOKER PAYS TOP RATE!
I'M PLAYING THINGS STRAIGHT NOW. I'M ON THE UP AND UP.
YEAH, WE HEARD, AND IT LOOKS LIKE IT'S WORKING OUT GREAT FOR YOU TOO, MAX BUDDY!
YOU'LL BE BACK WHEN YOU GET HUNGRY ENOUGH. YOU KNOW WHERE TO FIND US. TOODLES, LOSER!
DON'T DO IT.
BATMAN!
MAX GARNETT.

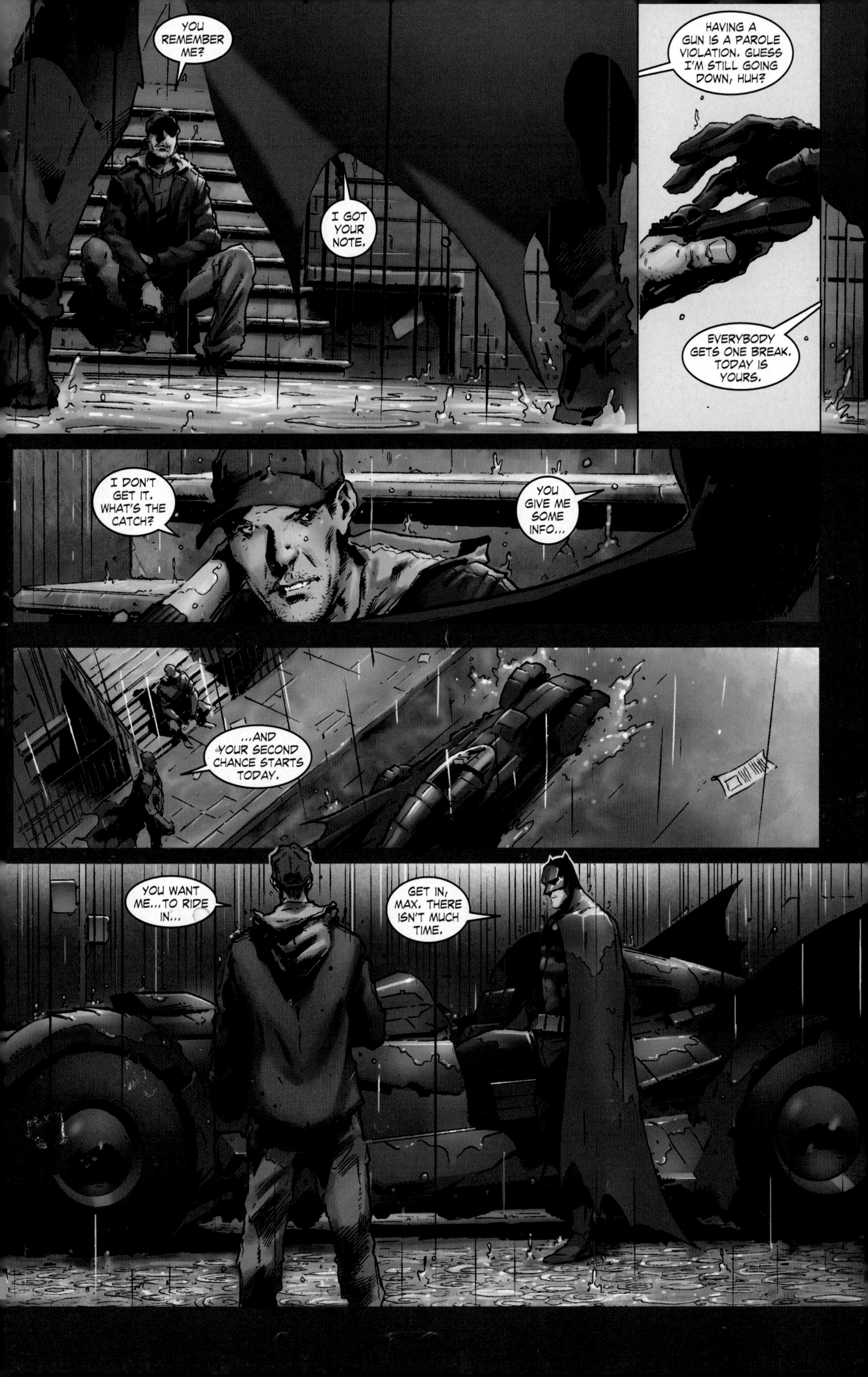
YOU REMEMBER ME?
I GOT YOUR NOTE.
HAVING A GUN IS A PAROLE VIOLATION. GUESS I'M STILL GOING DOWN, HUH?
EVERYBODY GETS ONE BREAK. TODAY IS YOURS.
I DON'T GET IT. WHAT'S THE CATCH?
YOU GIVE ME SOME INFO...
...AND YOUR SECOND CHANCE STARTS TODAY.
YOU WANT ME...TO RIDE IN...
GET IN, MAX. THERE ISN'T MUCH TIME.

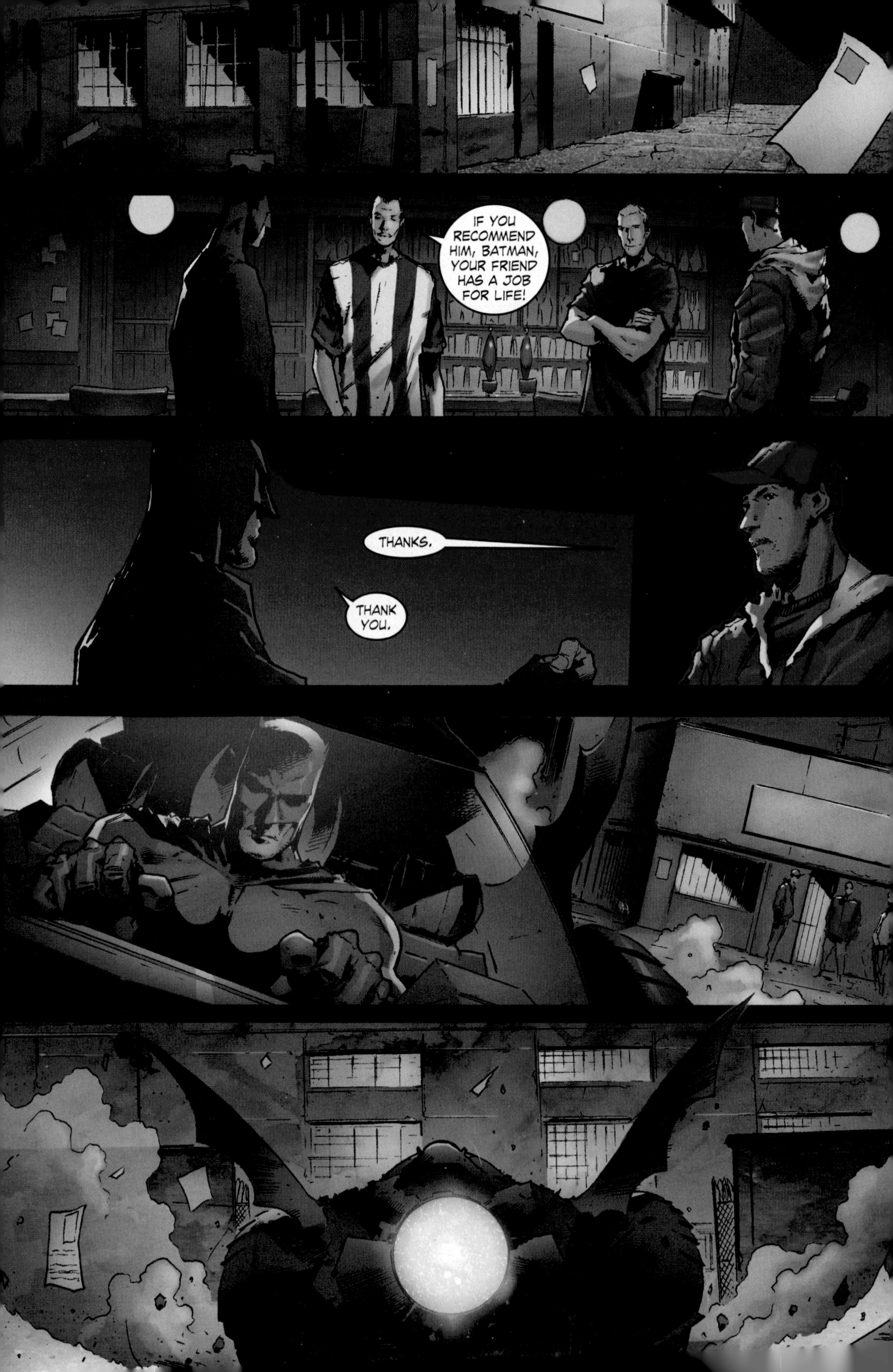
IF YOU RECOMMEND HIM, BATMAN, YOUR FRIEND HAS A JOB FOR LIFE!
THANKS.
THANK YOU.

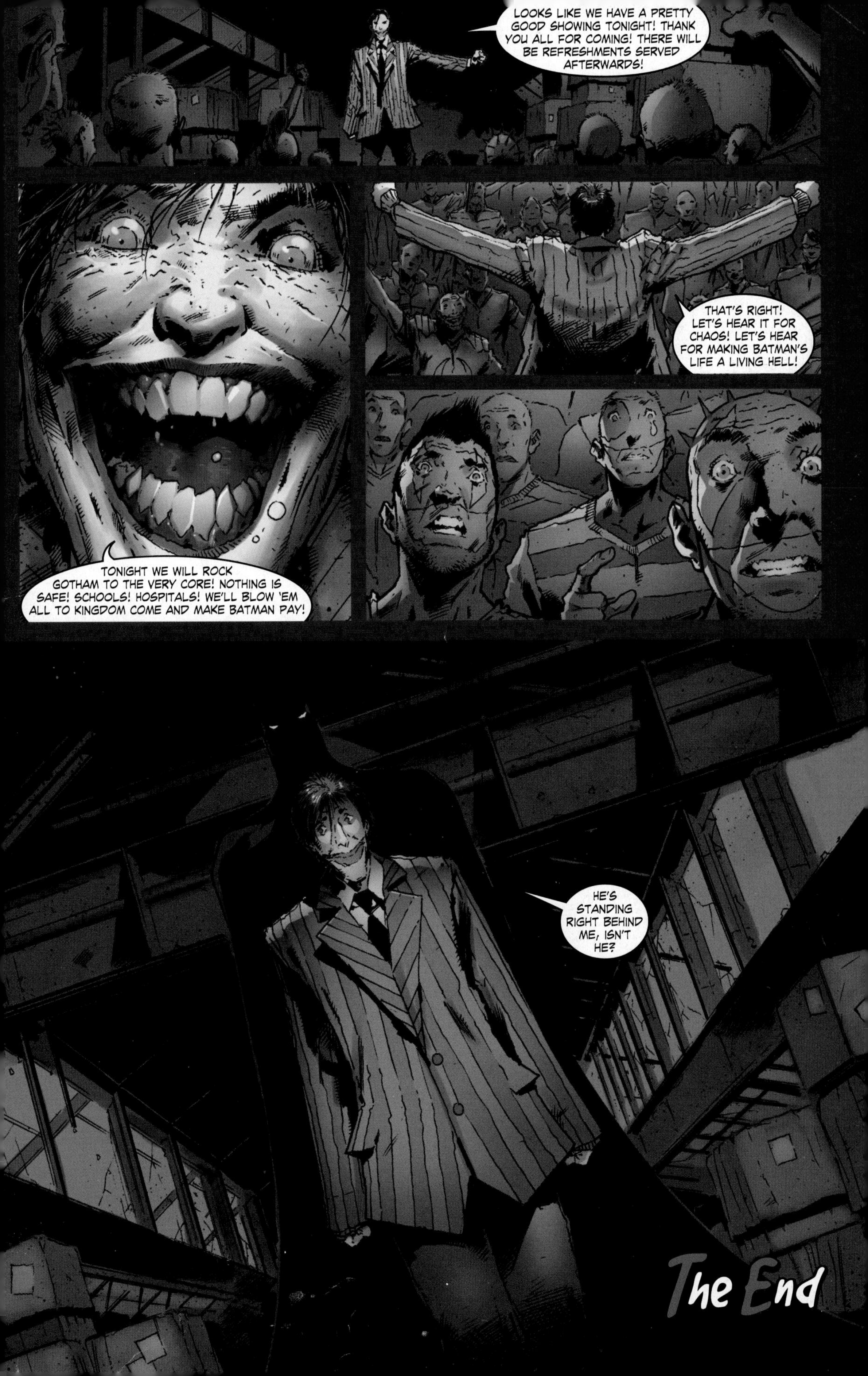
LOOKS LIKE WE HAVE A PRETTY GOOD SHOWING TONIGHT! THANK YOU ALL FOR COMING! THERE WILL BE REFRESHMENTS SERVED AFTERWARDS!
TONIGHT WE WILL ROCK GOTHAM TO THE VERY CORE! NOTHING IS SAFE! SCHOOLS! HOSPITALS! WE'LL BLOW 'EM ALL TO KINGDOM COME AND MAKE BATMAN PAY!
THAT'S RIGHT! LET'S HEAR IT FOR CHAOS! LET'S HEAR FOR MAKING BATMAN'S LIFE A LIVING HELL!
HE'S STANDING RIGHT BEHIND ME, ISN'T HE?
The End

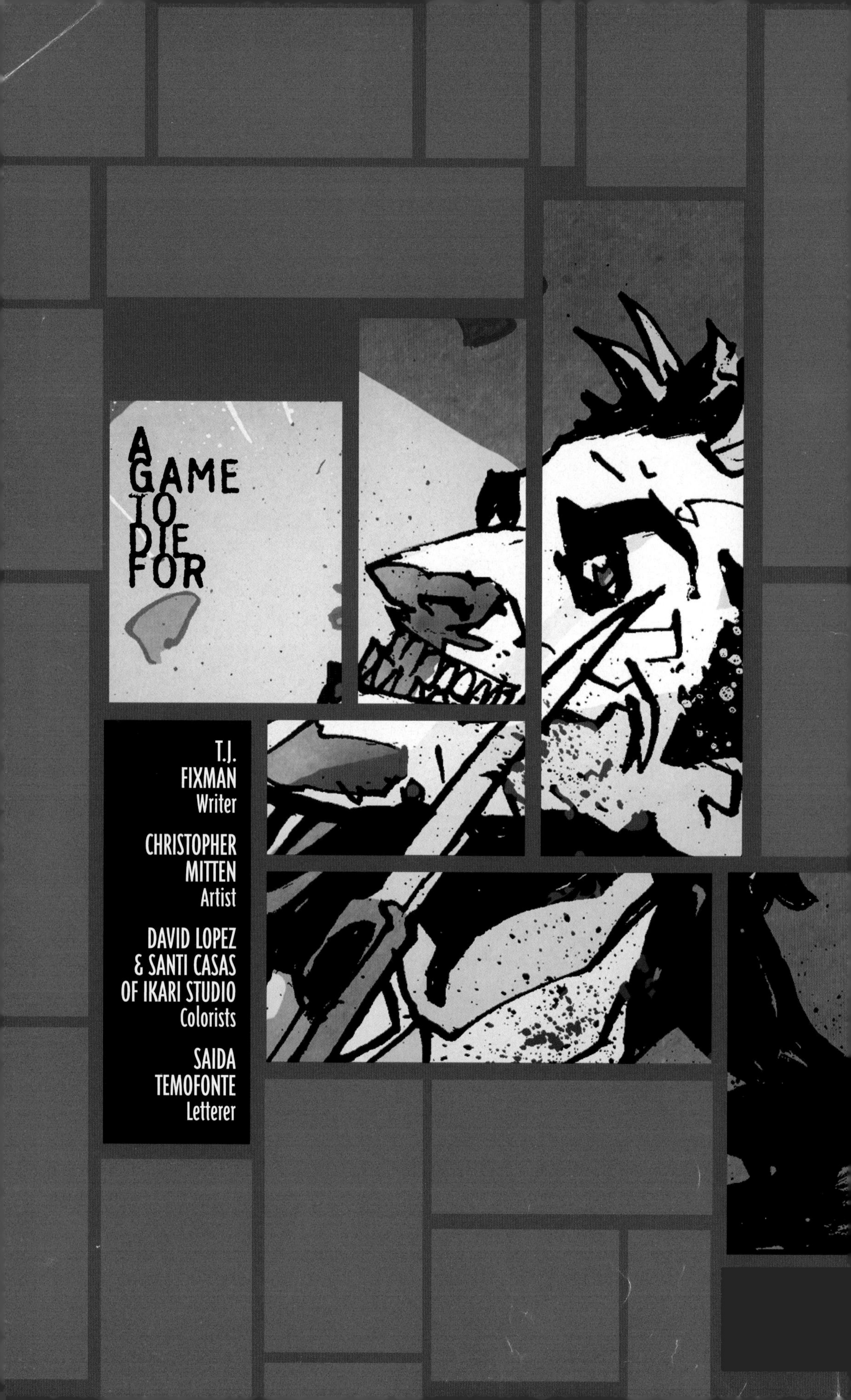
A GAME TO DIE FOR
T.J. FIXMAN
Writer
CHRISTOPHER MITTEN
Artist
DAVID LOPEZ & SANTI CASAS OF IKARI STUDIO
Colorists
SAIDA TEMOFONTE
Letterer

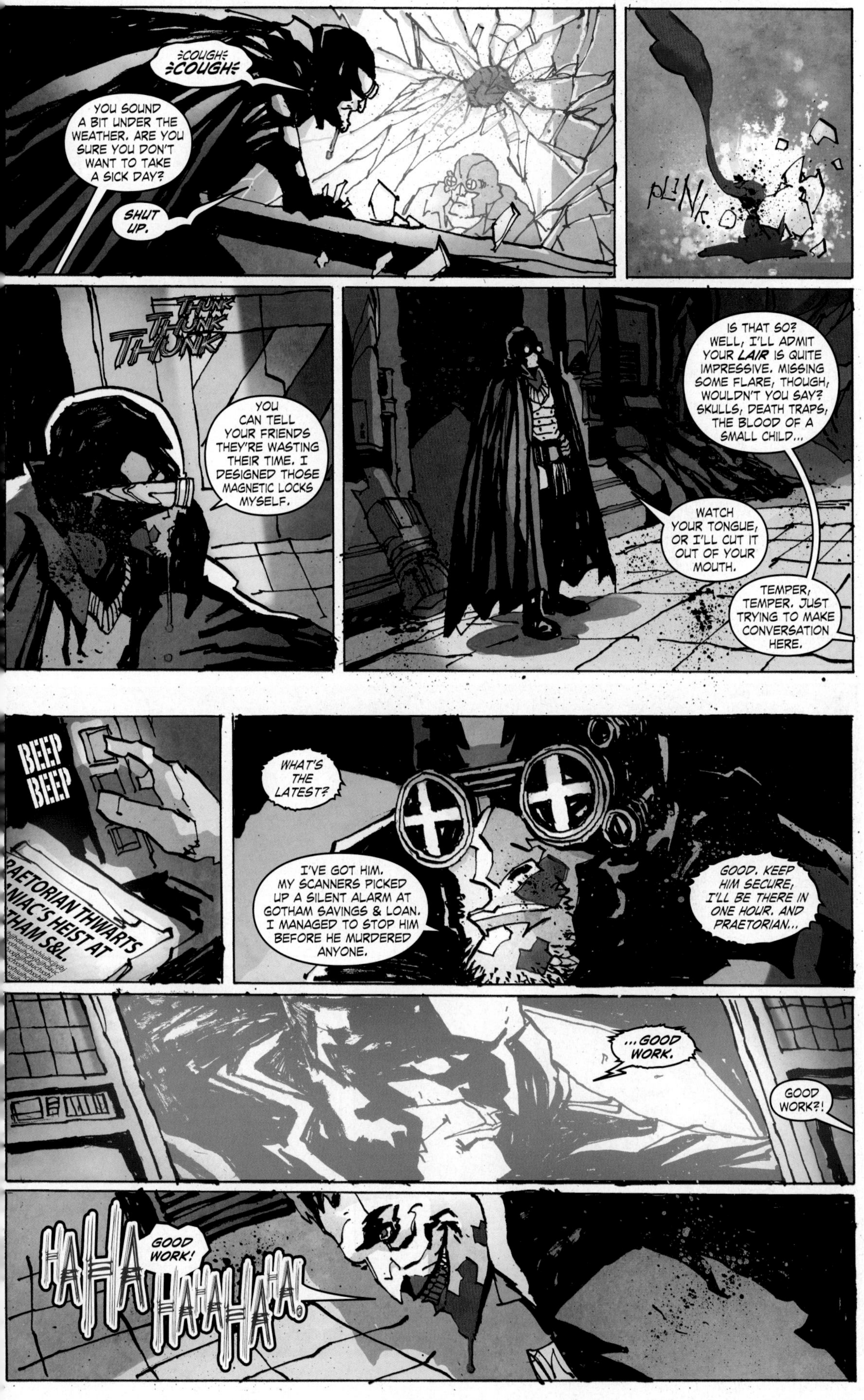

COUGH COUGH
YOU SOUND A BIT UNDER THE WEATHER. ARE YOU SURE YOU DON'T WANT TO TAKE A SICK DAY?
SHUT UP.
pLINK
THUNK THUNK THUNK
YOU CAN TELL YOUR FRIENDS THEY'RE WASTING THEIR TIME. I DESIGNED THOSE MAGNETIC LOCKS MYSELF.
IS THAT SO? WELL, I'LL ADMIT YOUR LAIR IS QUITE IMPRESSIVE. MISSING SOME FLARE, THOUGH, WOULDN'T YOU SAY? SKULLS, DEATH TRAPS, THE BLOOD OF A SMALL CHILD...
WATCH YOUR TONGUE, OR I'LL CUT IT OUT OF YOUR MOUTH.
TEMPER, TEMPER. JUST TRYING TO MAKE CONVERSATION HERE.
BEEP BEEP
PRAETORIAN THWARTS
NIAC'S HEIST AT
THAM S&L.
WHAT'S THE LATEST?
I'VE GOT HIM. MY SCANNERS PICKED UP A SILENT ALARM AT GOTHAM SAVINGS & LOAN. I MANAGED TO STOP HIM BEFORE HE MURDERED ANYONE.
GOOD. KEEP HIM SECURE, I'LL BE THERE IN ONE HOUR. AND PRAETORIAN...
...GOOD WORK.
GOOD WORK?!
HAHA
GOOD WORK!
HAHAHAHAHA

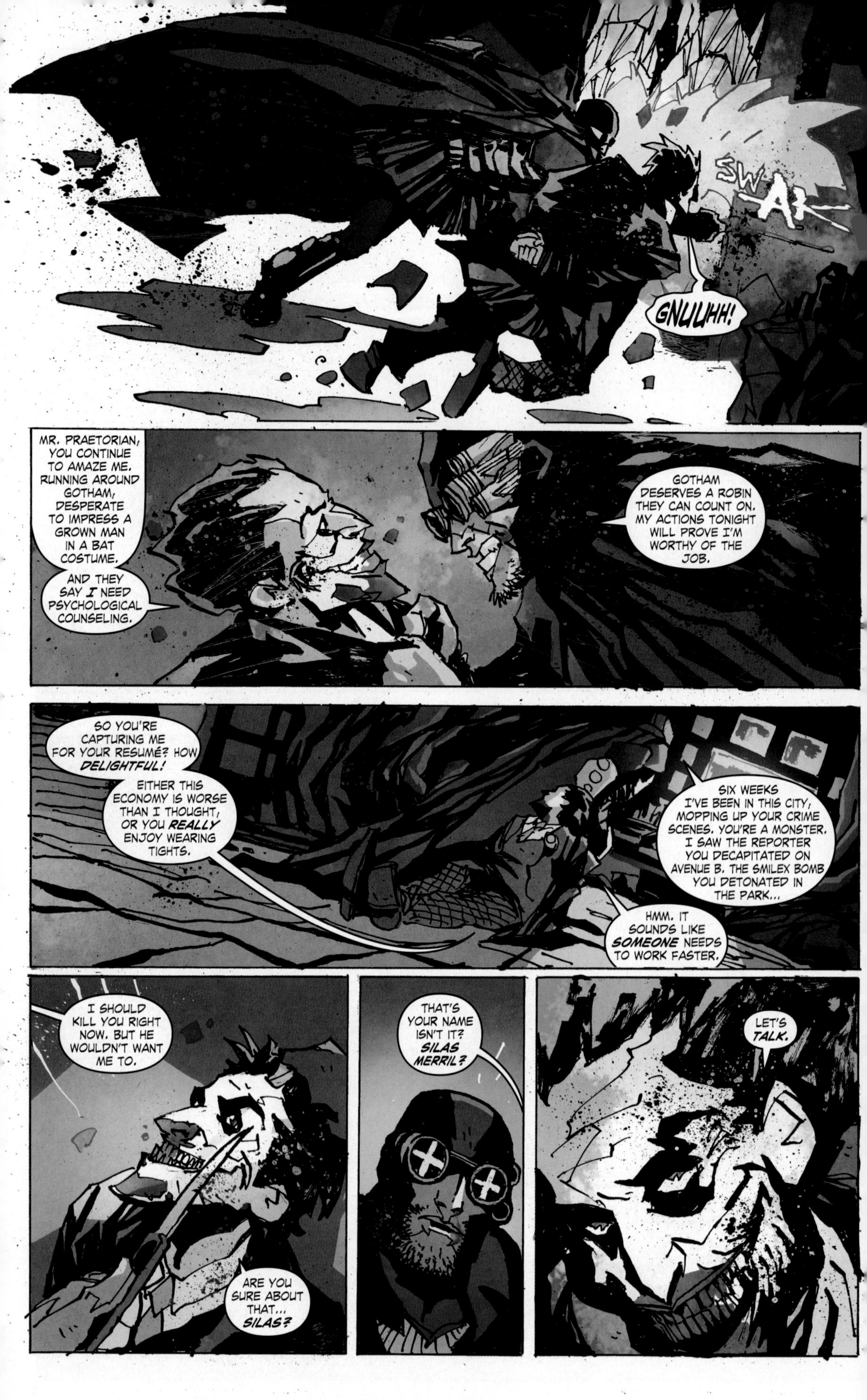
SWAK
GNUUHH!
MR. PRAETORIAN, YOU CONTINUE TO AMAZE ME. RUNNING AROUND GOTHAM, DESPERATE TO IMPRESS A GROWN MAN IN A BAT COSTUME.
AND THEY SAY I NEED PSYCHOLOGICAL COUNSELING.
GOTHAM DESERVES A ROBIN THEY CAN COUNT ON. MY ACTIONS TONIGHT WILL PROVE I'M WORTHY OF THE JOB.
SO YOU'RE CAPTURING ME FOR YOUR RESUMÉ? HOW DELIGHTFUL!
EITHER THIS ECONOMY IS WORSE THAN I THOUGHT, OR YOU REALLY ENJOY WEARING TIGHTS.
SIX WEEKS I'VE BEEN IN THIS CITY, MOPPING UP YOUR CRIME SCENES. YOU'RE A MONSTER. I SAW THE REPORTER YOU DECAPITATED ON AVENUE B. THE SMILEX BOMB YOU DETONATED IN THE PARK...
HMM. IT SOUNDS LIKE SOMEONE NEEDS TO WORK FASTER.
I SHOULD KILL YOU RIGHT NOW. BUT HE WOULDN'T WANT ME TO.
ARE YOU SURE ABOUT THAT... SILAS?
THAT'S YOUR NAME ISN'T IT? SILAS MERRIL?
LET'S TALK.

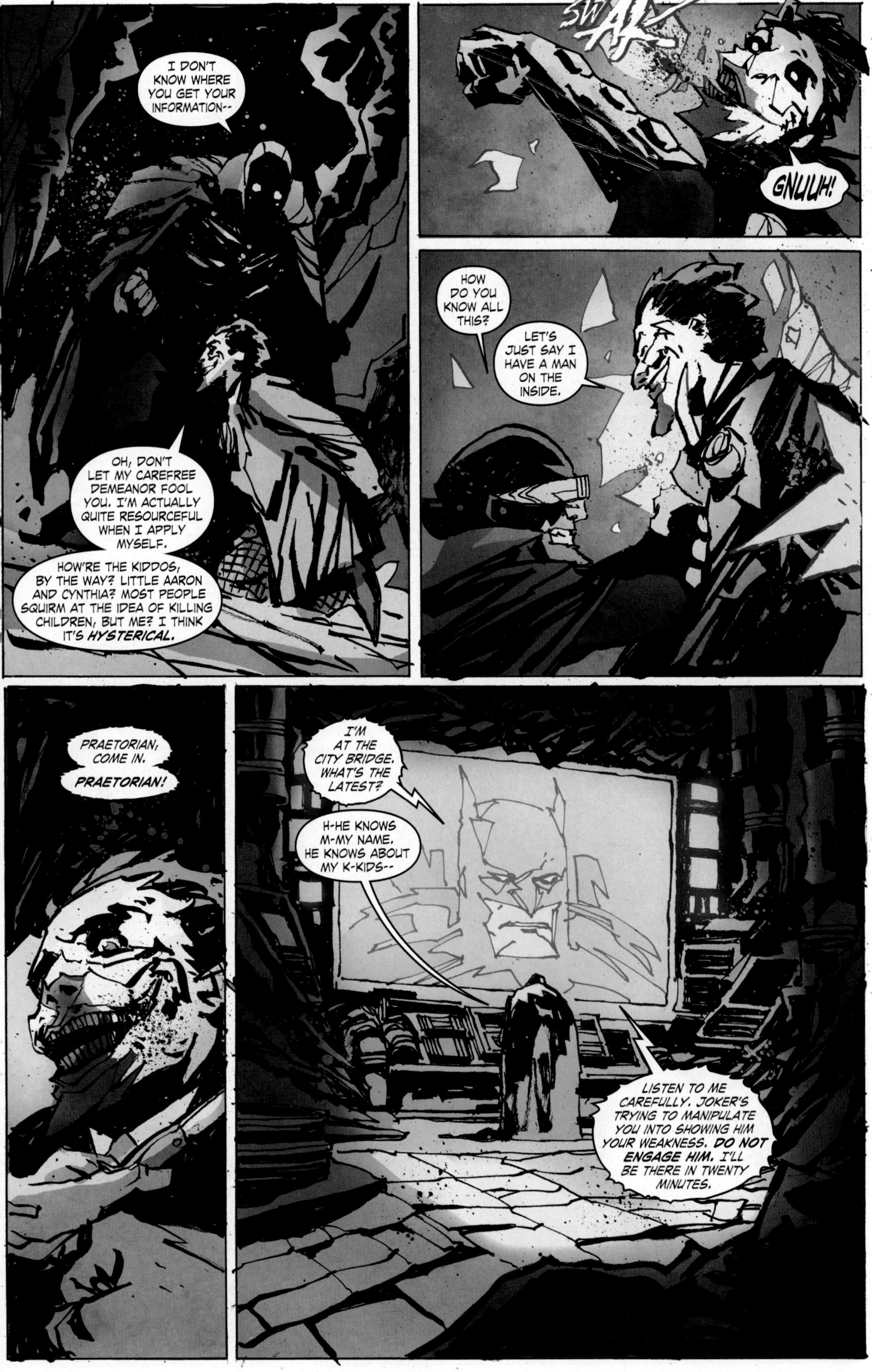
I DON'T KNOW WHERE YOU GET YOUR INFORMATION--
OH, DON'T LET MY CAREFREE DEMEANOR FOOL YOU. I'M ACTUALLY QUITE RESOURCEFUL WHEN I APPLY MYSELF.
HOW'RE THE KIDDOS, BY THE WAY? LITTLE AARON AND CYNTHIA? MOST PEOPLE SQUIRM AT THE IDEA OF KILLING CHILDREN, BUT ME? I THINK IT'S HYSTERICAL.
SWAK
GNUUH!
HOW DO YOU KNOW ALL THIS?
LET'S JUST SAY I HAVE A MAN ON THE INSIDE.
PRAETORIAN, COME IN.
PRAETORIAN!
I'M AT THE CITY BRIDGE. WHAT'S THE LATEST?
H-HE KNOWS M-MY NAME. HE KNOWS ABOUT MY K-KIDS--
LISTEN TO ME CAREFULLY. JOKER'S TRYING TO MANIPULATE YOU INTO SHOWING HIM YOUR WEAKNESS. DO NOT ENGAGE HIM. I'LL BE THERE IN TWENTY MINUTES.

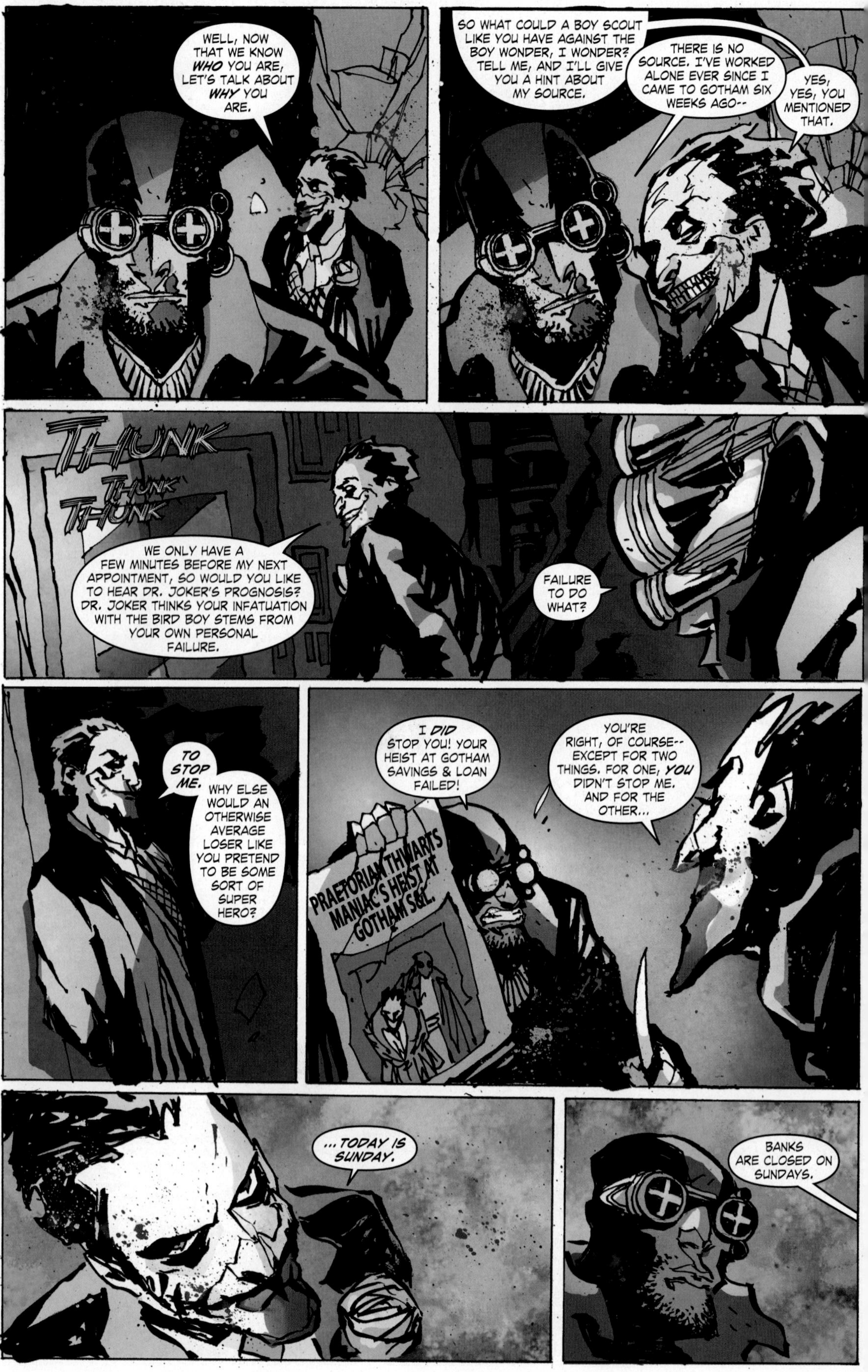
WELL, NOW THAT WE KNOW *WHO* YOU ARE, LET'S TALK ABOUT *WHY* YOU ARE.
SO WHAT COULD A BOY SCOUT LIKE YOU HAVE AGAINST THE BOY WONDER, I WONDER? TELL ME, AND I'LL GIVE YOU A HINT ABOUT MY SOURCE.
THERE IS NO SOURCE. I'VE WORKED ALONE EVER SINCE I CAME TO GOTHAM SIX WEEKS AGO--
YES, YES, YOU MENTIONED THAT.
THUNK
THUNK
THUNK
WE ONLY HAVE A FEW MINUTES BEFORE MY NEXT APPOINTMENT, SO WOULD YOU LIKE TO HEAR DR. JOKER'S PROGNOSIS? DR. JOKER THINKS YOUR INFATUATION WITH THE BIRD BOY STEMS FROM YOUR OWN PERSONAL FAILURE.
FAILURE TO DO WHAT?
TO STOP ME.
WHY ELSE WOULD AN OTHERWISE AVERAGE LOSER LIKE YOU PRETEND TO BE SOME SORT OF SUPER HERO?
I *DID* STOP YOU! YOUR HEIST AT GOTHAM SAVINGS & LOAN FAILED!
PRAETORIAN THWARTS MANIAC'S HEIST AT GOTHAM S&L.
YOU'RE RIGHT, OF COURSE-- EXCEPT FOR TWO THINGS. FOR ONE, *YOU* DIDN'T STOP ME. AND FOR THE OTHER...
...TODAY IS SUNDAY.
BANKS ARE CLOSED ON SUNDAYS.

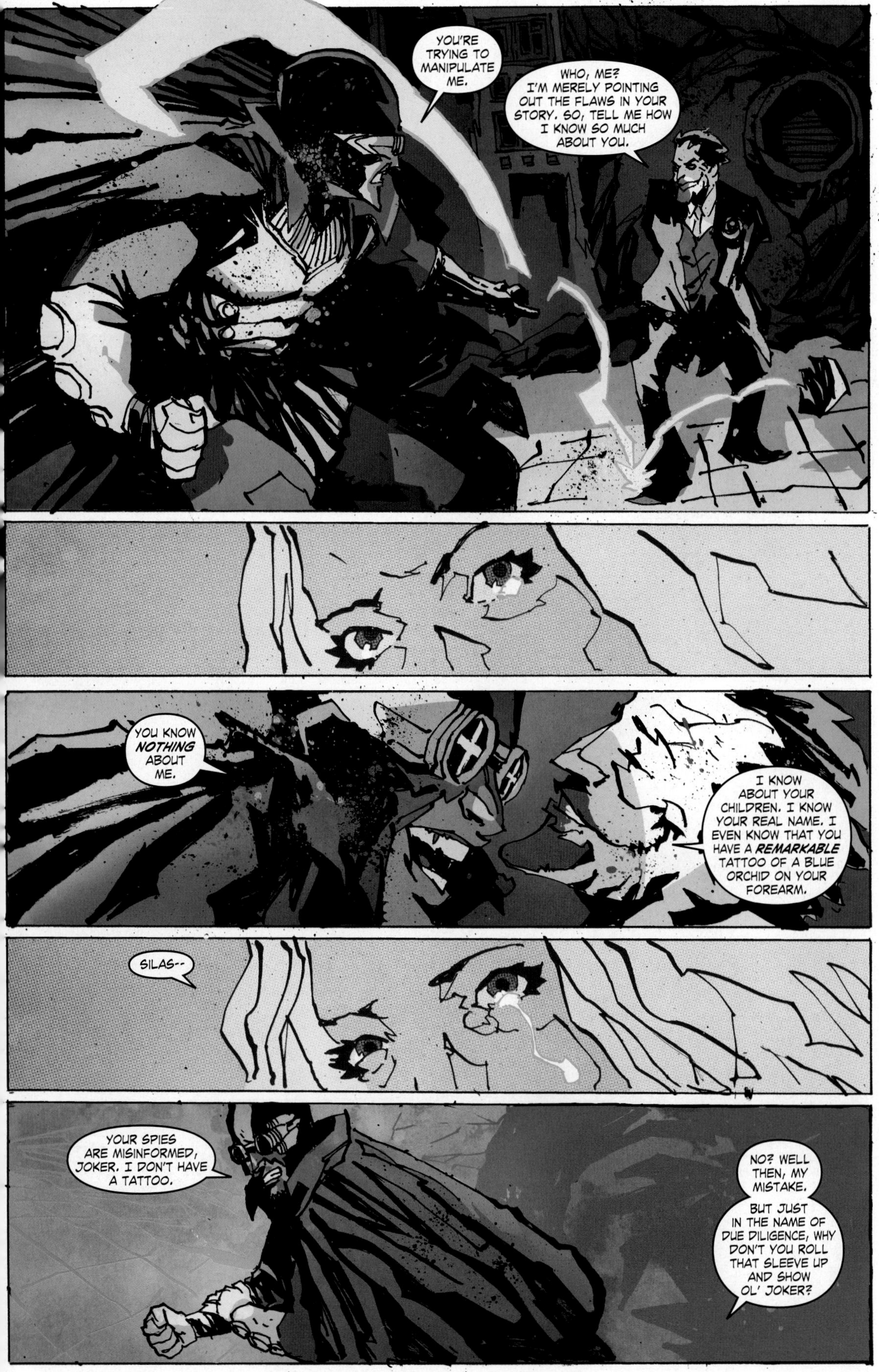
YOU'RE TRYING TO MANIPULATE ME.
WHO, ME? I'M MERELY POINTING OUT THE FLAWS IN YOUR STORY. SO, TELL ME HOW I KNOW SO MUCH ABOUT YOU.
YOU KNOW NOTHING ABOUT ME.
I KNOW ABOUT YOUR CHILDREN. I KNOW YOUR REAL NAME. I EVEN KNOW THAT YOU HAVE A REMARKABLE TATTOO OF A BLUE ORCHID ON YOUR FOREARM.
SILAS--
YOUR SPIES ARE MISINFORMED, JOKER. I DON'T HAVE A TATTOO.
NO? WELL THEN, MY MISTAKE.
BUT JUST IN THE NAME OF DUE DILIGENCE, WHY DON'T YOU ROLL THAT SLEEVE UP AND SHOW OL' JOKER?

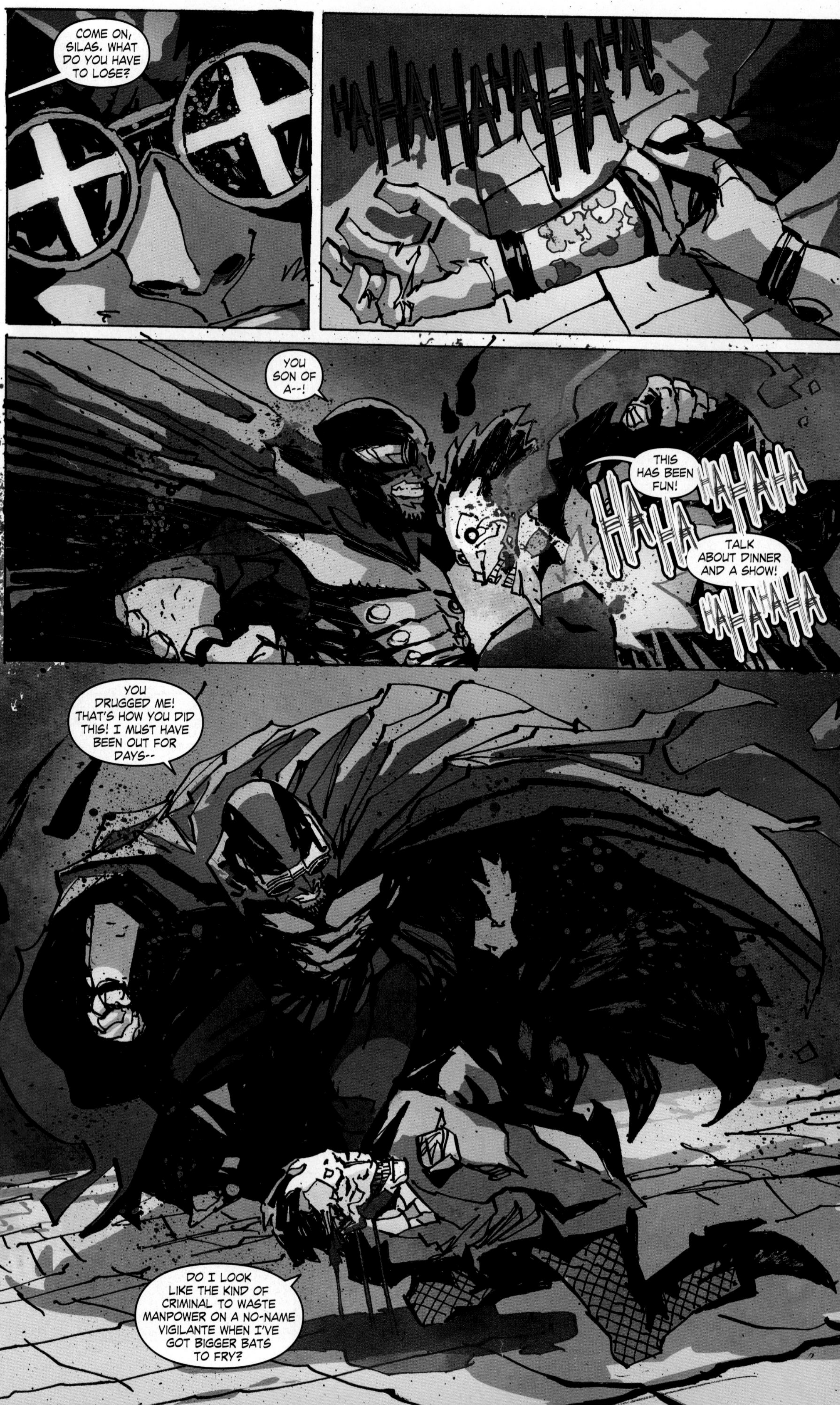

COME ON, SILAS. WHAT DO YOU HAVE TO LOSE?
HAHAHAHAHAHAHA!
YOU SON OF A--!
THIS HAS BEEN FUN!
HAHAHA HAHAHA
TALK ABOUT DINNER AND A SHOW!
HAHAHAHA
YOU DRUGGED ME! THAT'S HOW YOU DID THIS! I MUST HAVE BEEN OUT FOR DAYS--
DO I LOOK LIKE THE KIND OF CRIMINAL TO WASTE MANPOWER ON A NO-NAME VIGILANTE WHEN I'VE GOT BIGGER BATS TO FRY?

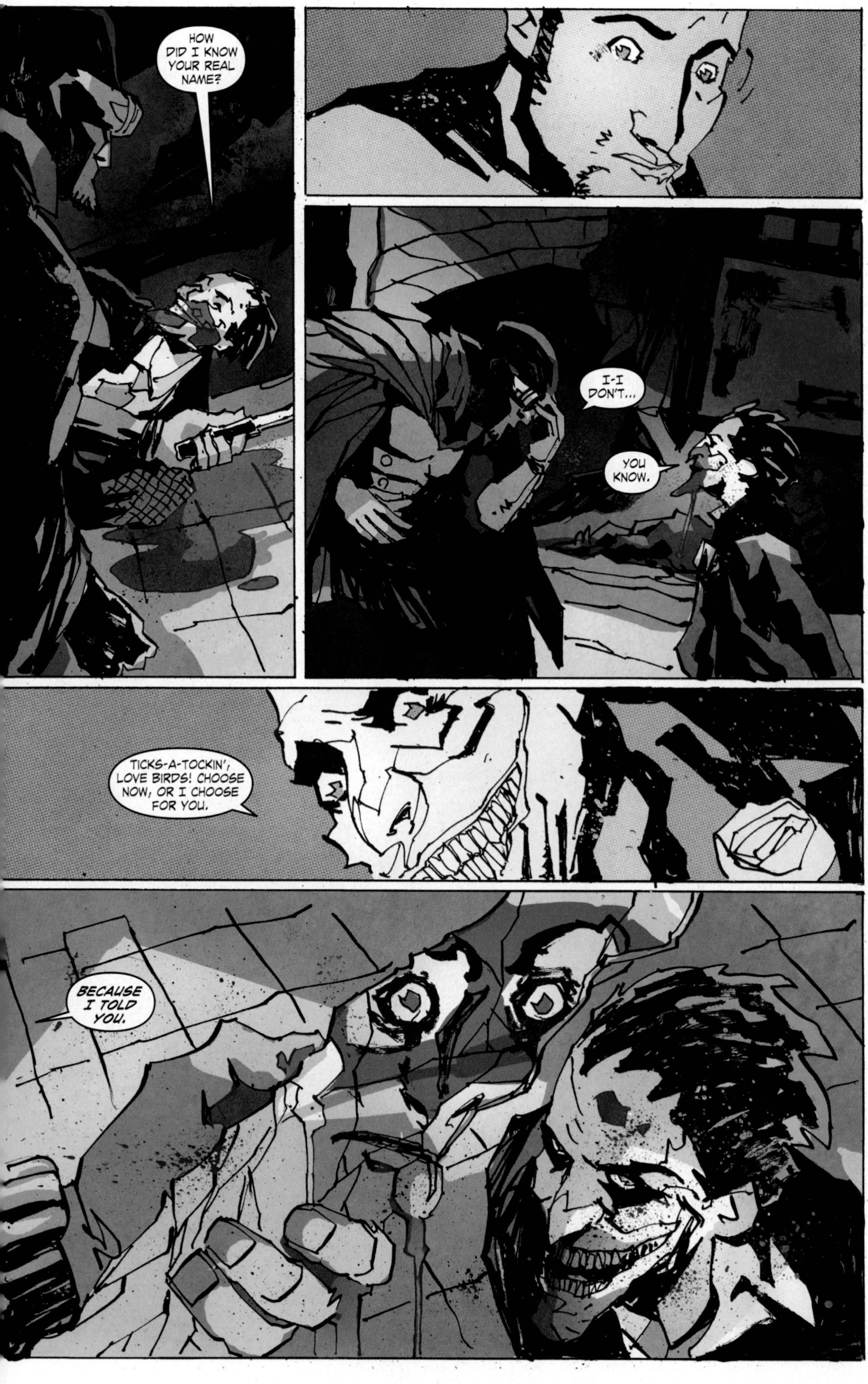
HOW DID I KNOW YOUR REAL NAME?
I-I DON'T...
YOU KNOW.
TICKS-A-TOCKIN', LOVE BIRDS! CHOOSE NOW, OR I CHOOSE FOR YOU.
BECAUSE I TOLD YOU.

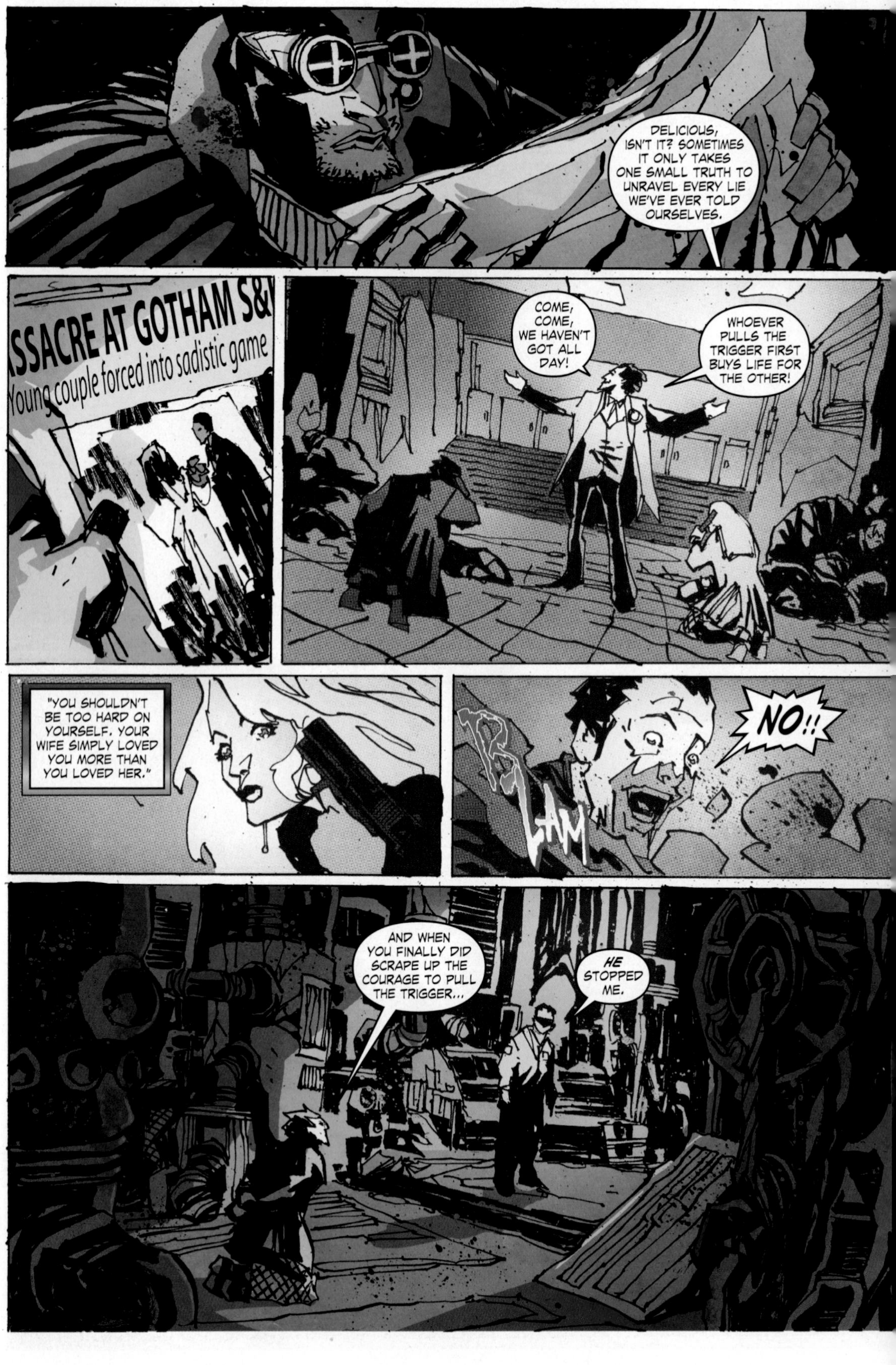
DELICIOUS, ISN'T IT? SOMETIMES IT ONLY TAKES ONE SMALL TRUTH TO UNRAVEL EVERY LIE WE'VE EVER TOLD OURSELVES.
ASSACRE AT GOTHAM S&
Young couple forced into sadistic game
COME, COME, WE HAVEN'T GOT ALL DAY!
WHOEVER PULLS THE TRIGGER FIRST BUYS LIFE FOR THE OTHER!
"YOU SHOULDN'T BE TOO HARD ON YOURSELF. YOUR WIFE SIMPLY LOVED YOU MORE THAN YOU LOVED HER."
BLAM
NO!!
AND WHEN YOU FINALLY DID SCRAPE UP THE COURAGE TO PULL THE TRIGGER...
HE STOPPED ME.

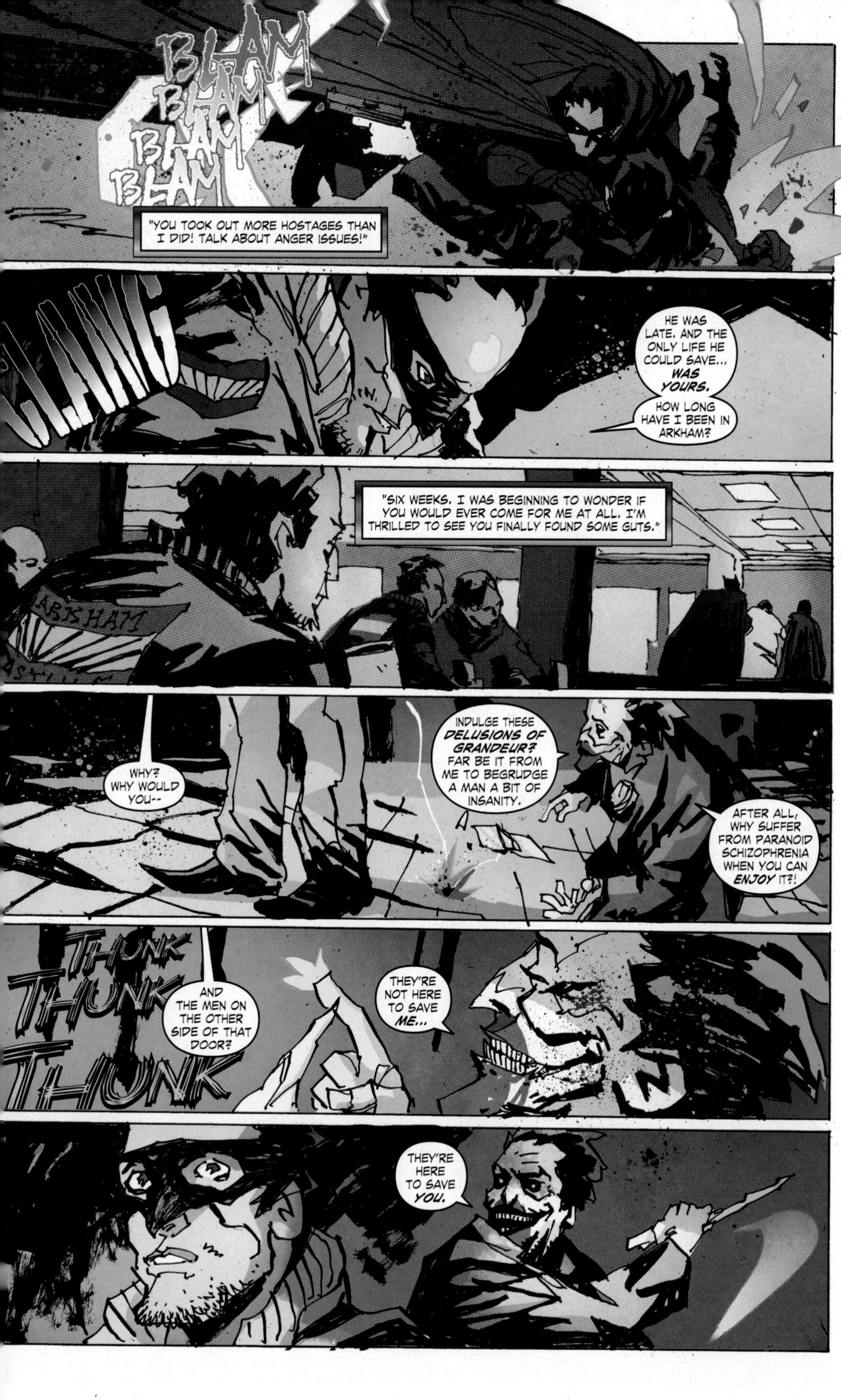
BLAM BLAM BLAM BLAM
"YOU TOOK OUT MORE HOSTAGES THAN I DID! TALK ABOUT ANGER ISSUES!"
WHANG
HE WAS LATE. AND THE ONLY LIFE HE COULD SAVE... WAS YOURS.
HOW LONG HAVE I BEEN IN ARKHAM?
"SIX WEEKS. I WAS BEGINNING TO WONDER IF YOU WOULD EVER COME FOR ME AT ALL. I'M THRILLED TO SEE YOU FINALLY FOUND SOME GUTS."
ARKHAM
WHY? WHY WOULD YOU--
INDULGE THESE DELUSIONS OF GRANDEUR? FAR BE IT FROM ME TO BEGRUDGE A MAN A BIT OF INSANITY.
AFTER ALL, WHY SUFFER FROM PARANOID SCHIZOPHRENIA WHEN YOU CAN ENJOY IT?!
THUNK THUNK THUNK
AND THE MEN ON THE OTHER SIDE OF THAT DOOR?
THEY'RE NOT HERE TO SAVE ME...
THEY'RE HERE TO SAVE YOU.

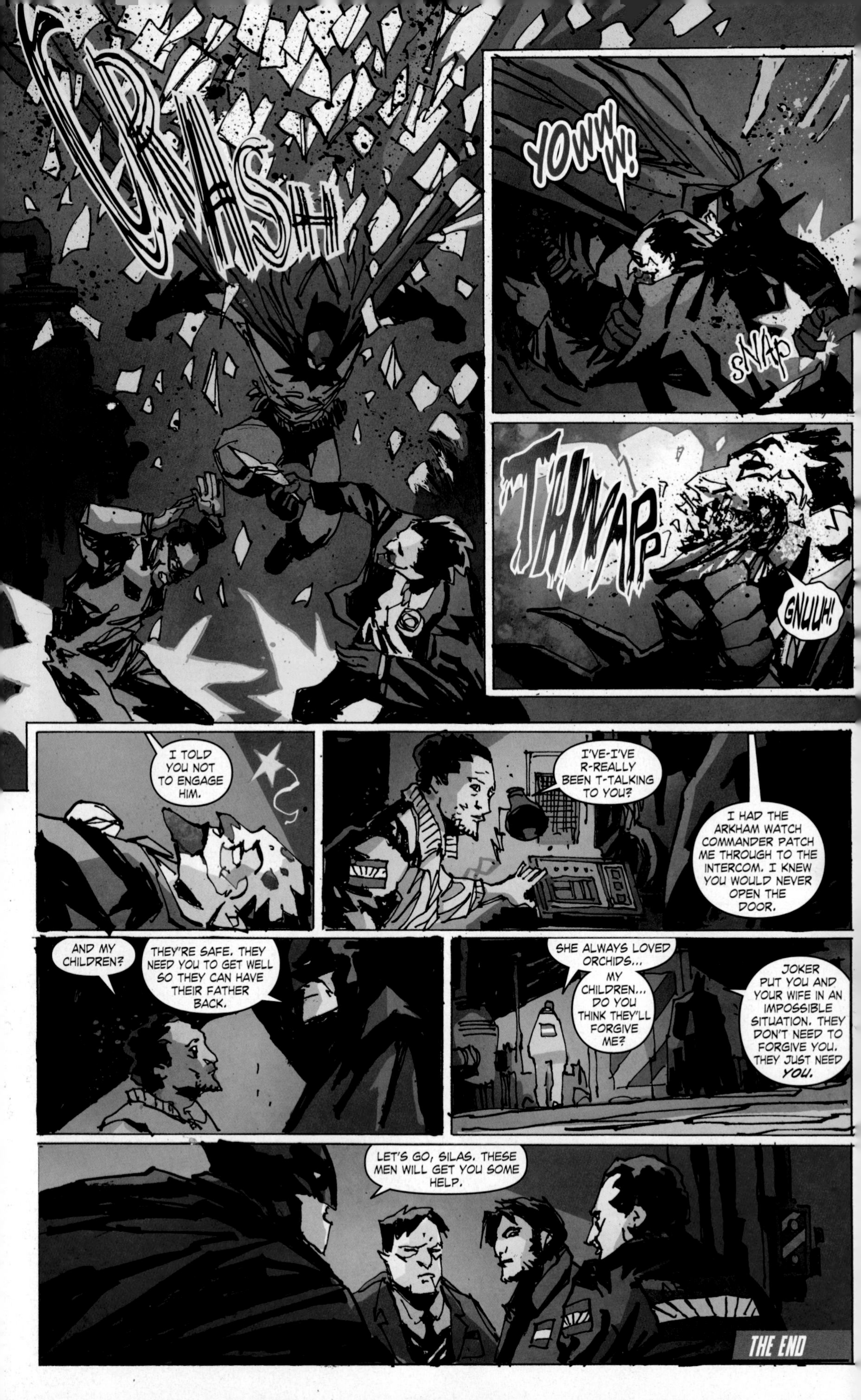
CRASH
YOWWW!
SNAP
THWAPP
GNUUH!
I TOLD YOU NOT TO ENGAGE HIM.
I'VE-I'VE R-REALLY BEEN T-TALKING TO YOU?
I HAD THE ARKHAM WATCH COMMANDER PATCH ME THROUGH TO THE INTERCOM. I KNEW YOU WOULD NEVER OPEN THE DOOR.
AND MY CHILDREN?
THEY'RE SAFE. THEY NEED YOU TO GET WELL SO THEY CAN HAVE THEIR FATHER BACK.
SHE ALWAYS LOVED ORCHIDS...
MY CHILDREN... DO YOU THINK THEY'LL FORGIVE ME?
JOKER PUT YOU AND YOUR WIFE IN AN IMPOSSIBLE SITUATION. THEY DON'T NEED TO FORGIVE YOU. THEY JUST NEED *YOU.*
LET'S GO, SILAS. THESE MEN WILL GET YOU SOME HELP.
THE END

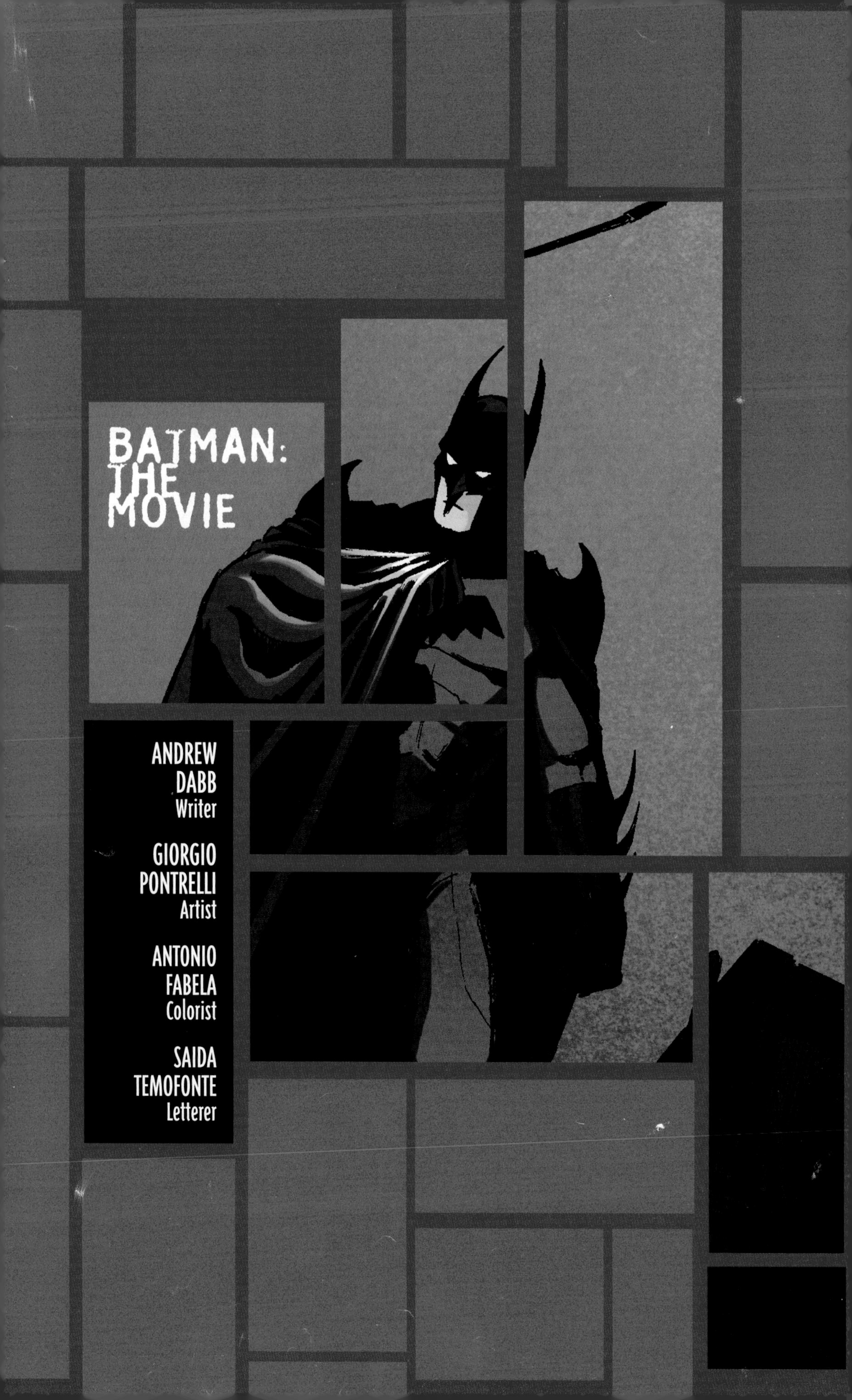
BATMAN:
THE
MOVIE
ANDREW
DABB
Writer
GIORGIO
PONTRELLI
Artist
ANTONIO
FABELA
Colorist
SAIDA
TEMOFONTE
Letterer

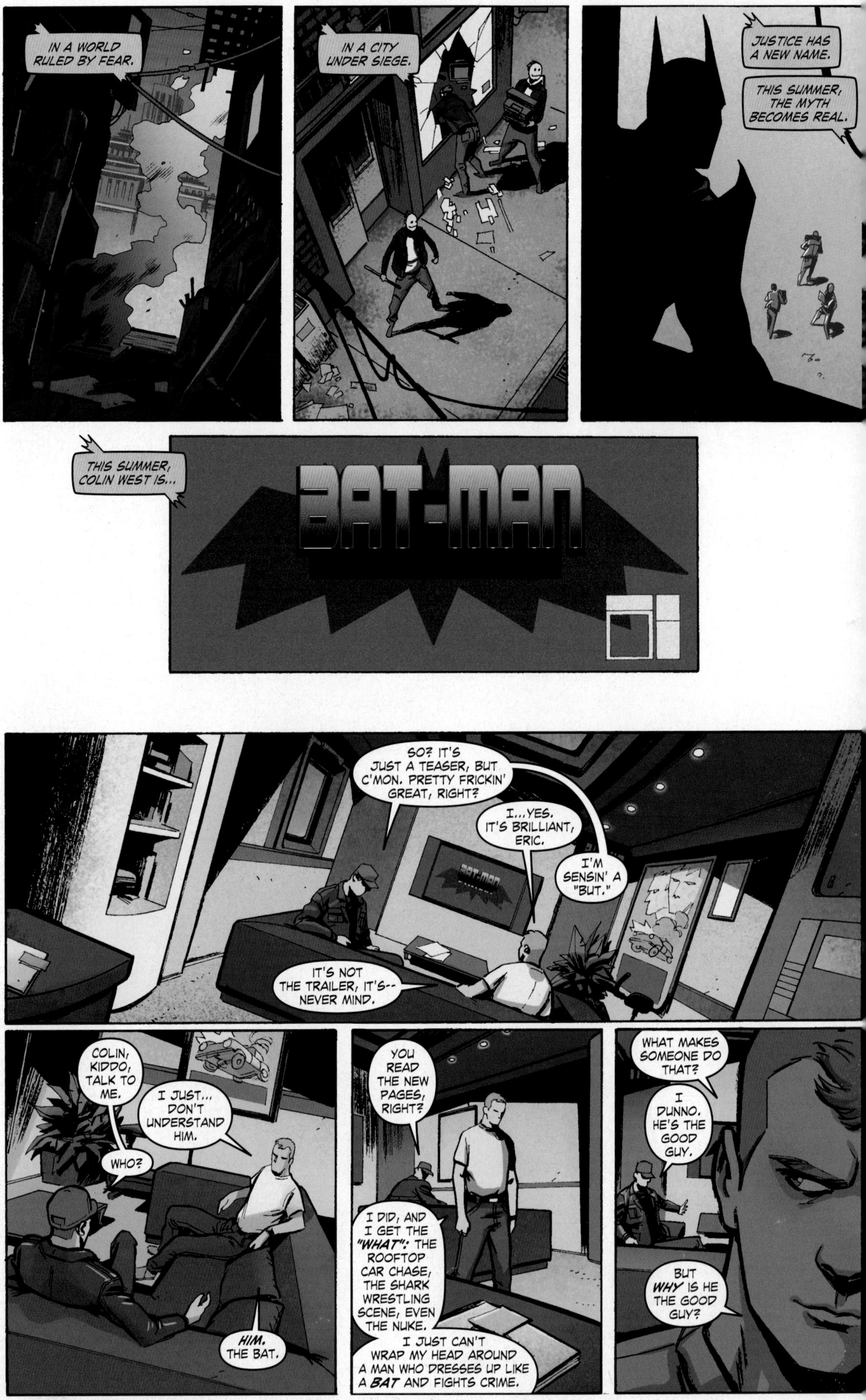

IN A WORLD RULED BY FEAR.
IN A CITY UNDER SIEGE.
JUSTICE HAS A NEW NAME.
THIS SUMMER, THE MYTH BECOMES REAL.
THIS SUMMER, COLIN WEST IS...
BAT-MAN
SO? IT'S JUST A TEASER, BUT C'MON. PRETTY FRICKIN' GREAT, RIGHT?
I...YES. IT'S BRILLIANT, ERIC.
I'M SENSIN' A "BUT."
IT'S NOT THE TRAILER, IT'S-- NEVER MIND.
COLIN, KIDDO, TALK TO ME.
I JUST... DON'T UNDERSTAND HIM.
WHO?
HIM. THE BAT.
YOU READ THE NEW PAGES, RIGHT?
I DID, AND I GET THE "WHAT": THE ROOFTOP CAR CHASE, THE SHARK WRESTLING SCENE, EVEN THE NUKE.
I JUST CAN'T WRAP MY HEAD AROUND A MAN WHO DRESSES UP LIKE A BAT AND FIGHTS CRIME.
WHAT MAKES SOMEONE DO THAT?
I DUNNO. HE'S THE GOOD GUY.
BUT WHY IS HE THE GOOD GUY?

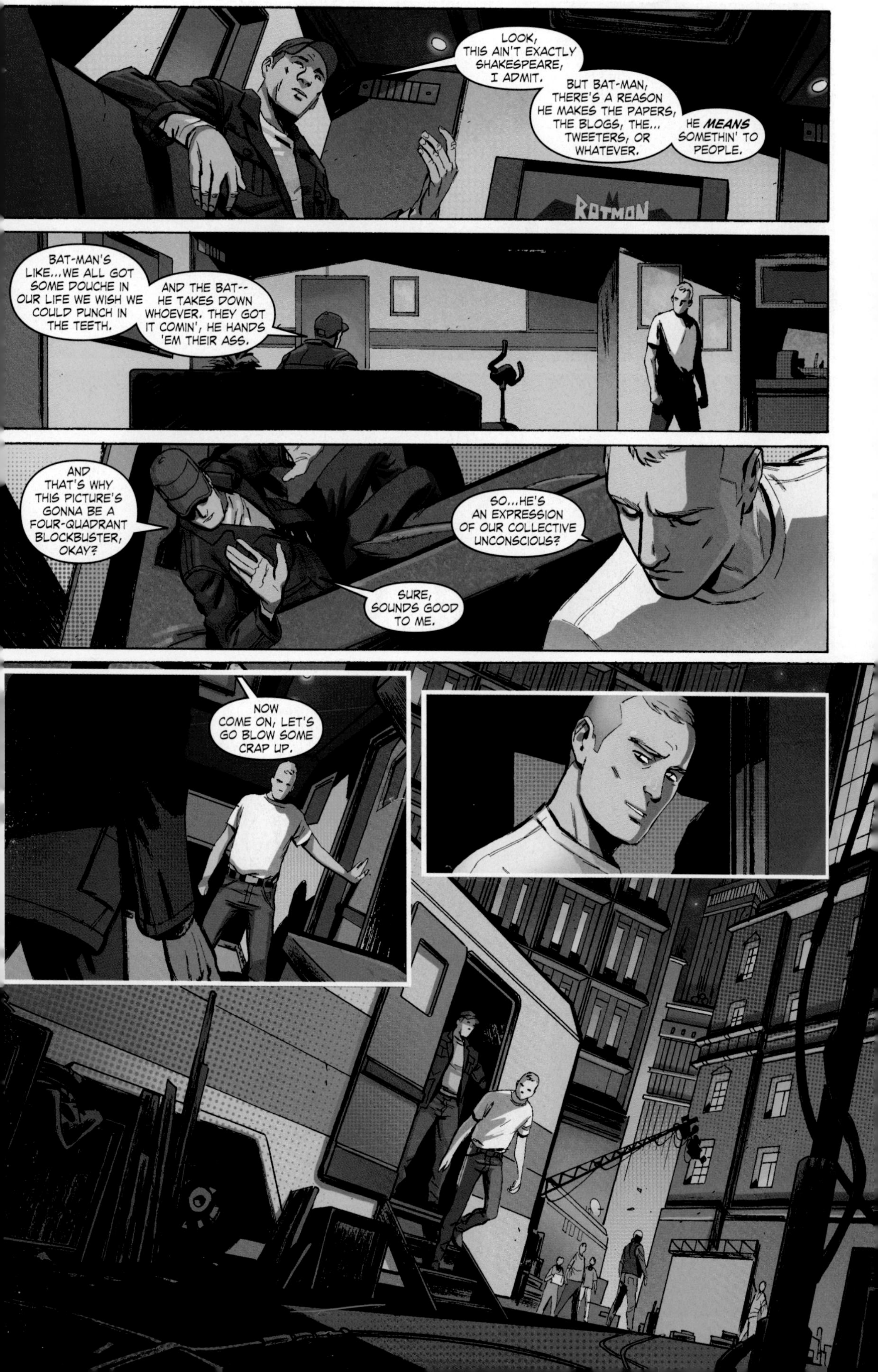
LOOK, THIS AIN'T EXACTLY SHAKESPEARE, I ADMIT.
BUT BAT-MAN, THERE'S A REASON HE MAKES THE PAPERS, THE BLOGS, THE... TWEETERS, OR WHATEVER.
HE **MEANS** SOMETHIN' TO PEOPLE.
BATMAN
BAT-MAN'S LIKE...WE ALL GOT SOME DOUCHE IN OUR LIFE WE WISH WE COULD PUNCH IN THE TEETH.
AND THE BAT-- HE TAKES DOWN WHOEVER. THEY GOT IT COMIN', HE HANDS 'EM THEIR ASS.
AND THAT'S WHY THIS PICTURE'S GONNA BE A FOUR-QUADRANT BLOCKBUSTER, OKAY?
SO...HE'S AN EXPRESSION OF OUR COLLECTIVE UNCONSCIOUS?
SURE, SOUNDS GOOD TO ME.
NOW COME ON, LET'S GO BLOW SOME CRAP UP.

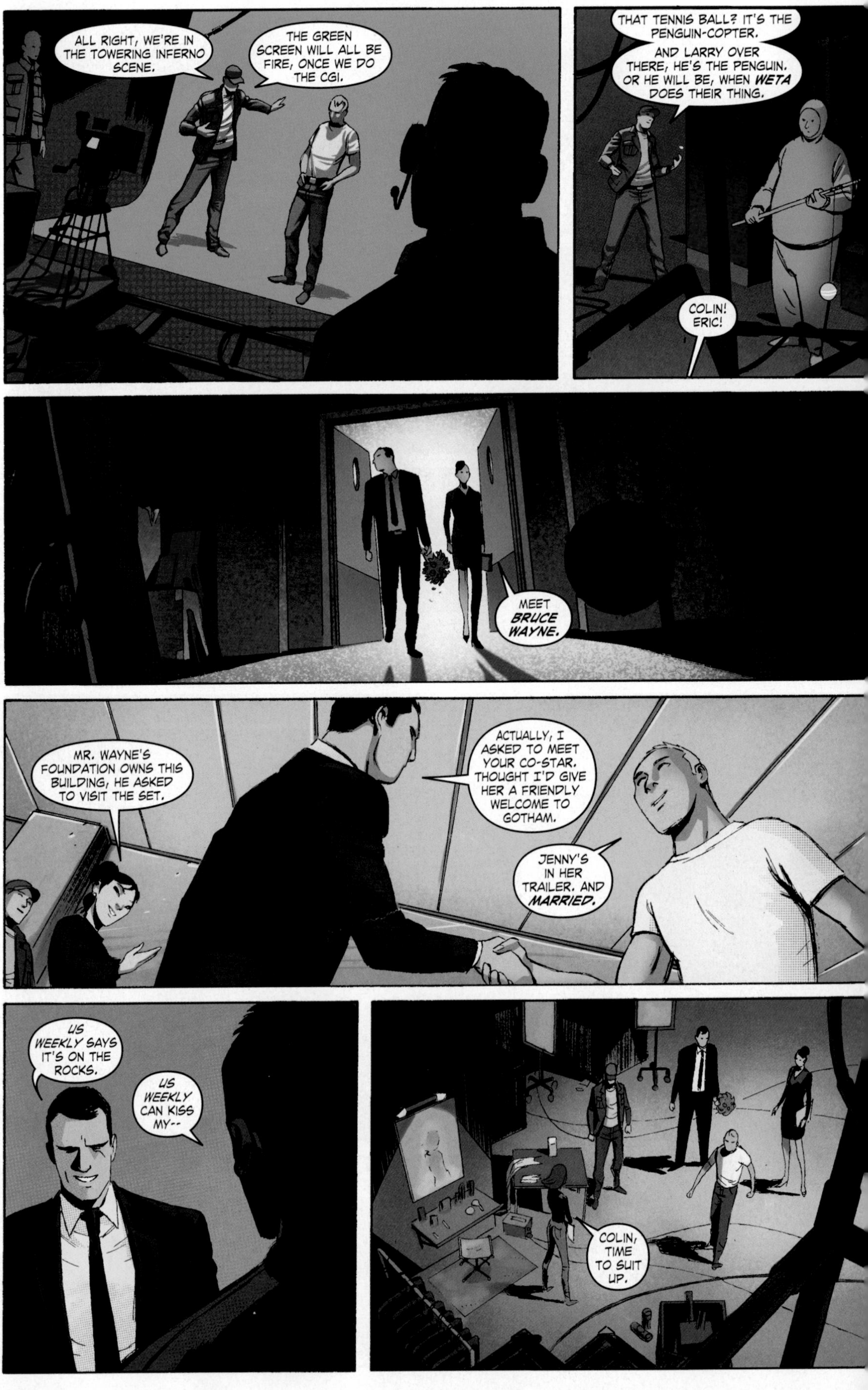
ALL RIGHT, WE'RE IN THE TOWERING INFERNO SCENE.
THE GREEN SCREEN WILL ALL BE FIRE, ONCE WE DO THE CGI.
THAT TENNIS BALL? IT'S THE PENGUIN-COPTER.
AND LARRY OVER THERE, HE'S THE PENGUIN. OR HE WILL BE, WHEN WETA DOES THEIR THING.
COLIN! ERIC!
MEET BRUCE WAYNE.
MR. WAYNE'S FOUNDATION OWNS THIS BUILDING, HE ASKED TO VISIT THE SET.
ACTUALLY, I ASKED TO MEET YOUR CO-STAR. THOUGHT I'D GIVE HER A FRIENDLY WELCOME TO GOTHAM.
JENNY'S IN HER TRAILER. AND MARRIED.
US WEEKLY SAYS IT'S ON THE ROCKS.
US WEEKLY CAN KISS MY--
COLIN, TIME TO SUIT UP.

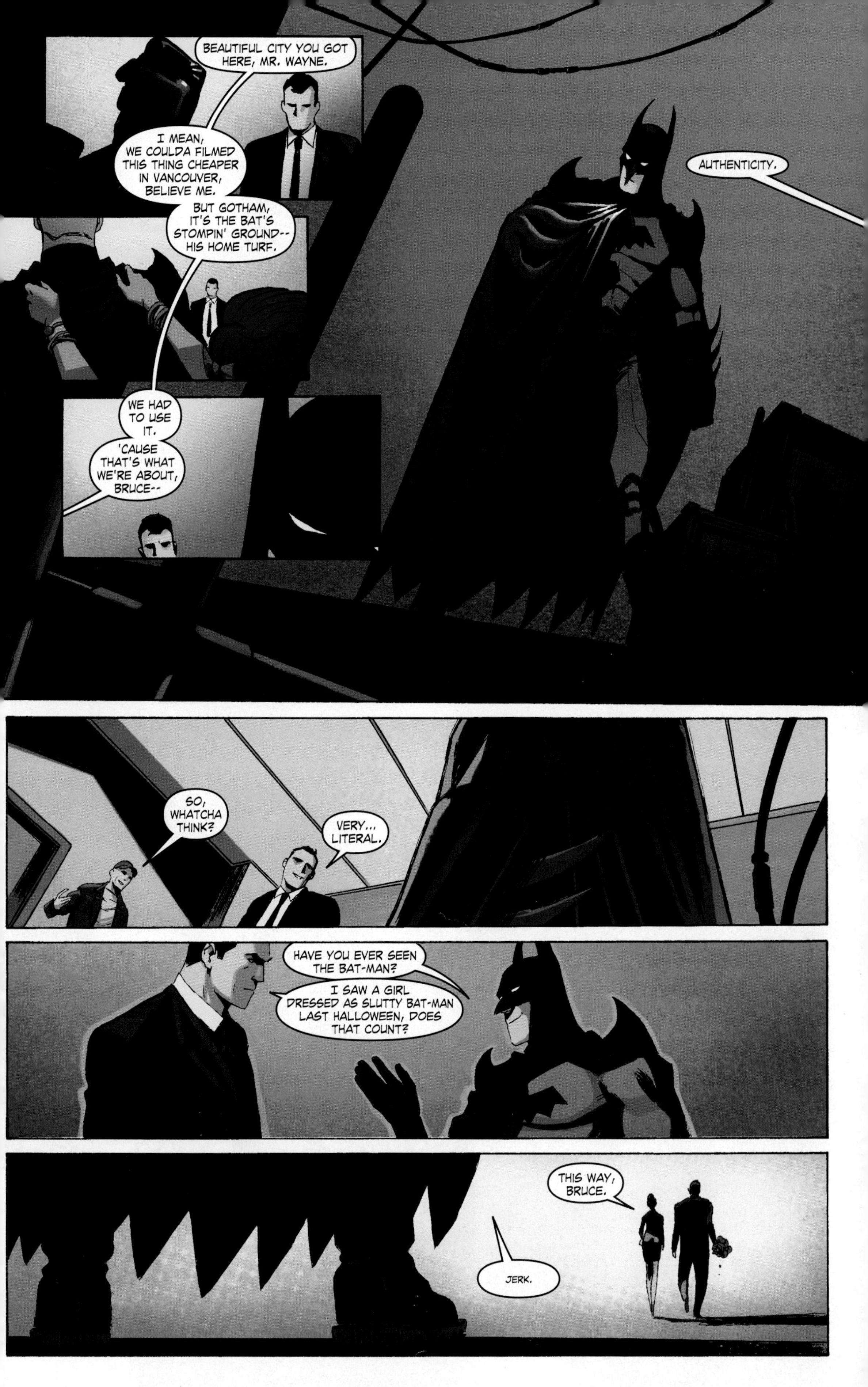
BEAUTIFUL CITY YOU GOT HERE, MR. WAYNE.
I MEAN, WE COULDA FILMED THIS THING CHEAPER IN VANCOUVER, BELIEVE ME.
BUT GOTHAM, IT'S THE BAT'S STOMPIN' GROUND-- HIS HOME TURF.
WE HAD TO USE IT.
'CAUSE THAT'S WHAT WE'RE ABOUT, BRUCE--
AUTHENTICITY.
SO, WHATCHA THINK?
VERY... LITERAL.
HAVE YOU EVER SEEN THE BAT-MAN?
I SAW A GIRL DRESSED AS SLUTTY BAT-MAN LAST HALLOWEEN, DOES THAT COUNT?
THIS WAY, BRUCE.
JERK.

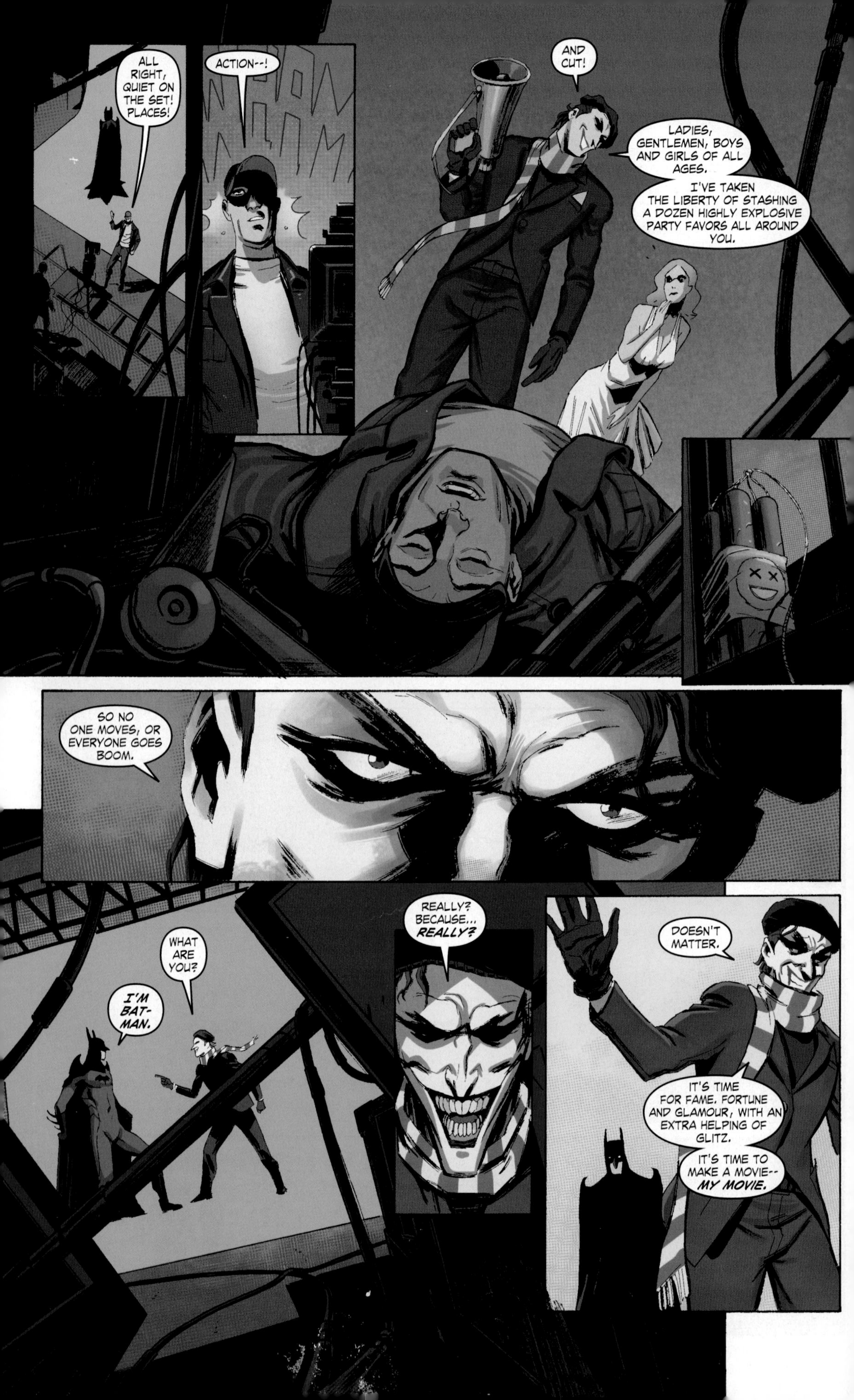
ALL RIGHT, QUIET ON THE SET! PLACES!
ACTION--!
AND CUT!
LADIES, GENTLEMEN, BOYS AND GIRLS OF ALL AGES.
I'VE TAKEN THE LIBERTY OF STASHING A DOZEN HIGHLY EXPLOSIVE PARTY FAVORS ALL AROUND YOU.
SO NO ONE MOVES, OR EVERYONE GOES BOOM.
WHAT ARE YOU?
I'M BAT-MAN.
REALLY? BECAUSE... REALLY?
DOESN'T MATTER.
IT'S TIME FOR FAME, FORTUNE AND GLAMOUR, WITH AN EXTRA HELPING OF GLITZ.
IT'S TIME TO MAKE A MOVIE-- MY MOVIE.

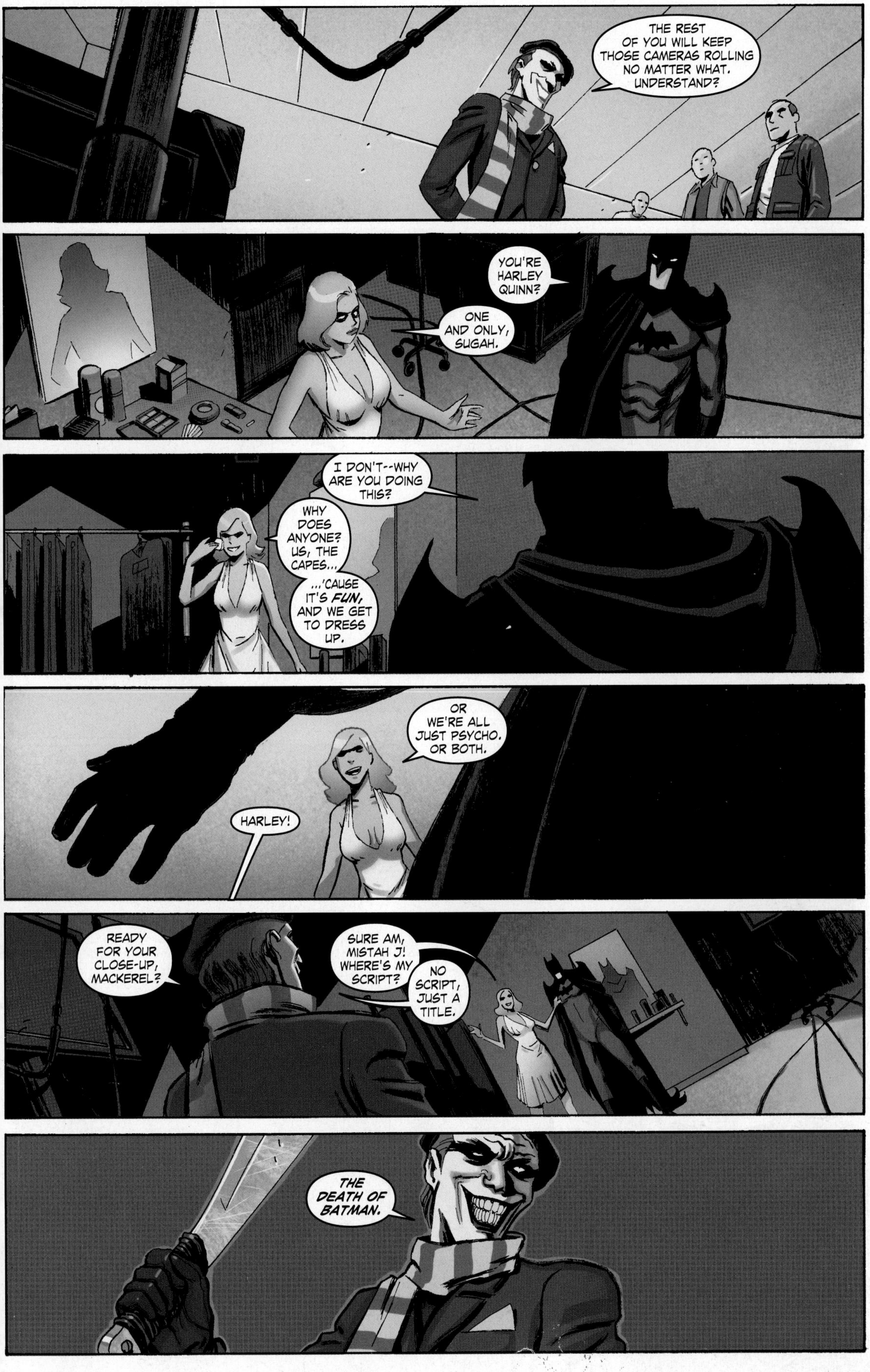
THE REST OF YOU WILL KEEP THOSE CAMERAS ROLLING NO MATTER WHAT. UNDERSTAND?
YOU'RE HARLEY QUINN?
ONE AND ONLY, SUGAH.
I DON'T--WHY ARE YOU DOING THIS?
WHY DOES ANYONE? US, THE CAPES...
...'CAUSE IT'S *FUN,* AND WE GET TO DRESS UP.
OR WE'RE ALL JUST PSYCHO. OR BOTH.
HARLEY!
READY FOR YOUR CLOSE-UP, MACKEREL?
SURE AM, MISTAH J! WHERE'S MY SCRIPT?
NO SCRIPT, JUST A TITLE.
THE DEATH OF BATMAN.

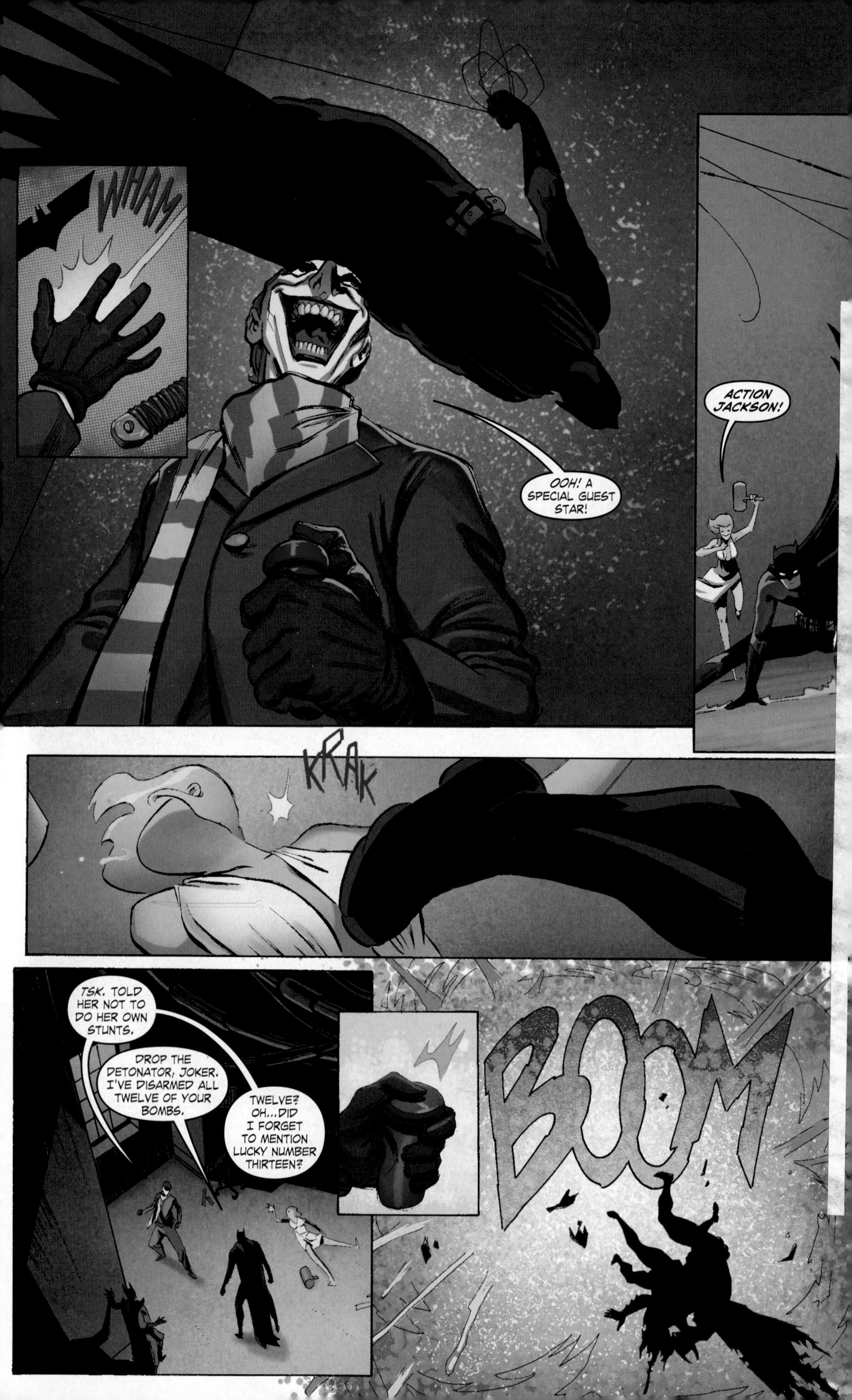
WHAM
OOH! A SPECIAL GUEST STAR!
ACTION JACKSON!
KRAK
TSK. TOLD HER NOT TO DO HER OWN STUNTS.
DROP THE DETONATOR, JOKER. I'VE DISARMED ALL TWELVE OF YOUR BOMBS.
TWELVE? OH...DID I FORGET TO MENTION LUCKY NUMBER THIRTEEN?
BOOM

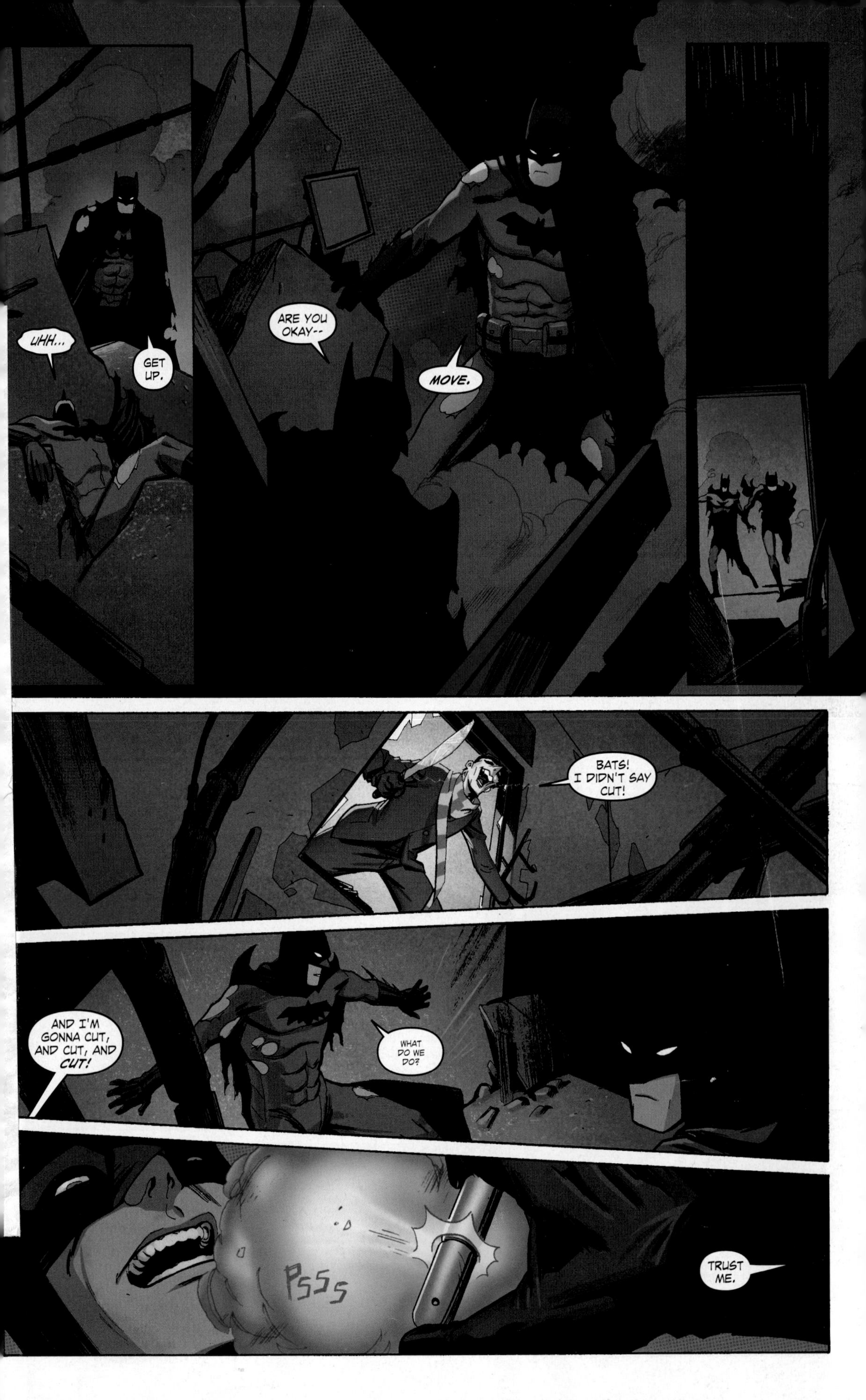
UHH...
GET UP.
ARE YOU OKAY--
MOVE.
BATS! I DIDN'T SAY CUT!
AND I'M GONNA CUT, AND CUT, AND CUT!
WHAT DO WE DO?
PSSS
TRUST ME.

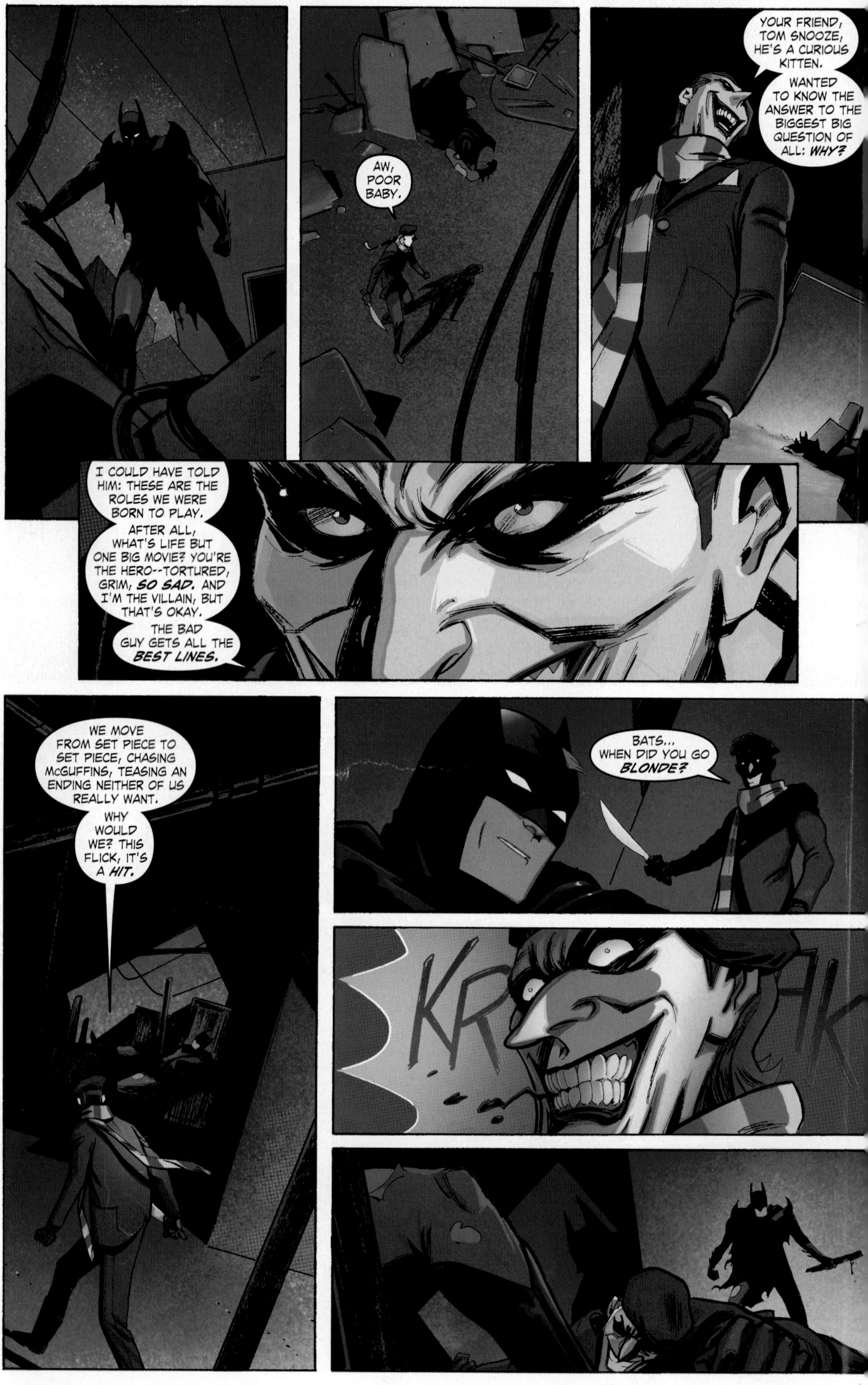
AW, POOR BABY.
YOUR FRIEND, TOM SNOOZE, HE'S A CURIOUS KITTEN.
WANTED TO KNOW THE ANSWER TO THE BIGGEST BIG QUESTION OF ALL: WHY?
I COULD HAVE TOLD HIM: THESE ARE THE ROLES WE WERE BORN TO PLAY.
AFTER ALL, WHAT'S LIFE BUT ONE BIG MOVIE? YOU'RE THE HERO--TORTURED, GRIM, SO SAD. AND I'M THE VILLAIN, BUT THAT'S OKAY.
THE BAD GUY GETS ALL THE BEST LINES.
WE MOVE FROM SET PIECE TO SET PIECE, CHASING McGUFFINS, TEASING AN ENDING NEITHER OF US REALLY WANT.
WHY WOULD WE? THIS FLICK, IT'S A HIT.
BATS... WHEN DID YOU GO BLONDE?
KRAK

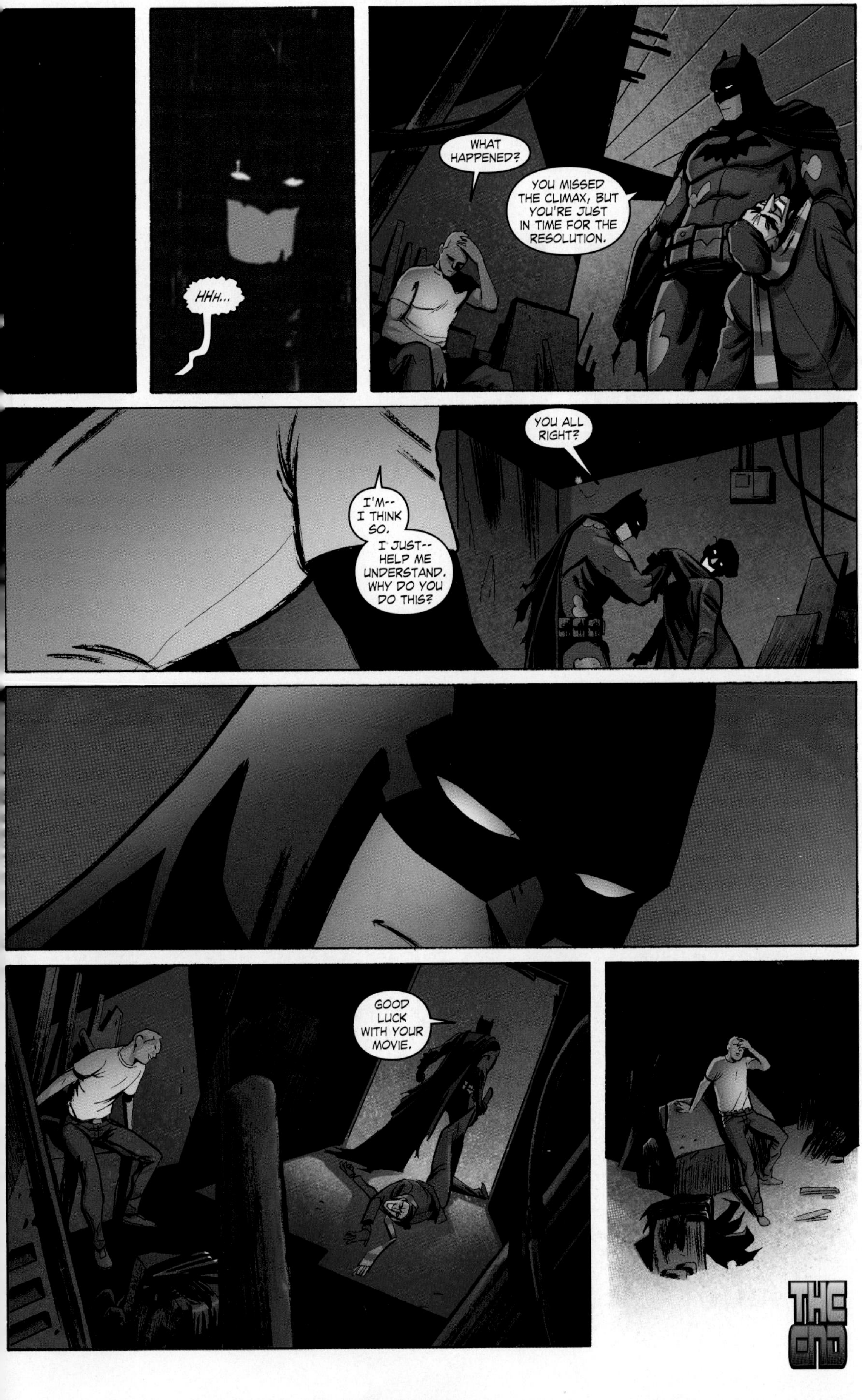
HHH...
WHAT HAPPENED?
YOU MISSED THE CLIMAX, BUT YOU'RE JUST IN TIME FOR THE RESOLUTION.
YOU ALL RIGHT?
I'M-- I THINK SO.
I JUST-- HELP ME UNDERSTAND. WHY DO YOU DO THIS?
GOOD LUCK WITH YOUR MOVIE.
THE END

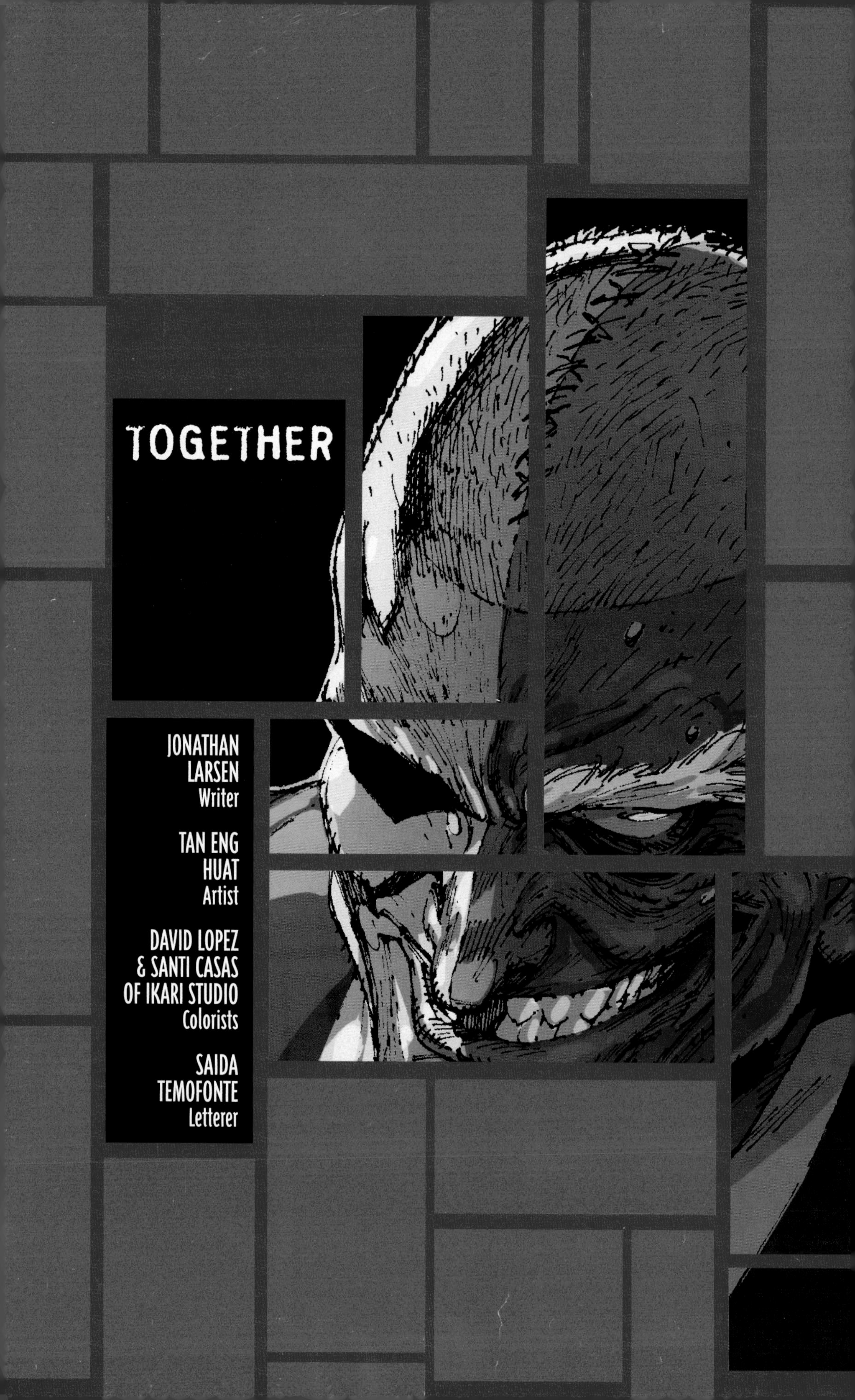
TOGETHER
JONATHAN LARSEN Writer
TAN ENG HUAT Artist
DAVID LOPEZ & SANTI CASAS OF IKARI STUDIO Colorists
SAIDA TEMOFONTE Letterer

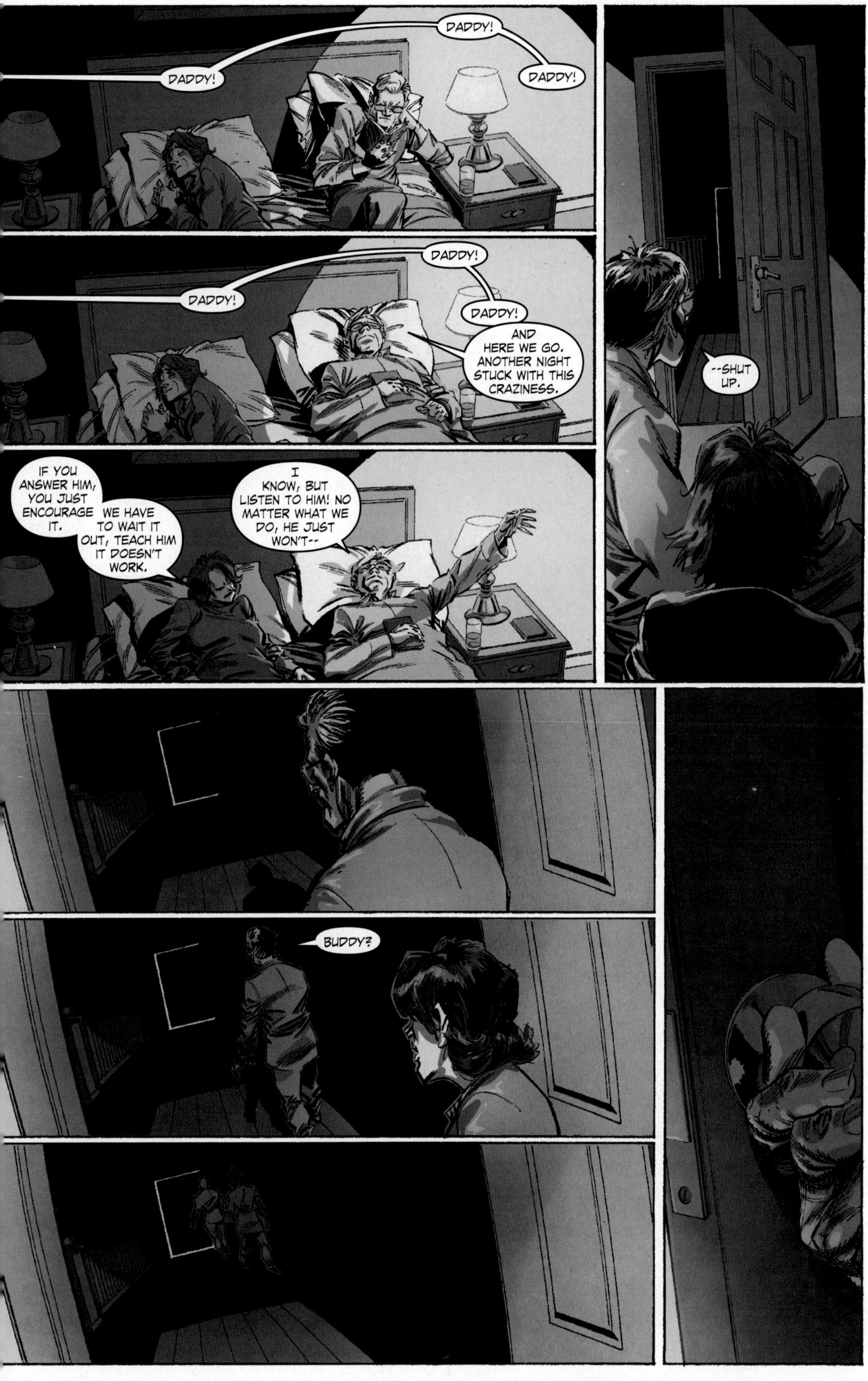
DADDY!
DADDY!
DADDY!
DADDY!
DADDY!
DADDY!
AND HERE WE GO. ANOTHER NIGHT STUCK WITH THIS CRAZINESS.
IF YOU ANSWER HIM, YOU JUST ENCOURAGE IT.
WE HAVE TO WAIT IT OUT, TEACH HIM IT DOESN'T WORK.
I KNOW, BUT LISTEN TO HIM! NO MATTER WHAT WE DO, HE JUST WON'T--
--SHUT UP.
BUDDY?

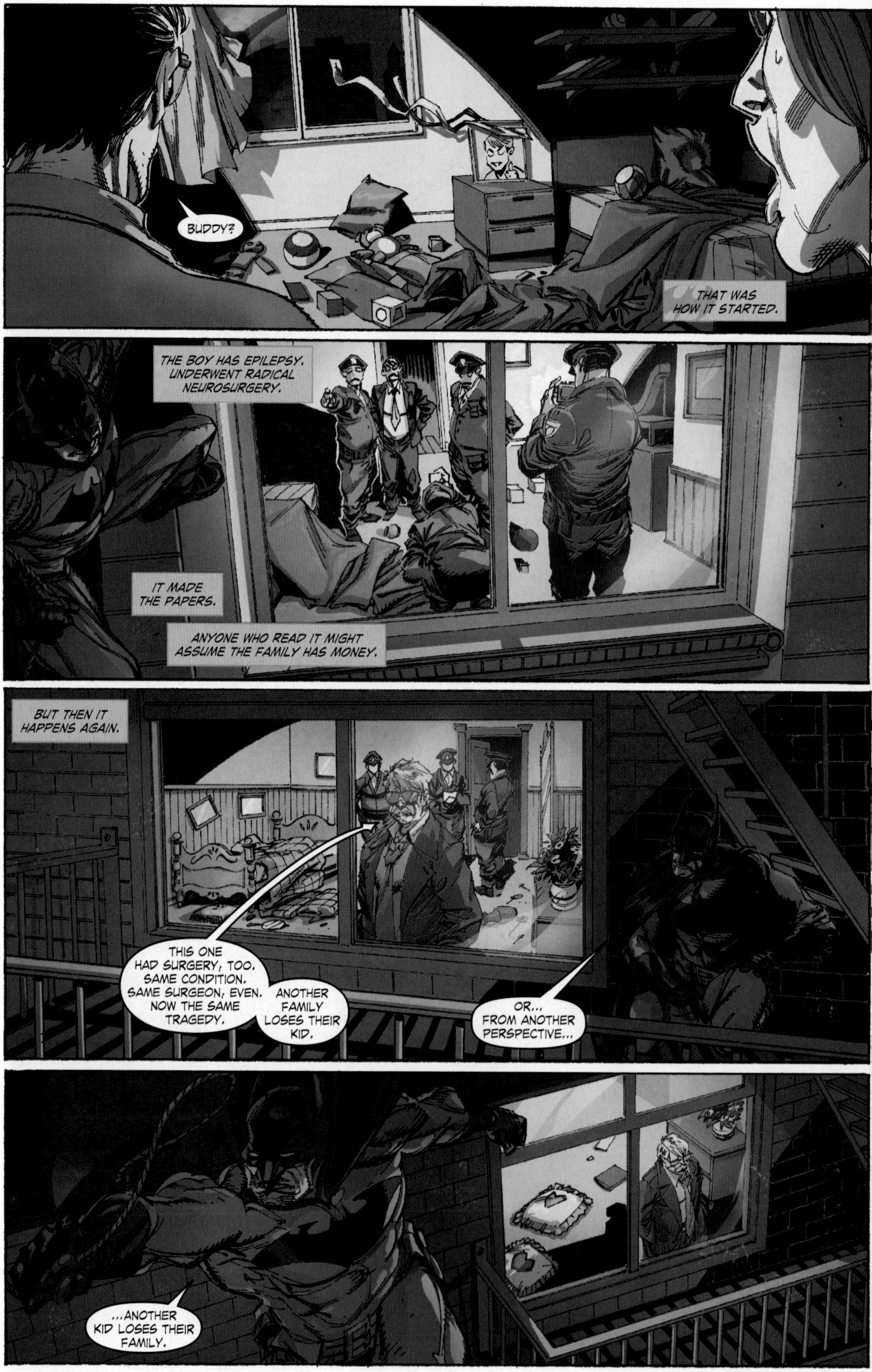
BUDDY?
THAT WAS HOW IT STARTED.
THE BOY HAS EPILEPSY. UNDERWENT RADICAL NEUROSURGERY.
IT MADE THE PAPERS.
ANYONE WHO READ IT MIGHT ASSUME THE FAMILY HAS MONEY.
BUT THEN IT HAPPENS AGAIN.
THIS ONE HAD SURGERY, TOO. SAME CONDITION. SAME SURGEON, EVEN. NOW THE SAME TRAGEDY.
ANOTHER FAMILY LOSES THEIR KID.
OR... FROM ANOTHER PERSPECTIVE...
...ANOTHER KID LOSES THEIR FAMILY.

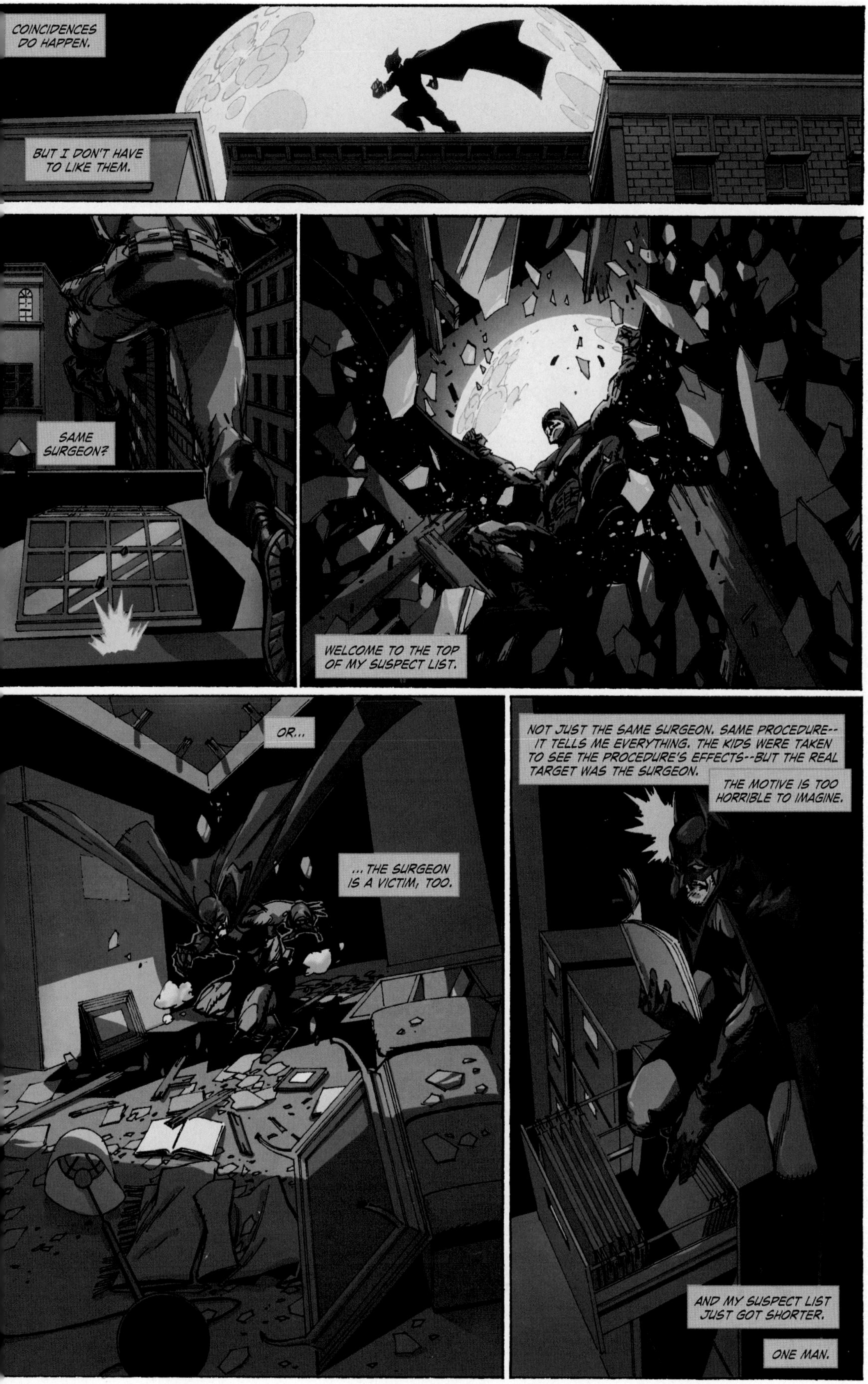
COINCIDENCES DO HAPPEN.
BUT I DON'T HAVE TO LIKE THEM.
SAME SURGEON?
WELCOME TO THE TOP OF MY SUSPECT LIST.
OR...
...THE SURGEON IS A VICTIM, TOO.
NOT JUST THE SAME SURGEON. SAME PROCEDURE-- IT TELLS ME EVERYTHING. THE KIDS WERE TAKEN TO SEE THE PROCEDURE'S EFFECTS--BUT THE REAL TARGET WAS THE SURGEON.
THE MOTIVE IS TOO HORRIBLE TO IMAGINE.
AND MY SUSPECT LIST JUST GOT SHORTER.
ONE MAN.

I HAVE TO STOP HIM.

AERIAL RECON OF THE SURGEON'S PRIVATE CLINIC TELLS ME HOW TWISTED HE IS NOW--HOW MUCH SICKER.

IT'S HIS LOOKOUT. THIS SHOULD BE UNTHINKABLE FOR HIM...

JUST ONE MAN.

THIS TIME THERE'S NO COMING BACK. IF HE GETS AWAY WITH IT.

IF I'M TOO SLOW.

DON'T DO IT. PLEASE.

DON'T LET HIM DO THIS TO YOU.

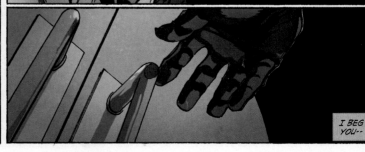

I BEG YOU--

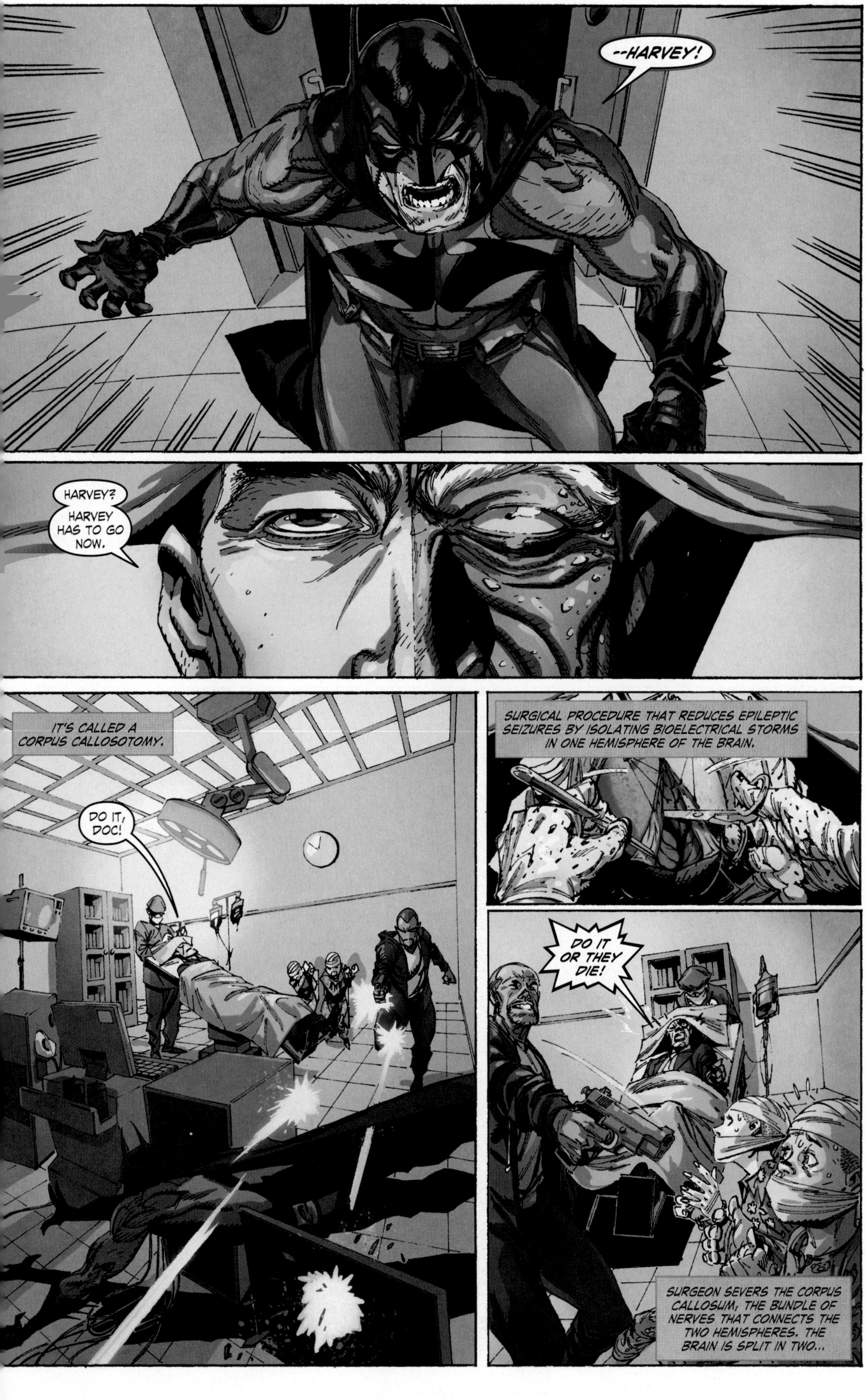
--HARVEY!
HARVEY? HARVEY HAS TO GO NOW.
IT'S CALLED A CORPUS CALLOSOTOMY.
DO IT, DOC!
SURGICAL PROCEDURE THAT REDUCES EPILEPTIC SEIZURES BY ISOLATING BIOELECTRICAL STORMS IN ONE HEMISPHERE OF THE BRAIN.
DO IT OR THEY DIE!
SURGEON SEVERS THE CORPUS CALLOSUM, THE BUNDLE OF NERVES THAT CONNECTS THE TWO HEMISPHERES. THE BRAIN IS SPLIT IN TWO...

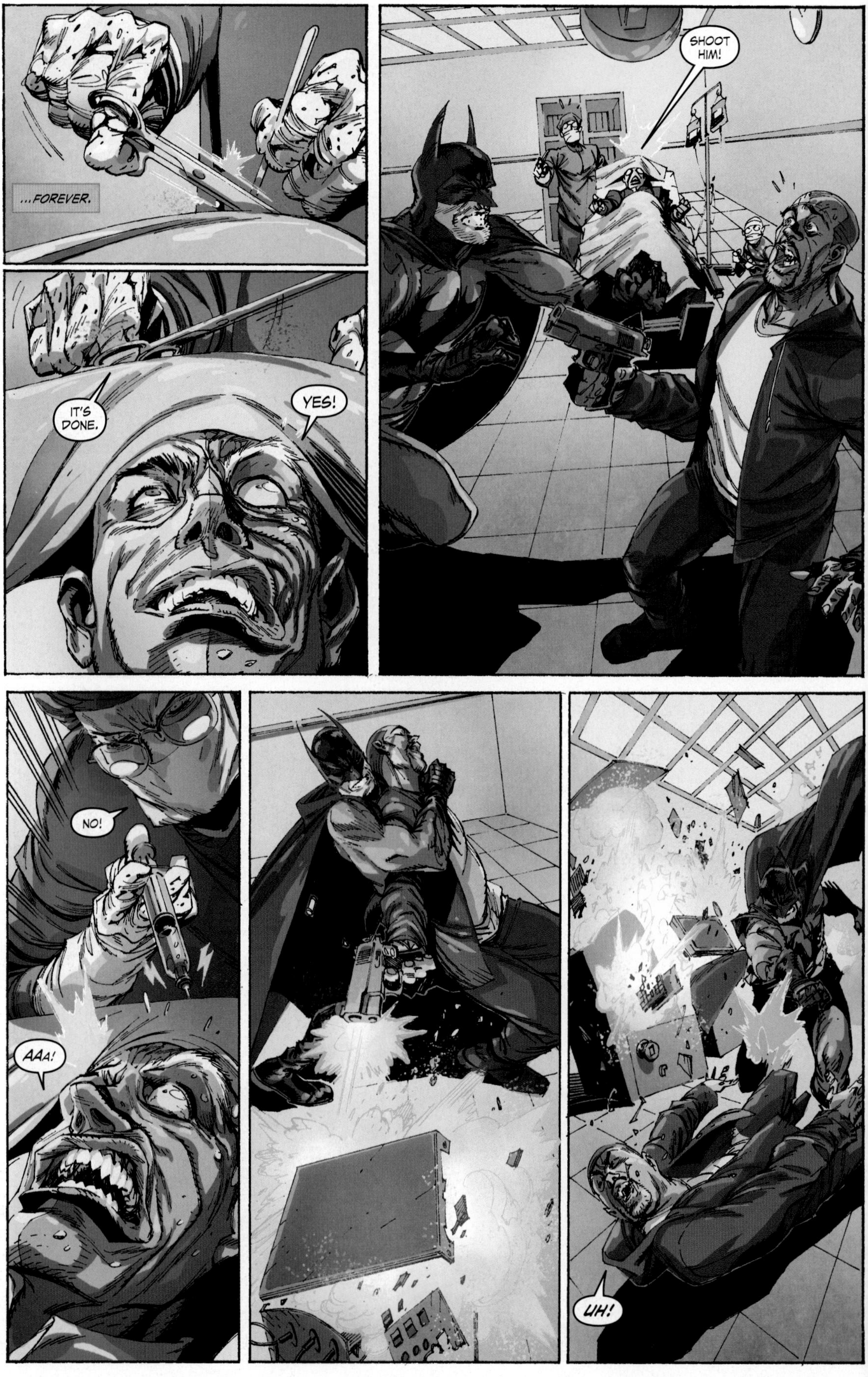
...FOREVER.
IT'S DONE.
YES!
SHOOT HIM!
NO!
AAA!
UH!

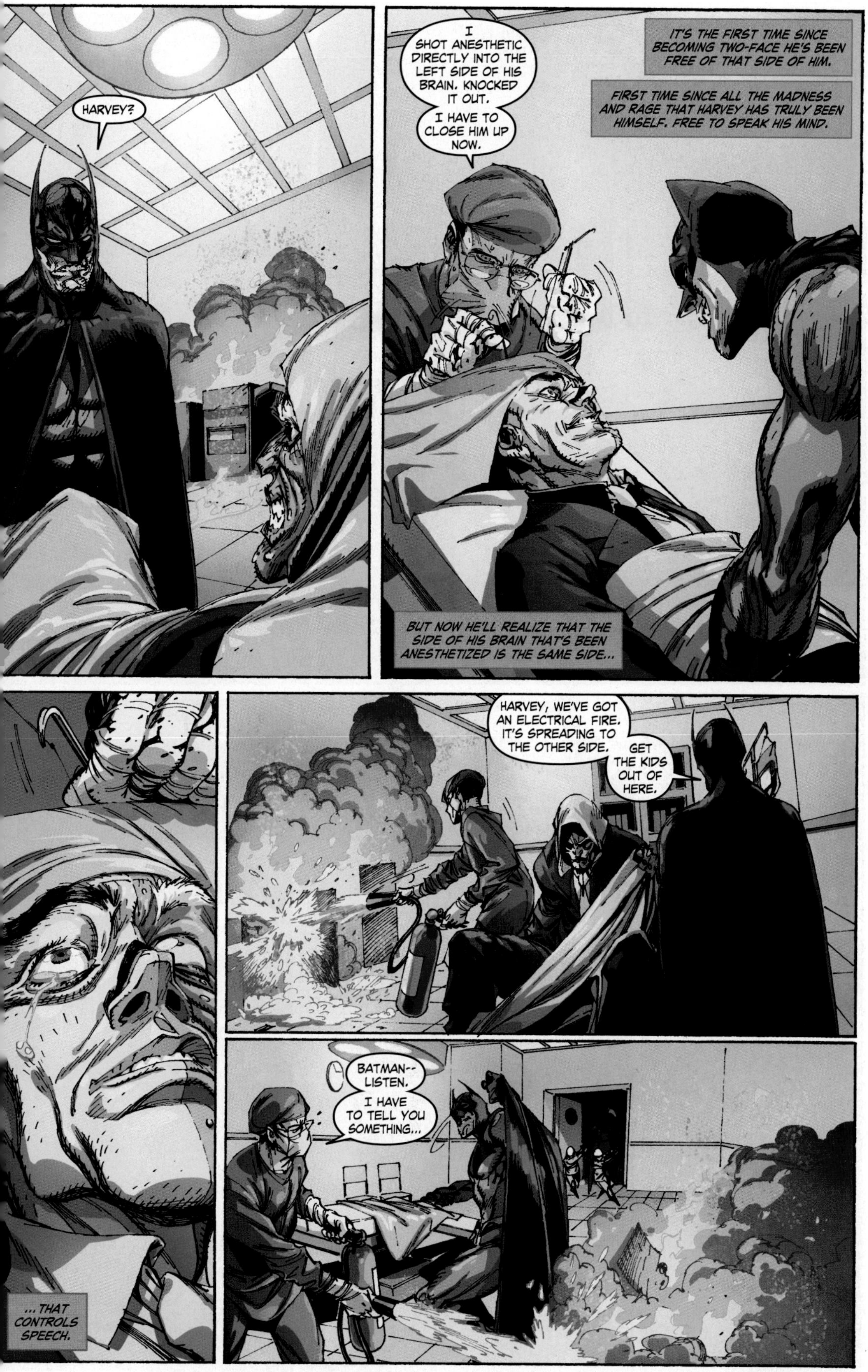
HARVEY?
I SHOT ANESTHETIC DIRECTLY INTO THE LEFT SIDE OF HIS BRAIN. KNOCKED IT OUT.
I HAVE TO CLOSE HIM UP NOW.
IT'S THE FIRST TIME SINCE BECOMING TWO-FACE HE'S BEEN FREE OF THAT SIDE OF HIM.
FIRST TIME SINCE ALL THE MADNESS AND RAGE THAT HARVEY HAS TRULY BEEN HIMSELF. FREE TO SPEAK HIS MIND.
BUT NOW HE'LL REALIZE THAT THE SIDE OF HIS BRAIN THAT'S BEEN ANESTHETIZED IS THE SAME SIDE...
...THAT CONTROLS SPEECH.
HARVEY, WE'VE GOT AN ELECTRICAL FIRE. IT'S SPREADING TO THE OTHER SIDE.
GET THE KIDS OUT OF HERE.
BATMAN-- LISTEN.
I HAVE TO TELL YOU SOMETHING...

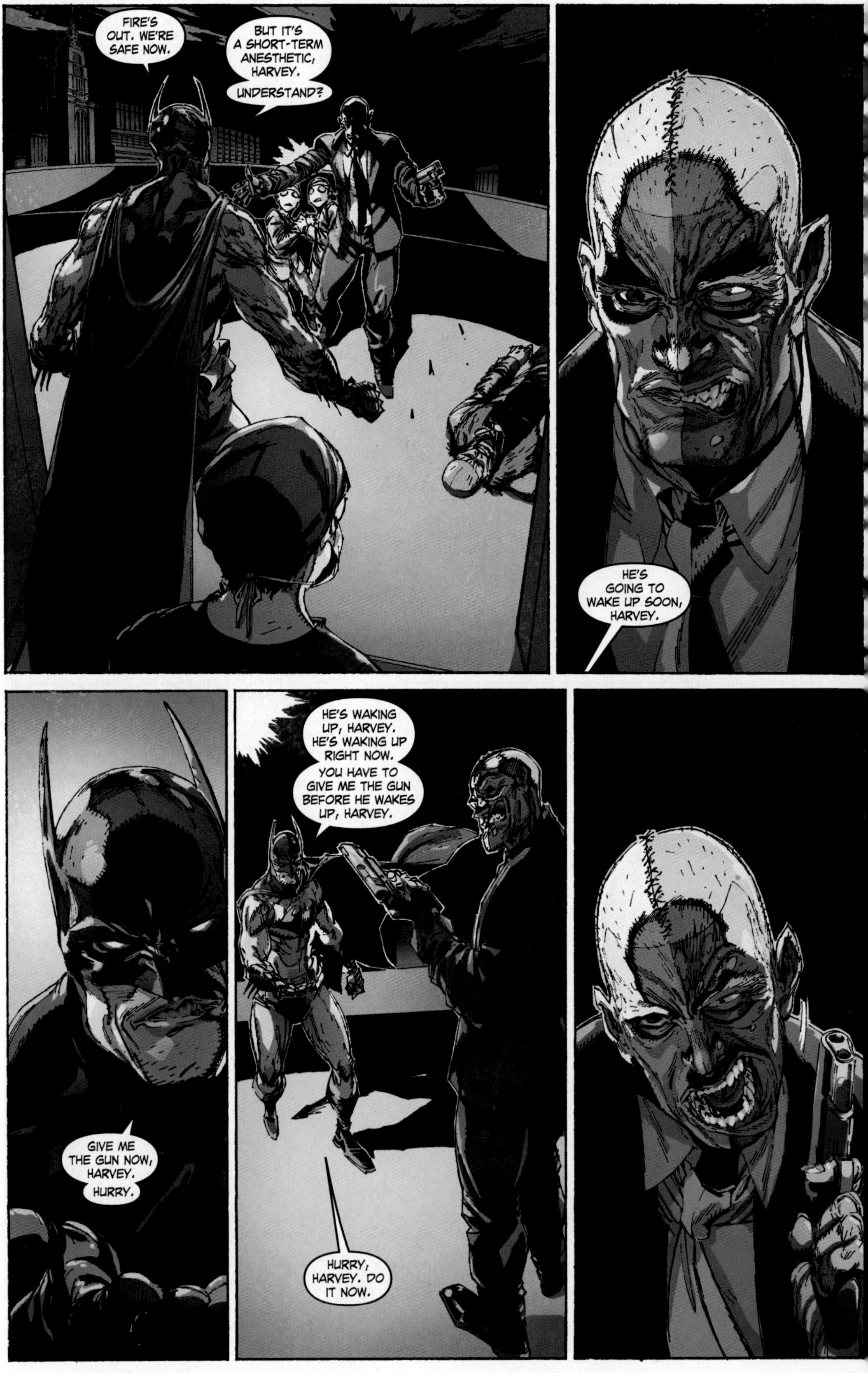
FIRE'S OUT. WE'RE SAFE NOW.
BUT IT'S A SHORT-TERM ANESTHETIC, HARVEY.
UNDERSTAND?
HE'S GOING TO WAKE UP SOON, HARVEY.
GIVE ME THE GUN NOW, HARVEY.
HURRY.
HE'S WAKING UP, HARVEY. HE'S WAKING UP RIGHT NOW.
YOU HAVE TO GIVE ME THE GUN BEFORE HE WAKES UP, HARVEY.
HURRY, HARVEY. DO IT NOW.

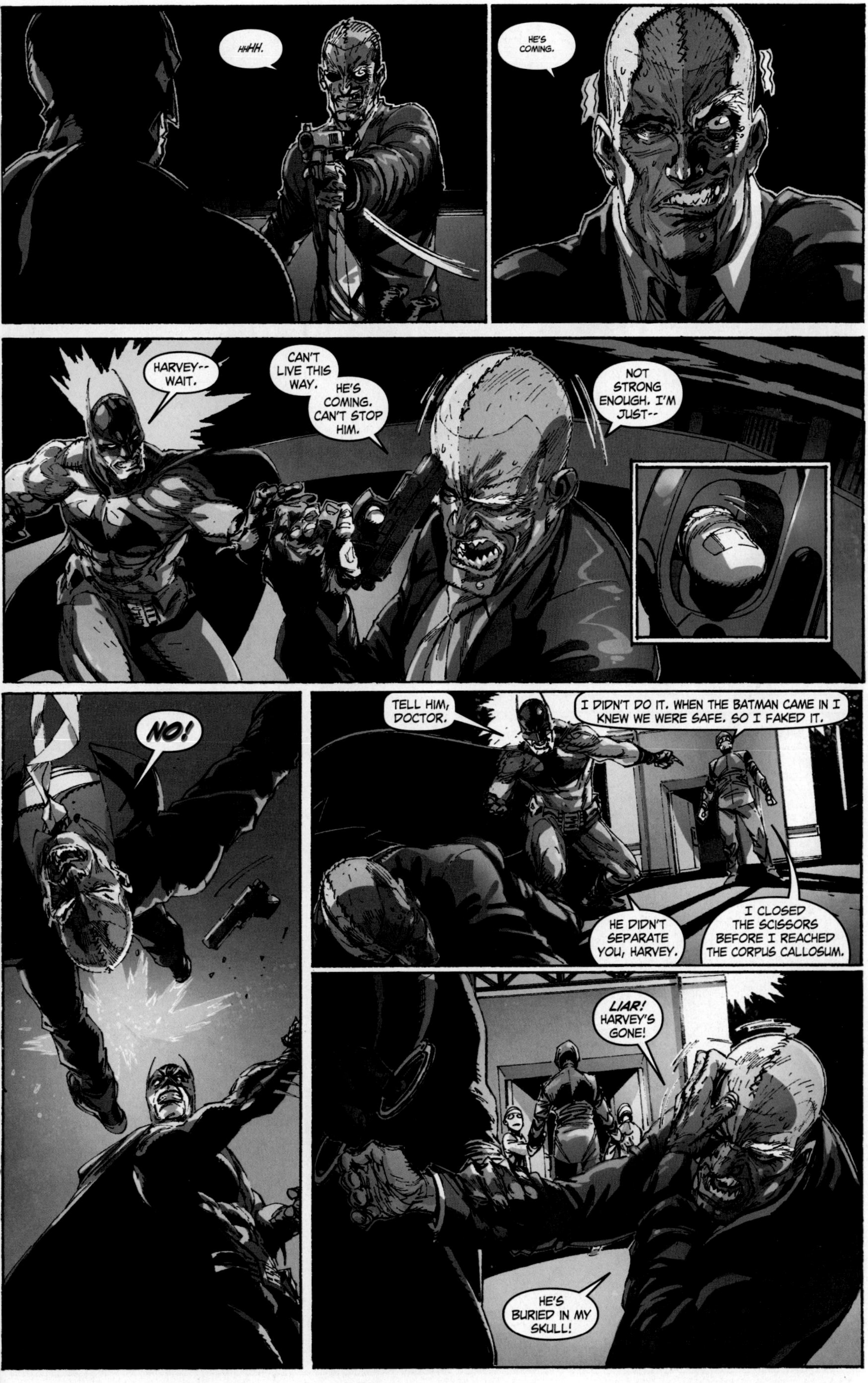
HHHH.
HE'S COMING.
HARVEY-- WAIT.
CAN'T LIVE THIS WAY.
HE'S COMING. CAN'T STOP HIM.
NOT STRONG ENOUGH. I'M JUST--
NO!
TELL HIM, DOCTOR.
I DIDN'T DO IT. WHEN THE BATMAN CAME IN I KNEW WE WERE SAFE. SO I FAKED IT.
HE DIDN'T SEPARATE YOU, HARVEY.
I CLOSED THE SCISSORS BEFORE I REACHED THE CORPUS CALLOSUM.
LIAR! HARVEY'S GONE!
HE'S BURIED IN MY SKULL!

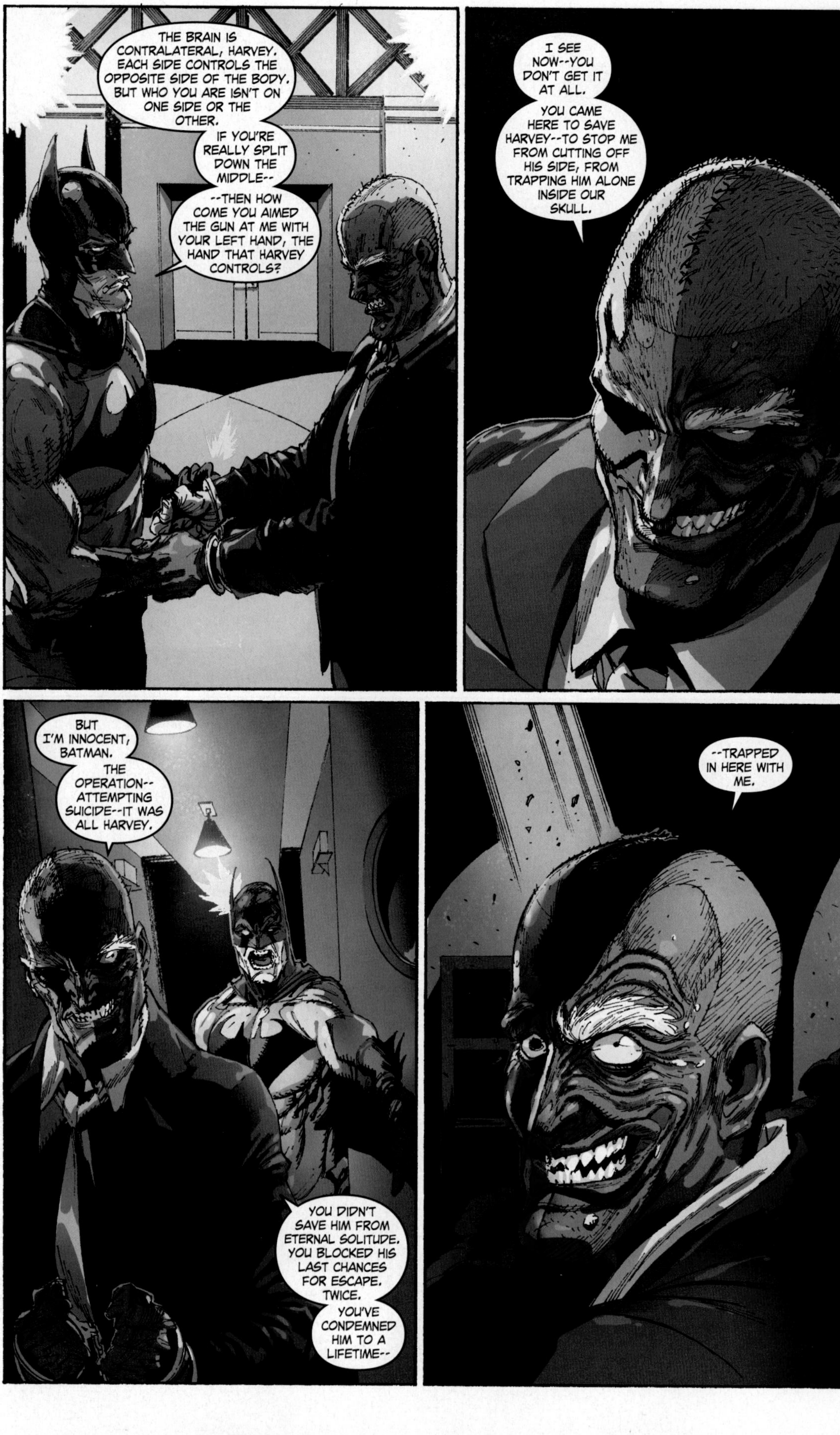
THE BRAIN IS CONTRALATERAL, HARVEY. EACH SIDE CONTROLS THE OPPOSITE SIDE OF THE BODY. BUT WHO YOU ARE ISN'T ON ONE SIDE OR THE OTHER.
IF YOU'RE REALLY SPLIT DOWN THE MIDDLE--
--THEN HOW COME YOU AIMED THE GUN AT ME WITH YOUR LEFT HAND, THE HAND THAT HARVEY CONTROLS?
I SEE NOW--YOU DON'T GET IT AT ALL.
YOU CAME HERE TO SAVE HARVEY--TO STOP ME FROM CUTTING OFF HIS SIDE, FROM TRAPPING HIM ALONE INSIDE OUR SKULL.
BUT I'M INNOCENT, BATMAN.
THE OPERATION--ATTEMPTING SUICIDE--IT WAS ALL HARVEY.
YOU DIDN'T SAVE HIM FROM ETERNAL SOLITUDE. YOU BLOCKED HIS LAST CHANCES FOR ESCAPE. TWICE.
YOU'VE CONDEMNED HIM TO A LIFETIME--
--TRAPPED IN HERE WITH ME.

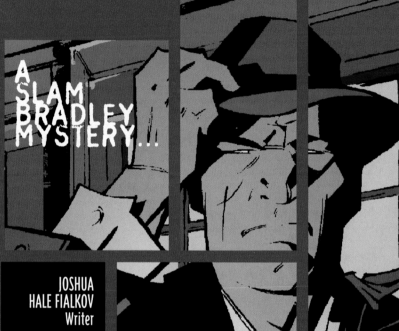

A SLAM
BRADLEY
MYSTERY...

JOSHUA
HALE FIALKOV
Writer

PHIL
HESTER
Penciller

ERIC
GAPSTUR
Inker

JIM
CHARALAMPIDIS
Colorist

SAIDA
TEMOFONTE
Letterer

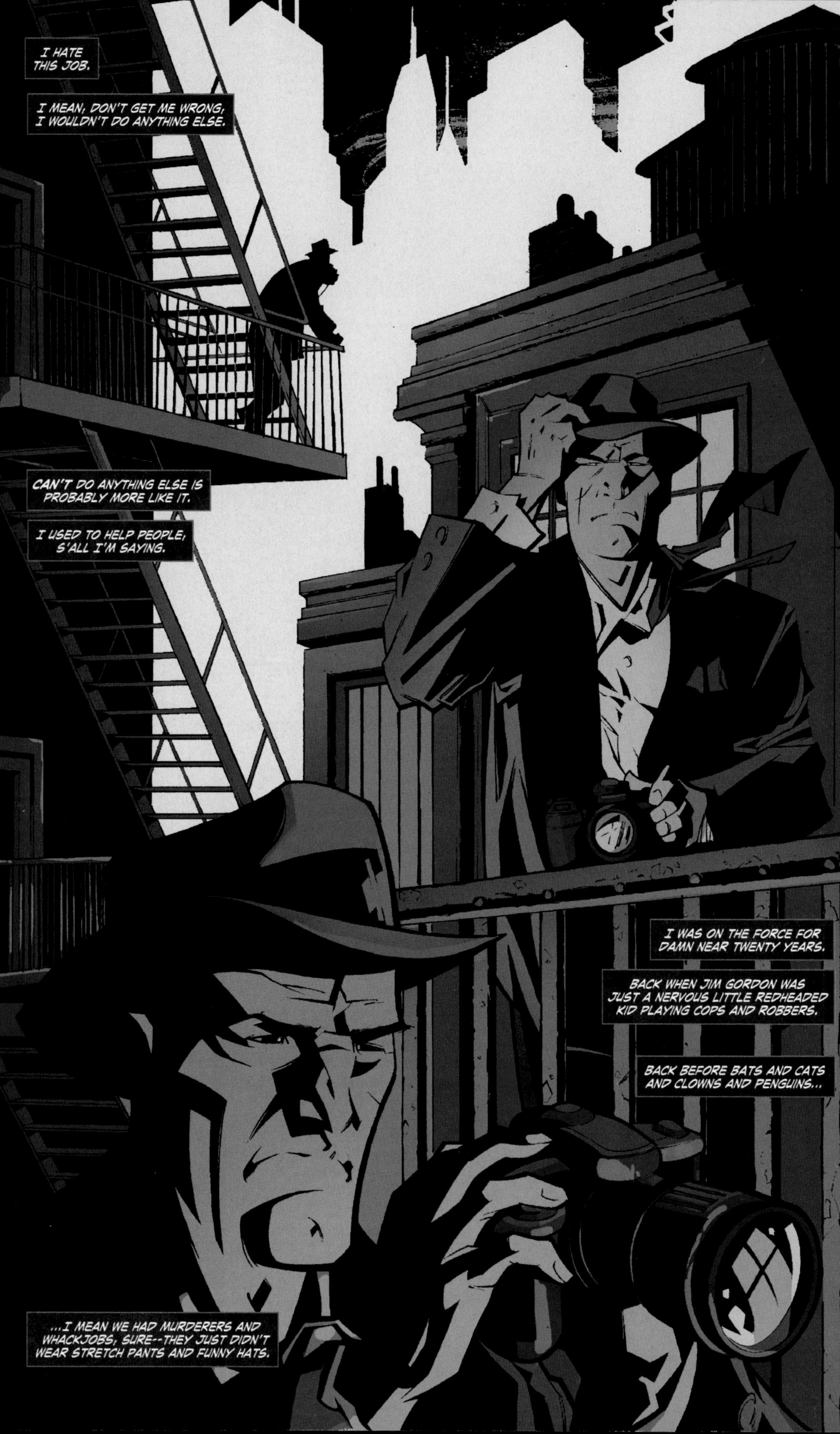
I HATE THIS JOB.
I MEAN, DON'T GET ME WRONG, I WOULDN'T DO ANYTHING ELSE.
CAN'T DO ANYTHING ELSE IS PROBABLY MORE LIKE IT.
I USED TO HELP PEOPLE, S'ALL I'M SAYING.
I WAS ON THE FORCE FOR DAMN NEAR TWENTY YEARS.
BACK WHEN JIM GORDON WAS JUST A NERVOUS LITTLE REDHEADED KID PLAYING COPS AND ROBBERS.
BACK BEFORE BATS AND CATS AND CLOWNS AND PENGUINS...
...I MEAN WE HAD MURDERERS AND WHACKJOBS, SURE--THEY JUST DIDN'T WEAR STRETCH PANTS AND FUNNY HATS.

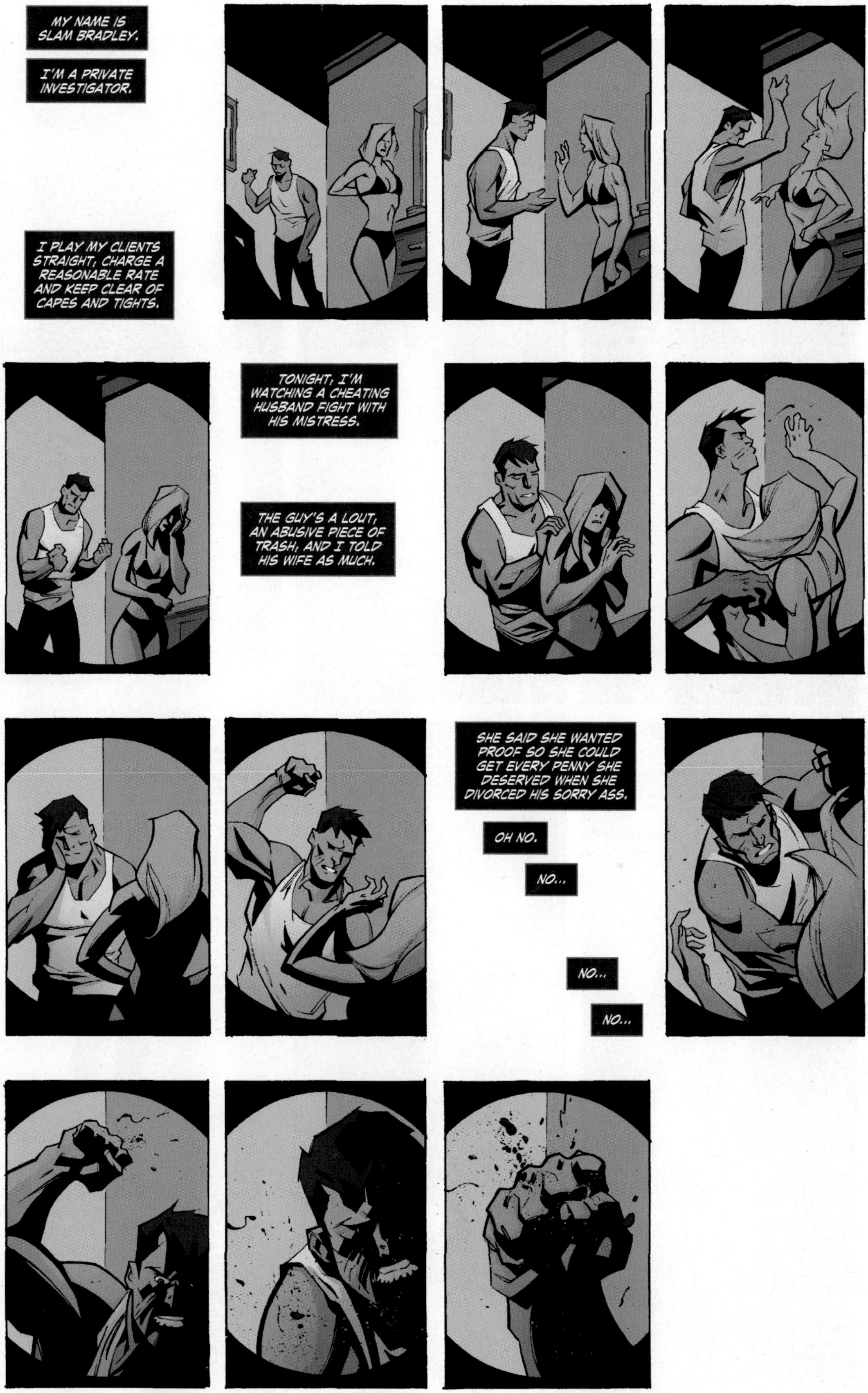
MY NAME IS SLAM BRADLEY.
I'M A PRIVATE INVESTIGATOR.
I PLAY MY CLIENTS STRAIGHT, CHARGE A REASONABLE RATE AND KEEP CLEAR OF CAPES AND TIGHTS.
TONIGHT, I'M WATCHING A CHEATING HUSBAND FIGHT WITH HIS MISTRESS.
THE GUY'S A LOUT, AN ABUSIVE PIECE OF TRASH, AND I TOLD HIS WIFE AS MUCH.
SHE SAID SHE WANTED PROOF SO SHE COULD GET EVERY PENNY SHE DESERVED WHEN SHE DIVORCED HIS SORRY ASS.
OH NO.
NO...
NO...
NO...

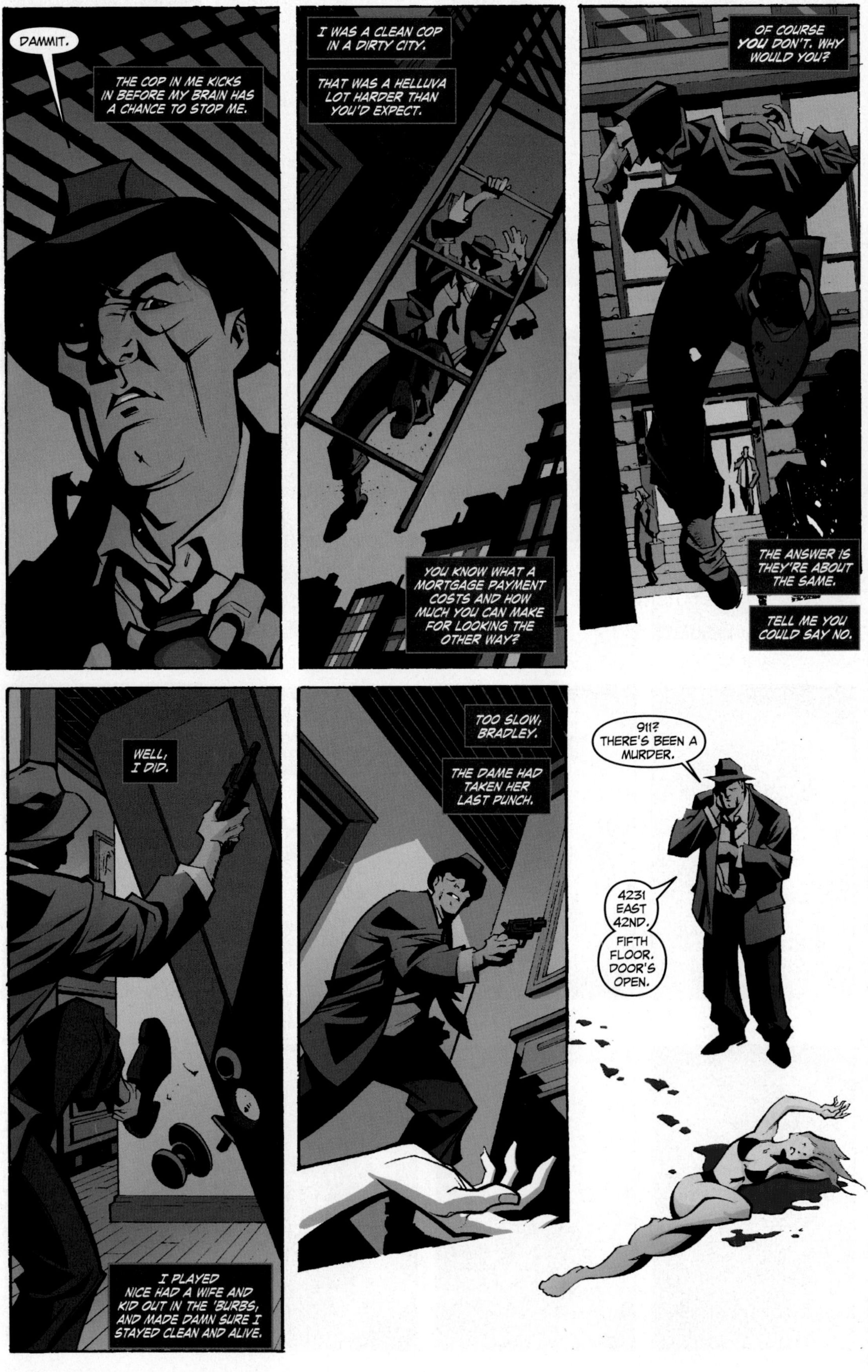
DAMMIT.
THE COP IN ME KICKS IN BEFORE MY BRAIN HAS A CHANCE TO STOP ME.
I WAS A CLEAN COP IN A DIRTY CITY.
THAT WAS A HELLUVA LOT HARDER THAN YOU'D EXPECT.
YOU KNOW WHAT A MORTGAGE PAYMENT COSTS AND HOW MUCH YOU CAN MAKE FOR LOOKING THE OTHER WAY?
OF COURSE YOU DON'T. WHY WOULD YOU?
THE ANSWER IS THEY'RE ABOUT THE SAME.
TELL ME YOU COULD SAY NO.
WELL, I DID.
I PLAYED NICE HAD A WIFE AND KID OUT IN THE 'BURBS, AND MADE DAMN SURE I STAYED CLEAN AND ALIVE.
TOO SLOW, BRADLEY.
THE DAME HAD TAKEN HER LAST PUNCH.
911? THERE'S BEEN A MURDER.
4231 EAST 42ND.
FIFTH FLOOR. DOOR'S OPEN.

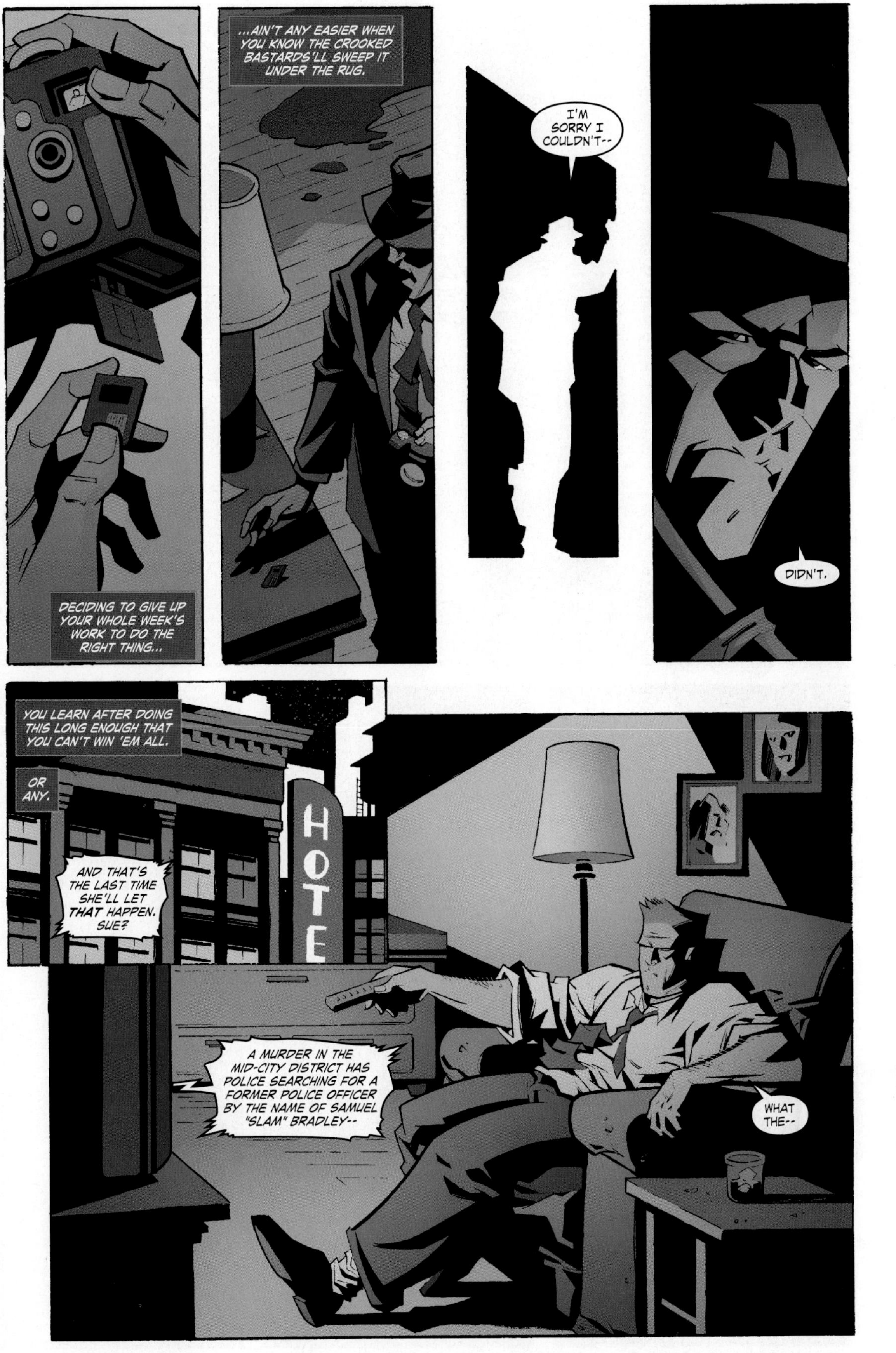

DECIDING TO GIVE UP YOUR WHOLE WEEK'S WORK TO DO THE RIGHT THING...
...AIN'T ANY EASIER WHEN YOU KNOW THE CROOKED BASTARDS'LL SWEEP IT UNDER THE RUG.
I'M SORRY I COULDN'T--
DIDN'T.
YOU LEARN AFTER DOING THIS LONG ENOUGH THAT YOU CAN'T WIN 'EM ALL.
OR ANY.
HOTE
AND THAT'S THE LAST TIME SHE'LL LET **THAT** HAPPEN. SUE?
A MURDER IN THE MID-CITY DISTRICT HAS POLICE SEARCHING FOR A FORMER POLICE OFFICER BY THE NAME OF SAMUEL "SLAM" BRADLEY--
WHAT THE--

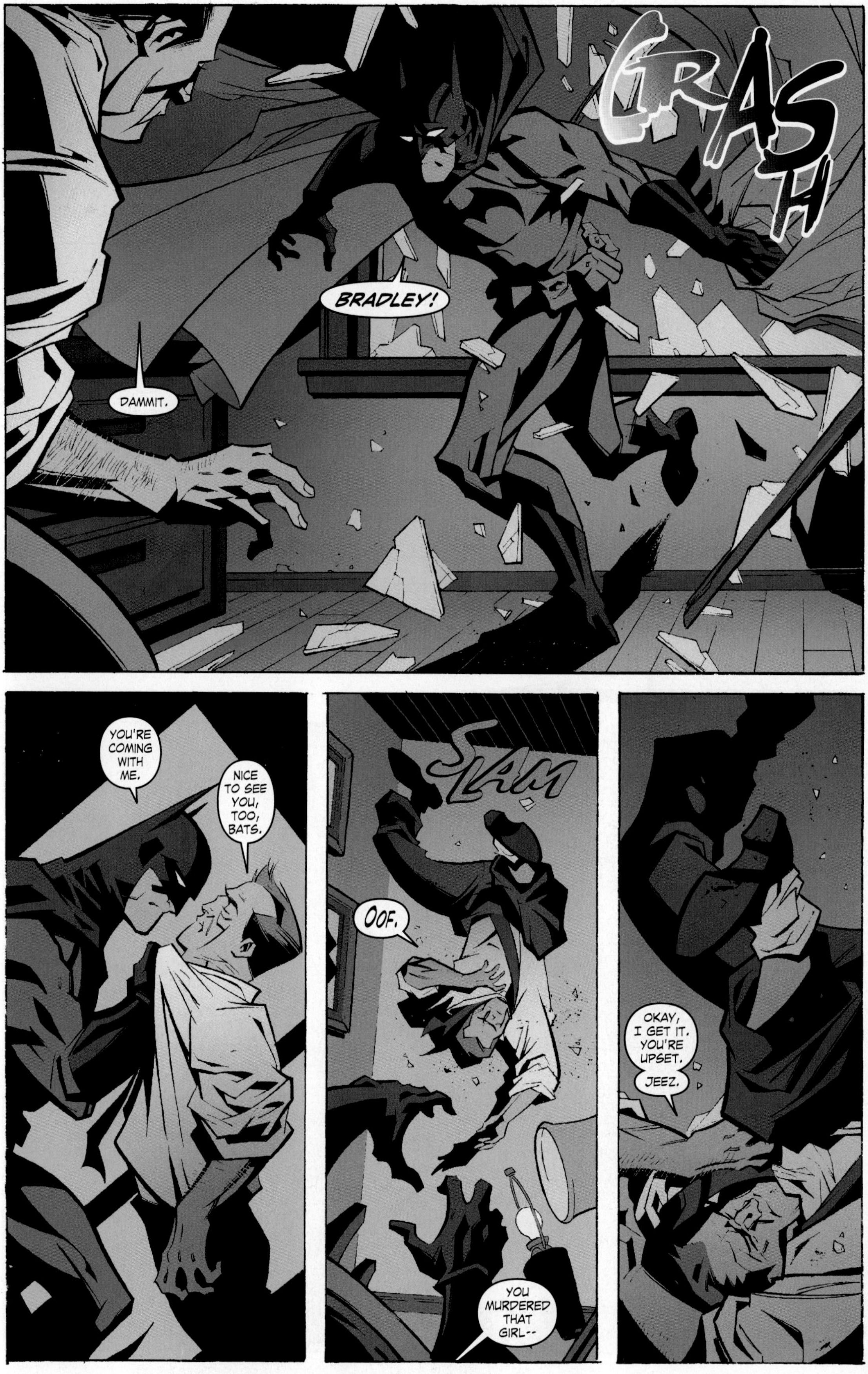
CRASH
BRADLEY!
DAMMIT.
YOU'RE COMING WITH ME.
NICE TO SEE YOU, TOO, BATS.
SLAM
OOF.
YOU MURDERED THAT GIRL--
OKAY, I GET IT. YOU'RE UPSET.
JEEZ.

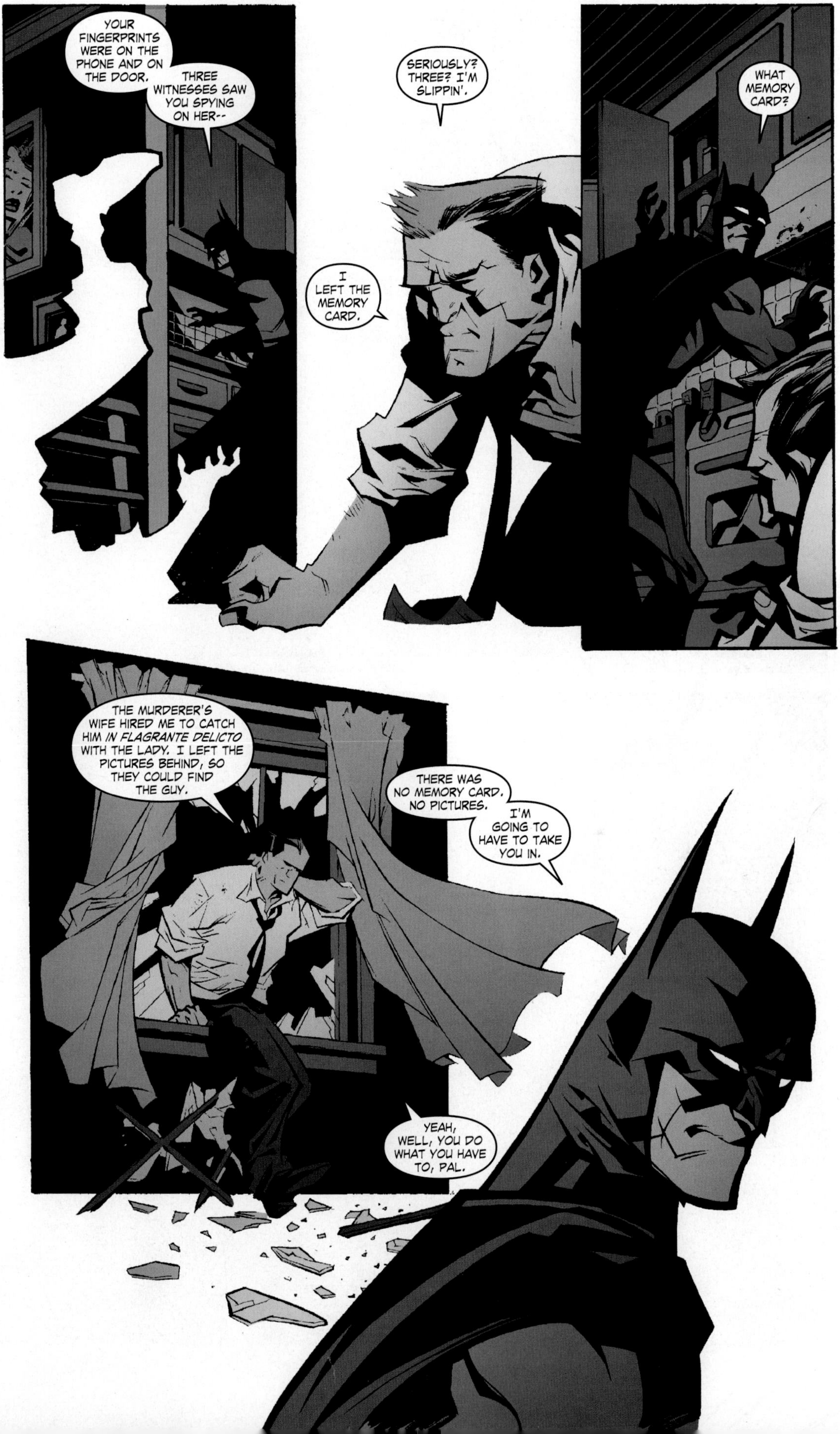
YOUR FINGERPRINTS WERE ON THE PHONE AND ON THE DOOR.
THREE WITNESSES SAW YOU SPYING ON HER--
SERIOUSLY? THREE? I'M SLIPPIN'.
I LEFT THE MEMORY CARD.
WHAT MEMORY CARD?
THE MURDERER'S WIFE HIRED ME TO CATCH HIM *IN FLAGRANTE DELICTO* WITH THE LADY. I LEFT THE PICTURES BEHIND, SO THEY COULD FIND THE GUY.
THERE WAS NO MEMORY CARD. NO PICTURES.
I'M GOING TO HAVE TO TAKE YOU IN.
YEAH, WELL, YOU DO WHAT YOU HAVE TO, PAL.

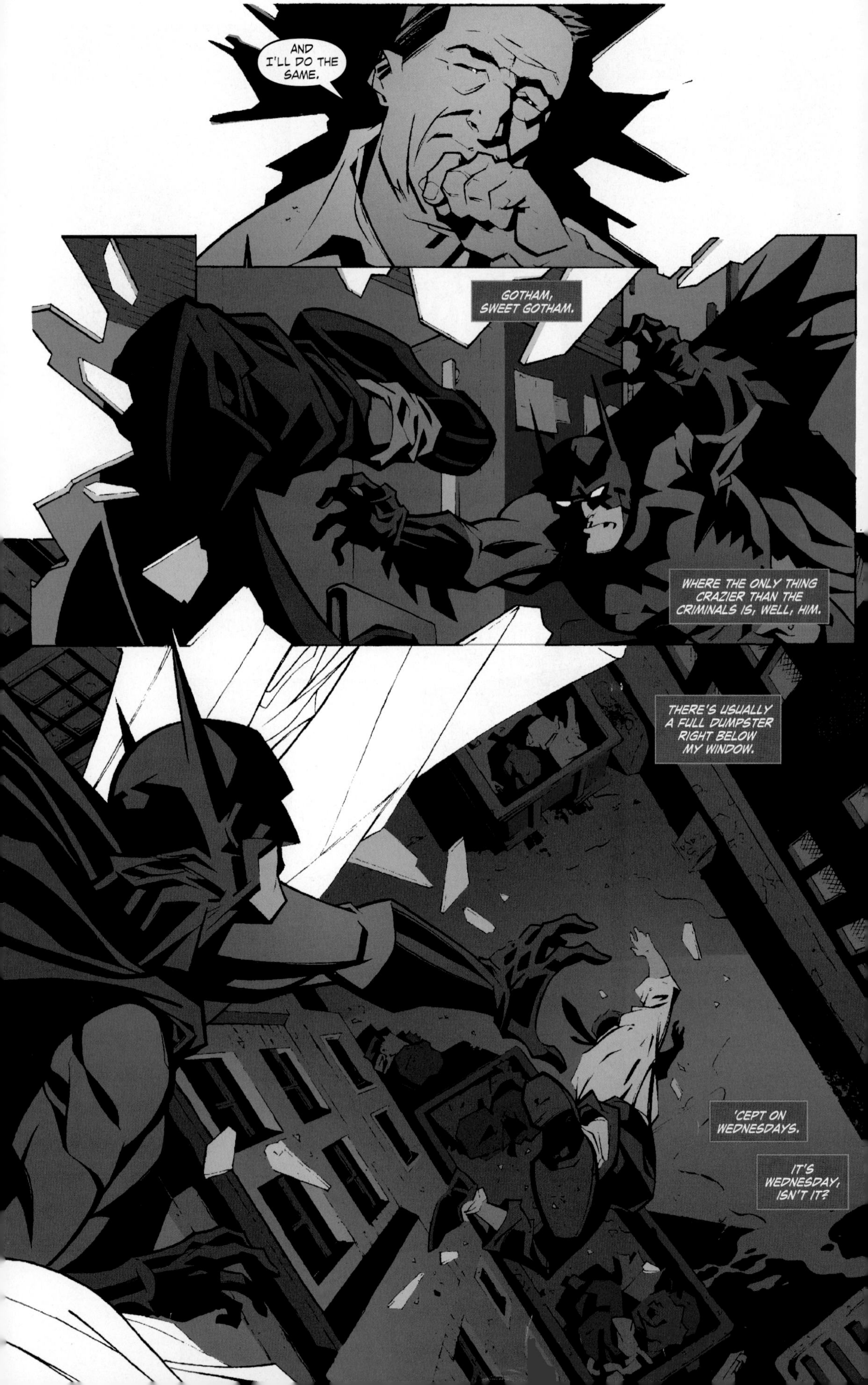
AND I'LL DO THE SAME.
GOTHAM, SWEET GOTHAM.
WHERE THE ONLY THING CRAZIER THAN THE CRIMINALS IS, WELL, HIM.
THERE'S USUALLY A FULL DUMPSTER RIGHT BELOW MY WINDOW.
'CEPT ON WEDNESDAYS.
IT'S WEDNESDAY, ISN'T IT?

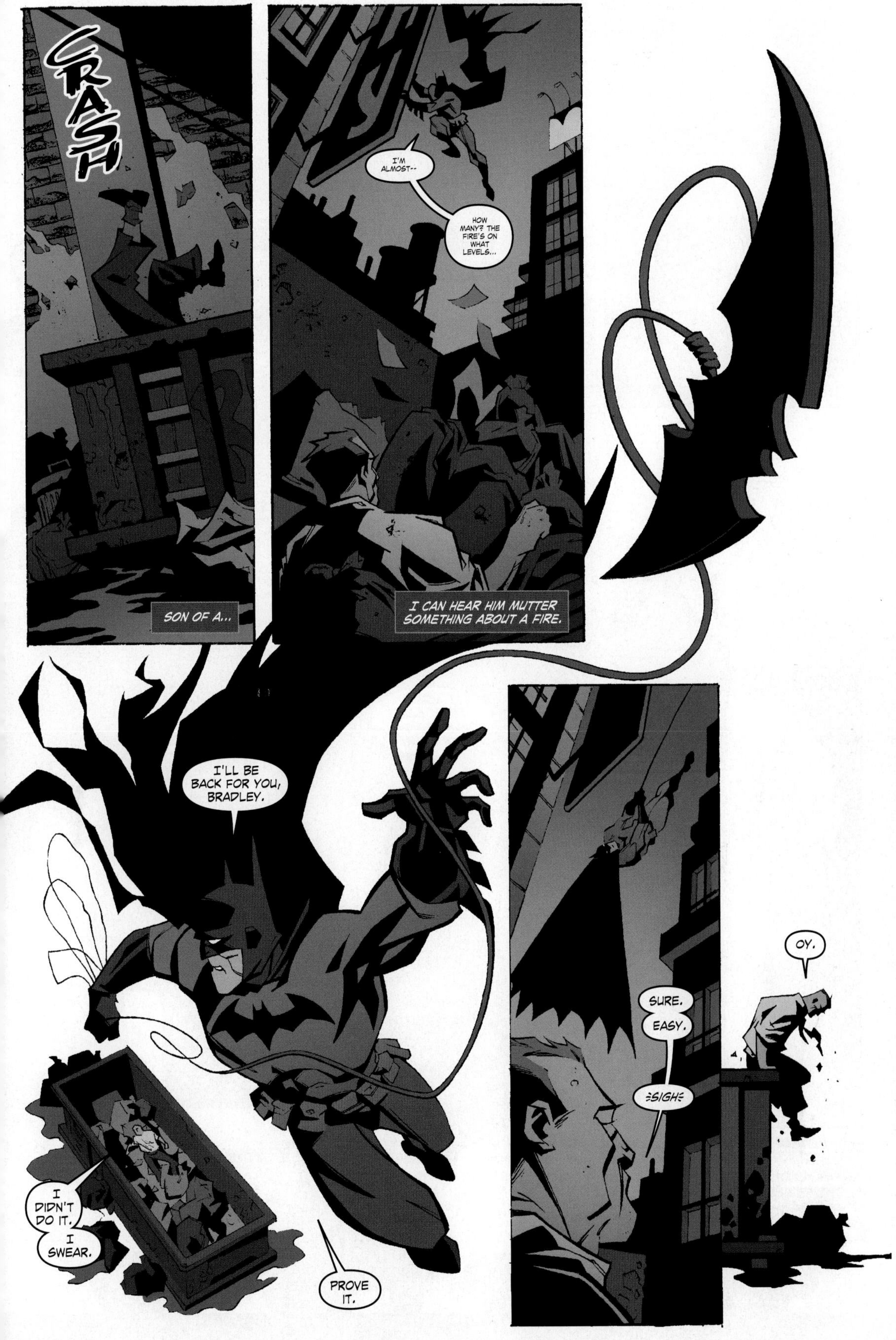
CRASH
SON OF A...
I'M ALMOST--
HOW MANY? THE FIRE'S ON WHAT LEVELS...
I CAN HEAR HIM MUTTER SOMETHING ABOUT A FIRE.
I'LL BE BACK FOR YOU, BRADLEY.
I DIDN'T DO IT.
I SWEAR.
PROVE IT.
OY.
SURE.
EASY.
SIGH

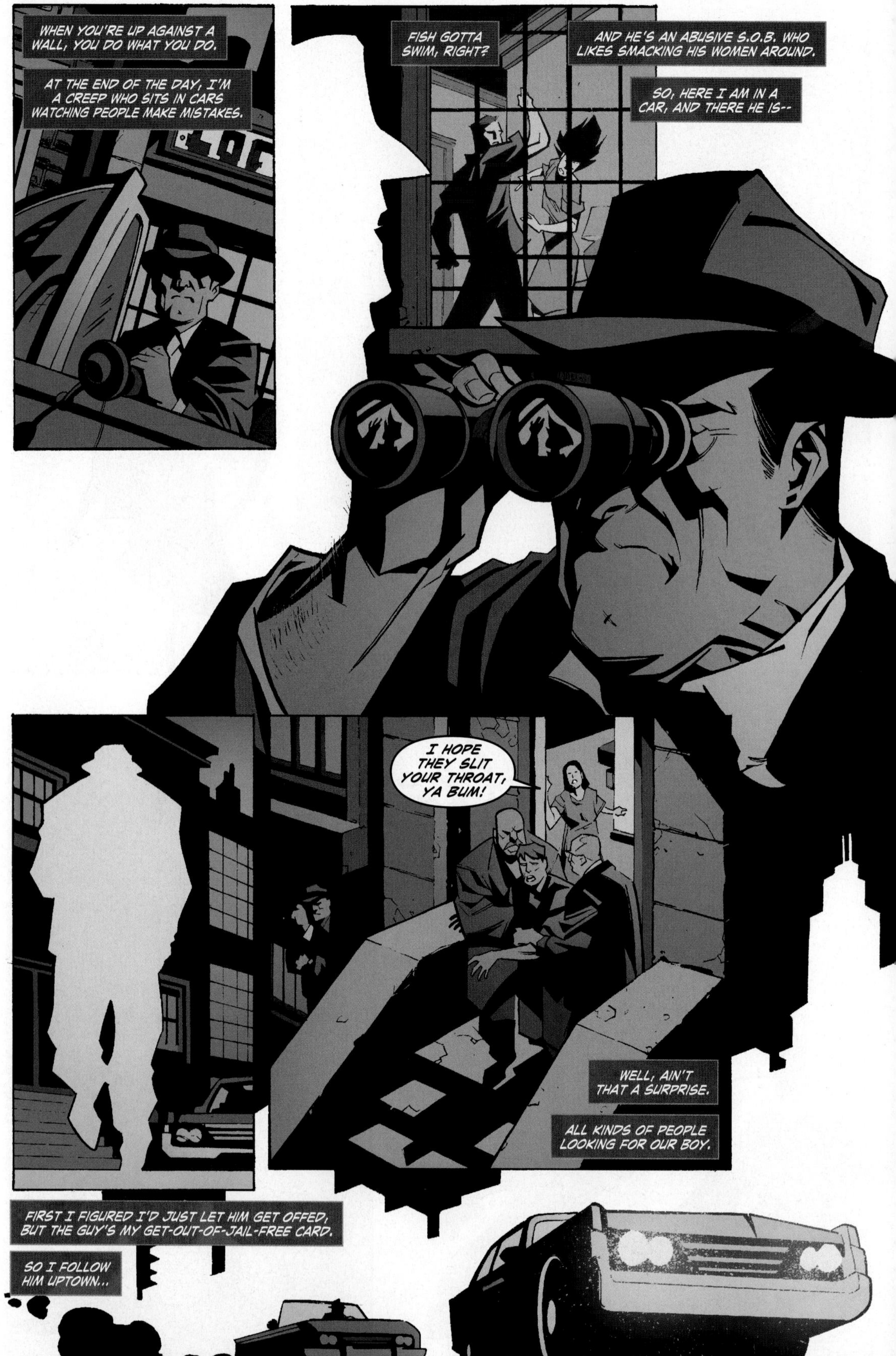
WHEN YOU'RE UP AGAINST A WALL, YOU DO WHAT YOU DO.
AT THE END OF THE DAY, I'M A CREEP WHO SITS IN CARS WATCHING PEOPLE MAKE MISTAKES.
FISH GOTTA SWIM, RIGHT?
AND HE'S AN ABUSIVE S.O.B. WHO LIKES SMACKING HIS WOMEN AROUND.
SO, HERE I AM IN A CAR, AND THERE HE IS--
I HOPE THEY SLIT YOUR THROAT, YA BUM!
WELL, AIN'T THAT A SURPRISE.
ALL KINDS OF PEOPLE LOOKING FOR OUR BOY.
FIRST I FIGURED I'D JUST LET HIM GET OFFED, BUT THE GUY'S MY GET-OUT-OF-JAIL-FREE CARD.
SO I FOLLOW HIM UPTOWN...

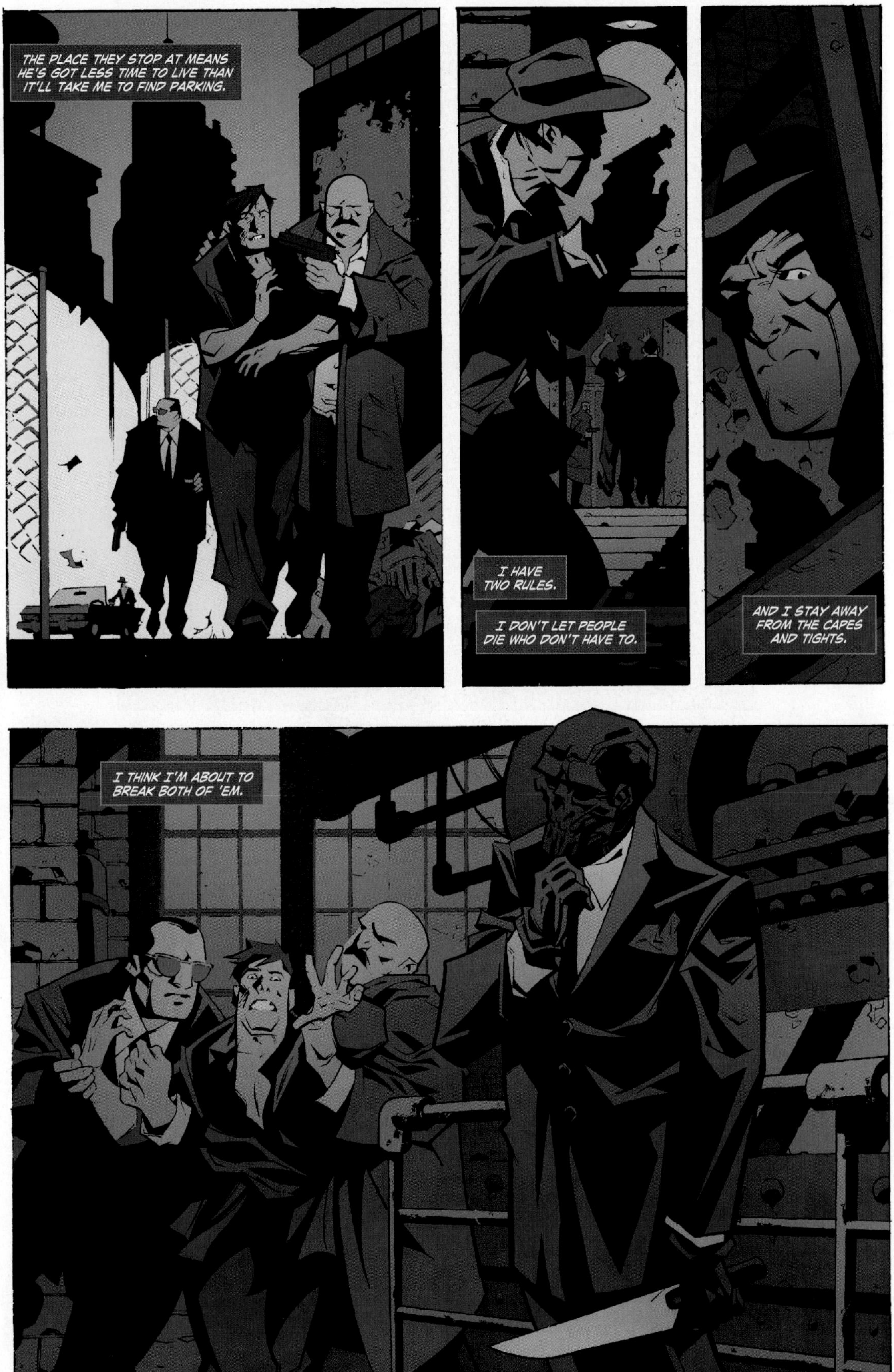
THE PLACE THEY STOP AT MEANS HE'S GOT LESS TIME TO LIVE THAN IT'LL TAKE ME TO FIND PARKING.
I HAVE TWO RULES.
I DON'T LET PEOPLE DIE WHO DON'T HAVE TO.
AND I STAY AWAY FROM THE CAPES AND TIGHTS.
I THINK I'M ABOUT TO BREAK BOTH OF 'EM.

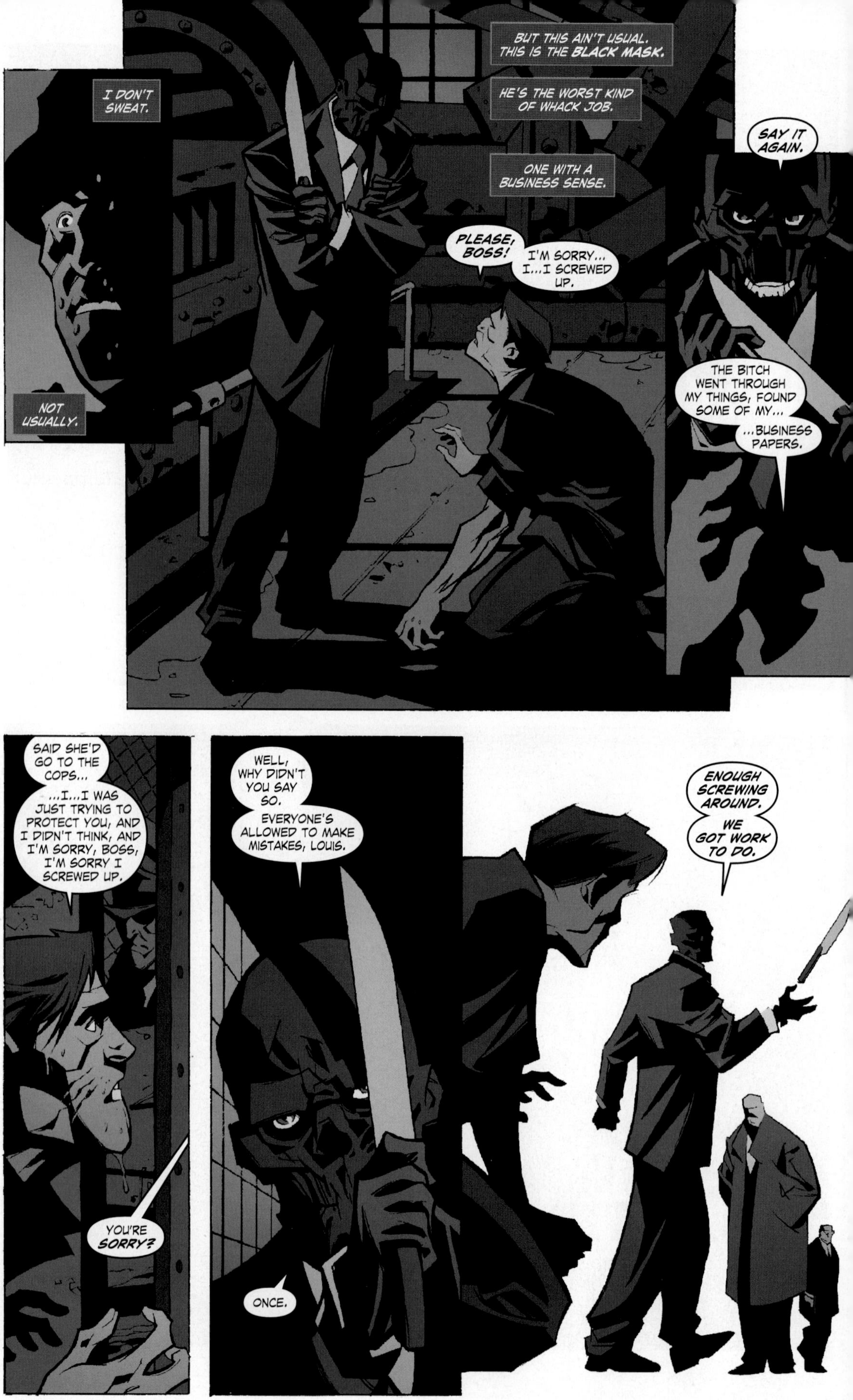
I DON'T SWEAT.
NOT USUALLY.
BUT THIS AIN'T USUAL. THIS IS THE BLACK MASK.
HE'S THE WORST KIND OF WHACK JOB.
ONE WITH A BUSINESS SENSE.
PLEASE, BOSS!
I'M SORRY... I...I SCREWED UP.
SAY IT AGAIN.
THE BITCH WENT THROUGH MY THINGS, FOUND SOME OF MY...
...BUSINESS PAPERS.
SAID SHE'D GO TO THE COPS...
...I...I WAS JUST TRYING TO PROTECT YOU, AND I DIDN'T THINK, AND I'M SORRY, BOSS, I'M SORRY I SCREWED UP.
YOU'RE SORRY?
WELL, WHY DIDN'T YOU SAY SO.
EVERYONE'S ALLOWED TO MAKE MISTAKES, LOUIS.
ONCE.
ENOUGH SCREWING AROUND.
WE GOT WORK TO DO.

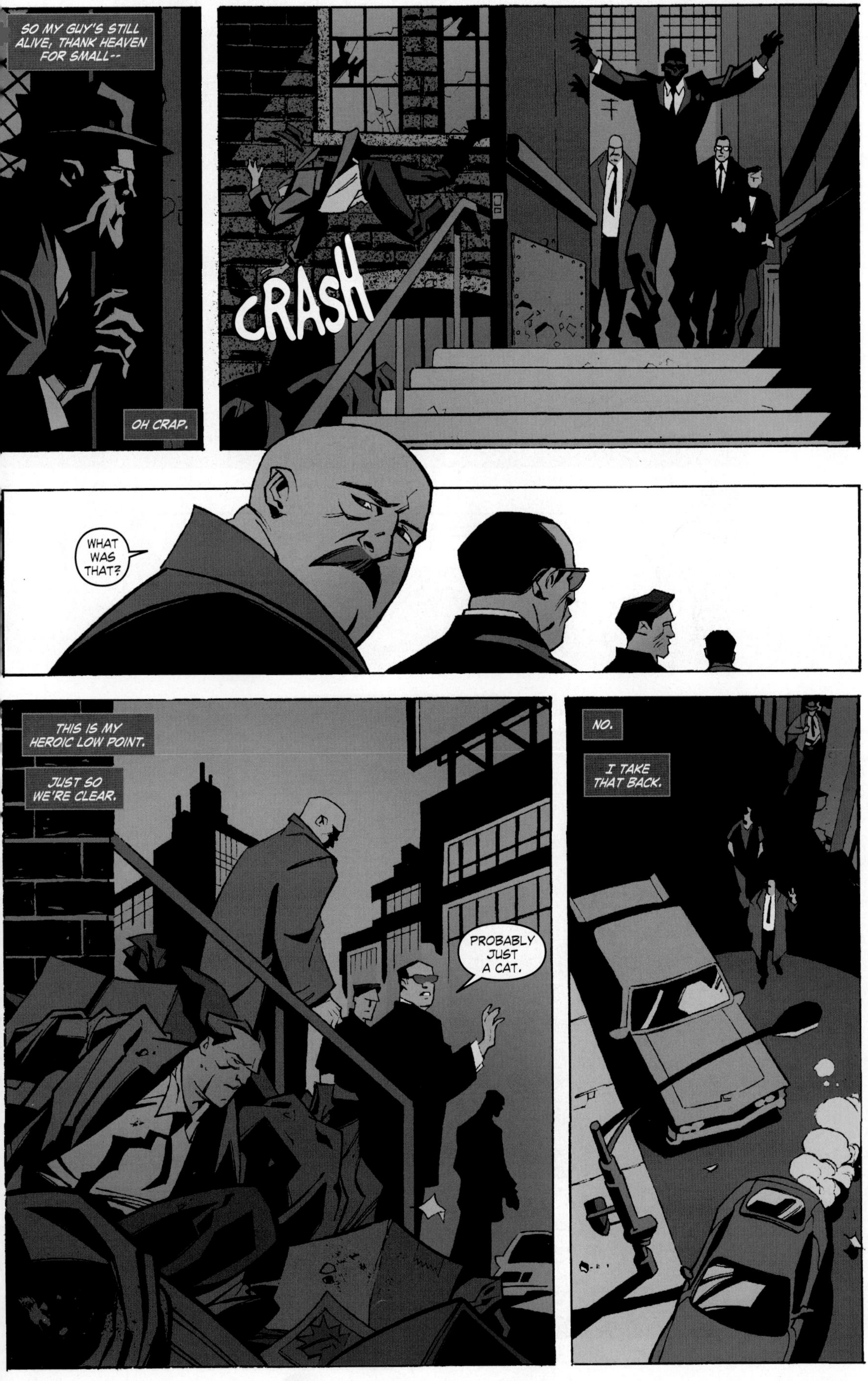
SO MY GUY'S STILL ALIVE, THANK HEAVEN FOR SMALL--
OH CRAP.
CRASH
WHAT WAS THAT?
THIS IS MY HEROIC LOW POINT.
JUST SO WE'RE CLEAR.
PROBABLY JUST A CAT.
NO.
I TAKE THAT BACK.

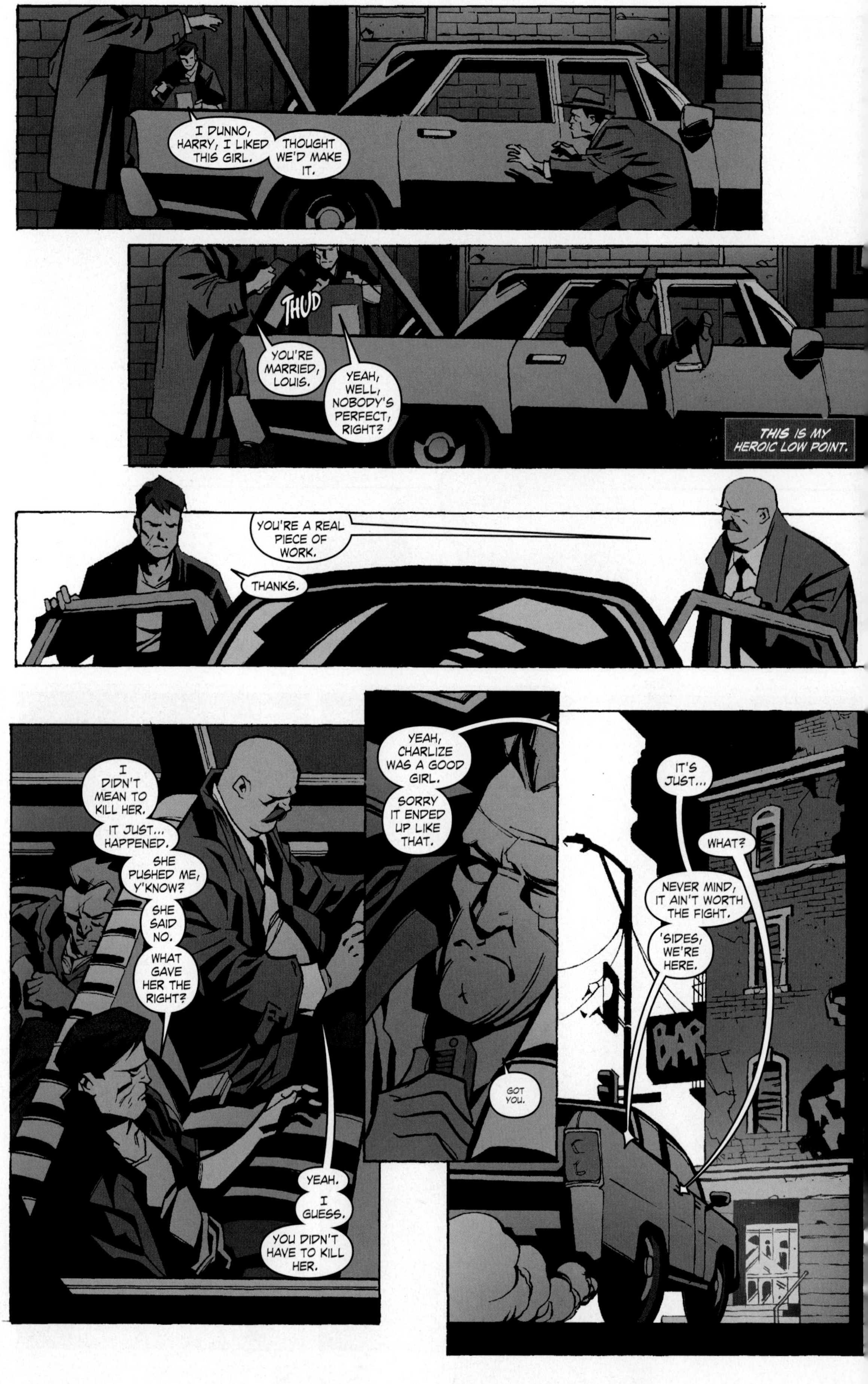
I DUNNO, HARRY, I LIKED THIS GIRL.
THOUGHT WE'D MAKE IT.
THUD
YOU'RE MARRIED, LOUIS.
YEAH, WELL, NOBODY'S PERFECT, RIGHT?
THIS IS MY HEROIC LOW POINT.
YOU'RE A REAL PIECE OF WORK.
THANKS.
I DIDN'T MEAN TO KILL HER.
IT JUST... HAPPENED.
SHE PUSHED ME, Y'KNOW?
SHE SAID NO.
WHAT GAVE HER THE RIGHT?
YEAH.
I GUESS.
YOU DIDN'T HAVE TO KILL HER.
YEAH, CHARLIZE WAS A GOOD GIRL.
SORRY IT ENDED UP LIKE THAT.
GOT YOU.
IT'S JUST...
WHAT?
NEVER MIND, IT AIN'T WORTH THE FIGHT.
'SIDES, WE'RE HERE.
BAR

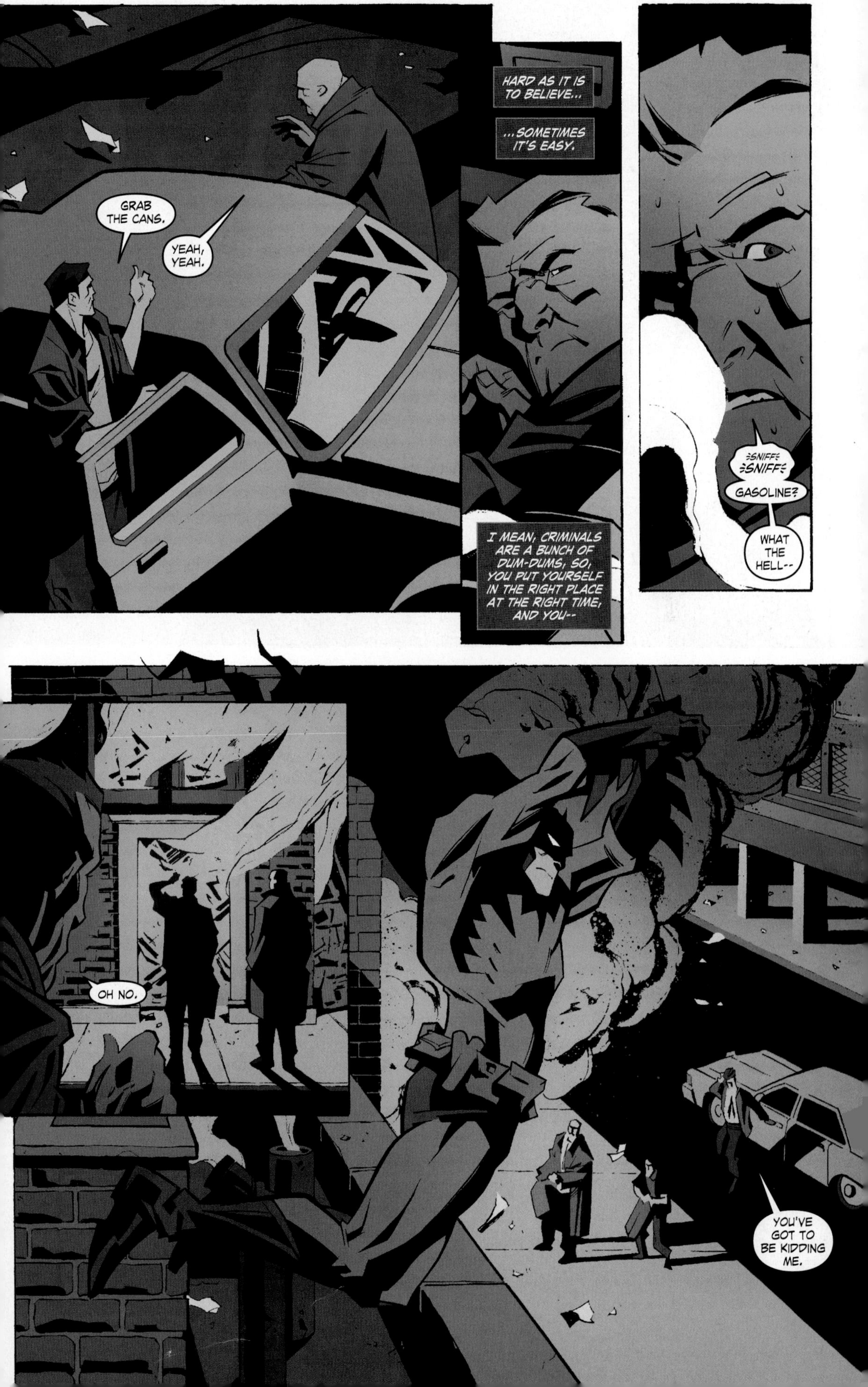
GRAB THE CANS.
YEAH, YEAH.
HARD AS IT IS TO BELIEVE...
...SOMETIMES IT'S EASY.
I MEAN, CRIMINALS ARE A BUNCH OF DUM-DUMS, SO, YOU PUT YOURSELF IN THE RIGHT PLACE AT THE RIGHT TIME, AND YOU--
SNIFF SNIFF
GASOLINE?
WHAT THE HELL--
OH NO.
YOU'VE GOT TO BE KIDDING ME.

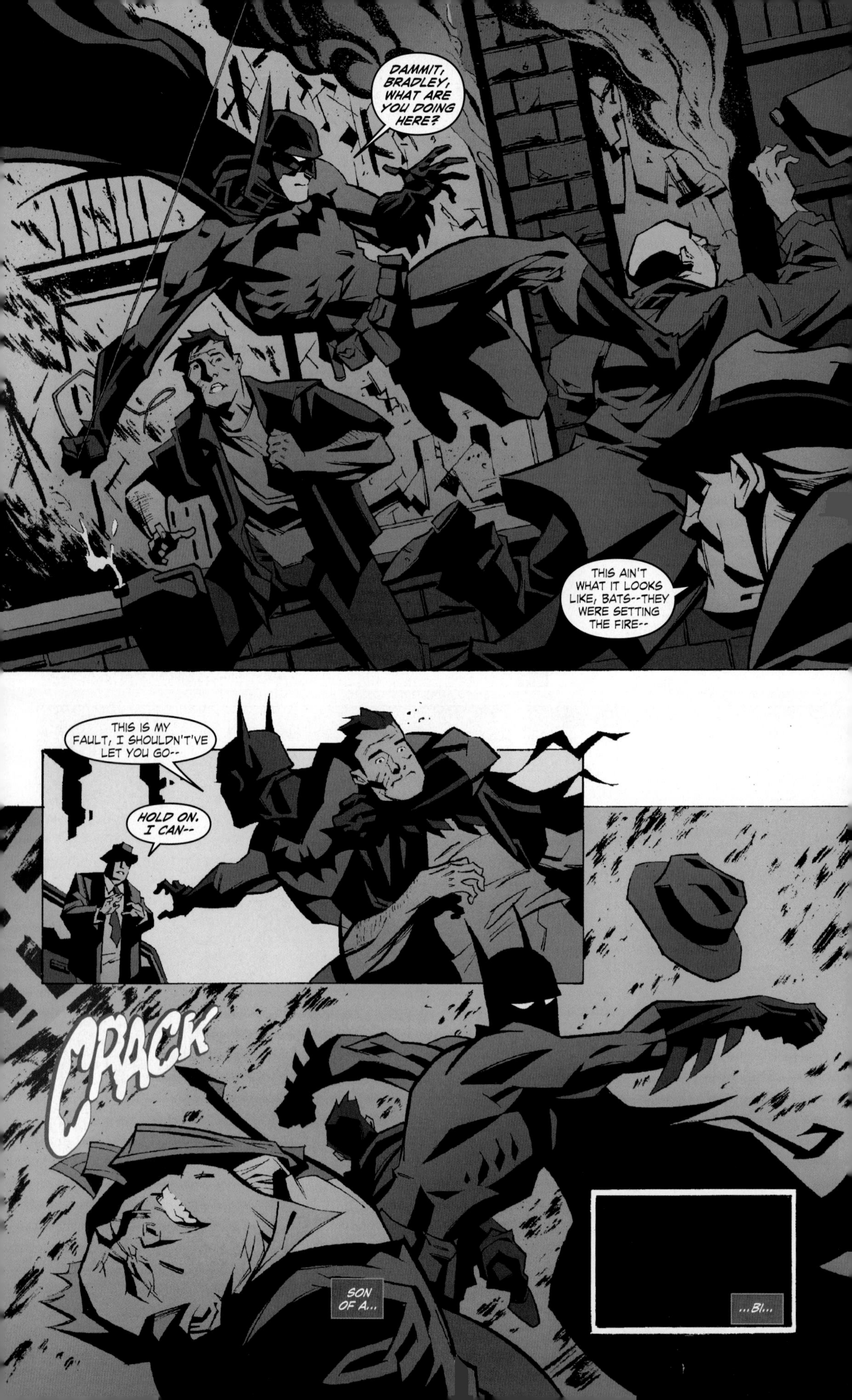
DAMMIT, BRADLEY, WHAT ARE YOU DOING HERE?
THIS AIN'T WHAT IT LOOKS LIKE, BATS--THEY WERE SETTING THE FIRE--
THIS IS MY FAULT, I SHOULDN'T'VE LET YOU GO--
HOLD ON. I CAN--
CRACK
SON OF A...
...BI...

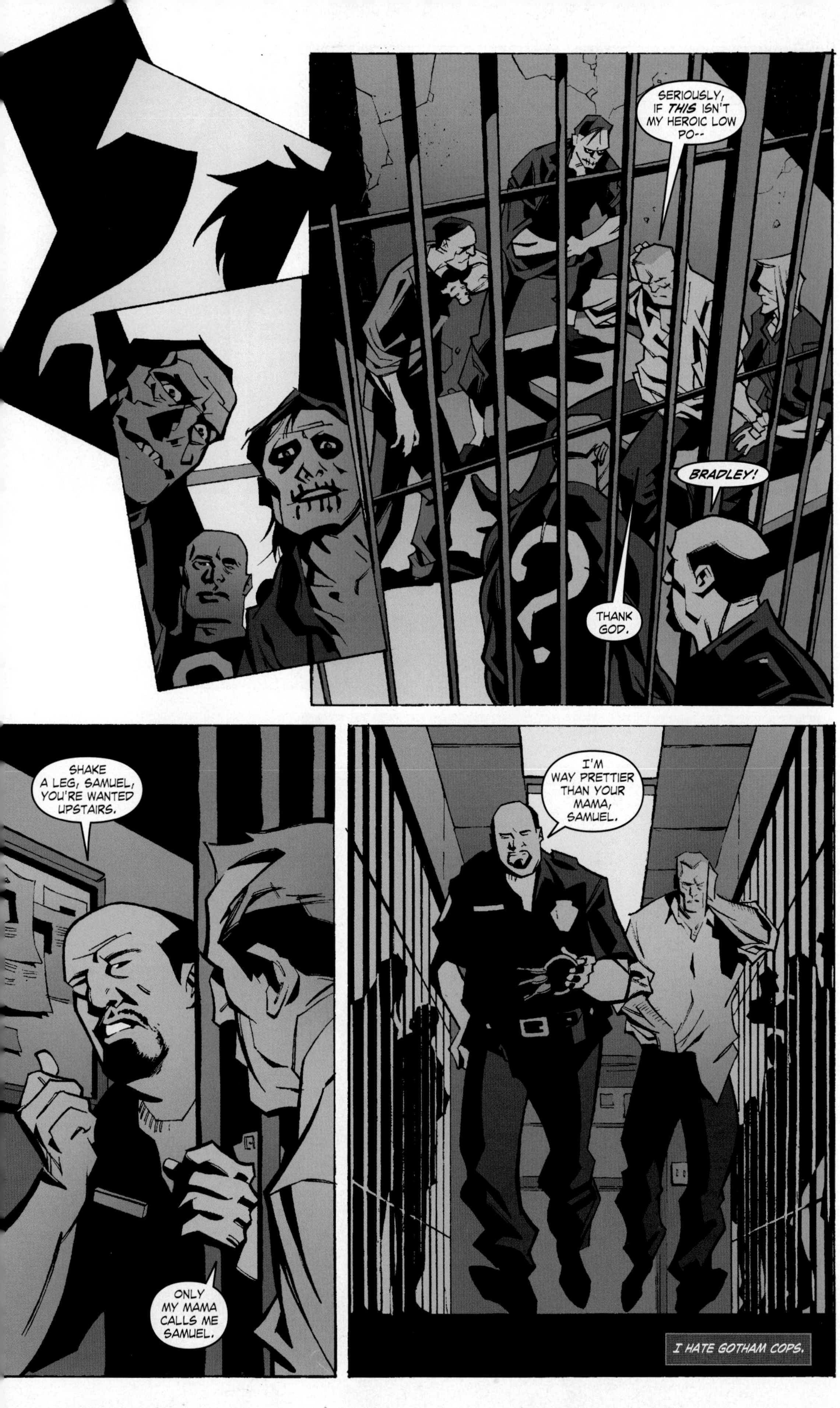
SERIOUSLY, IF THIS ISN'T MY HEROIC LOW PO--
BRADLEY!
THANK GOD.
SHAKE A LEG, SAMUEL, YOU'RE WANTED UPSTAIRS.
ONLY MY MAMA CALLS ME SAMUEL.
I'M WAY PRETTIER THAN YOUR MAMA, SAMUEL.
I HATE GOTHAM COPS.

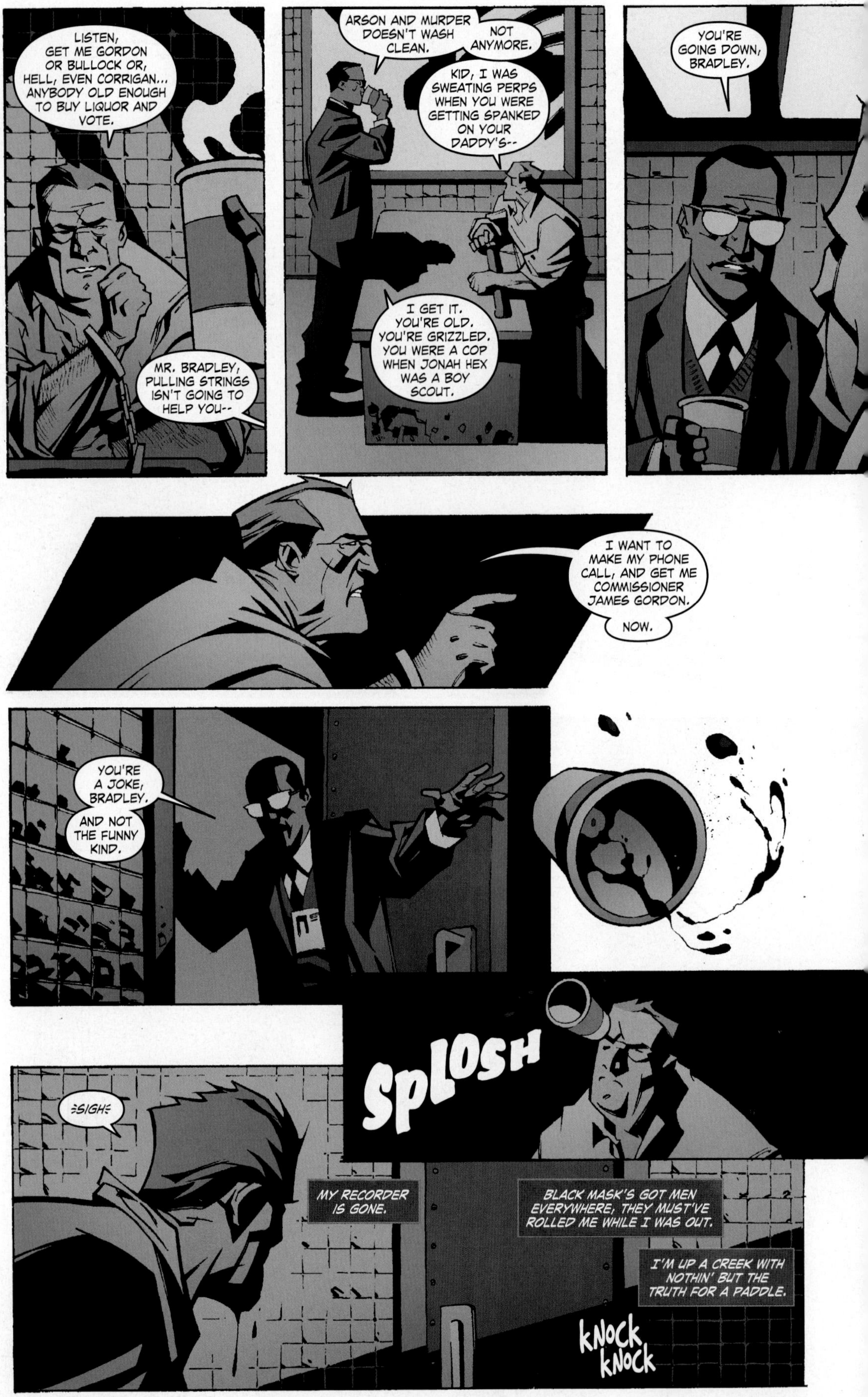
LISTEN, GET ME GORDON OR BULLOCK OR, HELL, EVEN CORRIGAN... ANYBODY OLD ENOUGH TO BUY LIQUOR AND VOTE.
MR. BRADLEY, PULLING STRINGS ISN'T GOING TO HELP YOU--
ARSON AND MURDER DOESN'T WASH CLEAN.
NOT ANYMORE.
KID, I WAS SWEATING PERPS WHEN YOU WERE GETTING SPANKED ON YOUR DADDY'S--
I GET IT. YOU'RE OLD. YOU'RE GRIZZLED. YOU WERE A COP WHEN JONAH HEX WAS A BOY SCOUT.
YOU'RE GOING DOWN, BRADLEY.
I WANT TO MAKE MY PHONE CALL, AND GET ME COMMISSIONER JAMES GORDON.
NOW.
YOU'RE A JOKE, BRADLEY.
AND NOT THE FUNNY KIND.
SPLOSH
SIGH
MY RECORDER IS GONE.
BLACK MASK'S GOT MEN EVERYWHERE, THEY MUST'VE ROLLED ME WHILE I WAS OUT.
I'M UP A CREEK WITH NOTHIN' BUT THE TRUTH FOR A PADDLE.
KNOCK KNOCK

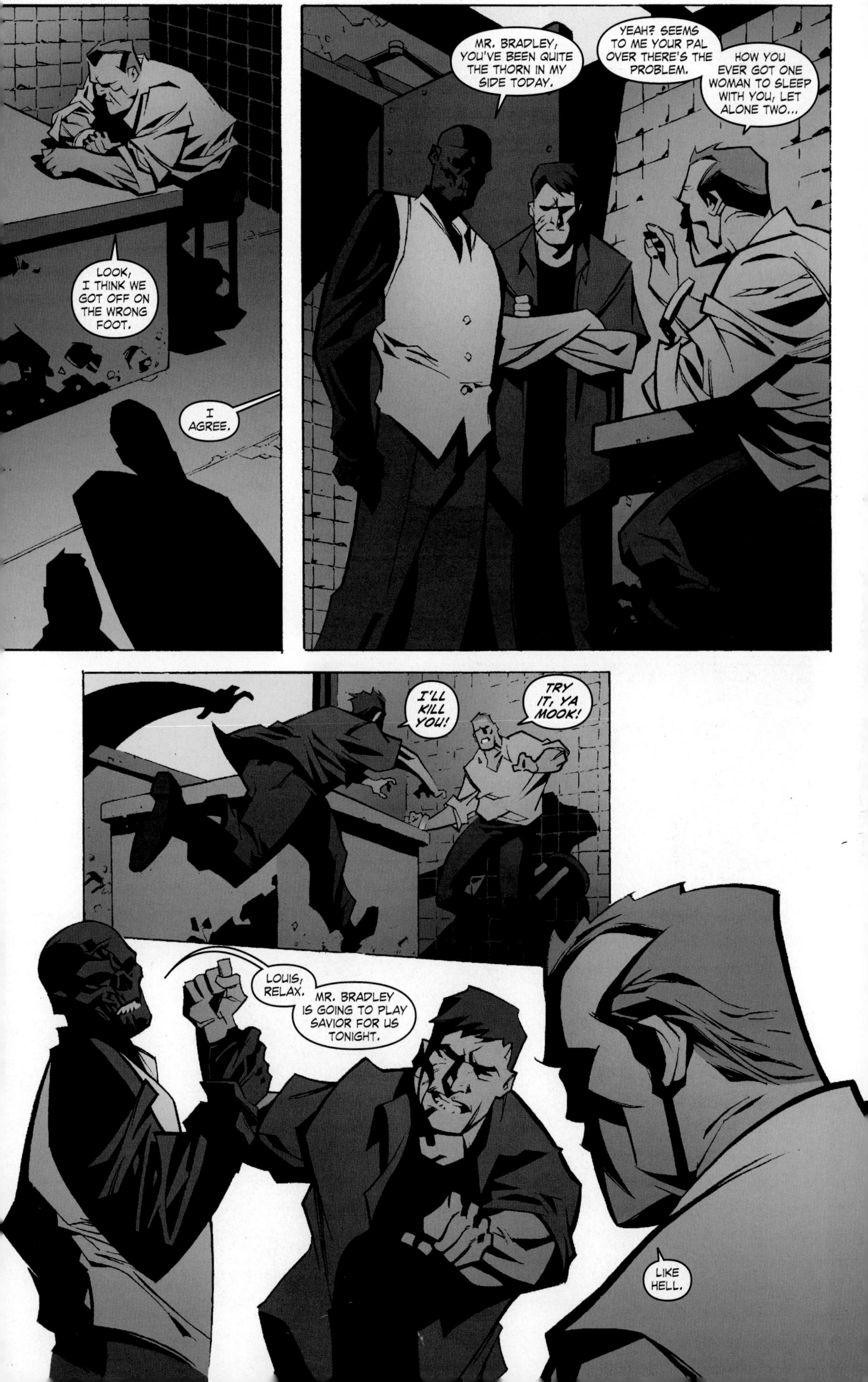
LOOK, I THINK WE GOT OFF ON THE WRONG FOOT.
I AGREE.
MR. BRADLEY, YOU'VE BEEN QUITE THE THORN IN MY SIDE TODAY.
YEAH? SEEMS TO ME YOUR PAL OVER THERE'S THE PROBLEM.
HOW YOU EVER GOT ONE WOMAN TO SLEEP WITH YOU, LET ALONE TWO...
I'LL KILL YOU!
TRY IT, YA MOOK!
LOUIS, RELAX.
MR. BRADLEY IS GOING TO PLAY SAVIOR FOR US TONIGHT.
LIKE HELL.

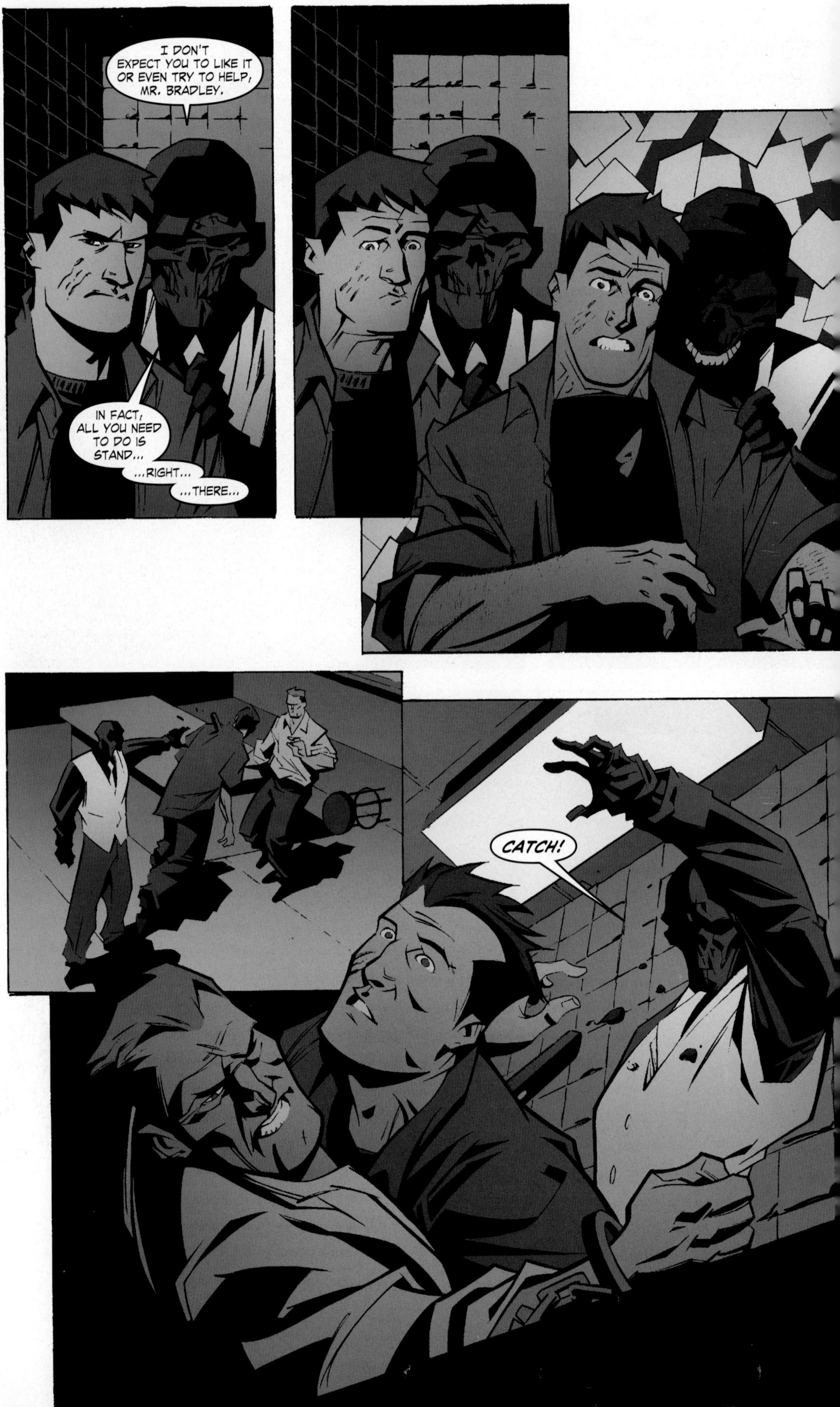
I DON'T EXPECT YOU TO LIKE IT OR EVEN TRY TO HELP, MR. BRADLEY.
IN FACT, ALL YOU NEED TO DO IS STAND...
...RIGHT...
...THERE...
CATCH!

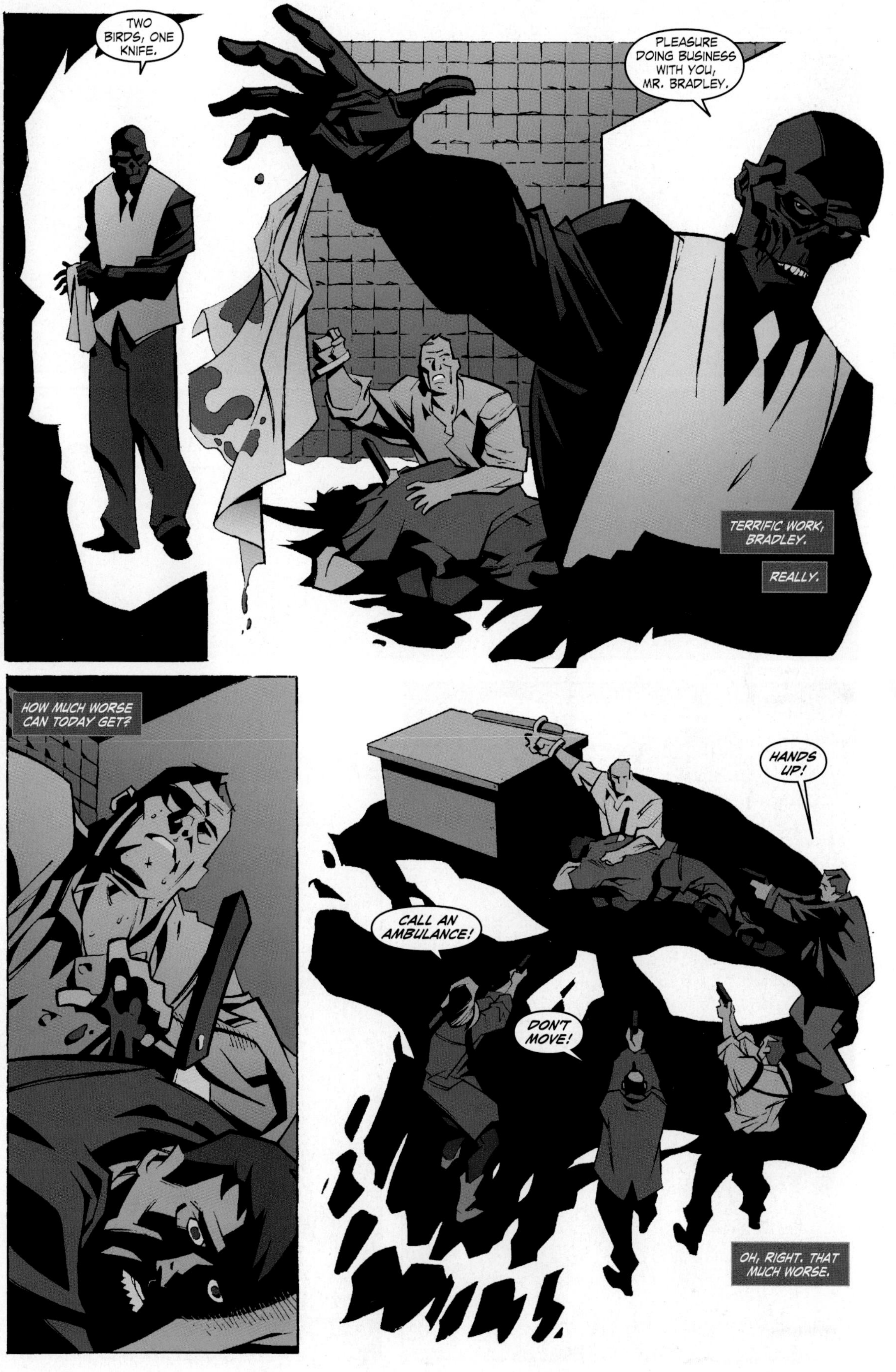
TWO BIRDS, ONE KNIFE.
PLEASURE DOING BUSINESS WITH YOU, MR. BRADLEY.
TERRIFIC WORK, BRADLEY.
REALLY.
HOW MUCH WORSE CAN TODAY GET?
HANDS UP!
CALL AN AMBULANCE!
DON'T MOVE!
OH, RIGHT. THAT MUCH WORSE.

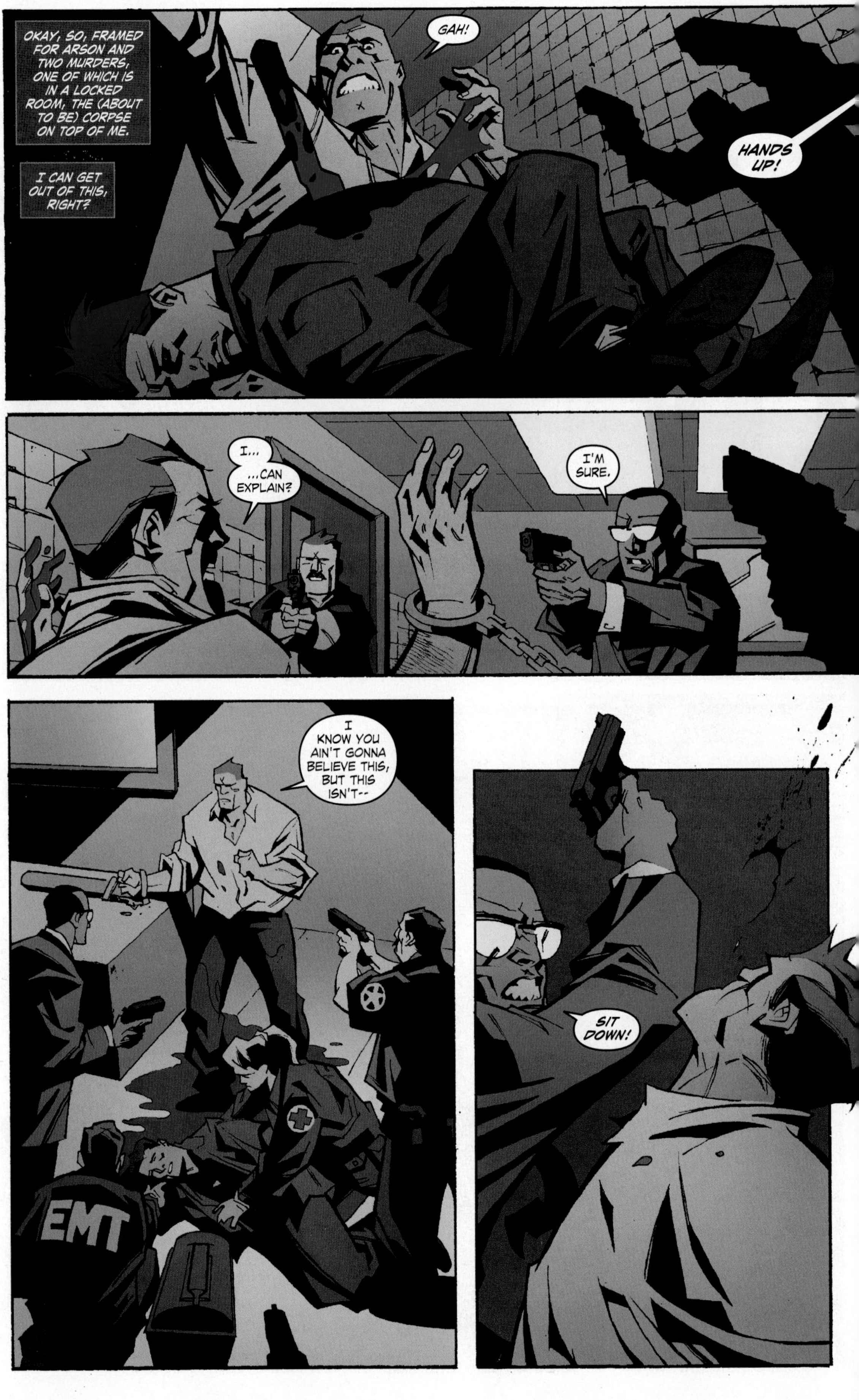

OKAY, SO, FRAMED FOR ARSON AND TWO MURDERS, ONE OF WHICH IS IN A LOCKED ROOM, THE (ABOUT TO BE) CORPSE ON TOP OF ME.
I CAN GET OUT OF THIS, RIGHT?
GAH!
HANDS UP!
I... ...CAN EXPLAIN?
I'M SURE.
I KNOW YOU AIN'T GONNA BELIEVE THIS, BUT THIS ISN'T--
EMT
SIT DOWN!

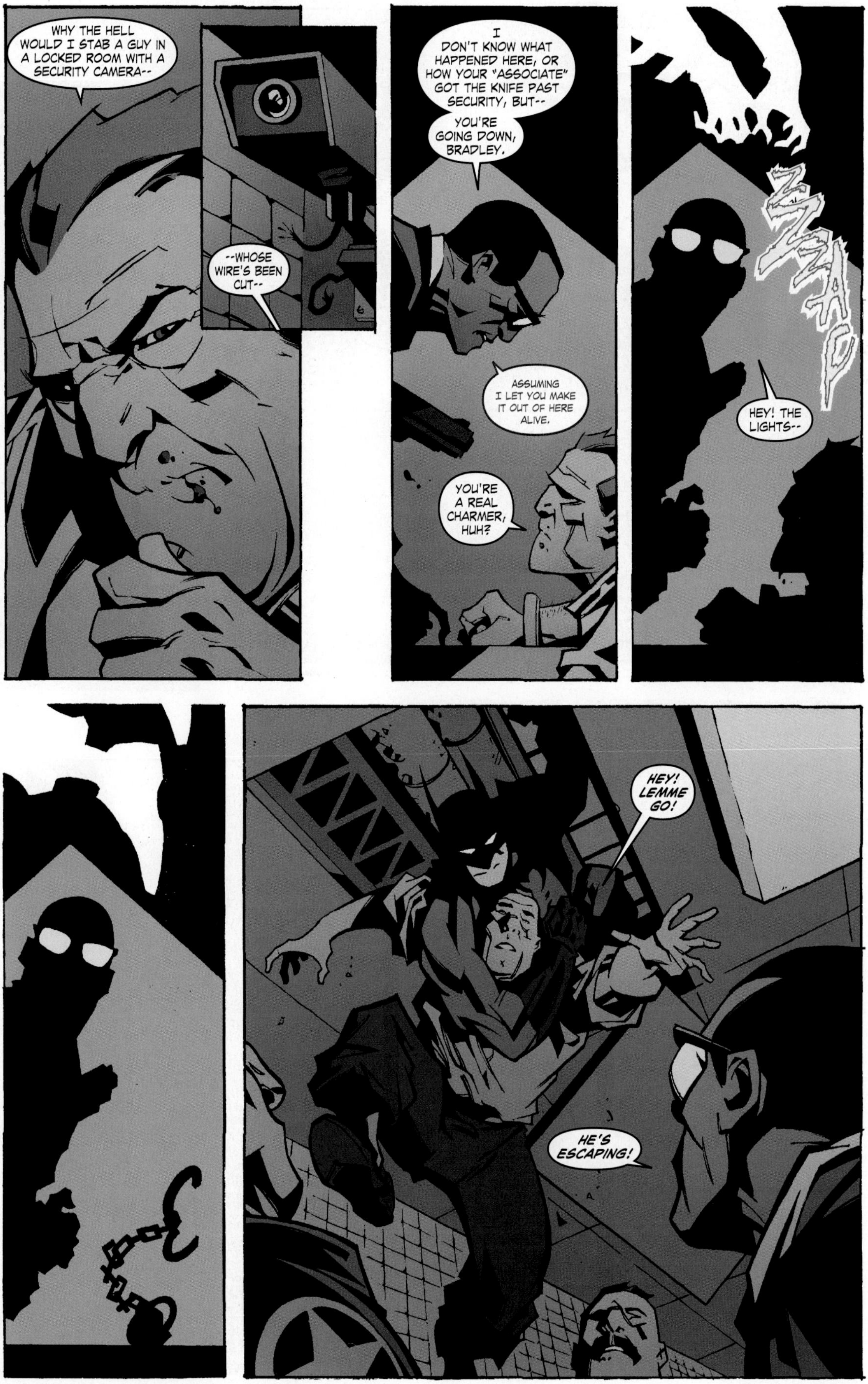
WHY THE HELL WOULD I STAB A GUY IN A LOCKED ROOM WITH A SECURITY CAMERA--
--WHOSE WIRE'S BEEN CUT--
I DON'T KNOW WHAT HAPPENED HERE, OR HOW YOUR "ASSOCIATE" GOT THE KNIFE PAST SECURITY, BUT--
YOU'RE GOING DOWN, BRADLEY.
ASSUMING I LET YOU MAKE IT OUT OF HERE ALIVE.
YOU'RE A REAL CHARMER, HUH?
ZZZAP
HEY! THE LIGHTS--
HEY! LEMME GO!
HE'S ESCAPING!

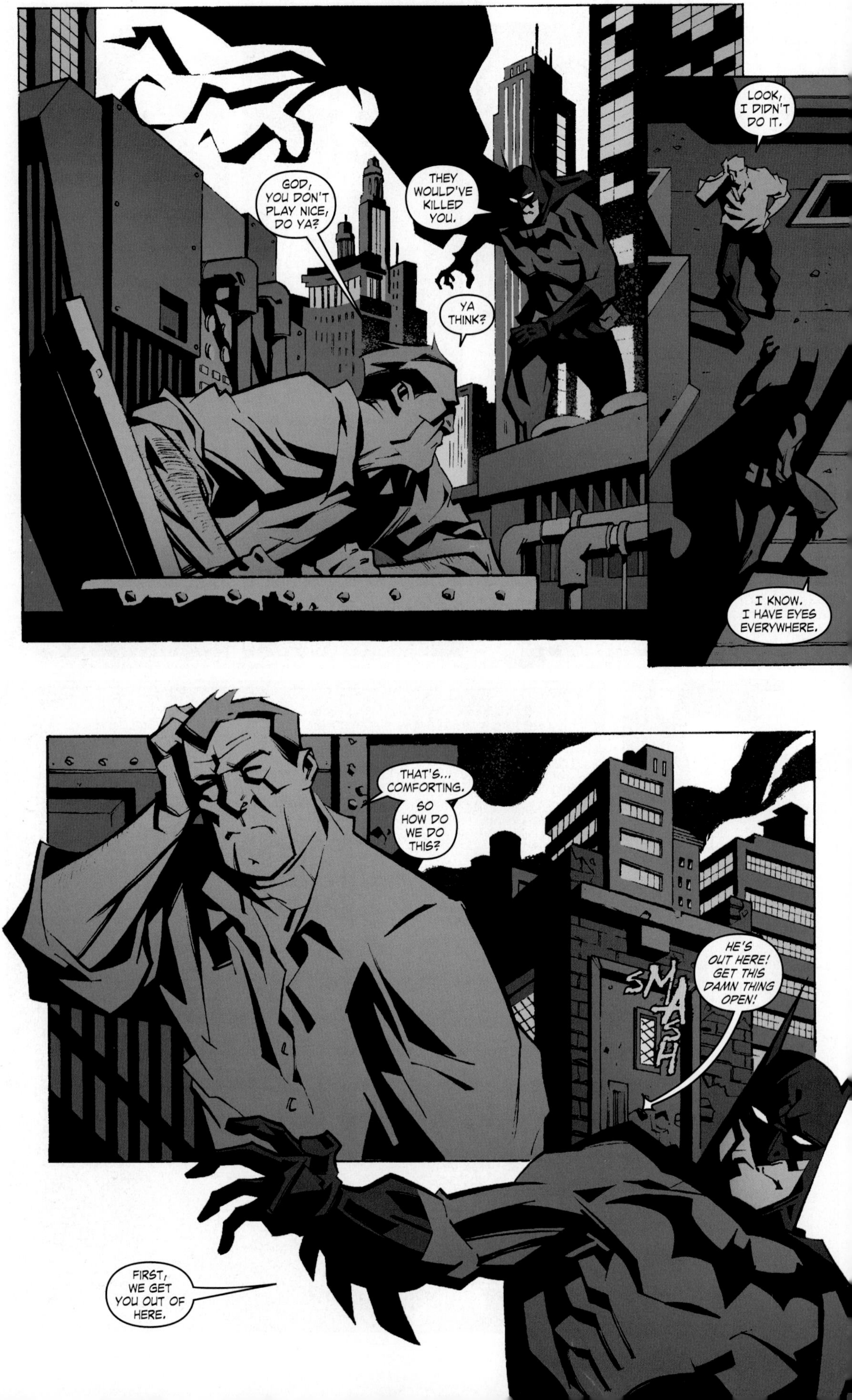
GOD, YOU DON'T PLAY NICE, DO YA?
THEY WOULD'VE KILLED YOU.
YA THINK?
LOOK, I DIDN'T DO IT.
I KNOW. I HAVE EYES EVERYWHERE.
THAT'S... COMFORTING.
SO HOW DO WE DO THIS?
HE'S OUT HERE! GET THIS DAMN THING OPEN!
SMASH
FIRST, WE GET YOU OUT OF HERE.

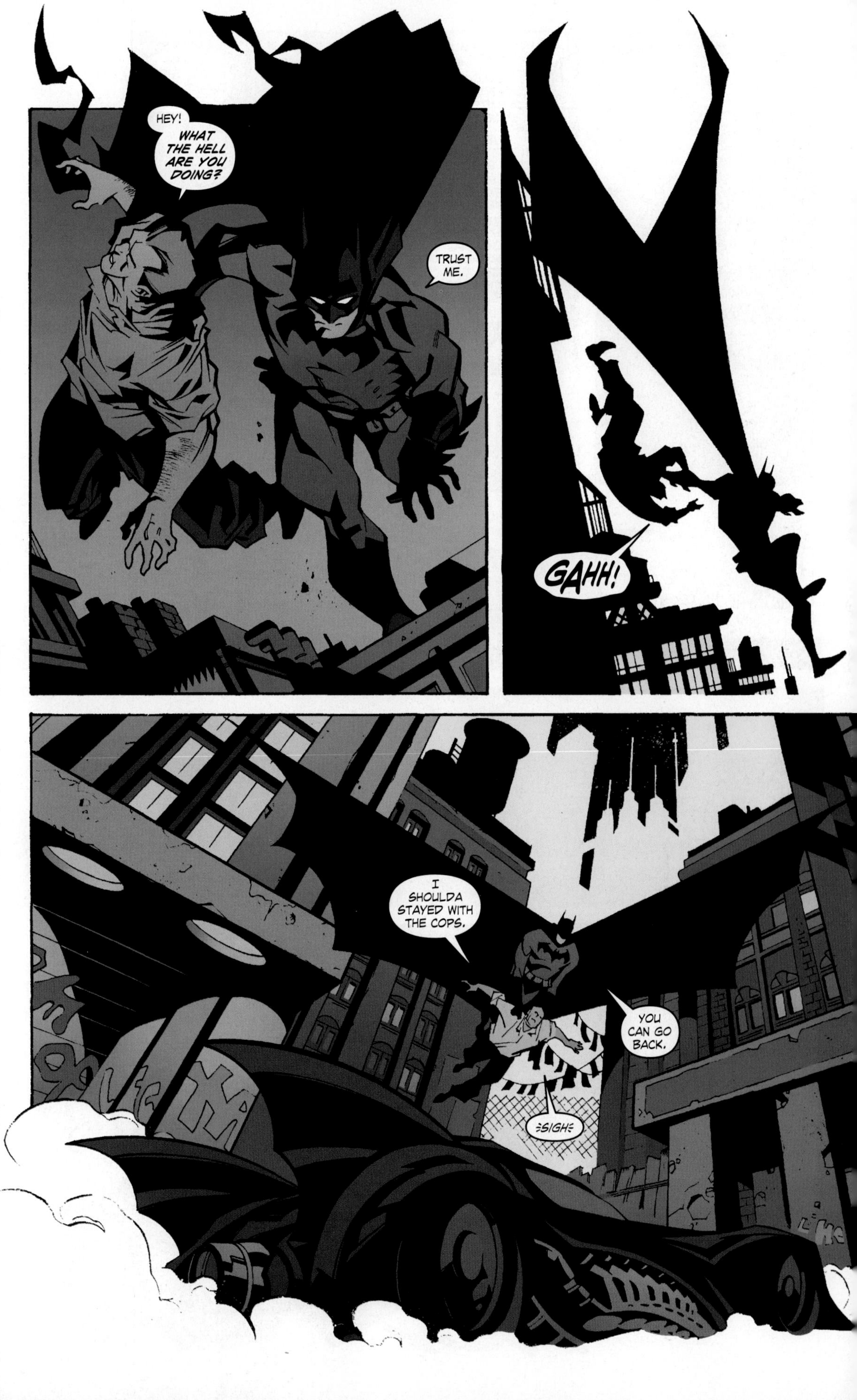
HEY!
WHAT THE HELL ARE YOU DOING?
TRUST ME.
GAHH!
I SHOULDA STAYED WITH THE COPS.
YOU CAN GO BACK.
SIGH

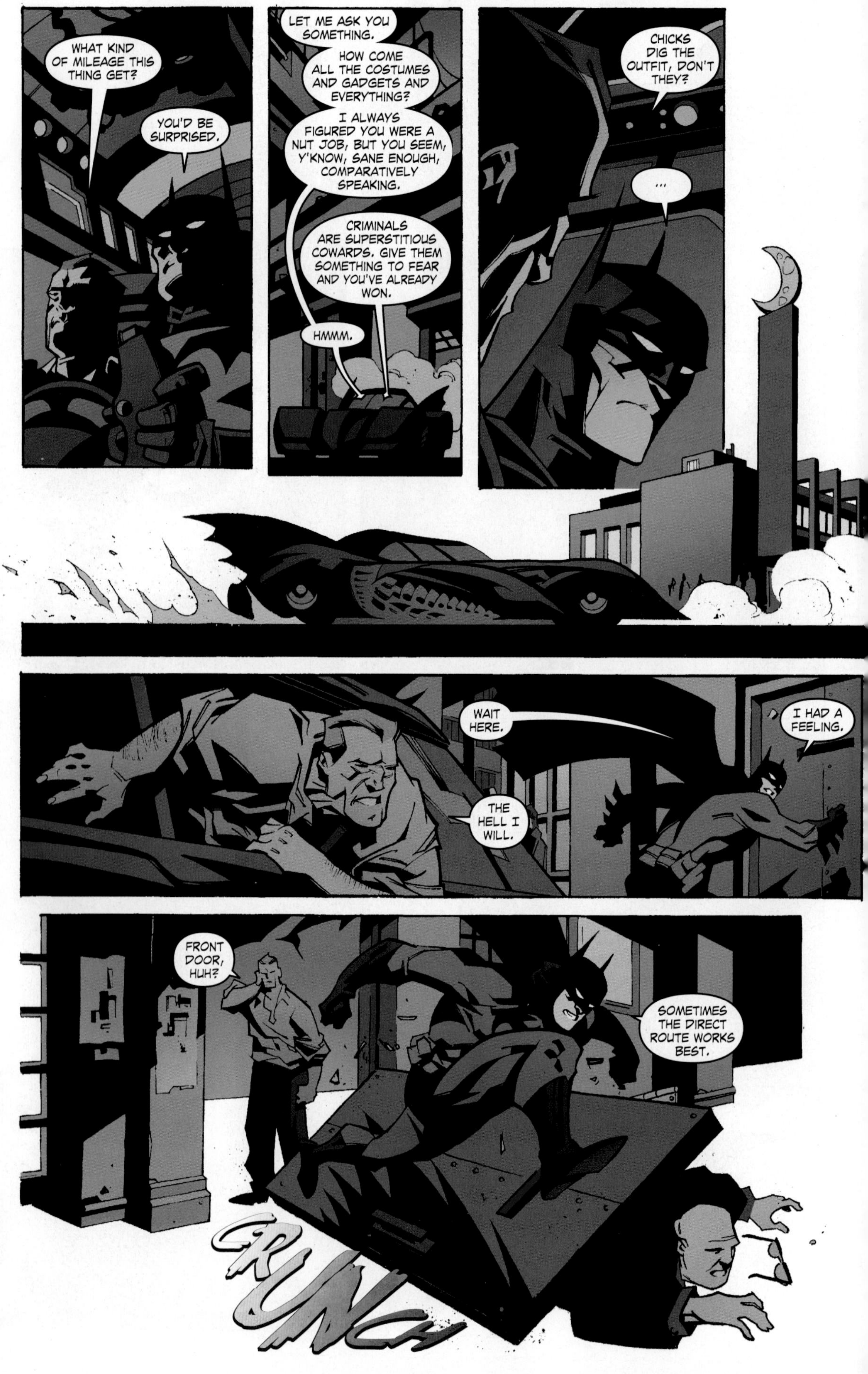
WHAT KIND OF MILEAGE THIS THING GET?
YOU'D BE SURPRISED.
LET ME ASK YOU SOMETHING.
HOW COME ALL THE COSTUMES AND GADGETS AND EVERYTHING?
I ALWAYS FIGURED YOU WERE A NUT JOB, BUT YOU SEEM, Y'KNOW, SANE ENOUGH, COMPARATIVELY SPEAKING.
CRIMINALS ARE SUPERSTITIOUS COWARDS. GIVE THEM SOMETHING TO FEAR AND YOU'VE ALREADY WON.
HMMM.
CHICKS DIG THE OUTFIT, DON'T THEY?
...
WAIT HERE.
THE HELL I WILL.
I HAD A FEELING.
FRONT DOOR, HUH?
SOMETIMES THE DIRECT ROUTE WORKS BEST.
CRUNCH

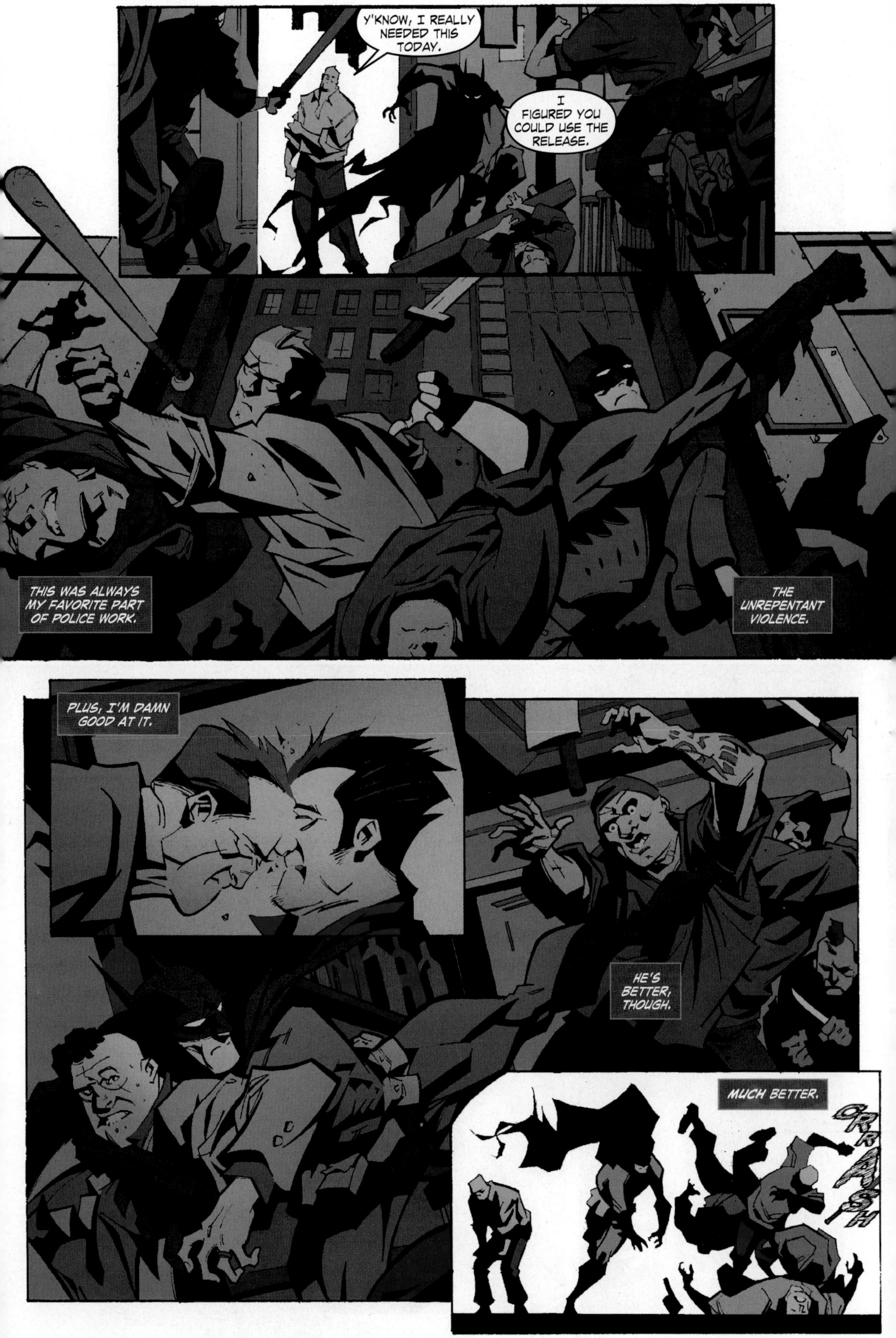
Y'KNOW, I REALLY NEEDED THIS TODAY.
I FIGURED YOU COULD USE THE RELEASE.
THIS WAS ALWAYS MY FAVORITE PART OF POLICE WORK.
THE UNREPENTANT VIOLENCE.
PLUS, I'M DAMN GOOD AT IT.
HE'S BETTER, THOUGH.
MUCH BETTER.
CRRASH

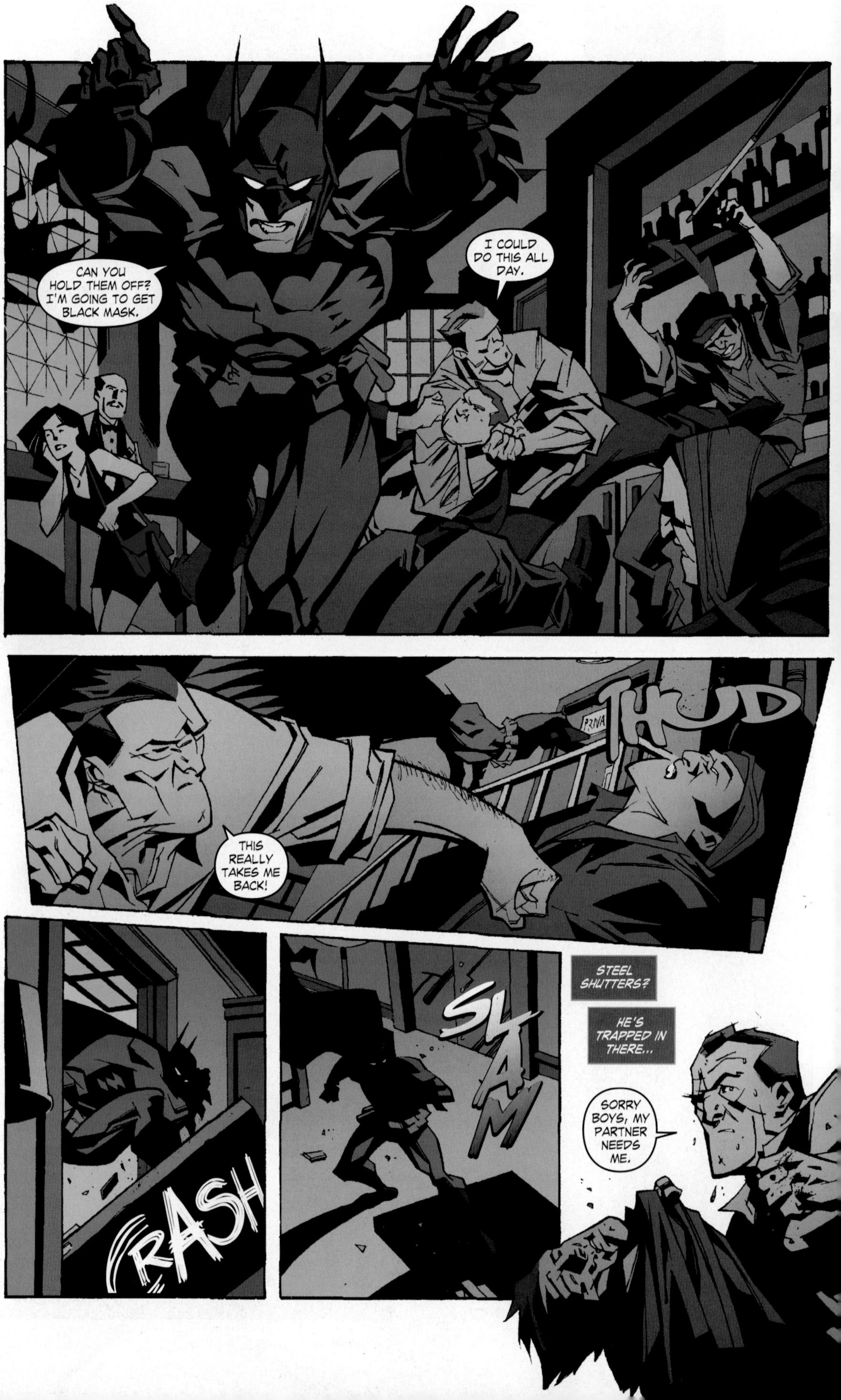
CAN YOU HOLD THEM OFF? I'M GOING TO GET BLACK MASK.
I COULD DO THIS ALL DAY.
THUD
THIS REALLY TAKES ME BACK!
CRASH
SLAM
STEEL SHUTTERS?
HE'S TRAPPED IN THERE...
SORRY BOYS, MY PARTNER NEEDS ME.

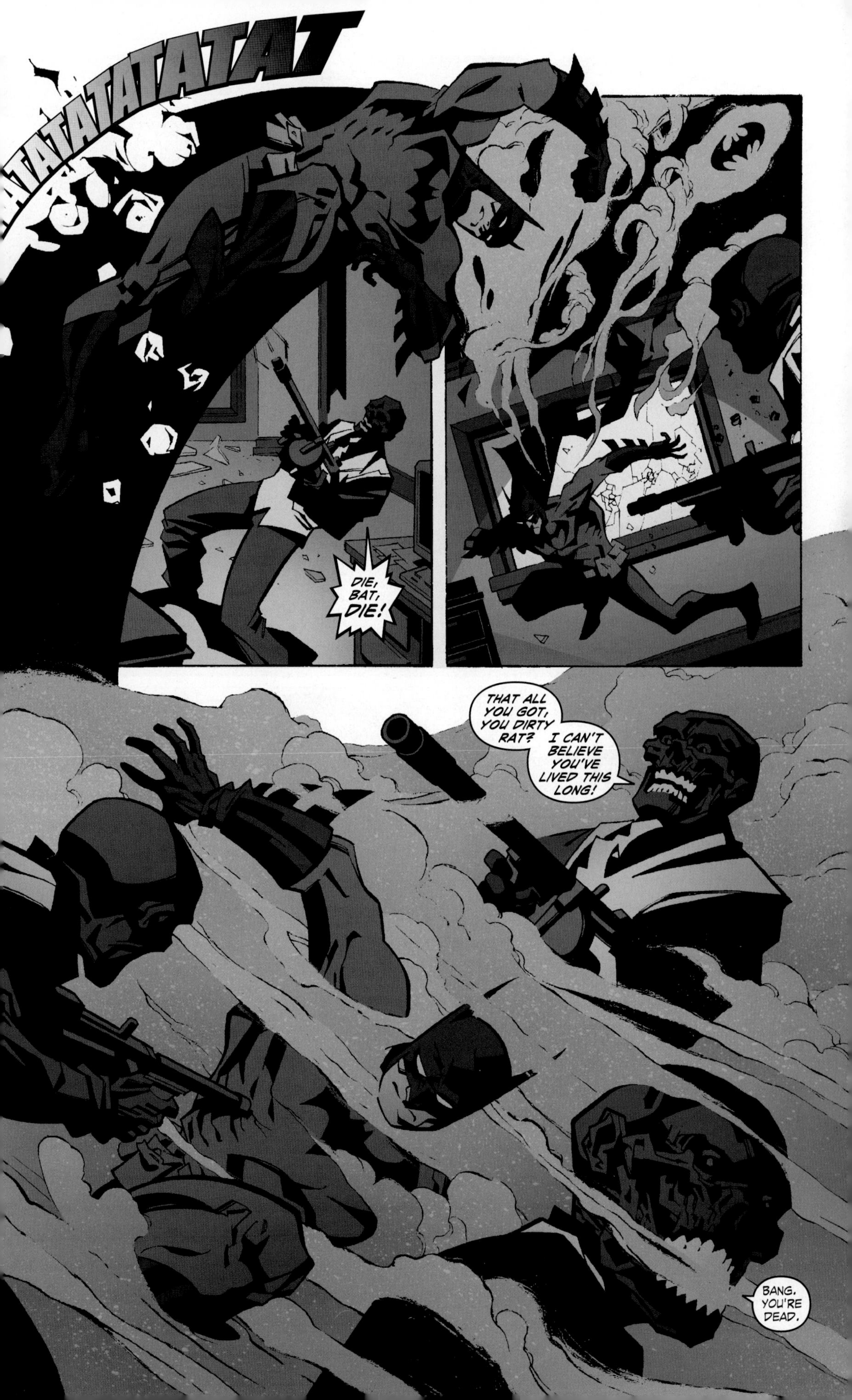
TATATATATATAT
DIE, BAT, DIE!
THAT ALL YOU GOT, YOU DIRTY RAT?
I CAN'T BELIEVE YOU'VE LIVED THIS LONG!
BANG. YOU'RE DEAD.

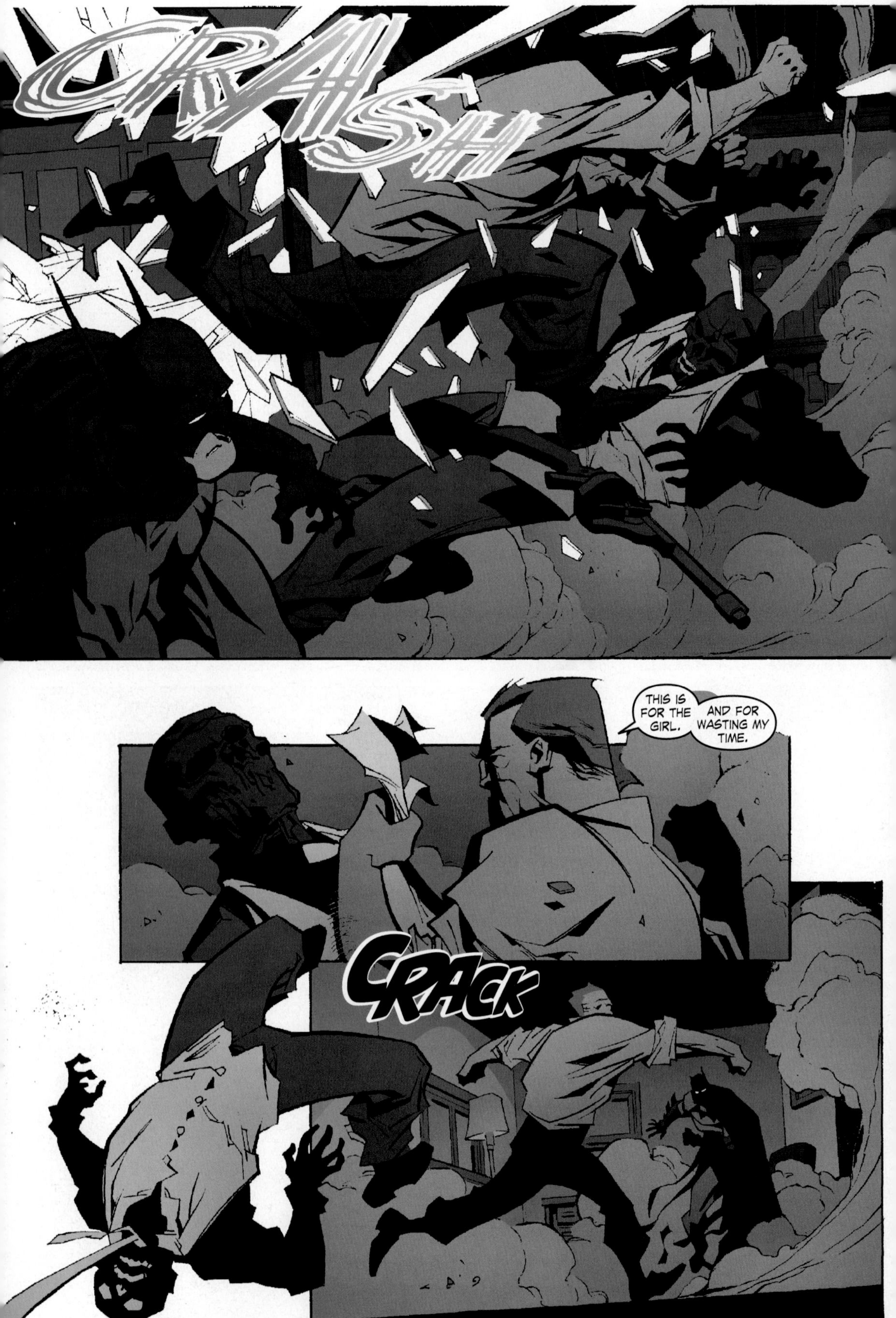
CRASH
THIS IS FOR THE GIRL.
AND FOR WASTING MY TIME.
CRACK

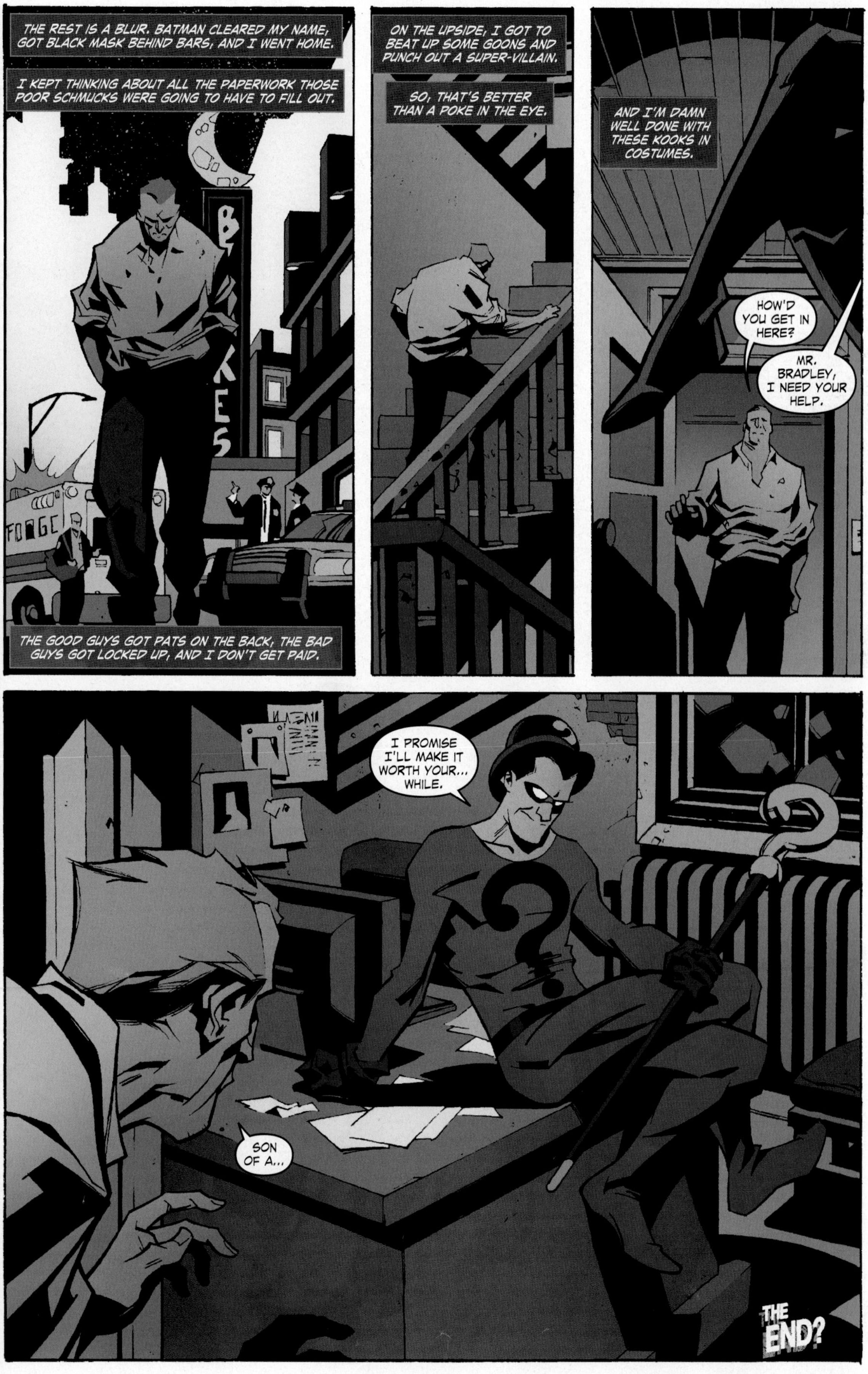
THE REST IS A BLUR. BATMAN CLEARED MY NAME, GOT BLACK MASK BEHIND BARS, AND I WENT HOME.
I KEPT THINKING ABOUT ALL THE PAPERWORK THOSE POOR SCHMUCKS WERE GOING TO HAVE TO FILL OUT.
THE GOOD GUYS GOT PATS ON THE BACK, THE BAD GUYS GOT LOCKED UP, AND I DON'T GET PAID.
ON THE UPSIDE, I GOT TO BEAT UP SOME GOONS AND PUNCH OUT A SUPER-VILLAIN.
SO, THAT'S BETTER THAN A POKE IN THE EYE.
AND I'M DAMN WELL DONE WITH THESE KOOKS IN COSTUMES.
HOW'D YOU GET IN HERE?
MR. BRADLEY, I NEED YOUR HELP.
I PROMISE I'LL MAKE IT WORTH YOUR... WHILE.
SON OF A...
THE END?

Legends of the Dark Knight #1 Variant Cover by Stephen Platt

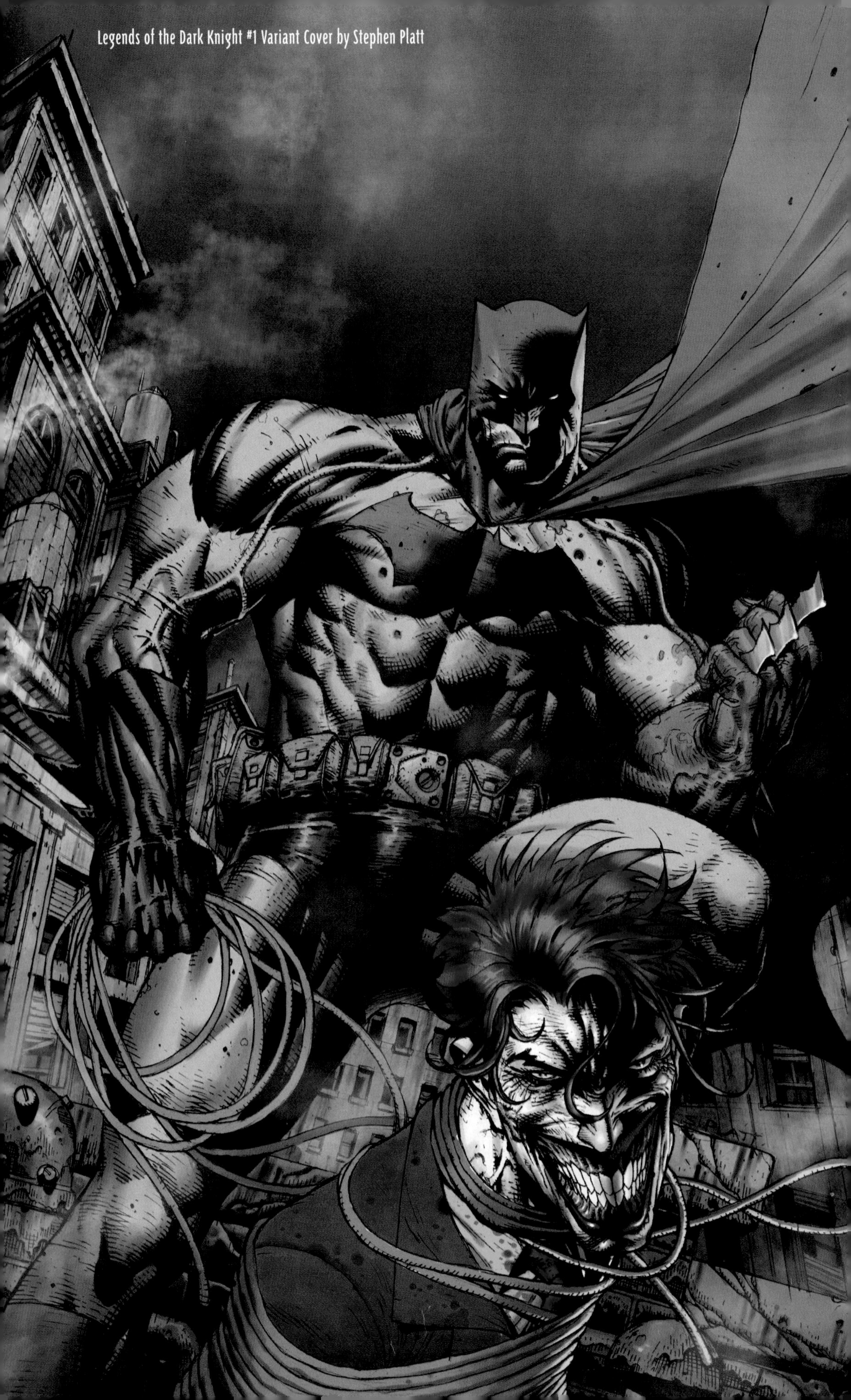

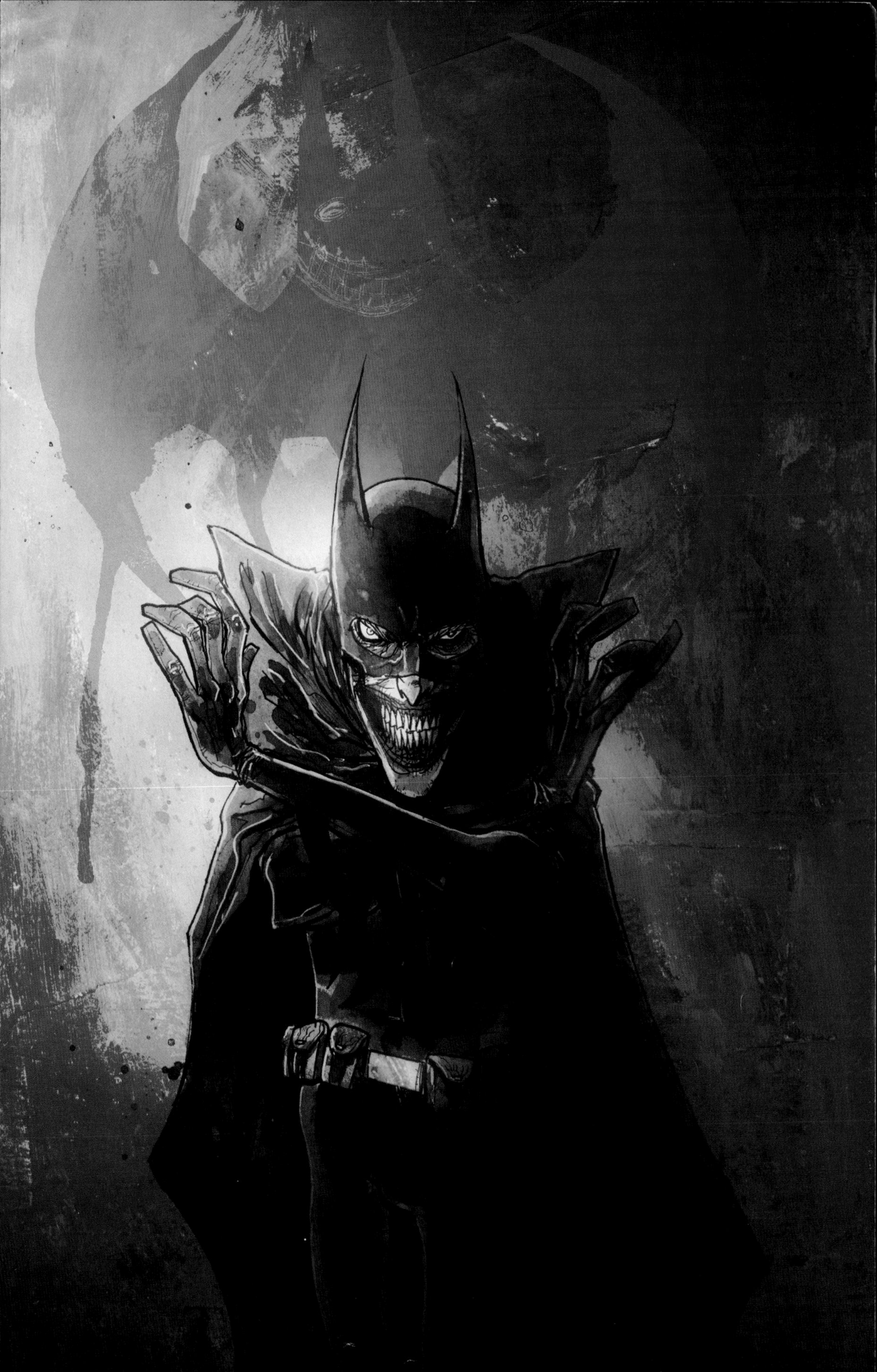

Legends of the Dark Knight #2 Cover by Ben Templesmith

Legends of the Dark Knight #3 Cover by Trevor Hairsine

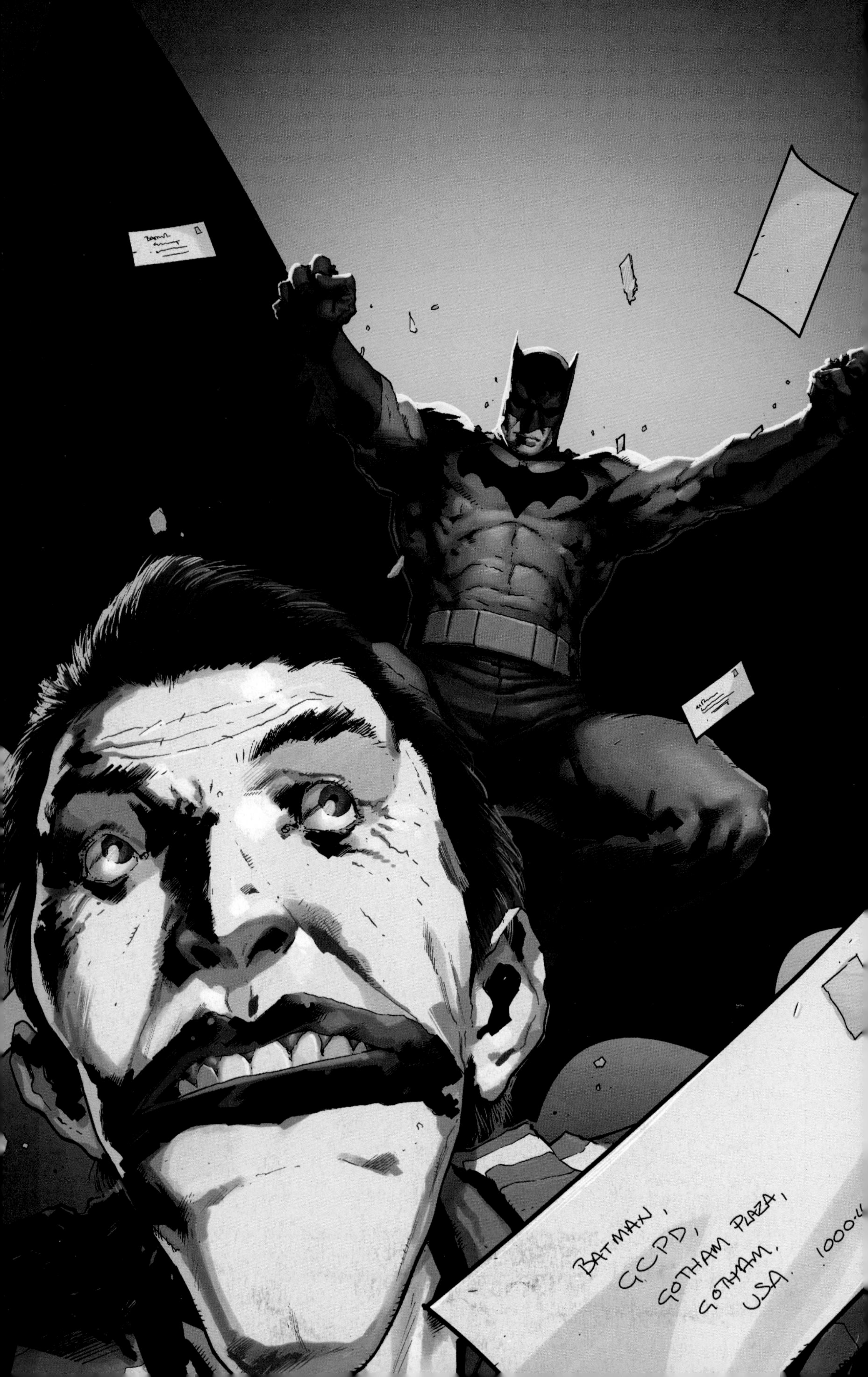
BATMAN,
G.C.P.D,
GOTHAM PLAZA,
GOTHAM,
USA.

Legends of the Dark Knight #4 Cover by Jheremy Raapack with David Lopez & Santi Casas of Ikari Studio

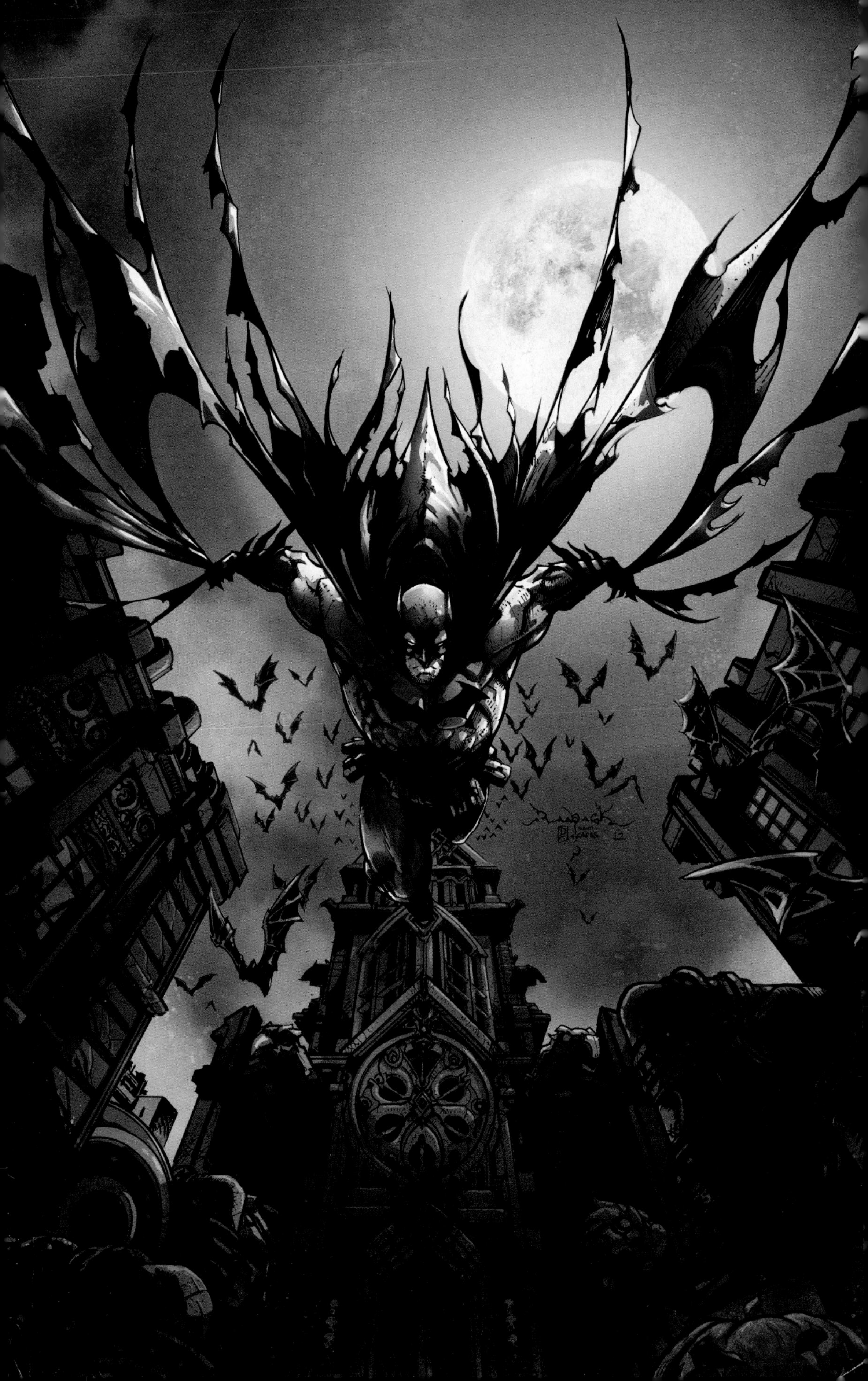

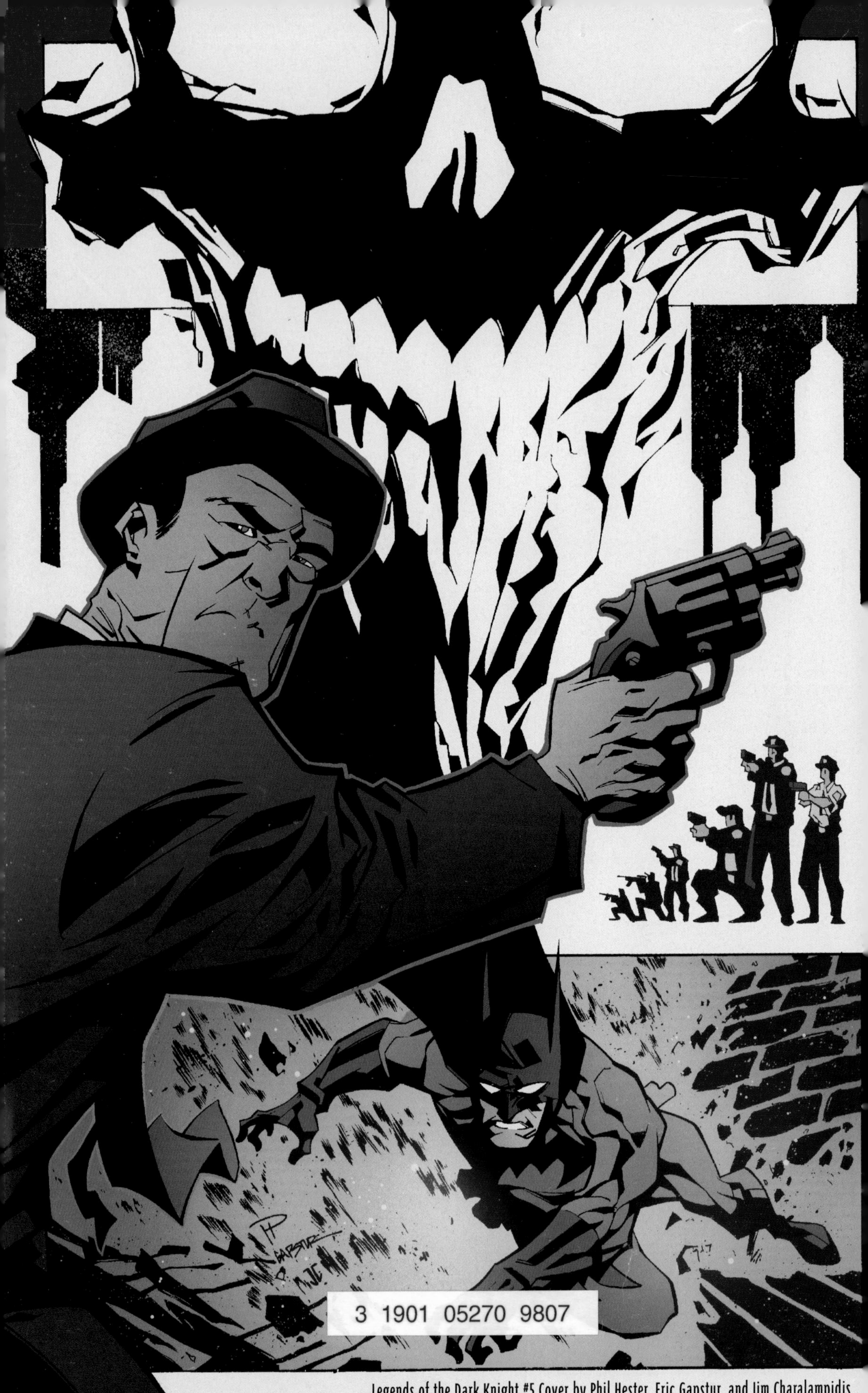

Legends of the Dark Knight #5 Cover by Phil Hester, Eric Gapstur, and Jim Charalampidis